THE FIRST EMANCIPATION

The First Emancipation

THE FORGOTTEN HISTORY OF ABOLITION IN REVOLUTIONARY FRANCE

Jeremy D. Popkin

PRINCETON UNIVERSITY PRESS
PRINCETON & OXFORD

Published by Princeton University Press
41 William Street, Princeton, New Jersey 08540
99 Banbury Road, Oxford OX2 6JX

press.princeton.edu

GPSR Authorized Representative: Easy Access System Europe - Mustamäe tee 50, 10621 Tallinn, Estonia, gpsr.requests@easproject.com

ISBN 9780691246925
ISBN (epub) 9780691287553
ISBN (PDF) 9780691246949

British Library Cataloging-in-Publication Data is available

Editorial: Priya Nelson, Emma Wagh
Production Editorial: Elizabeth Byrd
Jacket: Chris Ferrante
Production: Danielle Amatucci
Publicity: Maria Whelan (US), Carmen Jimenez (UK)
Copyeditor: Ashley Moore
Jacket image: Anne Louis Girodet De Roucy-Trioson, *Portrait of Jean-Baptiste Belley* (detail), 1797, oil on canvas. © Photo Josse / Bridgeman Images

Printed in the United States of America

10 9 8 7 6 5 4 3 2 1

CONTENTS

Introduction

ON 4 FEBRUARY 1794, the legislators of France's revolutionary government passed a historic decree: "The National Convention declares slavery abolished in all the colonies; as a consequence, it decrees that all men resident in the colonies, regardless of color, are French citizens, and will enjoy all the rights assured by the constitution."[1] With this one sentence, the deputies proclaimed the end of an institution that had been fundamental to the entire enterprise of European colonization in the Americas for the previous three centuries and that was still legal in the newly independent United States and the empires of Britain, Spain, Portugal, and the Netherlands. The French abolition decree, issued at a moment when there were more enslaved Black people in France's Caribbean colonies than in the thirteen states of the American republic, was the most radical such law in the entire history of the struggle against slavery. It not only granted immediate and unconditional freedom, it also elevated formerly enslaved Black people to full French citizenship, and it provided no compensation to former slave owners. As a token of their seriousness, the French lawmakers welcomed two men of African descent as voting members of the Convention. They and others would sit in the country's legislative assemblies throughout the next five years.

In revolutionary France, the law passed on 4 February 1794 was known as the decree of 16 pluviôse Year II, the date of its passage according to the revolutionary calendar adopted three months earlier. The calendar symbolized the revolutionaries' conviction that the proclamation of the French Republic on 22 September 1792 had marked the beginning of a new era in the history of humanity, and the decree of 16 pluviôse underlined their determination to transform not just their own country but the entire world. Members of the Convention predicted that their action would free not only the enslaved Black men and women in France's colonies but also those of the other European empires with which France was at war: Surely the news from France would lead to uprisings by the enslaved populations in the colonies of France's enemies.

Even as they congratulated themselves on passing their emancipation decree, the French legislators knew that abolishing slavery would not be as simple as the short text made it seem. A few years earlier, some of them had participated in France's first revolutionary legislature, the National Assembly, when it enacted its Declaration of the Rights of Man and Citizen in August 1789. Article 1 of that historic document stated that "men are born and remain free and equal in rights." When the declaration was passed, the National Assembly's most celebrated member, Count Honoré Gabriel Riqueti de Mirabeau, addressed France's colonists, telling them that the clear sense of the document was that "there cannot be, either in France, or in any other territory under France's laws, any men except *free men*, except *men equal to one another*."[2] And yet slavery continued in France's colonies, and on no fewer than three separate occasions before its session ended in September 1791, the same National Assembly that had written the Declaration of Rights affirmed its legal status. The passage of the decree of 16 pluviôse was an admission that the soaring rhetoric of the French Revolution's most famous statement of principles had not yet brought about any change to an institution that clearly violated the most basic of them.

As the deputies voted on 16 pluviôse, they also knew that they had little real choice in the matter. Before the introduction of the motion that led to their abolition of slavery, they had listened to a three-hour speech explaining that the nearly half a million Black people in France's most valuable colony, Saint-Domingue (today's independent nation of Haiti), had already obtained their freedom. For two and a half years, much of Saint-Domingue's Black population had been free in practice, thanks to the massive slave insurrection that had broken out there in August 1791, the start of what we now call the Haitian Revolution. In the summer of 1793, the two "civil commissioners" who represented the French government, Léger-Félicité Sonthonax and Etienne Polverel, recognized that they could not defeat the insurrection and that they needed Black support to oppose white colonists and invasions by the British and the Spanish. To win that support, they promised the Black population legal recognition of the freedom they had already obtained through insurrection.[3]

When the deputies in Paris took their vote in 1794, they also knew that its impact would depend on the outcome of the struggles that threatened the future of the revolution in France. Georges Danton, the deputy whose eloquence carried the day in favor of the motion to abolish slavery, was already locked in mortal combat with the members of the powerful Committee of Public Safety, who would send him to the guillotine two months later. Neither the committee's most famous member, Maximilien Robespierre, nor any of his colleagues was present in the Convention on 16 pluviôse. Would they actually implement such a far-reaching measure that had been passed without their approval? Even if they did, would revolutionary France emerge victorious from the war it was fighting against a coalition of all the other major powers of the European continent? A French defeat would certainly undo all of the Convention's radical measures, including the abolition of slavery.

And even if France triumphed over its foreign foes, would the country remain faithful to the principles laid out in the Declaration of Rights and radically broadened by the decree of 16 pluviôse? When the Convention proclaimed that liberty and equality should be extended to the enslaved populations of the colonies, it had already approved drastic restrictions to freedom in France itself, restrictions justified as necessary to win what Robespierre called "the war of liberty against its enemies." Five years later, many of the same deputies who voted for the abolition of slavery in 1794 voted to give dictatorial powers to a general who soon enacted a constitution that made no mention of the rights enshrined in the 1789 declaration. In 1802, after having drastically curtailed freedom in France itself, that general, Napoleon Bonaparte, revoked the freedom granted to enslaved Blacks by the decree of 16 pluviôse. To avoid being forced back into slavery, the Black population in Saint-Domingue would have to win a bloody war against French soldiers fighting under the tricolor flag that was supposed to symbolize freedom but that, in the Caribbean, had come to stand for its opposite. The Black populations in the other French colonies would have to wait until 1848, when France's Second Republic passed a second abolition decree freeing them.

Because of the complexity of revolutionary France's struggles about slavery and the short duration of the policy decreed on 16 pluviôse, the dramatic story of these conflicts has rarely received the attention it deserves. Histories of the international abolition movement in the revolutionary era, written for the most part by scholars from English-speaking countries, have privileged events in the United States and Britain, where the fights against slavery, no matter how slowly they proceeded, seem to vindicate Martin Luther King Jr.'s conviction that "the arc of the moral universe is long, but it bends toward justice."[4] The American and British abolition narratives are also attractive because they feature morally admirable figures, such as the Quaker Anthony Benezet, the tireless crusaders Thomas Clarkson and William Wilberforce, the Grimké sisters, and Frederick Douglass, as well as inspiring examples of collective action by ordinary people, such as the antislavery petition campaigns in Britain in the early 1790s and the Underground Railroad in America. The French abolition movement during the Revolution, by comparison, was smaller and more elitist, and the involvement of many of its leading figures in other aspects of the revolutionary movement, such as the pro-war campaign in 1791–92 and the Terror, makes it harder to depict them as inspiring moral exemplars.

In recent decades, the greatly increased attention paid to what is now known as the Haitian Revolution has also worked to obscure the significance of the campaigns against slavery and racial hierarchy in metropolitan France. Without the slave uprising in Saint-Domingue, it is indeed doubtful that the revolutionaries in France would ever have taken a step as drastic as they did in 1794. Figures such as Vincent Ogé, Boukman Dutty, Toussaint Louverture, Jean-Jacques Dessalines, Louis Delgrès, and the thousands of largely anonymous people of African descent who participated in the Haitian Revolution and the resistance to slavery in Guadeloupe played essential roles in forcing revolutionary France to confront the contradiction between its own ideals and the reality of colonial slavery and racism. Recognition of the agency of the enslaved populations in the Caribbean colonies is entirely justified, and I have contributed to the scholarship on the Haitian Revolution myself, but the focus on events in the colonies has had the effect of making the debates about abolition in metropolitan France seem somewhat irrelevant.[5]

Recognizing the importance of the Haitian Revolution, however, should not obscure the significance of the French revolutionaries' debates about slavery and particularly their radical decision to declare its abolition in 1794. The abolition of slavery did not come about only because of resistance on the part of the oppressed. Acceptance of the need to end slavery was a dialectical process that also required a transformation of mentalities within the white-dominated societies of the Western world. In France, debates about the legitimacy of slavery began several decades before the outbreak of the French Revolution, and political confrontations over the issue began even before the storming of the Bastille. The disruptions caused by those confrontations and by the revolutionaries' proclamation that "men are born and remain free and equal in rights" created the context in which the free people of color and enslaved Black populations in the colonies could imagine not just that their revolts might succeed but that the legitimacy of their demands might be recognized.

Until the passage of the decree of 4 February 1794, the freedom that the insurgents in Saint-Domingue had obtained for themselves was menaced from all sides. Not only the French but two other great imperial powers—Britain and Spain—were committed to restoring white supremacy in the troubled colony, and the United States, the newest player in the politics of the American world, was equally opposed to the Black movement. The Spanish had allied themselves with the Black rebels, but Madrid's aim was to defeat their French enemies, not to abolish slavery; the British, whose valuable slave colony of Jamaica was separated from Saint-Domingue by only sixty miles of ocean, were even less favorable to abolition. In revolutionary France itself, there were many, even among those who supported the Revolution, who were prepared to accept the occupation of the country's overseas colonies by foreign foes in order to preserve the system of slavery. Without the French decree of 4 February 1794, the Black fighters who had forced the end of slavery in Saint-Domingue would have been isolated in a hostile world.

Necessarily preoccupied with the struggle for their own freedom, the Black insurgents in Saint-Domingue had little reason to concern themselves with the implications of their movement for the wider world and few means for addressing audiences outside the island. Although the revolt's leaders were familiar with the language of the French Declaration of the Rights of Man and Citizen, they did not necessarily embrace its universalist principles. Even after the French civil commissioners Sonthonax and Polverel proclaimed the abolition of slavery in Saint-Domingue in the summer of 1793, the leaders of the insurrection maintained their loyalty to Spain, which was providing them with arms and ammunition. In August 1793 Toussaint Louverture denounced the French as "republican traitors" who had murdered their king and atheists who had "trampled under foot" the "unshakeable pillar" of the Catholic Church.[6] Had the Black movement and its Spanish allies defeated the French in Saint-Domingue in 1793, their victory would have been a triumph for the cause of "throne and altar," the principles of the European counterrevolution, rather than for the ideals of liberty and equality associated with the French Revolution.

Although it was the Black movement in Saint-Domingue that forced the French revolutionaries to take a stand against slavery, it was in the debates that followed the passage of the Declaration of the Rights of Man in 1789 and their translation into law in 1794 that slavery and racial discrimination were indelibly stamped as violations of universal natural rights. For five years after the passage of the 1794 abolition decree, France offered the world an unprecedented example of a multiracial polity spanning the Atlantic Ocean. Until Napoleon silenced talk of natural rights in France and reinstated slavery in its colonies, the weight of the most powerful European nation of the day was thrown onto the scales on the side of abolition. Napoleon's reversal of emancipation also had implications that went far beyond France. To justify reenslavement and counter the impact of the revolutionary experiment, French advocates of slavery became the most outspoken proponents of the pseudoscientific racist doctrines that pervaded the Western world for the next two centuries. Had Napoleon not deliberately sabotaged the experiment launched in 1794, the history of France and that of a Western world still invested in slavery might have taken a very different course.

Uncovering the history of the French revolutionary confrontation with race and slavery is important not just for understanding the wider history of the struggle for abolition but also for comprehending the history of the French Revolution. Mentions of the slave uprising in Saint-Domingue are now de rigueur in serious accounts of the period, but the full extent of what contemporaries called "the affair of the colonies" in the metropole remains less explored. Although revolutionary politicians had many other concerns, practically every prominent participant in revolutionary politics took an active part in debates about slavery and the colonies. The careers of a number of them, including not only the dedicated antislavery activist Jacques-Pierre Brissot and the staunch defender of colonial interests Antoine Barnave but also figures as important as Mirabeau, Robespierre, and Napoleon Bonaparte, were dramatically affected by their stands on these issues. Every one of the revolutionary-era legislative bodies, from the Estates General of 1789 to the assemblies of the Napoleonic Consulate, engaged in debates on these issues. As they organized campaigns to shape public opinion, supporters and opponents of slavery were pioneers in creating the Revolution's political culture. The two movements were among the first to form political clubs to support their causes. They deployed all the political media of the time to publicize their ideas and organize campaigns to influence legislators.[7]

Although the French Revolution's abolition of slavery resonated throughout the world at the time, it faded from historical memory once Napoleon repealed the abolition law in 1802. What was remembered instead of the revolutionary decree of 4 February 1794 was the uprising of enslaved Blacks in the French colony of Saint-Domingue that began in August 1791 and culminated, in 1804, in the declaration of the independence of Haiti. Today this "Haitian Revolution" is recognized, alongside the American and French

Revolutions, as one of the great movements for freedom that laid the bases for modern ideas of liberty and equality.[8] At the time and for decades afterward, however, lurid accounts that depicted Blacks, "with daggers in one hand and torches in the other," massacring planters and burning plantations shaped public reactions to slavery throughout the white world. With such images in their minds, it was difficult for Europeans and white Americans to think of the revolutionary abolition decree as anything but a disastrous mistake, like the campaign to abolish religion that the revolutionaries had undertaken at almost the same moment.

Even today, when an increasingly multiracial France is grappling openly with the place of slavery in its history, more is said about the second abolition of slavery under France's Second Republic in 1848 than about the decree of 16 pluviôse. To be sure, the 1848 law proved more durable than the one passed in 1794, but it was also less radical; among other things, it provided financial compensation to former slave owners. The date of France's annual national commemoration of "the memories of the slave trade, of slavery and of their abolition," 10 May, marks neither the anniversary of 4 February 1794 nor that of the 1848 abolition law, but instead the anniversary of the passage of the "loi Taubira" in 2001, a law named after Christiane Taubira, the Black French legislator who proposed it, that defines slavery as a violation of human rights.[9]

While the history of the French Revolution's confrontation with slavery is important because it led to the earliest abolition decree in the Western world, it is also important to understand the reasons why that decree proved so short-lived. As the United States Supreme Court's 2022 decision to overturn a previous ruling that established a right to abortion shows, individual rights can be taken away as well as expanded. Slavery was reintroduced in France in 1802 not by an arbitrary decree, like the *statut des Juifs* issued by the collaborationist Vichy government in October 1940, but by a legislative process during which Napoleon's henchmen took pains to persuade members of the regime's assemblies that repealing the decree of 16 pluviôse was necessary and desirable. Indeed, the debates about reimposing slavery in 1802 were more extensive than the hurried discussion that led the National Convention's decree in 1794. Napoleon's success in pushing through the law restoring slavery is a reminder that even rights loudly proclaimed as "natural" at one moment can be rescinded when political circumstances change.

Previous histories of the French Revolution's debates about race and slavery have adopted various strategies to make sense of the complexity of this story. The anticolonial activist Yves Bénot's *La Révolution française et la fin des colonies*, published in 1987, was a pathbreaking attempt to bring attention to the subject. Bénot chose to deal separately with the different issues involved in the "affaire des colonies," which sometimes obscured the connections between them and made it difficult for readers to understand the chronology of events. Florence Gauthier's *Triomphe et mort du droit naturel en Révolution 1789-1795-1802* and Jean-Daniel Piquet's *L'Emancipation des Noirs dans la Révolution française (1789–1795)* expanded on Bénot's work and did much to underline the importance of the issues of race and slavery. Both also made dubious claims about key issues, such as their assertion that Robespierre was a main contributor to the abolition of slavery in 1794, a contention that cannot be justified by the evidence. Like Bénot's earlier volume, Piquet's account also stops midway through the revolutionary decade. Tessie Liu's *A Frail Liberty: Probationary Citizens in the French and Haitian Revolutions*, published in 2022, extends into the Napoleonic period, but it is concerned primarily with the ideas of the French abolitionists, which are often treated in isolation from the political context in which they were put forward. If Piquet credits the revolutionaries with more radical views than they actually held, Liu tends to fault them for falling short of present-day standards of universal human rights.[10]

The French Revolution's confrontation with slavery is a story about how the revolutionaries came to decree the abolition of slavery in 1794, but is it the story of an abolitionist movement? The question is more complicated than it may seem. If one reserves the label of "abolitionist" for people who saw slavery as a violation of fundamental human rights and consequently advocated the immediate emancipation of its victims and the granting to them of all the rights held by whites, without any compensation for their owners, then it has to be said that there were few, if any, white abolitionists in the revolutionary period, either in France or anywhere else in the world, prior to the passage of the decree of 16 pluviôse. Even the Black leaders of the Haitian Revolution did not always embrace such an unqualified position. In negotiations with the white colonists at the end of 1791, after the first wave of the Saint-Domingue insurrection, the movement's leaders offered to end their movement in exchange for personal freedom for its leaders and a promise of more humane treatment and amnesty for the other Black participants, who would then return to work on their plantations. During the years when he held power as the appointed French governor of Saint-Domingue, Toussaint Louverture imposed a rigorous regime of forced labor on the majority of the colony's Black population, a regime that was not always easy to distinguish from slavery.[11]

As we will see, there were many French writers and politicians, before and during the Revolution, who denounced the evils of slavery in seemingly uncompromising terms and then gave various reasons why it could at best be phased out gradually, with compensation for slave owners, or "humanized" by limiting its "abuses." For this reason, some modern scholars prefer the term "antislavery," which defines an attitude, to "abolition," which suggests advocacy of a definite action.[12] It is sometimes difficult to distinguish such exponents of antislavery from its more moderate defenders, who often insisted that they, too, recognized slavery's inhumanity and hoped to find ways to make it less cruel. There was, nevertheless, a clear distinction, recognized by participants in the revolutionary debates, between those who sincerely aimed to promote the abolition of slavery, even if they considered immediate emancipation impractical, and those who were at best willing to envisage the end of slavery as a possibility in the distant future. Figures such as Brissot, Condorcet, and Henri Grégoire, the leaders of the Société des Amis des Noirs, even though they were all advocates of gradual emancipation, were unquestionably not in the same camp as men like Médéric Louis Élie Moreau de Saint-Méry, Pierre-Victor Malouet, or the other outspoken defenders of slavery. In 1794, however, the French legislators did declare the abolition of slavery, and from then on there was a clear distinction between those who defended Black freedom in the colonies and those who, even if they carefully avoided using the word "slavery," sought to confine the emancipated Blacks to a second-class status that often amounted to enslavement under other terms.

Even if we accept that the word "abolitionist" is appropriate for the French opponents of slavery of the revolutionary period, can we describe them as a "movement"? In Britain, from 1787 onward, there was a recognized abolitionist movement, led by Clarkson, Wilberforce, and their associates, which, in 1807, achieved its aim of pressuring Parliament to abolish the slave trade. This was the model Jacques-Pierre Brissot had in mind when he established the Société des Amis des Noirs in 1788. Even for its own leading members, however, the Amis des Noirs quickly became a secondary concern, overshadowed by political clubs and movements focused on a wider range of issues, such as the Jacobin Club. Many of the activists who plunged into the revolutionary debates about race and slavery were not members of the Amis des Noirs, and the organization had essentially ceased to exist by the time the law of 4 April 1792, which granted rights to free people of color, was passed. By 4 February 1794, when the National Convention voted to abolish slavery, almost all the prominent members of the Amis des Noirs had fallen victim to the Terror. Paradoxically, that radical emancipation decree was pushed through the Convention by politicians who had rarely shown much previous commitment to the abolitionist cause and who were careful to avoid any mention of Brissot or the Amis des Noirs. In contrast to Britain and the United States, abolition in France was achieved at a moment when there was nothing resembling a coherent movement advocating for it.

The victory of abolition in France in 1794 was especially surprising because, while there was no coherent group advocating for it, there definitely was an organized group opposing it: the representatives of the white colonists from the Caribbean, who were meeting with the members of the Committee of Public Safety at precisely the moment on 4 February 1794 when the National Convention passed its decree. The story of the French Revolution's struggles over slavery cannot be comprehended without taking into account the efforts of slavery's defenders, who proved themselves as adept as the abolitionists at exploiting the possibilities for political action created by the Revolution. Eventually, under Napoleon, they succeeded in reversing the emancipation decree and extending the era of slavery in most French colonies by nearly half a century. Without understanding the many groups and individuals who opposed the abolitionists, we cannot understand either the obstacles that stood in the way of emancipation or its fragility.

Fortunately, the sources for studying race and slavery during the French Revolution are abundant. Throughout the Revolution, both the advocates of reform and their opponents relied on the printing press to circulate their arguments, generating a voluminous library of pamphlets and newspaper articles, as well as caricatures and engravings. The period's often explosive legislative debates on these subjects are documented in the press and in the records of the revolutionary assemblies' proceedings. Figures ranging from the abolitionist Brissot to his bitter opponent Moreau de Saint-Méry preserved important materials that are now available in the French national archives and other repositories.

While sources are abundant, translating the language used to argue about race and slavery is a fraught issue, with the additional challenge of negotiating differences in usage in the United States and in France. In the revolutionary era, French authors used the terms *Nègre* (Negro) and *Noir* (Black) interchangeably for individuals of pure African ancestry; these words might or might not be capitalized, depending on the preference of individual authors. Advocates of abolition showed some preference for *Noir*, with a capital *N*, as opposed to *nègre*, which was more commonly used by defenders of slavery; nevertheless, *nègre* did not usually have the pejorative connotation of the American "N-word," and some committed abolitionists continued to use it.[13] *Africain* was another term sometimes used, often but not always with the purpose of implying that the individuals it described did not deserve to be considered French. In contrast to present-day American usage, revolutionary-era writers of all political persuasions normally capitalized *Blancs*, a practice I have not adopted here. No one at the time hesitated to employ the term *esclave* to describe enslaved individuals. In present-day American scholarship, it is now accepted that to describe someone as a "slave" is to imply that servitude was one of their inherent characteristics. I have followed current usage by using formulations such as "enslaved persons," except in translations of documents from the time and in phrases such as "slave uprising," where the clear implication is that the participants were revolting against the condition imposed on them.

A particularly complicated question of linguistic usage arises in describing the group that scholars of the French colonial empire sometimes describe as its "third race," people of partial or full African descent who were legally free before the revolutionaries' abolition of slavery in 1793–94. At the time, a wide variety of terms were used to refer to the members of this group. They were sometimes called *jaunes* or *rouges* ("yellows" or "reds") to distinguish them from Blacks. Whites, including some of their most outspoken allies, routinely referred to them as *mulâtres* (mulattos) or sometimes as *sang-mêlés* (mixed bloods). Defenders of the colonial system of racial hierarchy often labeled them *affranchis* (freedmen), implying that they all owed their freedom to the beneficence of the whites; members of the group vigorously objected to that term, insisting that many of them had been born free.

Representatives of this group in revolutionary France generally referred to themselves as *hommes* or *gens de couleur libres*, and sometimes as *hommes de couleur et nègres libres* (men of color and free Negroes), a formulation that distinguished those who had some white ancestry from those who did not. Translating these terms into present-day English presents difficulties. "Mulatto" is derived from the word for "mule," an unacceptable pejorative equating human beings with animals. "People of color" would be misleading: In current American usage, it refers to nonwhites generally, including Asians, Latinos, and Native Americans as well as Blacks, whereas in the French revolutionary context it was reserved for a much more specific group. (A small number of dark-skinned people of South Asian ancestry were sometimes included in the category, but it definitely did not take in East Asians or the various nonwhite populations of the Americas.)[14] To avoid undue linguistic contortions, except in translations of documents I have generally used the term "mixed race" even though it occludes the fact that some members of the group did not have white ancestry.

The account of the French Revolution's debates and decisions offered here seeks to put the ideas and actions of the French advocates of abolition and racial equality in the context of their chaotic times. I hope to have brought the protagonists of these tense, high-stakes struggles to life and to have made the reasons for what they said and did understandable. Even Condorcet and Henri

Grégoire—the two major abolitionists who, in 1989 at the celebration of the bicentennial of the French Revolution, were singled out for the honor of reburial in the Panthéon, France's shrine to its national heroes—were not perfect human beings. They sometimes felt compelled to compromise their principles, and they, like all the other politicians of the time, made some serious political misjudgments. Nevertheless, they and their even more problematic colleagues, figures such as Mirabeau and Brissot, made important contributions to the battle against the evils of slavery and racism that deserve to be understood.

CHAPTER ONE

Old Regime France and Its Slaves

"FRANCE, THE MOTHER of liberty, doesn't permit any slaves." So pronounced the judges of the Parlement de Bordeaux, the royal court in France's most important Atlantic port, in 1571. The Bordeaux court's edict, issued in response to the attempt of a French merchant to sell a cargo of enslaved Blacks brought from Africa, resulted in the freeing of his captives. It also established a precedent that would continue to be cited in French legal treatises for the next two centuries. A compilation of French laws issued in 1710 considered the full range of precedents relating to the issue of slavery in the country and concluded that "today every slave is free from the moment he sets foot in the kingdom."[1]

This claim was not completely accurate: Until 1748, the French Navy maintained a fleet of galleys in the Mediterranean whose oarsmen were a mixture of condemned prisoners and enslaved Muslim captives.[2] Nevertheless, in contrast to the United States, nowhere in Louis XVI's European domain did one see enslaved laborers toiling in the fields under the supervision of overseers armed with whips. The peasant farmers who made up some 80 percent of France's population at the moment of the revolution in 1789 had many complaints about their condition, but they were legally free, able to own property, to marry as they saw fit, and to engage in their own versions of the "pursuit of happiness" that the American Declaration of Independence had declared a fundamental natural right. Like slavery, race did not seem to be a major issue in late eighteenth-century France in the way that it was in the United States. There was a sprinkling of dark-skinned people of African ancestry living in the kingdom, but the vast majority of Louis XVI's subjects had probably never encountered a Black person in the flesh.

Even if the signs of engagement with slavery and race were largely invisible in the European territories of France, the kingdom was inextricably involved with Black people and the issues their enslavement raised. The editor of the 1710 legal treatise who had concluded that there were no slaves in France added that "this law is not in effect with regard to the negro slaves of our isles in America who come with their masters."[3] His acknowledgment of this exception to France's general laws reflected the fact that France was not just a kingdom in Europe; it was also the heart of a colonial empire whose prosperity depended on the enslavement of Black people. Starting in the early 1600s, the French laid claim to significant possessions in the Americas, on the coast of Africa, and in the Indian Ocean. Although they had only a shaky grip on the vast territories they claimed in North America, encompassing much of present-day Canada and the Mississippi valley down to New Orleans, the French established a solid foothold in the Caribbean. A first colony was established on the small island of Saint Christopher in 1626; then, in 1635, the ambitious Cardinal Richelieu, King Louis XIII's chief minister, oversaw the planting of settlements on two of the larger Windward Islands in the eastern Caribbean, Martinique and Guadeloupe, which remain parts of France today.

Possession of other territories in the Caribbean was ferociously contested during the many wars of the 1600s. In addition to Martinique and Guadeloupe, the French laid claim to a stretch of the South American mainland, referred to as Cayenne or Guiana. More important for the future of French involvement with slavery, however, was their success in occupying the western part of the large island of Hispaniola. Initially claimed for Spain by Christopher Columbus in 1492, Hispaniola had been virtually abandoned once the native population had been decimated and the island's natural resources pillaged. In the course of the 1600s, freebooters known as buccaneers created small settlements along the island's north coast. By this time, most of the cultivatable land in Martinique and Guadeloupe had been given out, and a growing number of would-be plantation owners turned their attention to what came to be called the colony of Saint-Domingue. The French monarchy saw an opportunity to extend its influence at the expense of its Spanish rival and sent officials to establish a presence in the area. In 1697 a treaty gave France possession of most of what is now the independent nation of Haiti, leaving the Spanish in possession of the eastern half of Hispaniola, today's Dominican Republic.

At the time when France gained possession of Saint-Domingue, the islands of the Caribbean were rapidly becoming among the most valuable pieces of real estate in the world. Initially, the main export crop grown in the region was tobacco, but by the last decades of the 1600s, a new product came to dominate: sugar. From the British-held island of Barbados, the first Caribbean colony to experience the "sugar revolution," sugarcane cultivation spread to Martinique and Guadeloupe; once the available land there had been turned into plantations, attention turned to Saint-Domingue. Considerably larger than the other French Caribbean colonies, Saint-Domingue offered seemingly inexhaustible possibilities for the expansion of production. By the time of the French Revolution in 1789, Saint-Domingue alone produced close to half of the entire world's supply of sugar.

Enslaved Africans were imported to the French Caribbean colonies from the outset; in 1642 Louis XIII granted a general authorization to French merchants to engage in the slave trade. Initially, as in many other colonies in the Americas, enslaved Blacks labored alongside poor European whites who had indentured themselves to landowners for a certain number of years and Indigenous people who were also subjected to forced labor, but within a few decades, planters came to rely almost exclusively on Black captives imported from the other side of the Atlantic. "A Black slave is much more useful than a French servant who is only [contracted] for three years, who needs clothing, asks for wages, and is not accustomed to the heat," a Jesuit priest wrote in 1640.[4]

France's Caribbean sugar islands became the jewels of an empire that also included slaving stations on the west coast of Africa, trading posts in India, and the Mascarene Islands in the Indian Ocean, known at the time as the Ile de France (today's independent nation of Mauritius) and the Ile Bourbon (today's French overseas department of Reunion). Slavery existed in all these colonies. In India and the Mascarenes, Blacks from Africa were imported, along with captives from South Asia. The French outposts on the African coast served the needs of slave traders purchasing captives for shipment to the Caribbean. Under Louis XIV, who reigned from 1648 to 1715, France vigorously pursued an aggressive colonial policy, and for a brief period, from 1700 to 1713, it also held the *asiento*, the official monopoly on supplying slaves to the vast Spanish empire in the Americas, which seemed to put the country in position to dominate the Atlantic slave trade.

The number of French who were directly involved with the colonies and slavery during Louis XIV's reign remained small, but the existence of the empire affected the metropole in many ways. One of the main motivations for the issuance of a 1669 decree regulating the use of the kingdom's forests, for example, was to make sure that the navy, the essential tool for the defense of the colonies, had an adequate supply of tall, straight tree trunks for ships' masts.[5] In 1685 royal legal experts were called on to draw up a lengthy edict that came to be known as the Code Noir to resolve the many questions that had already arisen concerning the consequences of the spread of plantation slavery. The various provisions of the Code Noir showed how many different issues the existence of slavery raised. The Catholic Church, whose theologians had declared, soon after the beginning of the African slave trade, that Blacks were human beings with souls that needed to be saved, agreed that enslavement could be justified if it was a means for bringing them to the Christian faith. A ruling in 1698 by the faculty of the Sorbonne, the highest French authority on Church doctrine, stated that "divine and human laws permit slaves; from which it follows that one can sell them, buy them, and exchange them like other goods."[6]

By 1685, it was already clear to Louis XIV's legal experts that, in the absence of white women, white colonists were having children with enslaved women of other races in the colonies. The Code Noir sought to discourage the practice, specifying that if free men fathered mixed-race children out of wedlock, the mother and the children would be confiscated for the benefit of the colonial hospital. If the father chose to marry the mother of his children, however, she and her offspring were to be declared free. According to article 59 of the code, they and other manumitted slaves were to have "the same rights, privileges and liberties enjoyed by persons born free," a clause that appeared to establish full equality among free persons regardless of their race. Article 58, however, obligated enslaved persons who were granted freedom "to retain a particular respect for their former masters, their widows and their children," thereby creating a distinction between free-born whites and other free people.[7] A century after they were first formulated, the contradictions between these two articles would generate explosive debates about race during the French Revolution.

A number of articles in the Code Noir specified punishments for enslaved Blacks whose behavior threatened white masters. Blacks could be whipped if they were found carrying weapons, if they gathered together with enslaved people from other plantations, or if they were found selling sugarcane, which was presumed to belong to their owners. They could not hold any public offices or appear in court cases, except as witnesses whose testimony could be disregarded if the judges so decided. "The slave who will have struck his master or the wife of his master, his mistress or their children to bring blood, or in the face, will be punished with death," according to article 33.[8] On the other hand, however, some of the code's articles attempted to establish a minimum of rights for enslaved people. They were to receive specified amounts of food each week and two sets of clothing each year, and, in theory, they had the right to complain to local officials if these rules were not observed. Slave owners could put their enslaved captives in chains or whip them, but they were prohibited from "torturing them or mutilating their bodies." Officially, only the courts had the right to order the execution of an enslaved person, in which case the owner was entitled to compensation for the value of his "property."[9] In practice, the enslaved population had no meaningful way to protest if owners ignored the protective provisions of the code, but these articles reflected at least some uneasiness on the part of the officials who drafted it about the consequences of giving slave masters unlimited authority.

While royal officials occupied themselves with creating a legal framework for the slave colonies in the distant Caribbean, written accounts allowed French readers to imagine life in the islands. The Dominican missionary Jean-Baptiste Labat's *Nouveau Voyage aux isles de l'Amérique*, published in 1722, continued to be cited as a source of information throughout the eighteenth century. As defenders of the slave trade would continue to claim for the rest of the century, Labat alleged that many of the Black captives purchased in Africa were either "criminals . . . who deserve death or some other punishment" or else prisoners of war, although he acknowledged that others were victims of "merchants who steal all the men, women, children they can catch."[10] Pierre-François de Charlevoix, another priest who spent time in Saint-Domingue early in the eighteenth century, assured readers that once an enslaved captive had adjusted to his situation, "he becomes more easily accustomed to slavery, [a condition] for which he seems to have been born; . . . all it takes to dominate him is to . . . make him feel with a few lashes that he has masters."[11]

Labat and Charlevoix were enthusiastic promoters of the sugar industry; during his stay in Martinique, Labat had run a plantation of his own, and his books included detailed engravings showing enslaved Blacks processing sugarcane into the syrup from which sugar was eventually refined. He acknowledged the brutal exploitation involved in the plantation economy, telling readers that the Blacks often labored for eighteen hours a day. The job of feeding the sugarcane stalks through the heavy rollers that squeezed out the cane juice was usually given to enslaved women, and Labat described how, "when exhausted by the day's work and overcome by fatigue, they fall asleep while pushing the canes . . . they find themselves caught and crushed before one can rescue them," often losing an arm or even being killed.[12] Labat's intention was not to arouse indignation about the cruelty of slavery, however. As apologists for the colonists would continue to claim down to the time of the French Revolution, he insisted that most plantation owners treated their enslaved laborers humanely.[13]

By the end of Louis XIV's long reign in 1715, the possession of overseas slave colonies had come to seem an essential feature of French life. Nevertheless, the decades following the end of Louis

XIV's final war, the War of the Spanish Succession, saw many ups and downs in the fortunes of France's overseas empire. The *asiento* was lost to the British in the 1713 peace treaty that ended that war, and it would be the British who would build up the largest slaving industry in the eighteenth century. As the French monarchy struggled to reduce the mountain of debt resulting from Louis XIV's wars, the regent Philippe d'Orléans, who headed the government during the years before Louis XV came of age, turned to a Scottish-born financier, John Law, who promised that the colonies held the solution to the problem. Law's Compagnie des Indes was part of a scheme meant to integrate the French slave trade and the management of the colonies; for a time, he managed to persuade French investors that profits from the overseas empire would easily pay off the royal debt. Despite the rapid collapse of Law's speculative scheme, the conviction that the colonies were a national asset survived.

For a quarter century after Louis XIV's death, France and its empire enjoyed a period of peace that allowed for steady growth in colonial production, fueled by a regular flow of enslaved captives from Africa. The manuscript journal kept by Lieutenant Robert Durand of the *Diligent*, a slaving vessel that sailed to the West African coast in 1731 and then to the Caribbean island of Martinique, allowed the American historian Robert Harms to reconstruct the routine, "distressingly ordinary in its own time and place," by which slaving voyages were organized and financed and Black prisoners were purchased, crammed into the ship's hold, carried across the Atlantic, and then sold.[14] For most of the eighteenth century, the city of Nantes, located on the Loire River, dominated the French slave trade. Of the 1,200,000 African captives known to have been transported on French ships, 538,818 were taken on ships launched from there.[15] Bordeaux, the largest Atlantic port, had a smaller share in the slave trade until the last decade before the French Revolution, but it was by far the largest participant in direct commerce with the colonies, shipping wine, wheat, and other products from its hinterland across the Atlantic and bringing back sugar, indigo, and other tropical specialties from the Caribbean.

One consequence of the growing connections between France and its colonies was the arrival in the metropole of a small number of enslaved Black people, usually brought as the domestic servants of wealthy colonists. Elegant noblewomen began to have portraits of themselves painted in the company of their Black servants, whose dark skin emphasized the whiteness of their employers' complexions.[16] Small as the number of Blacks in France was, it presented a problem for French officials: How could the principle that slavery was prohibited in the kingdom be reconciled with the interests of the colonists who claimed slaves as property and asserted their right to bring them to Europe? In 1715, after a local court in Nantes declared a Black female servant from the colonies legally free, Gérard Mellier, the mayor of the city, urged the royal government to regulate the conditions under which enslaved people could be brought to France.[17] The response was an edict issued in October 1716 that permitted colonists to bring enslaved servants to France, provided they registered them with the local admiralty court.[18]

For several decades after the issuance of the 1716 edict, French courts were not confronted with any cases regarding the status of enslaved people brought into the kingdom. In 1738, however, Jean Boucaux, a Black man who had been brought to France years earlier as a slave, brought a successful suit to claim his freedom. Soon after the verdict in the Boucaux case, a new royal declaration, issued on 15 December 1738, reasserted the rights of slave-owning colonists. The preamble to the new declaration expressed a concern that too many Blacks were being brought to France, where they "contract a spirit of independence . . . which may have troublesome results," and its provisions restricted the limited rights they had been able to claim under the 1716 edict.[19]

As the colonies and the slave trade became more important aspects of French life, discussions of the issues they raised became more frequent. The many editions of Jacques Savary's *Le Parfait Négociant* recognized that the slave trade "might seem inhumane" but reassured its practitioners that African captives would benefit if Christian purchasers "rescued them from a cruel slavery, and take them to the islands where they not only experience a gentler form of servitude, but also the knowledge of the true God and the path to salvation."[20] In 1734 the economist Jean-François Melon laid out nonreligious arguments that would be repeated and elaborated on by defenders of slavery for the rest of the century. "The colonies are necessary to the nation," he told his readers, "and the slaves are necessary to the colonies, where their numerical predominance over the colonists would be dangerous, if the customary gentleness of their treatment was not accompanied by military severity." Melon also addressed the issue of race. In the abstract, he admitted, it might be fair to treat all people the same, but "in spite of ourselves, we care more about Europeans than Africans." Although it would be desirable to increase the population of the colonies, he warned against the growing number of mixed-race children, "a new race of mulattos, whose deformity would be all the more dangerous, because there would be a continual comparison with the whites."[21] Richard Cantillon, another early contributor to the development of economic theory, made a sober calculation of the relative costs of employing enslaved and free laborers. Ignoring moral considerations, Cantillon concluded that "it will always be more profitable to the Proprietor to keep Slaves than to keep free Peasants, because when he has brought up a number too large for his requirements he can sell the surplus slaves as he does his cattle."[22]

The middle decades of the eighteenth century brought important changes in many aspects of French life, including attitudes toward the issues raised by the existence of the colonies. France came out of the first of the major wars fought under Louis XV, the War of the Austrian Succession in 1740–48, with most of its overseas colonies intact. The subsequent conflict that began in North America in 1754, where it was known as the French and Indian War, and in Europe in 1756, where it was called the Seven Years' War, ended in disaster for the country's empire. In the course of what has been called the first global war, the British conquered French Canada, the French trading posts in Senegal and their holdings in India, and the Caribbean islands of Martinique and Guadeloupe. In the peace settlement negotiated in 1763, the French managed to reclaim their Caribbean islands and one of their African slave-trading outposts, but only at the price of abandoning their holdings in North America and India.

On world maps drawn up after 1763, the remains of the French empire appeared insignificant compared with the holdings of its European rivals. Not only had France lost its territories in North

America and the Indian subcontinent, but the loyalty of the white colonists in its Caribbean islands had proved less than reliable. During the years when Guadeloupe had been occupied by the British, the local planters were able to buy African captives at lower prices than French slave traders demanded, and they had profited from the opportunity to sell their sugar on the British market instead of being forced to deal only with French merchants. Among officials in the bureau of the French naval ministry, which administered the colonies, there were questions about whether it was worth the cost of remaining in the colonial game. Members of the Physiocrats, a group of reformers devoted to the principle of free trade, suggested that France abandon its colonies and instead encourage the production of desirable commodities by free laborers in Africa. The Physiocrats' ideas appealed to some of the monarchy's policy experts.

The period of the Seven Years' War also generated new concern about the Black people present in France itself. In 1762 the king's representative to the Paris admiralty court, Guillaume Poncet de la Grave, complained to the judges that the 1738 edict requiring the registration of enslaved Blacks was not being enforced. "The introduction of too great a quantity of Negroes to France—whether in the quality of slaves, or in any other respect—is a dangerous consequence. We will soon see the French nation disfigured if a similar abuse is tolerated," he warned. The court responded by issuing a new ordinance, which differed from those of 1716 and 1738 because it required the registration of all persons of African ancestry, whether they were legally free or not; for the first time, a French law explicitly established race as a criterion for legal status. Among the Black people who had been living in France for some time without being registered and who now hurried to comply with the new regulations was the musically talented young Joseph Bologne, soon to become famous as the chevalier de Saint-George and known today as "the Black Mozart." Blacks threatened with being forcibly deported to the colonies brought legal cases contending that France's "freedom principle" should apply throughout the king's domains, prefiguring arguments that would be made during the revolutionary period.[23]

Surprisingly, far from signaling the end of France's overseas empire, the end of the Seven Years' War marked the beginning of a period in which the country's slave colonies took on greater importance than ever. In particular, Saint-Domingue, the largest of France's sugar islands, experienced a period of explosive economic growth that made it the largest and most intensive exploiter of slave labor in the Caribbean. In addition to sugar and the much-prized blue dyestuff indigo, French colonists began to cultivate another valuable crop, coffee. Britain's North American colonies developed into a major market for by-products of the sugar industry, molasses and rum, which did not interest French consumers. Determined to make the most of their remaining colonies, French ministers carried out reforms to their administrative systems and to the navy. By the time France entered the American Revolutionary War in 1778, these efforts had borne their fruit, and the French were able to hold their own against the British in the Caribbean while providing their American allies with crucial aid on the North American mainland.

In their efforts to support the Americans, the French even risked undermining the racial hierarchy in their own colonies: A unit of free men of color was formed in Saint-Domingue and served in the unsuccessful effort to capture Savannah in 1779. Some of these troops were taken to France after the failure of that campaign; the Saint-Domingue newspaper commented that "it must have seemed extraordinary in Europe to see people of color armed, disciplined, and war-ready."[24] By creating the prospect of lucrative trade with the newly independent United States, the conflict had the effect of making the Caribbean slave colonies seem more valuable than ever. The years that followed the end of the American war in 1783 were a period of unprecedented activity for French slave traders. The French government, eager to see the colonies prosper, actively promoted their activities. Slave traders received a bonus for every live captive they transported. Several edicts increased subsidies for traders supplying Martinique, Guadeloupe, and Saint-Domingue's South Province, areas where plantation owners complained about inadequate supplies, and allowed foreign traders to sell their captives in French ports.[25] Between 1783 and 1792, when the slave uprising in Saint-Domingue disrupted their business, the number of new captives carried on French ships averaged thirty-seven thousand per year, nearly double the highest rate achieved in any earlier period of the century. In 1789, the "Year 1 of French liberty" in revolutionary parlance, 130 French ships set off to purchase Black prisoners in Africa. By 1789, the number of enslaved laborers in Saint-Domingue alone had reached five hundred thousand, nearly twice as many as in 1780.[26]

Visiting France just before the Revolution, Banastre Tarleton, a British slave-trade advocate, enviously observed the advantages French policy gave to its slave traders:

> They are exempted from all import and export duties upon all manner of provisions, goods and merchandize included either in the outfit or cargo of the vessels. . . . They are entitled to a gratification of 40 livres per ton upon the measurement of every ship employed in African adventures . . . The French merchants are besides entitled to an additional bounty upon every head of Negroes imported in French vessels into the French colonies, to 160 livres for every Negro imported into the Windward Islands and 200 livres for every Negro landed at Port des Cayes Saint Louis in the southwest of the island of St. Domingo.[27]

Obviously jealous, Tarleton concluded, "The French government entertain a different opinion from that which is propagated by some people in this country and consider their African commerce . . . as a most important source of national wealth and the only natural support of their colonies."

A picture of how much the booming slave trade benefited the French economy can be derived from the manifests listing the cargo that slave ships took on board as they prepared to sail to Africa. The owner of the *Bon Père*, a vessel that sailed from La Rochelle in 1787, paid out 114,472 livres to get the ship ready for its voyage and to purchase the supplies of sea biscuits, rice, poultry, and salt meat that its crew would consume. In addition, the *Bon Père* left port carrying 295,000 livres' worth of trade goods to be exchanged for captives in Africa. Its inventory listed fifty-two different kinds of merchandise, including "textiles, liquor, glass of several different colors, knives, bowls, bells, Dutch pipes, 400 pounds of tobacco, mirrors, locks, stew pots, pottery, muskets together with flints and barrels of gunpowder, sabers, iron bars, lead, and umbrellas."[28] In La Rochelle, Nantes, and the other ports involved in the business, the slave trade was a major source of employment. Despite its known dangers—crews on slaving voyages died at rates comparable to those that affected the Black captives they helped transport—sailors do not seem to have been in short supply. The pay was low—20 to 30 livres a month—but it equaled what a peasant or an ordinary artisan could expect to earn. Ships' captains and officers were paid considerably more; a captain could come away from a single successful voyage with as much as 20,000 livres, several times the annual income of a typical lawyer or doctor of the period.[29]

To obtain the money to launch their costly ventures, slave traders depended on networks of investors, all of whom thereby came to have an interest in the prosperity of the business. Slave trading was an expensive affair involving major risks, and it might take years before a vessel completed the trip from France to Africa, the Middle Passage across the Atlantic, and the return voyage with a cargo of sugar and coffee whose sale would finally determine its profitability. Bankers in inland financial centers like Paris and Rouen were happy to put some of their capital to work this way. The number of individuals who had a monetary interest in the continued success of the slave trade thus greatly exceeded the number who were directly involved in outfitting the ships that embarked from France's ports.

Slave trading was a risky proposition: Some expeditions generated large profits, but a shipwreck or an outbreak of disease among the captives during the Middle Passage from Africa to the Caribbean could bring financial disaster. Direct trade in merchandise was safer, which explains why Bordeaux was content to let the smaller port of Nantes dominate the slave trade for much of the eighteenth century, until the 1780s when the possibilities in slave trading became so enticing that the Bordelais could no longer ignore them.[30] Nevertheless, both the slave trade and direct commerce with the colonies generated substantial profits, which were reflected in the prosperity of the cities along France's coasts. Many of the well-to-do members of France's bourgeoisie who would play important roles in the politics of the revolutionary period owed their prosperity to the empire.

The cargoes brought from the colonies by ships that had made the triangular voyage from France to Africa to the Caribbean and back, as well as the more numerous vessels engaged in direct trade with the islands, also generated economic activity in the metropole. Ironically, even as French colonial sugar and coffee production boomed in the 1780s, most of it was destined for reexport to other parts of Europe, particularly the Dutch Republic and northern Germany. The sale of sugar and coffee to foreign customers was essential to maintaining France's overall balance of trade, covering the cost of many products imported from outside the kingdom. There was a domestic sugar-refining industry, however, concentrated particularly in the Loire River city of Orléans south of Paris, where twenty-seven enterprises were operating in 1789.[31] Cotton and indigo, the other two principal products of the colonies, helped sustain textile manufacturing, the largest industry in the country at the time.

In addition to investing in slaving voyages, French men and women invested in colonial properties, even if they never intended to set foot on the islands. Both wealthy nobles and bourgeois commoners had properties overseas. Merchants in the port cities frequently lent money to plantation owners and sometimes wound up taking over their lands when their clients could not repay their debts. Other people in France inadvertently found themselves with claims to colonial property when relatives who had gone overseas died, leaving estates that often became the subjects of lengthy legal proceedings. Exploring the lives of a random collection of a few dozen eighteenth-century families in the quiet provincial town of Angoulême, for example, the American historian Emma Rothschild found at least a half dozen who became involved with such inheritance cases in the two decades before the Revolution.[32]

Paris, France's great metropolis, was as connected to the colonies as any other part of the country. "It is from Paris that we send them a considerable quantity of merchandise of all kinds, whose consumption keeps the arts, the manufactures and the commerce of this capital prosperous," one colonist wrote.

> It is in Paris that more than a thousand colonial property owners, their families and their children spend more than 50 million every year. It is in Paris that many daughters of wealthy colonists have made marriages

> that put a lot of wealth into circulation. It is in Paris that the colonists who seek redress, favors or justice, or who have left their country to come experience life in France, make their home. It is in Paris, finally, that those among them who have a large fortune show off their money and seek the advantages that wealth can only procure in a great capital.[33]

Not everyone in Paris was impressed with the wealth generated by these ties with the Caribbean, however. When one young aristocrat sought his estranged mother's consent for his marriage to a woman whose dowry consisted of properties in Saint-Domingue, his mother's lawyer objected that the value of such plantations was often exaggerated. Ironically, the young nobleman in this case was a certain Louis-Marthe Gouy d'Arsy, who never visited the Caribbean but who nevertheless drew on the status his wife's plantations gave him to become the leader of a campaign to obtain seats for the colonies in the revolutionary National Assembly of 1789.[34]

Interest in the colonies was frequently reflected in the period's visual culture. The *Encyclopédie* and other reference works included depictions of plantations that showed Black laborers at work. In 1785 a decorated faience plate made in the inland city of Nevers, a community with no obvious connection to the colonies, featured colorful scenes of Blacks working under the supervision of armed white overseers, with the motto "Long live good work in the isles of America"; presumably, these plates were intended for sale in the port cities (figure 1). Around the same time, the absentee owner of a Saint-Domingue sugar plantation commissioned an elaborate engraved map of his property there. The corners of the engraving were filled with detailed illustrations of colonial life, including a scene of a man with a raised whip pursuing a naked Black woman and another depicting a Black man with an iron collar around his neck. The owners of a slave ship that set sail from Nantes in 1770 commissioned detailed watercolor paintings showing how the captives were crammed into the hold and how they were supervised when they were brought up on deck for their meals.[35]

To some ambitious Frenchmen, the colonies, especially Saint-Domingue, had the allure of a place where one could find greater opportunities than in the metropole. An anonymous memoir from

FIGURE 1: *Le beau travalle de l'Amérique.* A pottery plate manufactured in the provincial city of Nevers in 1785 featured a white overseer and enslaved Black plantation laborers. *Credit:* © Musées d'Art et d'Histoire de la Rochelle, Max Roy.

the period relates the story of a young man who had resisted his parents' pressure to enter the priesthood. "I had a few ideas about the Americas . . . , having read a travel narrative about that country," he wrote. "My only thought and my only desire was to take a ship and to go Cap Français," the main city of Saint-Domingue. The parents of the rebellious teenager Victor Hugues, who would later play a major role in revolutionary politics in the Caribbean, shipped him off to an uncle in Saint-Domingue in 1777 to get him out of their house in Marseille. Other families deliberately encouraged their sons to think of seeking their fortune in the islands. René Levasseur, who in 1794 would make the motion that led to the National

Convention's decree abolishing slavery, claimed that his uncle, "a rich colonist," had promised him a share of his colonial estate, only to disinherit him when Levasseur "blamed the infamous slave trade in his presence."[36]

Another sign of France's increasing enmeshment with its slave colonies was the small but growing population of free people of color in the metropole. Some white colonists who had created "Atlantic families" by fathering children in the colonies sent them to Europe to be educated or even crossed the ocean as a family group. The most famous example is the family of the musician and swordsman Joseph Bologne, who arrived in France as a small boy in 1749 with his white father, a wealthy planter from Guadeloupe, together with his father's white wife and his own Black mother. Thanks to his family's wealth and connections—his father was officially received at the royal court in 1757—the young man was able to purchase a royal office in 1763, which entitled him to call himself the chevalier de Saint-George. Ten years later, having established himself as a virtuoso performer and composer, he became the conductor of the capital city's most celebrated musical ensemble. Saint-George was a unique case: No other person of mixed racial ancestry succeeded in breaking the country's racial barriers so dramatically. But even a recognized genius could face difficulties because of his race. In 1776 Louis XVI vetoed his appointment as director of the Royal Academy of Music when a group of female performers objected that "their honor and their delicate conscience would never permit them to be put under the orders of a mulatto."[37]

The greatest enemy of the mixed-race population in the metropole was the royal official Poncet de la Grave, who played a central role in pushing for greater restrictions against the admission of Blacks to France in 1762. He had support from some of the port cities: In Nantes, city authorities complained in 1770 that Blacks who were supposedly enslaved were finding ways to establish permanent residence. They "even form mixed unions," sometimes with the assistance of clergy who upheld their right to marriage, the complaint noted.[38] In 1776 Poncet de la Grave found a powerful ally in the new minister of the navy, Antoine Sartine. Sartine persuaded Louis XVI to issue a decree suspending any further freedom suits, pending a review of the legislation concerning the issue. Rather than referring to "slaves," the word that had always raised the hackles of French judges because it violated the venerable principle that "there are no slaves in France," Sartine drafted measures referring to "Blacks," introducing a racial criterion that would affect individuals regardless of their legal status. In August 1777 the king approved the final version of the *police des noirs* (regulation regarding Blacks). The justification for the measure that Sartine submitted used explicitly racist language: "Their marriages to Europeans are encouraged; the public houses are infected; the colors mingle together; the blood degenerates. . . . If they return to America, they carry with them the spirit of liberty, of independence and of equality that they communicate to the others; destroy the bonds of discipline and subordination and thereby prepare a revolution."[39]

These toughened regulations set off a rush on the part of owners and employers of Black servants to comply with its requirements: Lists from 1777 include over 1,400 individuals. In Bordeaux alone, there were 208 enslaved Black people and 94 with free status. Of the individuals registered in 1777, about one-quarter were characterized as "mulattos." Slightly over half of them had been born in the colonies, and almost a third were originally from Africa. Of those who indicated their legal status, 49 percent were free; the situation of the others was often unclear, given the contradiction between France's supposed "freedom principle" and the recognition of slave owners' rights. More than two-thirds of those registered in 1777 were men, mostly young, and the vast majority were domestic servants. In Paris many members of the nobility included Black servants in their households; in the port cities, ships' captains and merchants trading with the colonies had frequently brought Blacks back from their overseas voyages.[40]

In a matter of years, the *police des noirs*, like all previous attempts to limit the presence of Blacks in France, lost most of its effectiveness. The well-connected aristocrats who employed most of the Black servants in the capital were easily able to flout the regulations, and courts continued to grant freedom to most of the Black people who managed to get their cases heard. Among those who had succeeded in making themselves economically independent, the men were often hairdressers or cooks, while women earned their living as seamstresses. Only a minority were able to get around the regulations designed to discourage them from marrying; of those who succeeded, most were in racially mixed relationships. About one in seven of the Black people residing in France at the time of the 1777 survey was able to read and write.[41]

The treatment Black residents received from the surrounding population varied tremendously. A few were members of princely families from Africa, like Boudacan-Marc, from the kingdom of Warri, who visited both Paris and Saint-Domingue in 1784. The French government hoped to negotiate a trade treaty with his country, and the colonial legal expert Moreau de Saint-Méry delivered a lecture about him.[42] Many Blacks had originally been brought to France by colonial slave owners but had been granted their freedom by their former owners. Others were the mixed-race children of white colonists who had returned to France, like the children of the La Rochelle merchant Aimé-Benjamin Fleuriau, who brought them to his native city in 1763. His three sons eventually returned to Saint-Domingue, but his two daughters remained in the port city.[43] Some of the Black people in France lived quietly, accepted by their neighbors; if they were people of mixed race with light skin, they might even succeed in passing for white and disappearing into the general population. French judges generally favored Black plaintiffs who came to court claiming that they were being unjustly held as slaves or were being mistreated. Consulted by another American in 1786 about what problems he might encounter if he brought an enslaved servant to France with him, the American ambassador Thomas Jefferson warned that "the laws of France give him freedom if he claims it."[44] Other Blacks, however, experienced hostility and prejudice. In Paris in 1780, agents of a former colonist whose servant had won a legal judgment granting him his freedom attacked the man in the street, also beating up two other Black men they encountered for good measure.[45]

As they tried to accommodate and even strengthen France's connections with its overseas possessions in the 1780s and deal with issues such as the presence of Blacks in the metropole, royal authorities found it increasingly difficult to reconcile economic interests, racial prejudices, and a public opinion that was becoming receptive to criticisms of slavery. A memorandum prepared by one official in 1781 made the case that the treatment of slaves in the colonies needed to be ameliorated "so that their numbers can be regenerated regularly in our possessions, which Africa will soon be unable to supply," in view of the growing difficulty that slave traders were having in finding enough captives to meet the colonists' demands. As the French historian of colonial trade Jean Tarrade noted, the point of view expressed in this document was "strictly mercantile and not humanitarian," and it did not lead to any immediate reform measures; its author himself warned that "slavery is a kind of swamp which it is dangerous to stir up."[46]

In late 1780 the minister Sartine, who had started the discussions that led to the 1781 report, was replaced by Charles Eugène Gabriel de la Croix, the marquis de Castries. In 1784 Castries undertook to reform the regulations governing slavery in the colonies. The ordinance he issued on 3 December 1784 was in no sense an attempt at the abolition of slavery. Instead, it reaffirmed the provisions of the original Code Noir that were meant to assure enslaved laborers a minimum of decent treatment. Its most radical alteration to the Code Noir was an elaborate section on the administration of plantations, meant to ensure that the regulations were actually observed.[47]

Slave owners reacted violently to even this seemingly mild reform. "We sit here on top of a barrel of gunpowder, which can be set off by the slightest error in administration, and that is what will happen if the court does not change its policy," one of them wrote. "This edict violates the sacred rights of property and puts a dagger in the hands of the slaves, by giving control over their discipline and their regime to someone other than their masters."[48] Castries responded to complaints by persuading the king to reaffirm his measures in December 1785. Nevertheless, opposition, especially in the key colony of Saint-Domingue, remained powerful. In 1786 the government tried to repress dissent there by abolishing the Conseil supérieur in Cap Français and uniting it with the more tractable court in Port-au-Prince, a move that spurred even more resistance. It was clear that if any broader reforms to the monarchy allowed the Caribbean colonists an opportunity to voice their opinions, efforts to tinker with the regulation of slavery would face even stronger objections.

CHAPTER TWO

The Prerevolutionary Debate About Slavery

CARIBBEAN PLANTERS REACTED vehemently against the minister Castries's attempted reforms because, even in the midst of the boom in slave imports in the 1780s, they felt increasingly beleaguered. In addition to the fear of slave conspiracies that made them complain that they lived "on top of a barrel of gunpowder," they knew that slavery was coming under increased attack in the metropole. Since the middle of the eighteenth century, French writers had been forging ever more powerful arguments against the institution. Long before the outbreak of the French Revolution, the intellectual weapons that would be wielded on behalf of abolition were already familiar. Slavery was denounced as a flagrant violation of its victims' natural rights, as an outrage to sentiments of humanity, and as a drag on the French economy. Its defenders were ready with justifications for the institution, but they were fighting an uphill battle. In the age of Enlightenment, traditional appeals to Bible passages permitting slavery lost their effectiveness, forcing its proponents to turn to secular arguments about racial differences and to emphasize the practical obstacles to any change in the system.

The discussion of slavery in the Baron de Montesquieu's masterwork, *The Spirit of the Laws*, published in 1748, marked a turning point in French discussions of the issue. For the first time, an author recognized as one of the kingdom's major intellects delivered a sustained critique of the institution, devoting an entire section of his magnum opus to the questions it raised. Montesquieu was well acquainted with these questions. His native city of Bordeaux owed its fortune to overseas trade, and it has been claimed that he may have had financial interests tied to the colonies, although recent scholarship has disputed these assertions.[1] The first chapter of book 15 of Montesquieu's work began with an unambiguous condemnation of the very principle of slavery: "It is not good in its essence: it is neither useful to the master nor to the slave. To the master, because he contracts all sorts of bad habits with his slaves; he becomes accustomed to violating all the moral virtues, he becomes proud, hasty, hard, angry, obsessed with pleasure, cruel."[2] Montesquieu then traced the history of slavery, from Roman times onward. Despite historical precedents, he asserted, slavery was always contrary to natural law. He rejected arguments such as the claim that the purchase of captives in Africa was justified on the grounds that they were condemned criminals or prisoners of war.

When he came to the specific topic of "the slavery of Negroes," Montesquieu abruptly abandoned the sober style of the earlier parts of his discussion for what some readers took to be biting sarcasm, whereas others interpreted his language as evidence that he was not truly serious in denouncing the treatment of enslaved Blacks. "If I had to justify the right that we have to enslave the Blacks, here is what I would say: The peoples of Europe, having exterminated the inhabitants of America, had to put the Africans into slavery, to clear and work all that land"; the sugar that Europeans craved would be too expensive otherwise. The following lines in Montesquieu's text are the most controversial: "Those of whom we speak are black from their feet to their heads, and their noses are so flattened that it is almost impossible to feel sorry for them. One can hardly imagine that God, who is such a wise being, could have put a soul, especially a good soul, in an entirely black body." Was Montesquieu attempting to ridicule arguments for Black inferiority, or did he perhaps share his onetime Bordeaux academy colleague Jean-François Melon's opinion that blackness was a "deformity" that could justify depriving Black people of their rights?[3]

Having condemned slavery as an inherent violation of natural law and having singled out the particular issue of the enslavement of Africans in the European colonies, Montesquieu then complicated his own argument by suggesting that there were some parts of the world where the institution was nevertheless necessary. "There are countries where the heat enfeebles the body and weakens the spirit so much that men cannot be made to perform arduous duties except out of a fear of punishment. There, slavery is less of a shock to reason," he wrote.[4] Nevertheless, in a country with a free government, as France thought of itself, slavery was difficult to maintain. "Nothing puts men in a condition more like that of beasts than to be continually in contact with free men, and not to be one of them. Such men are the natural enemies of society, and it would be dangerous if there were a large number of them," he wrote. His chapter 17, "Regulations to Be Made Between the Master and the Slaves," reads like a summary of the protective provisions of the French Code Noir: "The magistrate should see that the slave has his food and his clothing; that should be regulated by the law." Masters should be obliged to care for their slaves in illness and old age, and they should not be allowed to put them to death without going through a legal procedure.[5] Although Montesquieu did not explicitly propose the abolition of slavery, he devoted a chapter to the question of manumissions. "One must not suddenly, and by a general law, grant a large number of manumissions," he wrote, but enslaved individuals might be given the opportunity to earn their freedom, and those who had the skills to support themselves could be made independent; he thus sketched out possibilities that later authors would develop into schemes for gradual emancipation that would compensate slave owners for the money they had spent to purchase their captive laborers or raise the laborers' children until they were old enough to work. Perhaps with the Code Noir's provisions about free people of color in mind, he recognized the issues posed by their place in society, writing that the law should be clear about what obligations they had to their former owners.[6]

One cannot classify Montesquieu as an abolitionist, and defenders of slavery frequently cited his argument that slavery was inevitable in tropical climates, but his work established a pattern that would recur in French discussions of slavery down to the years of the Revolution. Setting aside the religious considerations that pervaded the English abolitionist John Woolman's impassioned *Considerations on the Keeping of Negroes*, published six years after *The Spirit of the Laws*, Montesquieu treated the issue as a purely secular and moral one. Like most subsequent French Enlightenment authors, he wrote about slavery in two registers—one in which he treated it as an unmistakable violation of natural rights, and one in which he pragmatically accepted its existence and tried to limit its abuses—without finding a way to reconcile them. Even if what one scholar has called the "sinuosities of his reasoning" make it hard to decide what Montesquieu's intimate thoughts on the subject were, however, *The Spirit of the Laws* brought the issue of slavery into the center of public discussion in France in a way that no previous publication had done.[7]

Subsequent French authors borrowed liberally from Montesquieu's discussion of slavery. In 1755 Louis de Jaucourt, author of several articles on the subject in the celebrated *Encyclopédie*, the compendium of Enlightenment ideas edited by the two French men of letters Jean d'Alembert and Denis Diderot, freely acknowledged reprinting large extracts from *The Spirit of the Laws* in his treatment of the subject. In his article on the slave trade, Jaucourt denounced "this buying of Negroes, to reduce them to slavery," as a "business that violates religion, morality, natural laws, and the rights of human nature," and he coined a phrase destined to reverberate during the French Revolution: "Let the European colonies be destroyed rather than make so many unfortunate people."[8] In the Revolution's most heated debate about slavery in May 1791, Maximilien Robespierre would repeat Jaucourt's words, earning himself a reputation as an uncompromising enemy of slavery.

Just as Montesquieu had sometimes contradicted himself in his discussion of slavery, the multiauthor *Encyclopédie* included articles that expressed a wide range of views on race and slavery. Samuel Formey's article "Negro" alluded to the notion of separate races, opining that Blacks "seem to constitute a new species of humans" who displayed a range of skin tones but who were uniformly ugly. Diderot, the *Encyclopédie*'s principal editor and one of the most radical Enlightenment thinkers, did not think Blacks were the equal of whites, but he left no doubt about his dislike for slavery: "Although in general Negroes have little intelligence, they are not devoid of feeling. They react to good and bad treatment. . . . We have reduced them, I do not say to the condition of slaves, but to that of beasts of burden; and we are reasonable! And we are Christians!"[9] Despite his personal opposition to slavery, however, Diderot included in the *Encyclopédie* an article titled "Commerce in Negroes" that repeated customary justifications for the slave trade and warned purchasers of enslaved Africans that "their hard nature requires that one not treat them with too much indulgence." An article titled "Negroes, Considered as Slaves in the American Colonies" described the Blacks as naturally lazy and superstitious, but generally submissive and good-natured. Just as Robespierre would borrow a line from Jaucourt's denunciation of the slave trade, the revolutionary deputy Louis Dufay, whose speech on 4 February 1794 provoked the National Convention's decree abolishing slavery, would repeat this article's description of the Blacks as "generally honest, brave, compassionate, charitable, respectful of their parents . . . and very respectful to the elderly."[10]

Voltaire and Jean-Jacques Rousseau, who were, along with Montesquieu, the most famous authors of the French Enlightenment, had much less to say about slavery. Voltaire dashed off a few throwaway lines, especially a famous passage in his short novel *Candide* in which the title character meets an enslaved Black man who has been badly mutilated by a cruel slave master and who tells him, "This is the price at which you eat sugar in Europe." Perhaps because the Bible insisted so strongly on the common origin of the human species, the antireligious Voltaire espoused polygeneticism—the idea that whites and Blacks were separate species—and he did not hesitate, on occasion, to state openly that whites "seem to me superior to these Negroes, as these Negroes are to apes."[11] It has been claimed that Voltaire, a wealthy man, had investments in the slave trade; he did own some stock in the Compagnie des Indes but he does not seem to have put any money directly into slaving voyages.[12]

Rousseau's relationship to the issue of slavery was more complicated than Voltaire's. Rousseau's *Social Contract*, his most celebrated political work, famously begins with the line, "Man is born free, and yet everywhere he is in chains," leading readers to expect a polemic against slavery and other forms of oppression, but the second sentence of the work presents those chains as legitimate, since they represent the obligations imposed by the social contract to which all members of society have consented. Rousseau did emphatically refute the justifications of slavery advanced in earlier works on natural law, particularly those of Hugo Grotius and John Locke, concluding that "the words *slavery* and *right* are contradictory; they mutually exclude each other." Unlike Montesquieu, however, Rousseau had nothing to say about slavery as a historical phenomenon or an aspect of the world in which he lived. Furthermore, he conceded that, in order for free citizens to devote themselves to the welfare of their society, it might be necessary for them to rely on slaves to work for them, as had been the case in ancient Sparta.[13]

More influential in discussions about the issue of slavery during the middle years of the eighteenth century than the works of Voltaire or Rousseau was a now-forgotten volume by Victor Riqueti, marquis de Mirabeau, the father of the famous revolutionary orator. The elder Mirabeau's *L'Ami des hommes* (The Friend of Mankind) went through twenty editions in the years that followed its first publication in 1756. Unlike Montesquieu's *Spirit of the Laws*, *L'Ami des hommes* was an out-and-out polemic, designed to promote the dogma of unrestricted commercial freedom that was the mantra of the school of French economic writers known as the Physiocrats. Whereas Voltaire and Rousseau had little firsthand knowledge about conditions in the French colonies, Mirabeau was well informed thanks to his brother Jean-Antoine, who served as governor of Guadeloupe from 1753 to 1757. The planters' treatment of the Blacks revolted Jean-Antoine. "One cannot reconcile slavery with Christianity," he told his brother. "I know that if I were made minister of the navy tomorrow, I would have an edict passed that would declare every Negro free upon being baptized."[14]

Encouraged by his brother's jaundiced view of the colonies, Victor Mirabeau denounced the "monstrous system that constitutes the current policy of Europe in the Americas." His condemnation of slavery was part of his overall tirade against the whole colonial enterprise. He was not motivated by any great humanitarian concern for Black people, whom he called "a separate race, distinguished and separated from our species by the most permanent characteristic . . . , color." Nevertheless, he was disgusted by the way enslaved Blacks were treated in the colonies. "They are tossed into stables where their fellows are crowded together, they are overworked for the benefit of their masters, and from this system of customs and usages there is born . . . in a century that considers itself the epitome of enlightenment, the harshest and, I would dare to say, the most impious of servitudes."[15]

In the years following the publication of *L'Ami des hommes*, members of the Physiocrat group with which Victor Mirabeau associated himself took up and extended his campaign against the French colonial system and his critique of the economic disadvantages of slavery. Expanding on the Physiocrats' boundless faith in the liberating power of free trade, Pierre-Joseph-André Roubaud, editor of the *Journal de Commerce*, outlined an idea that would pervade French discussions about slavery, colonization, and Africa down to the revolutionary era and beyond. "Will it not be more humane to introduce Christian Religion, commerce, and the Arts to the inhabitants of Africa & provide them with a taste for commodities & the pleasures of life, than to buy them to turn them into slaves, & leave uncultivated such a beautiful region only to continue a commerce so contrary to all Christian doctrines & to common notions of conscience?"[16] Bringing Africa into the sphere of European-style capitalism would eliminate both the need for expensive colonies and the demand for enslaved laborers.

These early critiques of slavery alarmed defenders of the institution and inspired defenses of it. In 1764 the Marseille merchant Auguste Chambon's manual for traders acknowledged the moral issues that the slave trade raised, showing, as the American scholar Lauren Clay has said, "that for the first time, those making money from slavery found themselves on the defensive."[17] A theologian, Jean Bellon de Saint-Quentin, repeated the religious arguments that had been used for centuries to justify the institution. "One doesn't aggravate the conditions of the enslaved Negroes, and one does them no injury in transferring them to our islands. . . . They are given the opportunity to know Jesus Christ and his evangel, and thereby to escape from the spiritual slavery that is infinitely worse, that leaves them in thrall to the devil and to sin," he wrote.[18]

Bellon de Saint-Quentin at least pretended to care about the salvation of Black people's souls. The naturalist Jacques-Philibert Rousselot de Surgy made it clear that, in his view, they did not deserve such consideration: "All the travelers who have spent time among them, all the writers who have described them, agree in representing them as a nation that has . . . souls as black as their bodies. . . . No capacity for reasoning among the Negroes, no intelligence, no aptitude for any kind of abstract study. . . . Force is the only way to make them obey, and fear is the only thing that makes them act." Adapting the polygeneticist hypothesis to the defense of slavery, he concluded, "One would be tempted to believe . . . that the Negroes form a race of creatures that serves as the intermediate step by which nature seems to go from the orangutans, the chimpanzees, to man."[19] An illustration of where this kind of racist thinking could lead can be found in the unpublished papers of Emmanuel Sieyès, who would later become one of the most prominent figures in the French Revolution and a member of the abolitionist Société des Amis des Noirs. At some point in the years before the Revolution, Sieyès wrote a note to himself that he titled "Slaves. For another species that would have fewer needs and be less capable of exciting human compassion," in which he speculated about the possibility of creating a "species between men and animals" by mating apes with Negroes. These "anthropomorphic monkeys" could be used as slaves without raising the moral issues generated by the existing system of slavery.[20]

A more provocative case in favor of slavery was put forth by Simon-Nicolas-Henri Linguet, one of the period's literary celebrities. In his *Théorie des lois civiles* (Theory of civil laws), published in 1767, Linguet contended that "slavery is inseparable from the existence of society, that it always exists, though it may change its appearance." Linguet's argument was in some ways an extreme extension of Rousseau's denunciation of the evils of society and civilization, but he was not just making an abstract case. In passages that attracted the attention of later socialist theorists, notably Karl Marx, Linguet denounced the exploitation of supposedly free laborers in European societies. Far from making the condition of the poor better, he maintained, the abolition of slavery and serfdom had left them worse off. "They never have any part of the abundance that flows from their work . . . all that they have gained is to be continually tormented by the fear of dying of hunger. . . . The slave mattered to his master because of the money that he had cost him. But the free laborer doesn't cost the rich man who hires him anything."[21]

In several places in his treatise, Linguet commented explicitly on the situation of the enslaved populations in the French colonies. He admitted that an enslaved captive had the right to resist, but he also wrote that slave owners had a right to try to recapture their human property. The survival of the colonies was of no particular concern to Linguet: "What danger would there be for the universal social order, if all the Negroes of our islands took flight; if they preferred . . . the company of poisonous snakes . . . to the labor of processing the cane they have cultivated, and of which they are not even permitted to taste the sugar?" But a generalized revolt of the enslaved Blacks in the colonies would be a disaster. "It would not be an injustice, but it might be the cause of a great revolution," he wrote.[22]

Linguet had nothing but scathing contempt for those who thought the inevitable condition of humankind could be changed. "All the philosophical declamations that combat this maxim [the inevitability of slavery] are senseless, useless and even dangerous," he wrote. The critics' "lamentations about the enslavement of Negroes have not reduced by a single shilling the funds of the company that, from the coffeehouses of London, sends orders to buy them in Guinea and sell them in America." Since reform efforts were inevitably bound to fail, "one happily lets them have the glory of having well defended a cause in which they certainly will not prevail."[23] Despite his virulent disdain for the philosophes of the Enlightenment, Linguet gave the most "philosophical" justification of slavery produced at the time. He was determined to meet its critics on their own ground, insisting that they recognize that once humanity left the original state of nature, all laws did nothing but codify the right of the stronger.

Linguet's argument for slavery was aimed in part at the Physiocrats or "economists" who had critiqued slavery as part of their advocacy for an unfettered market economy based on free labor. For their part, the Physiocrats amplified and extended their criticism of slavery after 1763. Among the most influential of the Physiocrats' critiques of slavery was an article published in the *Ephémérides* by another member of the group, Pierre Samuel du Pont de Nemours, in 1771. Du Pont claimed to demonstrate that the cost of importing enslaved captives from Africa to the Caribbean, supervising them strictly enough to force them to do involuntary labor, caring for them in old age, and subsidizing the raising of their children far exceeded the cost of employing free laborers. "The slave is lazy, because laziness is his only pleasure, and the only way to recover a part of his personal autonomy, which the master has stolen. The slave is clumsy, because he has no interest in developing his intelligence. The slave is ill-intentioned, because he is in a continuous state of war with his master," du Pont wrote. "It would not be the same with free workers, who would keep what they earned. The desire to increase these earnings, and to merit preference over their rivals, would make them enterprising and intelligent."[24] Although even some of his friends, such as the reforming minister Etienne-François Turgot, questioned his calculations, du Pont's claims were widely repeated; modern scholarship indicates that he grossly underestimated the cost of free labor.[25] His assertions enabled critics to argue that slavery could be painlessly eliminated by persuading plantation owners to emancipate their laborers and turn them into free workers whose own economic interest would lead them to strive harder in order to earn more.

The growing collection of texts questioning the morality and the economic profitability of slavery and the slave trade presented the issues in an abstract fashion, without reference to the personal experiences of the Black victims of these institutions. As French writers became increasingly concerned with the issue of slavery, some of them were inspired to produce depictions of the injustice of slavery shaped to appeal to readers' emotions as well as their reason. The most successful French story of this sort was Jean-François Saint-Lambert's novella *Ziméo*, which appeared in 1769. Set in the British Caribbean colony of Jamaica, where the uprising known as Tacky's Rebellion, the largest slave rebellion in the Caribbean before the Haitian Revolution, had taken place in 1760, *Ziméo* features a handsome Black hero who reminds the narrator of Greek statues of Apollo. Ziméo is tricked into slavery by European merchants and taken to the Caribbean, along with his beloved, a young woman named Ellaroé. Saint-Lambert spared his readers none of the horrors of the Middle Passage, including a scene in which the white slave traders, having run out of food during the voyage, kill the sicklier Black prisoners and force the others to eat their flesh. On arrival in Jamaica, Ziméo is forcibly separated from Ellaroé, which drives him to despair.[26]

Unwilling to suffer the cruelty of the Jamaican slave owners, Ziméo puts himself at the head of a violent insurrection, described by the fictional narrator in language that would become all too familiar in France after the outbreak of the Haitian uprising in 1791: "Most of the houses were in flames; two or three hundred pillars of dark red fire reached from the plain to the summit of the mountains. . . . With sabers in their hands, furious Negroes pursued my unfortunate fellow citizens . . . ; from the plain, the cries of the slaughtered whites and the Negroes avid for carnage reached my ears." Arriving at the narrator's plantation, Ziméo discovers that its Blacks are preparing to defend their kind master. Instead of attacking, he takes the opportunity to explain himself. "I have taken revenge for my race and myself," he announces. But he asserts that he is not cruel by nature. He insists that "the Negro, born to love, becomes a tiger, a leopard, when he is forced to hate, and I have become one."[27]

Published before better-known evocations of the "liberator of the New World" in Louis-Sébastien Mercier's futuristic *L'Année 2440* and "the great man whom nature owes to its vexed, oppressed, tormented children" in the abbé Guillaume Thomas François Raynal's *Histoire des deux Indes*, *Ziméo* predicted that resentment against the cruelty of slavery would bring forth a leader who would launch a revolt against it. What was lacking in the story was any hint of what the white readers to whom *Ziméo* was addressed might do in response to the strong feelings Saint-Lambert's prose evoked. His story, which was reprinted several times in the two decades before the Revolution and inspired similar works, including a play by Olympe de Gouges, the future author of the 1791 "Declaration of the Rights of Women," and an unpublished story by the young Germaine de Staël, contributed to the creation of an atmosphere critical of slavery, but not to any concrete movement.[28]

Between the years 1770 and 1789, numerous authors repeated and extended the forceful arguments against slavery produced in the two previous decades, and public opinion appeared increasingly critical of the institution. For the first time, concrete proposals for the abolition of slavery were put forward. They were cautious and reflected assumptions about Black racial backwardness, but they nevertheless began the process of moving from abstract discussions of natural law and emotional denunciations of injustice to thinking about how significant change could be brought about. Public opinion was far from unanimous on the subject, however. Defenders of the slave trade and of the colonial order also became increasingly outspoken, developing a range of arguments that were less dependent on religious authority and more attuned to the ideas of the Enlightenment. As they sharpened their rhetorical weapons, would-be abolitionists and their opponents mingled freely in Paris salons and in institutions like the Musée de Paris, where the abolitionist Condorcet lectured on mathematics while the proslavery jurist Médéric Louis Élie Moreau de Saint-Méry explained that since "the enslaved are and must be the enemies of their masters," the Blacks needed to be kept under strict control.[29]

The year 1770 was marked by the appearance of the first edition of a work destined to provoke more discussion about the institution of slavery than any other publication of the period: the *Histoire philosophique des deux Indes* (Philosophical history of the two Indies). At first glance, this multivolume compilation of historical and statistical information about the European overseas empires hardly seemed destined to become one of the great bestsellers of the Enlightenment era. It had none of the satirical bite of Voltaire or Montesquieu and none of the emotional pathos of Saint-Lambert. Nevertheless, the *Histoire des deux Indes* became a sensational publishing phenomenon. Thirty-six editions appeared between 1770 and 1779, and an additional seventeen in the decade that followed.[30] The *Histoire des deux Indes* was translated into every major European language and inspired numerous published responses. Catholic critics condemned it as antireligious, particularly because of its denunciations of the Church's role in justifying the destruction of the New World's Indigenous populations and the institution of slavery. Governments denounced its scathing portrayal of their colonial policies; merchants and shippers debated its positions on the proper regulation of overseas trade.

Although the first two editions of 1770 and 1774 were published anonymously, the *Histoire des deux Indes* was associated from the start with the name of Guillaume Thomas François Raynal, a well-known figure in French literary circles and a habitué of Paris salons, such as that run by Madame Necker, the wife of the influential banker and future royal minister.[31] "No one knew more about the slave trade than the abbé Raynal, since he had made profitable investments in it," Louis-Sébastien Mercier, who sometimes attended the "celebrated luncheons" at which Raynal held forth, wrote. He remembered Raynal speaking in "his rustic accent, not letting any proposition go unchallenged, interrupting everyone."[32]

How much of the work's content actually came from Raynal's pen and how many of its more controversial passages accurately reflect his personal views remain subjects of controversy. Many of the work's most quotable passages about slavery are now thought to have been written either by Jean-Joseph de Pechméja, a minor man of letters of the period, or by Denis Diderot, the editor of the *Encyclopédie*, who took the opportunity to insert attacks on despotism and slavery without having to take public responsibility for them.[33] Whatever the truth about its authorship, the *Histoire des deux Indes* was central to every discussion concerning the colonial world throughout the years preceding the French Revolution.

Slavery was not the only or even the principal theme in the *Histoire des deux Indes*, but it was extensively discussed. In keeping with the tradition of French considerations of the subject dating back to Montesquieu, the work's approach was ambiguous and confusing, as du Pont complained in his review of the first edition: "Sometimes he expresses horror at slavery; he calls it useless and harmful as well as odious; and sometimes he tries to prove the need for slave labor, and the imaginary advantages of the slave trade."[34] The 1770 and 1774 editions parroted the conventional wisdom of the day about the physiological differences between whites and Blacks, claiming that the latter were by nature "more effeminate, lazier, weaker and unfortunately more suited to slavery" than other varieties of the human species. All three editions repeated the assertion, probably borrowed from Jean-Baptiste Labat, that

HISTOIRE
PHILOSOPHIQUE
ET POLITIQUE
DES ÉTABLISSEMENS ET DU COMMERCE
DES EUROPÉENS DANS LES DEUX INDES.

Par GUILLAUME-THOMAS RAYNAL.

TOME TROISIEME.

A GENEVE,
Chez JEAN-LEONARD PELLET, Imprimeur de
la Ville & de l'Académie.

M. DCC. LXXX.

FIGURE 2: The frontispiece of Raynal's *Histoire philosophique et politique des établissemens et du commerce des Européens dans les deux Indes*. The best-selling *Histoire des deux Indes* contained passages and images underlining the cruelty of slavery and warning of a possible slave revolt. *Credit:* Wikimedia Commons.

Black captives with humane masters "spontaneously embrace his interests."[35] More than these recyclings of familiar justifications for slavery and the colonial system, however, it was the book's denunciatory passages, which became more outspoken in each successive edition, that captured readers' attention. "Nothing is more horrible than the condition of the Blacks throughout the American archipelago. . . . Deprived of everything, [they are] condemned to unremitting toil, in a burning climate, under the constantly brandished whip of a ferocious driver," read the 1770 edition. In an example of how the book became more vehement over the years, by 1780, a line was added to this paragraph describing how "one begins by marking them with the ineffaceable seal of slavery, by branding them with a hot iron on their arms or their breasts with the name or the symbol of their oppressor."[36] Illustrations included in the work underlined the message about the cruelty of slavery (figure 2).

The most celebrated passage of the *Histoire des deux Indes*, both at the time and in every recent study of slavery, was one predicting that if the oppressive system on the plantations was not reformed or abolished, it would provoke a devastating revolt. These lines appeared first in the 1774 edition: "All the Blacks need is a leader courageous enough to lead them to vengeance and carnage. Where is he, this great man, who nature owes perhaps to the honor of the human race? Where is he, this new Spartacus? . . . Then the *Code noir* will disappear; how terrible the *Code blanc* will be, if the victor uses the right of reprisal!" In 1780 the reference to the "new Spartacus" was cut in favor of a line prophesying the arrival of a "great man": "He will appear, do not doubt it, he will show himself, he will raise the sacred banner of liberty. This venerable signal will rally his companions in misfortune around him. More impetuous than the torrents, everywhere they will leave indelible traces of their just resentment . . . all their tyrants will fall prey to the sword and the flames. The fields of America will eagerly be intoxicated with blood that they have awaited for many years."[37]

The trope of the Black liberator was another of the borrowings that characterized the *Histoire des deux Indes*: Saint-Lambert had employed it in *Ziméo*, and in his utopian novel, *The Year 2440*, published in 1771, Louis-Sébastien Mercier had imagined a statue in the Paris of the twenty-fifth century dedicated to "the Avenger of the New World," a Black man honored because he had "broken the chains of his compatriots" and "spilled the blood of their tyrants."[38] In the *Histoire des deux Indes*, the intended meaning of the passage was ambiguous. It was certainly not meant as an incitement to a slave revolt, both because enslaved Blacks in the Caribbean were unlikely to have the opportunity to read a multivolume work on European colonialism and because, as the passage itself stated, "your slaves have no need of your generosity, nor of your advice, to break the sacrilegious yoke that oppresses them." The evocation of a devastating slave uprising served rather as a warning of what would happen if the whites themselves did not take steps to ward off the danger. In all three editions, the passage about a possible slave revolt followed several sentences calling on the sovereigns of Europe to unite to support a program by which enslaved Blacks would be "given their liberty, but only one after the other, as a recompense for their savings, their conduct, their work": In other words, they would have to earn their freedom by their individual efforts.[39]

Whatever the ambiguities and hesitations of its message, the *Histoire des deux Indes* made the questions it treated central themes of public discussion. Its success inspired numerous other authors, including several who would go on to play a role in the French Revolution's debates on slavery, to take up the topic. A particularly significant recruit to the cause was Marie Jean Antoine Nicolas de Caritat, the marquis de Condorcet, the first of the prerevolutionary abolitionists who would live long enough to play a major role in the French Revolution. Elected to the Royal Academy of Sciences in 1769 at the age of twenty-four, and made its secretary in 1773, Condorcet occupied a central position in French intellectual life until the early years of the Revolution. The minister Etienne-François Turgot, who attempted to implement some of the ideas of the Physiocrats during his two years in office, from 1774 to 1776, brought Condorcet into politics by appointing him as inspector general of the royal mint in 1774. Among the ambitions Turgot expressed was the hope to "gradually eliminate, through wise laws, the slavery of the Negroes, the shame of modern nations." Writing in praise of his former patron in 1786, Condorcet said that Turgot "knew that . . . the example given by a great nation would lead all the others, and would win for the minister who gave it the gratitude of all of humanity."[40]

Why Condorcet developed a special detestation of slavery is unclear. He never visited the colonies, and it is not clear that he had any personal encounters with Black people until the Revolution. Like most French schoolboys of his generation, he had been subjected to severe discipline from his teachers, and he, like his future colleague in the Société des Amis des Noirs Jacques-Pierre Brissot, strongly condemned the practice of whipping students; such personal experiences may have made him sensitive to the cruelty of the punishments used on plantations.[41] Condorcet first wrote against slavery in 1776, in an unlikely context: the notes appended to his edition of the seventeenth-century philosopher Blaise Pascal's *Pensées*. In words that equaled or surpassed the strongest passages of the *Histoire des deux Indes*, he denounced the cruelty of slavery: "Tear men away from their homes, through treachery and violence, in order to sell them in public markets like beasts of burden; become accustomed to treating them like animals; force them to work by beating them; feed them, not so that they can live, but so that they can make money for us; abandon them when they are old or sick. . . . Permit them to become fathers only in order to give life to children destined to the same misery. . . . That's how we treat other men!"[42]

Burying a declamation against slavery in notes to a reprint of a century-old philosophical work was hardly an effective strategy for influencing public opinion. In 1781 Condorcet made a more serious effort to promote the abolitionist cause by publishing, under the pseudonym of a fictitious Protestant pastor named Joachim Schwartz, a pamphlet devoted exclusively to the subject. As forcefully as any author who had treated the subject, he proclaimed that "reducing a man to slavery, buying him, selling him, keeping him in servitude, are true crimes, crimes worse than theft."[43] Condorcet went further than any previous French author by putting forward an actual plan for emancipation. In the first place, he proposed banning the slave trade; like the American and British advocates of abolition who were beginning to campaign for such a measure, he reasoned that if planters could not purchase new captives from Africa, they would have to treat their laborers more humanely and encourage them to have children. He considered the possibility of declaring enslaved Black people free immediately, which, he conceded, would be difficult. The government would have to step in, both to overcome the opposition of the slaveholders and to deal with the fact that the victims of slavery would have been, in Condorcet's judgment, so damaged psychologically by their oppression that they would need a long period of apprenticeship before they would be ready to enjoy their freedom. "Are they not in the situation of unfortunates whom barbaric treatment has, in part, deprived of their reason; and so, whatever the cause that has made them unable of being men, what the legislator owes them, is less the use of their rights than the assurance of their welfare?" he asked.[44]

Because the complete and immediate abolition of slavery seemed both improbable and risky, Condorcet then turned his attention to what he called "ways of gradually destroying the slavery of the

Negroes." The plan he offered involved declaring any children of enslaved women whose color revealed that they had been fathered by whites to be free immediately, thus discouraging the sexual exploitation of enslaved women. Other children born after the enactment of his proposed law would be freed at the age of thirty-five, by which time they would have amply compensated their owners for the costs of raising them. Under these arrangements, Condorcet calculated that slavery would be completely abolished after seventy years, when the last child born to the last woman born into the condition of slavery would have turned thirty-five. Condorcet's proposal resembled the law passed by the legislature of the American state of Pennsylvania in 1780, which foresaw the gradual extinction of slavery over a period of forty-eight years.[45]

In 1784 the principle of abolition received another important endorsement from Jacques Necker, who had followed Turgot as royal finance minister from 1776 to 1781. For the first time, a man who had held one of the highest positions in the French government openly condemned slavery and the slave trade. "We preach humanity, and every year we go to impose chains on 20,000 inhabitants of Africa!" Necker exclaimed. "We take pride in the grandeur of man . . . but a small difference in the hair, or the color of the skin, is enough to change our respect into contempt, and to make us consider beings like us as if they were animals without intelligence." Necker admitted that it would be difficult for any one country to do away with the institution on its own, since rivals that maintained it would gain an economic advantage, but he asked whether it would not be possible to make a "general agreement, under which all nations would come together to abandon the slave trade?"[46]

Another French institution, the Catholic Church, also began to seem like a potential source of opposition to the institution of slavery. In his twelve-volume *Traité historique et dogmatique de la vraie religion* (Historical and dogmatic treatise on the true religion), published in 1780, the abbé Nicolas Bergier denounced Raynal's work, but not because of its critique of slavery. Enlightenment critics, Bergier argued, had things all wrong: It was Christianity that promoted the abolition of slavery. "If the authority of the Church had been stronger, slavery would have ceased to exist a long time ago," he claimed. In a later publication, which noted that

Bergier was the "confessor of Monsieur, brother of the king," the abbé drew together the remarks scattered throughout his earlier twelve-volume opus to produce a sharper denunciation of slavery, whose continued existence, he asserted, reflected the predominance of secular concerns: "Ever since commerce taught men to adore only the God of money, and since philosophy came along to reinforce this attitude, we can predict that slavery will be neither tempered nor diminished."[47]

By the mid-1780s, writing about slavery had become a familiar way for young authors, such as the future feminist firebrand Olympe de Gouges and the future literary celebrity Madame de Staël, Necker's daughter, to make their debuts in the literary world. Olympe de Gouges recognized that the injustice of slavery was a theme bound to attract sympathy. Her 1784 play *Zamore and Mirza, or the Fortunate Shipwreck*, although its protagonists were identified as Indians rather than Blacks, recycled sentimental themes about the reconciliation of noble enslaved people and humane whites familiar from *Ziméo*. In 1786 the young Germaine Necker, the daughter of the ex-minister, devoted one of her first literary efforts to a story in the same vein, set in Africa.[48] The *Encyclopédie méthodique*, a massive project meant to replace the Diderot *Encyclopédie*, reflected the way in which criticism of slavery had become common wisdom. Even though the tone of the work was far less polemical than that of its predecessor, articles justifying slavery and the slave trade were largely absent. The editor of the volumes on "commerce" was the Physiocrat Nicolas Baudeau, who opined that "it is difficult to justify the commerce in Negroes otherwise than by the law of the strongest." Jean-Nicolas Démeunier's volumes on "political economy and diplomacy" asserted that the American states were ridding themselves of slavery and that "the honest citizens of the United States lament the selfishness of the southern provinces, which put up obstacles to this emancipation." The abbé Bergier, entrusted with the *Encyclopédie méthodique*'s volumes on theology, brought together the religious critiques of slavery that had been scattered throughout his earlier publications.[49]

In the face of the growing number of attacks on slavery, its defenders realized that they, too, needed to become more vocal. The most outspoken defenders of slavery and the slave trade were writers who were themselves directly involved with the colonies. In two books published in 1776 and 1777, Emilien Petit, a colonial jurist, took direct aim at the *Histoire des deux Indes* and at the claim that slavery was more expensive than free labor. Petit's argumentative strategy, like that of many of the prerevolutionary defenders of the colonial status quo, was to concede a few points to the opposition but to maintain that their claims were exaggerated and that, in any case, the colonies could not survive if any major changes were made to the institutions that made them profitable. Although Petit admitted that "it is not difficult to demonstrate that the state of slavery is contrary to nature" and that "humanity will always suffer from the precautions that the whites are forced to take against the possible enterprises of the Blacks," he took it for granted that Europeans had become dependent on the products of the colonies and that whites were unfit to do agricultural work in tropical climates. He added that once enslaved Blacks had been imported, Europeans could not be expected to work alongside them, "without compromising white blood by subjecting them to the same discipline and labor."[50]

Like Petit, Michel René Hilliard d'Auberteuil, another Saint-Domingue colonist, conceded that "the idea of servitude is the hardest thing for man to conceive." He added, "I will not stop to examine whether this kind of property is legitimate; it is in any case advantageous, and if [the slaves] are treated with humanity, their slavery will not be unhappy." He accused the critics of slavery of hypocrisy. "The philosophers grumble about it, and nevertheless they participate in this evil, since they have not withdrawn into the deserts."[51] David Duval-Sanadon's *Discours sur l'esclavage des nègres, et sur l'idée de leur affranchissement dans les colonies*, whose author would become one of the leading defenders of slavery once the Revolution started, argued that the abolition of colonial slavery was simply impossible. "The respect due to property rights, would be the first, and the most insurmountable, barrier that would have to be broken," he announced. A unilateral French decision to abolish slavery would ruin its relations with other countries. It would never be practical to ship all the Blacks back to Africa, but if they remained in the colonies as free people, "what chaos! What anarchy! What terrible disorder! What power would be strong enough to restrain these freedmen, intoxicated by their new condition, in a hurry to claim all their rights, and whose number is ten times that of the whites?"[52]

Pierre-Victor Malouet, a colonial administrator who was destined to play a major role during the Revolution, differed from most of slavery's defenders on the question of the treatment of the free population of color. Although he did not think they should be made fully equal with the whites, he considered them essential allies in warding off any possible slave revolt. He wanted to "give them their own honors and distinctions, admit the most notable of them to certain honorific positions, and guarantee to all the rights of freedom which are too often violated when they come in conflict with whites." He even thought it would be a good idea to encourage intermarriage between poorer members of the white population and free Blacks. "One would thus increase the class who have children and who work," he argued.[53] Malouet's advocacy of intermarriage was part of a larger debate about the status of the mixed-race population whose development had been recognized as one of the inevitable by-products of France's colonial system since the early days of overseas settlement. The *Supplément à l'encyclopédie*, published in 1776, noted,

> This class of free people is, beyond any doubt, at all times the strongest ally of the whites against slave rebellions. If they have even a small amount of property, they treat the Negroes with the air of superiority of the whites, which they would have to give up if the slaves threw off the yoke, and in times of war, the mulattos furnish a good militia for the defense of the coastline, since they are almost all robust men and more able than the Europeans to endure the fatigues of the climate. The consumption of French products that they make, for which they employ all the profit from their work, is one of the main resources of colonial commerce.[54]

In contrast with the United States, where some free Blacks and even a handful of enslaved people in the northern states were able to publish newspaper articles and books arguing for their rights, enslaved Blacks in France's colonies had no direct way of addressing the metropolitan French public.[55] In 1783, however, the royal governor of Saint-Domingue helped Julien Raimond, a member of an influential mixed-race family in the Aquin parish in Saint-Domingue's South Province, embark for France with the explicit goal of lobbying for an improvement of his group's status. In 1786, after several years of preparation, Raimond submitted four lengthy memoranda to the navy minister Castries. He was in no sense arguing for the abolition of slavery, although he echoed the white French critics of the institution by asserting that "the Blacks are born free in their country, and it is only the Europeans' desire for gain that has made them slaves." But, he asked, "does that make it necessary to treat even the sixth generation of these unfortunates with contempt and humiliate them?" He contended that the discriminatory laws against people of mixed race were relatively recent, dating only from the years following the Seven Years' War. The laws for free people, he insisted, "should be the same for all subjects of the same ruler."[56]

Castries reacted cautiously to Raimond's memoranda, knowing that any attempt to change the system of racial hierarchy in the colonies would stir up protests. He shared the first three of the documents with the administrators of Saint-Domingue, the governor César-Henri de La Luzerne, who would soon succeed Castries as navy minister, and the civil intendant of Saint-Domingue, François Barbé-Marbois, and once he had received their replies, he asked Saint-Lambert, the author of *Ziméo*, to prepare a report. Saint-Lambert's report, which was kept secret, went far beyond anything the minister or even Julien Raimond would have approved. "In order to prepare a general emancipation," he wrote, "one should immediately bring the mulattos closer to the whites, so that some day the Blacks can be brought closer to the mulattos." Decades before the Church would begin to ordain Black priests, Saint-Lambert urged such a measure, which would "considerably elevate the Black race."[57] By the time Saint-Lambert submitted his suggestions, the French government was completely consumed by the domestic crisis that would soon lead to the calling of the Estates General and set the stage for the events of 1789, but his radical proposals were a sign of how attitudes to race were changing, at least among a small elite in the country.

In the last years before the outbreak of the Revolution, French thinking about slavery was also affected by developments in the new American republic that had come into existence with French aid during the recent war. Although French publications did not follow all the details of the extensive American debates on the subject in the various states following the start of the American Revolution, some French commentators realized that several states, particularly Pennsylvania, had passed laws designed to phase out the institution. The young marquis de Lafayette optimistically convinced himself that George Washington and the other Americans he admired because of their devotion to liberty were bound to espouse the cause of emancipation. In 1783 he wrote to Washington urging that they "unite in purchasing a small estate where we may try the experiment to free the Negroes, and use them only as tenants—such an example as yours might render it a general practice, and if we succeed in America, I will cheerfully devote a part of my time to render the method fashionable in the West Indies."[58] The French émigré J. Hector Saint-Jean de Crèvecoeur's widely read *Letters of an American Farmer*, published in English in 1781 and translated into French in 1784, introduced French readers to the antislavery ideas of the Quaker Anthony Benezet and mentioned the measures against slavery in Pennsylvania and Massachusetts during the American Revolution. Crèvecoeur's chapter on slavery in South Carolina added to the voluminous literature emphasizing the barbarous cruelty of the institution.[59]

The publication of a book by an aristocratic French officer who had served in the American war, the marquis de Chastellux, set off a debate, both about the character of the new United States and about the future of slavery there. In contrast to Crèvecoeur, whose *Letters of an American Farmer* had portrayed the Americans as "new men" devoted to the ideal of freedom, Chastellux depicted them as a people lacking culture and sophistication who hardly deserved to be held up as models for the nations of Europe. He also doubted that the Americans would succeed in doing away with slavery. Chastellux came close to embracing the claim that Blacks were a separate species, writing that "the more we regard the Negroes, the more must we be persuaded that the difference between them and us, consists in something more than complexion." If they were freed, they "would unquestionably form a distinct people, from whom neither succor, virtue, nor labor, could be expected." His conclusion was "that there is no other method of abolishing slavery, than by getting rid of the negroes."[60]

In 1786 Thomas Jefferson, the author of the Declaration of Independence and also a major slaveholder, arrived in Paris as the American ambassador to the court of Versailles. He was determined to counter the negative impression of his country purveyed in Chastellux's publication. Just a year earlier, Jefferson had published his *Notes on the State of Virginia*, in which he had expressed his own ambivalence on the issue of slavery, arguing on the one hand that Blacks were racially inferior to whites and that the two races could never live together peacefully, but on the other hand claiming, "I tremble for my country when I reflect that God is just," and expressing his hope that "the spirit of the master is abating, that of the slave rising from the dust, his condition mollifying, the way I hope preparing, under the auspices of heaven, for a total emancipation."[61]

In France, where he did not have to confront fellow Virginians committed to defending slavery, Jefferson stressed the latter aspect of his thinking on the subject. In correspondence with Jean-Nicolas Démeunier, who was compiling a volume about the constitutions of the American states, Jefferson explained that the time was not right to propose an emancipation bill in Virginia, but he supplied Démeunier with a forceful statement on the subject that the French author incorporated directly into his work: "What a stupendous, what an incomprehensible machine is man! who can endure toil, famine, stripes, imprisonment & death itself in vindication of his own liberty, and the next moment be deaf to all those motives whose power supported him thro' his trial, and inflict on his fellow men a bondage, one hour of which is fraught with more misery than ages of that which he rose in rebellion to oppose." Démeunier added an optimistic statement of his own: "When one sees the force of reason and the humanity of the statesmen who, by their personal influence and their writings, guide the councils of the new republics, one cannot doubt the victory of their generous spirits over the selfish interests of their fellow citizens."[62]

Démeunier was only one of the authors who spread the impression that the Americans were in the process of preparing the abolition of slavery. In an early part of his four-volume *Recherches historiques et politiques*, Jefferson's friend Filippo Mazzei assured readers that "since the Revolution, [the slaves'] situation has been more or less improved, and everywhere there are plans to abolish slavery, as soon as circumstances permit." When he realized that he had been too hopeful about the prospects of immediate abolition in the United States, Mazzei confessed that readers "should be astonished to learn, that in spite of the principles established in these new governments, which are imbued with liberty and equality, slavery can still exist in the United States." Nevertheless, Mazzei concluded that "justice demands . . . that one give freedom to the slaves as soon as possible, as well as the right of citizenship, which should be regarded as being restored to them and not as a gift, according to the sacred principle contained in the first article of our declaration of rights: that all men are born equally free and independent." Mazzei ended by commending Condorcet's 1781 pamphlet against slavery, "fit to persuade whoever loves reason, and does not prefer his own private advantage to humanity and justice."[63]

The debate about the prospects for ending slavery in the United States begun by Chastellux's work also provoked Jacques-Pierre Brissot, soon to become France's most active antislavery activist, to make his first public statement on the issue. A young and ambitious man of letters, Brissot, at the age of thirty-two in 1786, already had a long and complicated career behind him. By the time he turned thirty in 1784, he had published works on philosophy, theology, and legislation; thrown himself into an unsuccessful revolutionary movement in the Swiss city of Geneva; spent two years living in London; edited several periodicals; and found himself confined to the Bastille in Paris for two months. Despite his frenetic energy, however, Brissot was still largely unknown to the public by the mid-1780s. In London he had met several Quakers who were active in opposing slavery, but he had not yet engaged himself in any antislavery campaign.

After having been freed from prison thanks to his wife's connection with the entourage of the duc d'Orléans, Louis XVI's cousin and a patron of various figures willing to help advance his numerous projects, Brissot supported himself and his family by turning out pamphlets on French financial affairs, many of them commissioned by Honoré Gabriel Riqueti de Mirabeau, the son of the author of *L'Ami des Hommes* and future revolutionary. By 1786 Brissot had obtained a position of some importance: The marquis du Crest, who administered the duc d'Orléans's complicated financial affairs, hired him as his secretary. Whatever the obligations of that job, Brissot still found time to express his radical opinions. He was convinced that the newly independent American republic across the Atlantic was about to give the world the first example of a society based on the doctrine of natural rights, in which all men would be free and happy, and he seized the opportunity to refute Chastellux's opinions about slavery, as well as his criticism of the Quakers and his doubts about whether men in general were truly fit for freedom.

Brissot's denunciation of slavery was uncompromising. "Let us cease to make laws for the Blacks that are different from our own," he thundered, "since Heaven has put them on the same level as us, has created them equal to us, because they are brothers." If Blacks in the colonies appeared less intelligent and less enterprising than whites, it was because of the treatment inflicted on them, and if they resorted to violence against their oppressors, they were entirely justified. "You call your atrocities, rights, and the courage with which they resist you, crime! What an inversion of ideas! What horrible logic!" he wrote. Conscious of the economic shock that would come from ending the institution, he had no ideas for offsetting it. In a rhetorical maneuver that would be characteristic of his treatment of the subject throughout the years to come, he announced that he would "reserve that for another work."[64]

Perusing the library of works on race and slavery that France had produced by the mid-1780s could easily have led an observer to conclude that, in spite of the efforts of proslavery authors like Linguet, Malouet, and Emilien Petit, the issue had been settled in French minds. French authors, starting with Montesquieu, had produced an abundant literature on these topics. In contrast to the strongly religious tone characteristic of many British and American abolitionists, the French literature had a more secular cast. The fact that so many of the French writers who treated the subject were closely connected to the milieu of officials in the French government concerned with the colonies had the effect of persuading many antislavery authors to couple vehement denunciations of slavery in the abstract with strikingly moderate proposals for its eventual abolition. When all was said and done, however, there was no denying that French readers were exposed to a thorough airing of the questions posed by the existence of slavery in their empire. Nevertheless, as Linguet had remarked twenty years earlier, the noisy debates about slavery and race had had no impact on actual conditions in the colonies. Now, however, that was about to change.

CHAPTER THREE

Colonial Issues During the Prerevolutionary Crisis

THE NEWS HIT the French political world like a thunderbolt: On 29 December 1786, King Louis XVI announced that he was summoning an "Assembly of Notables," an institution that had not met since 1626, to advise him on "ideas for the relief of my people, the reform of numerous abuses, and the regulation of my finances."[1] For 150 years, French kings and the ministers who carried out their will had insisted that France was an "absolute" monarchy, in which the ruler alone enacted laws and set policy. Now, faced with a financial crisis so serious that his chief minister, Charles-Alexandre de Calonne, told him that only a drastic change in basic features of government and society could ward off a disastrous bankruptcy, the king was appealing for advice and consent from his subjects. It was the beginning of a series of retreats from the precepts of absolutism that would culminate, two years later, in a total revolution that would affect every part of French society, including its colonies.

Just three days after Louis XVI's announcement convoking the Assembly of Notables, Jacques-Pierre Brissot convened a meeting of his own. The idea came from his friend Hector Saint-Jean de Crèvecoeur, the author of the *Letters of an American Farmer*, but Brissot quickly made himself the central figure in the group, which originally consisted only of himself, Crèvecoeur, Brissot's Genevan banker friend Etienne Clavière, and Nicolas Bergasse, another man of letters who had been associated with Brissot in some of his pamphlet campaigns. The purpose of the gathering was to create an organization that would "confer about the public welfare and relations of France and the United States." Promoting trade between the two nations was in line with French government policy, but from the start, Brissot and his friends had broader ambitions. The news of the convocation of the Assembly of Notables "could be an opportunity to awaken ideas and useful projects in many minds," Brissot remarked at the group's second meeting. He also explained that he was already in touch with James Philips, one of the British Quakers involved in efforts to promote the abolition of slavery. In subsequent meetings in February and March 1787, Brissot and his colleagues discussed a number of ideas to improve the lives of ordinary French people and to diminish the risk of war. Brissot was especially interested in one particular subject, however, and at the group's last meeting, on 3 April 1787, he told the other members that he had wanted to bring up "the destruction of Negro slavery, or how to cooperate with this destruction that is being carried out by the Quakers. I intended to submit to you a vast plan on this subject, which demands ardor and, above all, persistence to not become worn down and discouraged by the obstacles that will be put in our way." Alas, he said, there was no time to discuss the matter at that meeting.[2]

The short-lived Société Gallo-Américaine was the first of many efforts Brissot would make to promote the abolitionist cause. Although he would not survive to see the revolutionary French government decree the end of slavery in 1794, no one else devoted so much time and energy to the campaign against slavery and racial prejudice. Given the importance of Brissot's role regarding these issues, as well as many other aspects of the Revolution, one would expect him to occupy a major place in narratives of the period's history, alongside figures like Honoré Gabriel Mirabeau and Maximilien Robespierre. Instead, he has been largely forgotten.[3] In 1989, at the time of the bicentennial of the Revolution, Condorcet and Henri Grégoire, allies of his in the debates about race and slavery, were honored with reburial in the Panthéon, France's shrine to its national heroes, but there was no mention of Brissot's contribution to that movement. Brissot's minor place in historical memory reflects the fact that, unlike Condorcet and Grégoire, he was associated not only with causes that now seem admirable but also with some of the most questionable aspects of the Revolution, particularly the decision to embark on an aggressive war to export the movement's ideals in 1792. The one conclusion about Brissot that almost all scholars of the Revolution agree on is that he had poor political judgment, as shown by his naïve assumption in 1792 that the populations of other countries would eagerly embrace the French revolutionaries.

In the summer of 1793, as he sat in prison awaiting the trial that he knew would result in his execution, Brissot wrote recollections of his early life and a lengthy speech defending his actions during the Revolution. Later editors cobbled these documents together with excerpts from his pamphlets and newspaper articles to produce a composite text published as his memoirs, in which Brissot was presented as a consistent defender of liberty whose actions during the Revolution had always been justified.[4] A few modern scholars have endorsed Brissot's view of himself. Impressed by the idealism of Brissot's early writings, Leonore Loft argued "that as a reformist he should be viewed as comparable to such icons of our time as Dr. Martin Luther King, Jr., and Nelson Mandela." The historian of the Enlightenment Jonathan Israel sees "the Brissotins," Brissot and his closest associates, as "the founders of the modern human rights tradition" and "the first organized champions of democratic, rights-based, secular modernity"; he attributes their defeat solely to the unscrupulous machinations of their enemies.[5] Other scholars have recognized that Brissot made serious mistakes that contributed to his failure as a leader and to his contested reputation after the Revolution.[6]

In addition to his shortcomings as a political leader, Brissot has been neglected because he was not as striking a personality as many of his fellow revolutionaries. It is symptomatic of the challenge Brissot presents that books about him say little or nothing about his appearance and the impression he made on others. When he was arrested in 1793, the police in the provincial town of Moulins described him as "five feet tall, hair dark brown, flat and thinning . . . a long nose, somewhat prominent, medium-sized mouth . . . oval-shaped face, narrow at the chin," features that would hardly have made him stand out.[7] Jérôme Pétion, another revolutionary politician who had known Brissot since childhood, wrote that "it was impossible to dress more plainly than he did, to have a less elegant apartment, a more frugal table, and to spend less money."[8] For biographical drama, Brissot's private life, as a happily married man and the father of three children, hardly compares with Mirabeau's serial affairs or with the mystery of Robespierre's celibacy.

From an early point in his life, Brissot did display a knack for making useful connections, and he had devoted friends, although he also had an unfortunate talent for accumulating enemies because of the harshness with which he treated his opponents. Madame Marie Jeanne Phlipon Roland, the brilliant and politically astute woman who was accused of having been the real center of the Girondin political faction with which Brissot became identified, accurately identified her friend's strengths and weaknesses. In her memoirs, she recalled the rapidity with which Brissot could put words on paper: "He composed a treatise the way someone else would copy a song." But in a letter written at a critical juncture during the Revolution, as foreign troops were advancing on Paris and as other revolutionaries were nerving themselves up for the assault on the monarchy that would take place on 10 August 1792, she was less admiring. No one, she told Brissot, believed more strongly than she in "the purity of your soul, of your total devotion to the public welfare, and of all that you possess in abilities and talents, as well as courage and virtue." Nevertheless, she told him, "you don't take the effort to foresee the bad, even in events; as a result a kind of optimism and hope that misleads you, even on the edge of precipices." A tendency to hesitate at moments of crisis meant that the public didn't regard him as "a constant defender, in the way it would like to see you."[9]

In the spring of 1787, Brissot was still far from imagining the revolution that was going to raise him to political prominence and then cost him his life. Indeed, his first effort to start a political movement petered out. In April 1787, after Brissot's remarks on slavery, the Société Gallo-Américaine suspended its meetings for the summer. As the Assembly of Notables became bogged down in acrimony and France lurched further into crisis, the group dissolved. That fall, Brissot had to take refuge in England to avoid arrest for having written a pamphlet attacking the French government for contemplating a declaration of bankruptcy. During his stay in London, he renewed his contacts with the British opponents of slavery, who were in the process of forming an organization, the Society for the Abolition of the Slave Trade, to press for an act of Parliament banning the purchase of Black captives in Africa. They urged Brissot to establish a parallel group in France, which could cooperate with them to promote the cause, and named him and his associate Etienne Clavière as their official correspondents in France. Having already attempted something similar even before he learned of the British initiative, Brissot eagerly took up the challenge, although he warned the British abolitionists that, in France, the cause would have "more obstacles to overcome."[10]

On 19 February 1788, Brissot and his friends created the Société des Amis des Noirs, an organization exclusively devoted to the issue of slavery. By this time, Brissot had considerably enlarged his circle of supporters. The list of those at the first meeting included Clavière and Bergasse from the Société Gallo-Américaine but also the future revolutionary journalist Jean-Louis Carra, the Dutch exile Antoine-Marie Cerisier, the future National Convention deputy Xavier Valady, and several others; the marquis de Lafayette wrote that he would have attended had he not been called away by other business. Lafayette was actually engaged in his own effort to promote abolition: He had purchased several plantations in the colony of Guiana and embarked on what proved to be an unsuccessful plan to allow their enslaved Blacks to earn their freedom. Brissot would later boast that his group's openness to reform-minded slave owners was one way in which it was trying to create a consensus on the need for abolition.[11] Brissot also tried to recruit another prominent slaveholder: Thomas Jefferson, the American ambassador to France. Jefferson responded that "no one desires more ardently than me to see not only the abolition of [the slave trade], but of slavery." Given that he represented a country where slavery was legal, however, he declined to join the group, saying, "It is my obligation not to make too public my desire to see it abolished."[12]

When the Société des Amis des Noirs was formed, Brissot's most important ally was Honoré Gabriel Mirabeau, son of the author of *L'Ami des Hommes*, one of the pioneering French critiques of slavery.[13] The younger Mirabeau and his now-deceased father had detested each other, to the point where the elder Mirabeau had obtained *lettres de cachet* to have his son imprisoned, but they shared a hostility toward slavery. Sensing that a revolution in French affairs was about to unfold, Mirabeau was determined at all costs to play a leading role in it. Born into a prominent noble family, he might have hoped to rise to a significant position under the old regime, but his often outrageous behavior had quashed any chance of his gaining office through normal paths. He had made a name for himself with a series of pamphlets in which he exalted the ideal of liberty in impassioned language. Better than anyone else in France, Mirabeau had grasped what methods politicians would have to adopt in a world where the old rules no longer applied. He had assembled a political team, his "atelier" or workshop, ready to help him publicize himself, and in the fall of 1787 he had intrigued to get official permission to launch his own periodical, the *Analyse des papiers anglois*, claiming that he would only publish translations of articles that had originally appeared across the Channel. In practice, he printed whatever he wanted, and even before the official inauguration of the Amis des Noirs, the journal's issues included a variety of articles denouncing slavery.[14]

Having lived in England, with its uncensored press, Brissot fully shared Mirabeau's conviction about the importance of printed propaganda. When Mirabeau, who knew no English, got the privilege to publish his paper, Brissot volunteered to help him, even though he considered the dissolute nobleman "the most egoistic and the most depraved of all men."[15] Mirabeau's reputation and his journal made him an indispensable partner. The speech Brissot gave at the opening meeting of the Société des Amis des Noirs was immediately published in the *Analyse* and circulated as a pamphlet, and he and other members of the group promptly began placing articles in prerevolutionary France's only daily newspaper, the *Journal de Paris*. Brissot's speech did not lay out a detailed plan for the abolition of slavery, but it did set forth a comprehensive program for putting the issue on the public agenda. The time was ripe, Brissot claimed: In addition to the formation of the British abolition society, slavery had been abolished in four northern states in the United States, and even in the American South the "best minds" were turning against it. "By what right could they insist on keeping other men in slavery, they who had given their blood to uphold this eternal truth: *All men are born free and equal*?" he demanded.[16]

The beginning of the French Revolution was still a year away when Brissot formed the Société des Amis des Noirs, but his initiative was itself a revolution in the struggle against slavery. For the first time in France, abolition became a tangible goal to be promoted through deliberate and systematic action. The structure of the group and the methods it adopted to push for its goals were themselves revolutionary. As the historian of the prerevolutionary French philanthropic movement Catherine Duprat wrote, "Freedom of entry, publicity, appeals for public debate, the democratic character of its internal operations, a network of correspondents and sister societies, a desire to affect public opinion . . . the Amis des Noirs thus offer, in their actions and their structure, the first model of the political groups that would appear in 1789."[17] For its members, as the historian of the French abolitionist crusade Marcel Dorigny wrote, the society was "a political apprenticeship without precedent in France at the time."[18] The group admitted women, and all members had a voice in determining its policies.

Although the name Friends of the Blacks avoided any explicit reference to abolition, the programmatic speech Brissot delivered at its inaugural meeting left no doubt about his conviction that the abolition of both slavery and the slave trade was not only inevitable but imminent; he even hinted that there would be no reason to oppose "conjugal unions of whites and Blacks, which the freedom restored to the latter would make more frequent." Whereas the British reformers had made a deliberate decision to target only the slave trade, calculating that its obvious cruelty would make its abolition an easier goal, Brissot's frequent references to "the first of all truths: [that] all men are born free" emphasized the evil of slavery itself. He was careful, near the end of his speech, to concede that "the freeing of the Negroes can only be done in stages and after experiments," but this concession was clearly out of tune with the general thrust of his presentation.[19]

Convinced of the rightness of his cause, Brissot took aim at all the arguments against the idea of total emancipation. As he would continue to do throughout the next five years of his campaign against slavery, he assured his audience that there was no reason to fear vengeance from emancipated slaves. “Why fear . . . the hand of a man whom one has willingly freed, whom one embraces as a brother, whom one seats by one’s side, to whom one restores all his rights, above all the right to use his reason to pursue his happiness?” The justice of the abolitionist cause was so evident that the planters could hardly counter it: “They themselves feel the general sense of horror inspired by their bloody claim of property.” France needed to act swiftly to keep up with the British, who, in Brissot’s optimistic view, would soon be benefiting from the increase in productivity that was sure to follow from the replacement of slave labor and the development of peaceful trade with Africa.[20]

To promote the abolition cause, Brissot went on, France needed a well-organized group with a clear plan of action. One priority would be to translate the antislavery publications that the London committee had sent, but the society should also bring back into print the best French works on the subject. In addition, members would carefully study the arguments put forward by the defenders of slavery and refute them. Society members would prepare articles for the press and cultivate relationships with journalists. They would maintain regular contact with their colleagues in Britain, and, like the British abolitionist Thomas Clarkson, they would gather reliable data about the French slave trade and the treatment of enslaved Blacks in the colonies.[21]

“We will be told that such a society is useless in France,” Brissot warned, since “the fate of the Negroes depends on the ministry.” But this was not a valid argument: If matters were left to the king’s ministers, they would inevitably succumb to propaganda from “the sellers of Negroes,” and if the cause of slave emancipation was defended only by isolated people of good will, they would become discouraged by the lack of immediate response to their efforts. “To all these obstacles, there is only one remedy: to unite all the forces of well-intentioned people, in order to direct them to a common cause.” The struggle might be long, but Brissot was convinced that it could be won. Sooner or later, “when it sees the nation convinced that the enslavement of Negroes is a crime, and that nature has widely attached more real advantages to free labor than to enslaved labor, will the ministers hesitate to themselves propose to the sovereign a universal wish, which his heart would embrace with enthusiasm?" he concluded.[22]

The printed version of Brissot's speech may have reached only a limited audience, but the articles he and his friends succeeded in placing in the *Journal de Paris*, France's only daily newspaper, brought the group and its program to the attention of a much wider public. The *Journal de Paris*, founded in 1777, was a censored publication that carried little overtly political news. Instead, it served as the organ for what would now be called a developing civil society, the burgeoning number of groups aiming to ameliorate France's various social ills. Unlike these other philanthropic efforts, however, the abolitionist campaign directly challenged a major social institution in which many of France's elites, including many of the *Journal de Paris*'s readers, had a direct interest. At a moment when debates about France's own political problems were still being framed primarily with reference to the country's traditional constitution, the paper's first article about the Amis des Noirs adopted a different language, that of natural rights. "After they have attacked the slave trade," it proclaimed, the group "will attack slavery itself. Between a form of servitude so harsh that it destroys future generations even in the midst of prosperity and the full enjoyment of the rights that Nature has given to all men, there is an immense distance that must be bridged."[23]

Although the goals and methods of the Société des Amis des Noirs had radical implications, the group hoped to achieve its goals through France's existing institutions. On 18 March 1788, Clavière reported that he had met with Louis XVI's principal minister, Loménie de Brienne, who had succeeded Calonne after the failure of the Assembly of Notables in 1787. The minister, Clavière claimed, had said that "it pained him to see that the slave trade and the slavery of the Negroes were continuing, that it would be desirable to find a way to abolish them . . . and that a society formed for the purpose of seeking and finding this solution could not fail to enjoy the protection of the government." Brienne insisted, however, that any abolition proposal would have to "prove that it was in the interest of the planters and the treasury to substitute free labor for that of slaves," adding that "the society would have to be prudent and sensible in its assemblies, its actions, its writings."[24]

Within a few months, Brissot's group had picked up a number of new members. On 4 April 1788, Lafayette brought a particularly important recruit to their meeting: Condorcet.[25] Older than Brissot and Lafayette and solidly anchored in the country's academic institutions, Condorcet might have seemed a more logical person than Brissot to take the lead in a campaign against slavery. He had been writing condemnations of the institution for more than a decade and had been the first French author to offer an actual plan for its gradual elimination. A regular participant in the capital's most prestigious salons, he knew all of France's most distinguished intellectuals. He also had governmental experience, having served as an assistant to the reforming minister Etienne-François Turgot in 1774–76 and having held a post at the royal mint since 1775.[26]

What Condorcet lacked, compared with Brissot, were the skills of a good publicist and an effective politician. Already in 1774, Turgot, who had brought Condorcet into politics, had called him an "enraged sheep" given to making radical proposals without any idea of how to implement them.[27] Condorcet and Brissot had found themselves in opposite camps on a number of occasions during the 1780s. Brissot had been an enthusiast for the ideas of Franz Mesmer, whose claims about curing disease through "animal magnetism" attracted a large following, whereas Condorcet, a defender of scientific orthodoxy, had overseen the Academy of Sciences' panel that condemned "mesmerism" as a fraud. They were also very different personalities. Brissot may not have been one of the period's great orators, but he always spoke with confidence; Condorcet was pathologically shy in front of audiences. Unlike Brissot, he wrote carefully and laboriously. What he brought to the abolitionist cause was his unswerving commitment to the ideals of human freedom and equality. On some questions, he was considerably more radical than Brissot: Whereas Brissot did not hesitate to proclaim that "among a serious people, women confine themselves to their homes, and do not get involved in public affairs," Condorcet advocated full equality between the sexes.[28] Despite their different personalities and backgrounds, however, Brissot and Condorcet would become firm allies in the campaign against slavery and racial prejudice and on a number of other issues until both fell victim to the Terror.

In 1788, however, in a pattern that would become characteristic of the Revolution's interaction with colonial affairs, a domestic crisis distracted both the Société des Amis des Noirs' members and their audience from the slavery issue. On 3 May 1788, the king's chief minister Loménie de Brienne and the justice minister Lamoignon de Malesherbes, their patience exhausted by the refusal of the parlements, or royal courts, to accept their proposals to deal with the financial crisis, attempted to replace the recalcitrant judges with a single "plenary court." This drastic reshaping of France's traditional institutions awakened fears that the government, instead of recognizing a role for public opinion in making laws, as the summoning of the Assembly of Notables had suggested, was instead broadening its claim to absolute power. Would-be reformers were shocked, and on 6 May, the Amis des Noirs decided to postpone the publication of any more translated English abolition tracts "until the current troubles have ended."[29]

By this time, Brissot had also notified his colleagues of a decision on his part that handicapped the group's campaign for the rest of the year: He was stepping down as its secretary in order to make a trip to the United States. The main purpose of his trip was to negotiate a complicated financial deal concerning the American debt to France stemming from the American Revolutionary War, an arrangement in which his friend the banker Clavière was involved. Brissot promised the society that he would use the opportunity to "discover in the New World further evidence of the harshness of the torturers of the Negroes, of the absurdity of the calculations on which slavery is founded." He was sure that the news of the founding of an abolitionist society in France would cause rejoicing among the American Quakers and among the "Negroes who I will encounter and inform that the masters in this capital . . . are planning to at least improve their condition, and to some day make them free. I am sure, tears of joy will flow from their eyes," he concluded.[30]

Brissot did not actually leave Paris for nearly two months after this announcement, and the society continued to meet, but most of its time was spent in tedious arguments about its own bylaws and the election of officers. In the meantime, however, opponents of abolition, alarmed by the appearance of an organized campaign against slavery and recognizing that the French monarchy's crisis might result in changes to the colonial system, were also beginning to mobilize. In Saint-Domingue, white colonists remained vehemently opposed to the edicts of 1784 and 1785 that had sought to limit their authority over their enslaved workforce, and Castries's effort to abolish the Conseil supérieur in Cap Français had added to the agitation there. The merchants of France's port cities had their own grievances, directed especially at an edict of 30 August 1784 that had permitted the Caribbean colonists to trade directly with the United States, thereby undermining the *exclusif*, the set of laws designed to reserve the colonial market for French traders.

On 20 April 1788, a group of Saint-Domingue colonists drafted an appeal to the king voicing their concerns about the future of slavery. Since the number of enslaved Blacks in the colonies greatly exceeded that of the whites, they insisted that it was necessary that "the power of the master be without limits in the mind of the slave." Unfortunately, from their point of view, the Castries edicts of 1784 and 1785 had made it clear to the Blacks that "the power of [their] master was subject to rules," and even if enslaved Blacks did not know what those rules were, the belief in their existence was encouraging disobedience "by slaves who interpret everything in favor of the freedom, the impatient desire for which nags at them. . . . A few more years, and perhaps there will be no more slaves." According to the colonists, the treatment of the captives on their plantations was already becoming less oppressive, and in any event, what was at stake was not so much their right of property as their power to "compel a man to work, and this right is not really so contrary to nature as the enthusiasts of liberty make it seem."[31] Médéric Louis Élie Moreau de Saint-Méry, one of the many signatories to this document, was tasked with taking it to France.[32]

A few years older than Brissot, Moreau de Saint-Méry would emerge as one of the leading opponents of the abolitionist movement in the first stages of the French Revolution. Born in Martinique in 1750, he had studied law in France before starting a career in Saint-Domingue's largest city, Cap Français. In the years before the Revolution, Moreau de Saint-Méry shuttled back and forth between Saint-Domingue and France, where the royal administration provided him with support for his project to publish a collection of the laws affecting the colonies. Like Brissot, he embraced many of the progressive ideas of the Enlightenment. In Cap Français, Moreau was the leading spirit of the Cercle des Philadelphes, the first learned society in the Caribbean; he was also a member of the Conseil supérieur of Cap Français, the body the minister Castries had tried to suppress in 1787. During one of his stays in Paris, he joined the Lycée de Paris, a gathering place for those interested in new ideas, whose members included sympathizers with abolition such as Condorcet. Diligent and organized, Moreau was even appointed as the Lycée's secretary. To counter the abolitionists' influence in the organization, Moreau helped arrange for the publication of the Saint-Domingue colonist David Duval-Sanadon's defense of slavery in 1785.[33]

When Moreau reached Paris on 2 July 1788, he found the kingdom's politics in a chaotic state. On 5 July, the government, in a desperate effort to regain control of the situation, announced that elections would be held for a meeting of the Estates General, an institution that had lain dormant even longer than the Assembly of Notables. The summoning of the Estates General meant that nearly the entire male population of the kingdom would be invited to choose deputies to represent them at Versailles and to draft *cahiers de doléances*, in which they could voice their own proposals for reform. Both the advocates and the opponents of abolition recognized the opportunity that this event offered them. Not only was there now a possibility of raising the issue of slavery in an assembly that would be pronouncing on every aspect of the kingdom's laws, but, for both advocates of abolition and defenders of colonial interests, there was now the prospect of being elected to a body that might change the course of French history.

Even before Moreau's arrival and the announcement of the Estates General, proposals were circulating to give the whites of Saint-Domingue control over their own affairs, such as the *Essai sur l'administration des colonies* reviewed in the *Journal de Paris* and the *Mercure de France* in March 1788, notable for its proposal to rename a part of the colony Aïti, the label victorious Black revolutionaries would choose for the country after their victory over Napoleon's forces in 1804.[34] The provincial resistance to the abolition of the parlements in France and the announcement of elections for the Estates General inspired some of the white colonists to work for a specific goal: representation of the colonies in that assembly.

According to Moreau de Saint-Méry's subsequent account, he met with several wealthy colonial plantation owners a week after he reached Paris and told them he intended to start a campaign to demand that the colonies be allowed to elect deputies to the upcoming Estates General. The idea was eagerly embraced by a number of the attendees, and the Comité colonial met four days later, on 16 July, at the initiative of an ambitious absentee proprietor, the marquis Louis-Marthe Gouy d'Arsy, who would dominate its proceedings throughout its campaign. Moreau himself was cautious about appearing publicly as a leader of the group, since he was also being paid by the government for his work on colonial laws.[35] Gouy d'Arsy, on the other hand, was an aggressive self-promoter who had crossed swords with Brissot and Clavière during a nasty struggle for the concession to build a water system in Paris during the late 1780s. Although he had never visited Saint-Domingue, his marriage to a wealthy heiress had made him the owner of a plantation there. Presenting himself as an advocate for the right of Saint-Domingue to choose deputies was an opportunity to build a reputation and win a seat in the Estates General.[36]

As the document drafted by the white colonists in Saint-Domingue in April 1788 showed, they were committed to an uncompromising defense of slavery. This explicit defense was dropped from the "Lettre au roi" later submitted to the National Assembly: The colonists undoubtedly realized that it could turn public opinion against them.[37] A revised "Lettre au roi" laid out the arguments Gouy d'Arsy and his allies would press until the final resolution of the issue by the Constituent Assembly on 4 July 1789. Saint-Domingue, the colonists argued, "has become the most valuable province of France." Its industrious plantation owners had succeeded in spite of an oppressive and inconsistent royal administration, and they therefore deserved a place "in the assembly of the great family."[38]

By mid-August 1788, the Amis des Noirs realized that they would need to modify their own strategy to counter the proslavery colonists' campaign. The government was hesitating to approve the abolitionist group's bylaws and allow them to publish an official statement of their program because of "the opposition of the colonists, who complain that the Negroes, enlightened about their right to liberty, and the efforts being made to restore it to them, murmur on the plantations and seem to foreshadow revolts."[39] In the absence of Brissot and with many of its other leading members fully occupied with the issues raised by the summoning of the Estates General, the Amis des Noirs lost a good deal of their momentum. The *Journal de Paris*'s laudatory review of the reprint of Condorcet's *Réflexions sur l'esclavage des Nègres* on 19 August 1788 was the paper's last article on a topic that had been one of its main themes for the previous six months. The *Journal de Paris*'s summary made the work sound more daring than it really was: "The author proves that legislators have no right to permit slavery, and that as a result they have the power to end it, on condition that they take precautions so that those who find themselves free have definite means of subsistence and cannot infringe on the legitimate properties of the former masters."

While the Amis des Noirs were marking time, their proslavery rivals were ramping up their own campaign. Between early August and mid-November 1788, while the antislavery group met only seven times, their opponents held twenty-one sessions. Like the Amis des Noirs, the Comité colonial initially petitioned the king and his ministers. In particular, they sought to persuade the comte de La Luzerne, Castries's successor as the minister for the colonies, to support their demand for deputies to the Estates General. At the same time, however, Gouy d'Arsy and his colleagues decided that "it was necessary to overcome the prejudice of the ministers by taking control of public opinion." In order to do this, they concluded that they needed to keep their concern about slavery secret and limit themselves to demanding representation in the Estates General. In demanding the right to establish a colonial assembly and to send deputies to the Estates General, the colonists explicitly associated themselves with the French provinces that were defying royal authority during the summer of 1788. "Brittany, Dauphiné, Provence, Béarn, have opposed all unconstitutional actions, and they have preserved and protected their constitution. Let their history be a lesson for our colony," Gouy d'Arsy wrote at the end of September 1788.[40]

Like the Amis des Noirs, the Comité colonial realized the importance of printed propaganda to answer attacks like Condorcet's pamphlet against slavery, which struck the comte Jean-François de Reynaud as "extremely dangerous for the authority and the lives of the colonial plantation owners."[41] Unlike their opponents, however, Gouy d'Arsy and his colleagues decided that they lacked the talent to write their own appeals and instead sought out hired pens. Jacques-Vincent Delacroix, a veteran scribbler, wrote their first pamphlet, *Voeu patriotique d'un Américain sur la prochaine assemblée des Etats Généraux*, which presented the case for colonial representation without mentioning the topic of slavery. Then the Comité colonial sought out an even more prominent spokesman. On 26 September 1788, the group charged Reynaud and Gouy d'Arsy "to try to engage Count Mirabeau who is, without contradiction, the best writer we have, to take on the task of writing, on the basis of materials they will furnish him, a brochure answering all the silly objections that poorly informed or ill-intentioned people are spreading among the public."[42] In addition to organizing publicity for their cause, the group sought to recruit allies among the merchants in France's port cities. On 6 October, Gouy d'Arsy told his colleagues that he had written to Le Havre, Nantes, Rochefort, La Rochelle, Bordeaux, Marseille, Brest, and Toulon. At subsequent meetings, however, he had to admit that this initiative had had little success: Traditionally at loggerheads with the planters over economic issues, the merchant community was not eager to join a campaign that might complicate their own efforts to influence the Estates General.[43]

Mirabeau, despite his public identification with the antislavery cause, did not reject the idea of defending the colonists out of hand. Their offer came at a moment when, desperate for money and determined to find some way to get himself elected to the upcoming assembly, he was pursuing a number of unsuccessful schemes that preceded his campaign for a seat in the Third Estate delegation from his native Provence.[44] In his biography of Mirabeau, published in 1832, the great tribune's nephew Lucas de Montigny mentioned having seen a manuscript draft of the colonists' address demanding representation in the Estates General, with numerous corrections in Mirabeau's handwriting.[45] On 16 October, the colonists were hoping that he would soon have their pamphlet completed, and on the 25th, assured by Reynaud that "this celebrated author is eager to have the honor and the glory of being among the number of the colony's deputies," they even discussed the possibility of electing him to represent them. "He needs to purchase a plantation, along with fifty Negroes, to become eligible," Reynaud noted.[46] Perhaps it was the realization that he would have to become a slave owner that led Mirabeau to end his relations with the group.

Not everyone on the proslavery side agreed that it was good strategy to avoid mentioning the subject. In the same session in which they discussed the possibility of helping Mirabeau acquire a plantation, the colonists' group debated the wisdom of the colonial administrator and future *monarchien* leader Pierre-Victor Malouet's desire to publish a pamphlet openly defending slavery. They decided to urge him to hold off until the Estates General had actually convened and granted the colonies representatives. Malouet replied by stressing the urgency of countering Condorcet's publication. "The colonies are lost," Malouet told Gouy d'Arsy, "if public opinion is turned against them." For his part, Malouet warned the group to set aside colonial grievances that would be poorly received in France: In his view, the colonists should say nothing about their opposition to the trade regulations of the *exclusif*.[47] Gouy d'Arsy's group also had to allay doubts that some of the Saint-Domingue planters harbored about the wisdom of seeking seats in the Estates General: They feared that an assembly in which the colonists would be only a small minority might make decisions without regard for their interests.

In the late summer and fall of 1788, the white plantation owners and their French allies pursued a two-track plan. In Saint-Domingue itself, those whites who favored the colony's representation in the Estates General prepared to choose deputies, even without authorization from the royal administration and despite opposition from colonists who did not want to entrust their interests to the leaders of the Paris committee, "four lawyers who are strangers to us and the colony."[48] In France, the Comité colonial lobbied the royal ministers and other influential figures. Their lobbying campaign became an exercise in frustration. The colony's governor general, Marie-Charles du Chilleau, said that the Estates General did not concern Saint-Domingue. La Luzerne, the minister of the navy, warned that if they were granted representation in an assembly that was going to have to approve increases in taxation, they would "be in danger of being assessed more heavily than they were, given the belief about their riches."[49] La Luzerne then reported to the king that he doubted whether the Comité colonial actually represented the views of most whites on the island; he also pointed out that no other European country had granted its colonies such a privilege. His clinching argument was that if the king decided the question on his own, he would be usurping the powers of the Estates General. On 11 September 1788, the royal council decided that the colonies would not be invited to send deputies to the upcoming meeting.[50]

Unsuccessful in their approach to the government, the colonists looked for support elsewhere. On 10 September 1788, their representatives met with the duc d'Orléans, who, like many French nobles, owned property in the Caribbean. In early October, they talked to Jacques Necker, who had been recalled to the ministry in place of Loménie de Brienne six weeks earlier, after the royal treasury had truly reached the brink of bankruptcy. When the convocation of a second Assembly of Notables, charged with determining the procedures to be followed at the Estates General, was announced, they prepared a petition emphasizing the importance of the colonies to the French.[51] Nevertheless, the royal administration stood firm in its refusal to take action in their favor and forbade the Notables from considering the matter. In Saint-Domingue, the pro-representation faction went forward with its unauthorized plan to choose deputies. Some of their nominees, like Gouy d'Arsy, were absentees, while others were colonial residents. By the beginning of April, the colonial delegates were en route to France, where the British ambassador reported that their efforts "may meet with success at so important a juncture."[52]

While the colonists were pursuing their campaign in the fall of 1788, the Amis des Noirs were largely inactive. Brissot was still in America—he would not return to France until late

January 1789—and many of the other members of the group were busy debating what other measures the Estates General should take to reform the country. Condorcet, Mirabeau, Clavière, Lafayette, the duc de Larochefoucauld-Liancourt, the abbé Emmanuel Sieyès, and a number of other group members also belonged to the Society of Thirty, a gathering of leading "Patriots" who hoped to see France converted into a constitutional monarchy. Despite the significant overlap in the two groups' membership, the questions of slavery and colonial representation do not seem to have come up in the Society of Thirty's discussions, or in the most widely circulated pamphlets written by group members, such as Sieyès's celebrated *What Is the Third Estate?* with its denunciation of the system of legal privileges that had structured French society for so many centuries.[53] These debates were unfolding in the context of a mounting social crisis: A disastrous grain harvest and an exceptionally harsh winter combined to drive up food prices and spark widespread popular unrest. For starving peasants and unemployed urban workers, issues concerning the colonies undoubtedly seemed far away.

The intertwined political and social crises that were pushing France toward revolution intensified in the last days of 1788, which explains why the longest and most comprehensive argument for abolition yet to appear in any language, the Protestant minister Benjamin Frossard's *La Cause des esclaves nègres et des habitans de la Guinée* (The cause of the Negro slaves and the inhabitants of Guinea), attracted little notice when it was published at the very end of that year. Frossard had had contacts with other members of the abolitionist milieu for a number of years. He encountered Brissot in 1782, and, during a stay in England in 1785, he met Granville Sharp and was deeply impressed by visits to several slave ships.[54] Although there was little that was original in Frossard's two-volume work, he provided a more systematic overview of all aspects of the subject than any previous author, including the British abolitionists. The proslavery advocate Malouet, who was alerted to the pending appearance of Frossard's work, was alarmed by the danger it posed to his party.[55] The first volume of Frossard's work was a comprehensive history of the institution of slavery, from ancient times to the present. The chapter headings of his second volume give a succinct summary of his argument: "The enslavement of the

Negroes is contrary to the laws of justice . . . The enslavement of the Negroes is contrary to all the teachings of the Christian religion . . . The enslavement of the Negroes is contrary to the prosperity of states and the interests of individuals . . . Ways of gradually abolishing slavery in America . . . Ways of reducing the rigor of slavery in the colonies, by abolishing the slave trade . . . Responses to some objections to the project of abolishing the slave trade."[56]

As the title of his chapter on "ways of gradually abolishing slavery" indicated, Frossard shared the conviction that, while "the freeing of the Negroes in our colonies is necessary, . . . the time for it has not yet arrived. . . . If it was sudden, it would endanger the colonies—One must first work to civilize the Negroes—Teach them the duties of citizens—And those of the Christian." He added that "it will be necessary that the masters have recovered the cost of the purchase of their slaves." Nevertheless, Frossard laid out a detailed program by which enslaved Blacks would be given the means to earn the money to pay for their freedom; he also wanted to set a date after which any future children born to enslaved parents would be considered free.[57] The newspaper in Lyon said that Frossard's work was "written with eloquence and many interesting facts about one of the most important causes that has ever occupied sensitive souls," and the Amis des Noirs voted to thank him for "the useful work that he has published."[58] Unfortunately for Frossard, the timing of his publication could hardly have been worse. His seven-hundred-page opus had to compete for attention with the flood of polemical pamphlets about the crises shaking the country, and a work that deserved to occupy an important place in the canon of the period's antislavery literature went almost unnoticed.

By January 1789, the attention of activists on all sides was focused on the local assemblies that were going to choose deputies to the Estates General and draft *cahiers de doléances*. The Amis des Noirs resumed meeting regularly at the end of the month, under the presidency of Condorcet. Brissot rejoined them on 3 February, and a week later, he delivered a lengthy report on the progress toward abolishing the slave trade in the United States and the status of freed Blacks in the northern states. His intention was to galvanize the French movement by showing that the reforms the Amis des Noirs were advocating could in fact be implemented without causing turmoil.[59] Rather than throwing his energy into the cause, however, Brissot then took off again for several weeks on a trip to the Netherlands; he did not even find time to get his report printed until the end of 1789. Instead, he put his energy into the composition of a nearly three-hundred-page tract outlining a "plan of conduct for the deputies of the people in the Estates General."[60] Only at the last minute, when the work was about to be published in May 1789, did he add an appendix on the slavery issue.

While Brissot was occupied with these other concerns, the Amis des Noirs became bogged down in procedural debates about the drafting of an open letter to the electoral assemblies urging them to condemn slavery in their cahiers. After much hemming and hawing, the letter was finally circulated in March, when many of the assemblies had already met. Following the familiar pattern of French antislavery polemics, the short pamphlet combined unqualified denunciations of slavery and the slave trade with acknowledgments that "there are injustices that cannot be repaired in a day, that . . . can only be destroyed with precautions necessary to assure the good, and not make it costly." The Amis des Noirs appealed to the participants in the electoral assemblies to instruct the deputies they chose to have the Estates General "examine ways to end the slave trade, and to prepare the end of slavery." "You will hear that this issue doesn't concern you," Condorcet added, "as if anything that humanity and justice demand could be foreign to noble and sensitive souls."[61] Meanwhile, the Comité colonial put out a series of pamphlets of its own arguing that "the intention of his Majesty is that all the provinces of his kingdom should send deputies to the Estates General" but avoiding mention of slavery.[62]

Both supporters and opponents of abolition campaigned actively to get themselves elected to the Estates General. Having abandoned the idea of being nominated to represent Saint-Domingue, Mirabeau returned to his native Provence in the South of France. Resoundingly rejected by his fellow nobles, he stirred up the commoners of the Third Estate and was chosen as one of their deputies.[63] He might have had the celebrated author Guillaume Thomas François Raynal as one of his colleagues, but the elderly compiler of the *Histoire philosophique des deux Indes* declined appeals to stand; he recommended that voters choose a certain Bertrand who was the director of the Compagnie d'Afrique, an enterprise involved in the slave trade.[64] Lafayette easily won election among the nobles of Auvergne, in the same province where the proslavery advocate Malouet was chosen as a deputy for the Third Estate.[65] Condorcet, on the other hand, was rejected by the nobility of Mantes and then by the nobles of Paris; he told a friend that he had been defeated by "the aristocrats, the *parlementaires*, the plantation owners, the devout Catholics and half of the slave traders."[66]

Brissot's childhood friend and fellow supporter of abolition, Jérôme Pétion, was elected in their native town of Chartres. Brissot, on the other hand, was frustrated in his own pursuit of a seat. He presided over the electoral assembly of the Third Estate in his Paris neighborhood but was not chosen to take part in the citywide electoral assembly.[67] Jean-Nicolas Démeunier, who had corresponded with Jefferson about slavery in the United States, did win a seat from Paris.[68] Moreau de Saint-Méry, the expert on colonial law, was a member of the central Paris electoral assembly, where he worked successfully to gain support for the idea of allowing the colonies to have deputies in the Estates General and to ward off any motion concerning slavery; he would eventually be seated as a representative of Martinique.[69] Meanwhile, Gouy d'Arsy and the other plantation owners who had appointed themselves as deputies for Saint-Domingue waited to see whether they would actually be admitted once the Estates General convened.

The selection of deputies ensured that both the abolitionists and their enemies would be represented in the Estates General, but at first glance, the evidence would seem to indicate that neither group had much success in getting its concerns reflected in the cahiers. Among the thousands of demands and requests in those documents, only around fifty concerned issues related to the colonies. Thirty-two metropolitan cahiers directly addressed the question of slavery, fourteen mentioned the question of representation for the colonies, and six took up issues concerning colonial trade regulations. Nevertheless, the cahiers' scattered references to colonial issues are more significant than they might seem. In the first case, the relative absence of the slavery issue in the cahiers does not fully reflect the importance of the issue in their debates. The cahiers from the metropolitan communities where the colonies mattered the most, the port cities, are remarkable for the absence of reference to these questions. This is certainly not because the citizens of Nantes, Bordeaux, Le Havre, La Rochelle, Saint-Malo, and Marseille were uninterested in such matters. As a French scholar has written about the cahiers of Havre and Rouen, "There was a voluntary and strategic silence, which betrays the unease of their opinion in the face of challenges to the legitimacy of slavery and the slave trade."[70]

What was said about these issues in the cahiers that do mention them is also significant. The Third Estate of Amiens was unequivocal about its principles: "The assembly, having considered the commerce with the coast of Africa and our colonies, has agreed that the slave trade is the source of the most atrocious crimes, that a man cannot be made, in any way, the property of another man, that justice and humanity equally condemn slavery." It was, to be sure, more cautious about how those principles should be implemented: "Convinced that an amelioration of this nature cannot be done in a day, and that its wish should not lose sight of the needs of cultivation in the colonies and the property rights of the colonists, whose prosperity it does not wish to destroy . . . [the assembly] has charged its deputies to ask the Estates General to discuss the best ways of abolishing the slave trade and preparing the abolition of the slavery of the Blacks."[71]

The Amiens Third Estate's cahier was the longest discussion of the issue, but other cahiers also strongly condemned slavery. The clergy of Melun said that "since, in the eyes of religion the difference of skin colors cannot create any distinction among its children, its ministers cannot stop themselves from objecting to the slavery of the Negroes in the colonies."[72] The Third Estate of Mont-de-Marsan hoped that the Estates General would "take into consideration the state of the Blacks in our colonies, search for the quickest methods of restoring their liberty, to which they have as much right as we do, since they are our fellow human beings," and the clergy of Metz denounced the slave trade as "contrary to natural law and all the laws of humanity."[73] Anticipating Robespierre's assertion, in May 1791, that if colonial interests could not be reconciled with human rights, it would be better to let the colonies perish than to abandon basic principles, the clergy of Reims was prepared to "sacrifice a barbaric policy to the essential rights of humanity."[74]

The noblesse of Mantes, influenced, no doubt, by Condorcet, said, "We are allowed to hope that France will have the honor of erasing the last traces of the degradation of human nature."[75] Mantes's clergy used even stronger language in condemning "the atrocious right that man has given himself to buy his fellow man, to deprive him of his liberty, to subject him to hard and unremitting labor, and to make him the victim of his caprices and cruelties for the whole term of his life. The king will therefore be asked to encourage the work of the respectable Société des Amis des Noirs and to authorize it to seek out and propose to the government the best methods for abolishing the infamous commerce of the slave trade."[76] Cahier demands concerning slavery often came up in the context of discussions about serfdom, indicating that some assemblies saw the parallel between these two violations of individual autonomy and liberty. The Third Estate of Reims argued that "the Third Estate, which, seven centuries ago, was in a condition of slavery almost equal to that of the Blacks nowadays, ought to take an interest in their situation."[77]

Although only two cahiers referred directly to the Amis des Noirs,[78] many of the cahier demands clearly echoed Amis des Noirs arguments, especially those that adopted its formula of demanding an immediate end to the slave trade but allowing for a more gradual abolition of slavery itself. The ten clergy cahiers that referred to the issue show that the Amis des Noirs was not the only source of antislavery sentiment, however. Although Catholic clergy played a minimal role in the group's prerevolutionary activities—the celebrated abbé Henri Grégoire only joined the society in December 1789—Christian beliefs clearly motivated some priests to condemn the institution.[79] Whether they were motivated by religion, by a devotion to the doctrine of natural rights, or by a philanthropic desire to improve the lot of humanity, when the drafters of the cahiers in 1789 did ponder slavery, they recognized that it was incompatible with the values they wanted to see institutionalized by the Estates General.

While the references to slavery in the cahiers showed a recognition of the seriousness of the issue, they also reflected the contradictory impulses that had already surfaced in the propaganda issued by the Amis des Noirs and that would complicate the revolutionaries' later attempts to deal with the subject. Under the influence of Alexandre Lameth, a member of the Amis des Noirs but also a plantation owner, the cahier of Péronne called for "a law concerning the slave trade and the regulation of Blacks that reconciles political interests with the sacred rights of liberty," a formula also adopted in Thimerais.[80] Chateau-Thierry qualified its ringing declaration against slavery by calling for "measures to be taken so that the fields of the colonies are not abandoned."[81] The Third Estate of Versailles looked to the abolition of slavery as its ultimate goal, but in the meantime it was willing to settle for changes in the regulations regarding enslaved captives' ability to purchase their freedom.[82]

No cahier suggested that France should simply abandon its colonies, and a certain number—although only about half as many as those that objected to slavery—endorsed the Saint-Domingue colonists' demand for representation in the Estates General. A few cahiers, such as those of the Third Estates of Versailles and Paris, condemned slavery while also calling for such representation.[83] Whereas demands critical of slavery came from widely scattered regions of the country, support for the Comité colonial's demands was concentrated in the Paris region, a reflection of the large number of absentee plantation owners in the capital. The language of the cahiers that mentioned the representation issue was almost always that of the Comité colonial's own proposals. The noblesse of Paris, for example, asked that "the French colonies be regarded from now on as provinces of France, removed from the arbitrary control of the ministry of the navy, assimilated to the other provinces, and participating like them in all the advantages that they should expect from the constitutional laws."[84] Whereas the discussions of slavery in the cahiers indicate that the issue did strike a chord with public opinion when it was brought up, the mentions of colonial representation sound more like the results of a determined lobbying group's efforts. The Amis des Noirs tried to counter these efforts: On 7 April 1789, Brissot warned the group about "the danger that would result from the admission of colonists as deputies to the Estates General . . . the spirit that the planters would bring with them, and all the woes that would result for the unfortunate Blacks."[85]

None of the French port cities mentioned either slavery or colonial representation in their cahiers. The Third Estate cahiers of six major cities—Bordeaux, La Rochelle, Lille, Nantes, Rennes, and Rouen—all demanded the abrogation of the edict of 30 August 1784, which had opened some colonial ports to trade with other countries.[86] The Bordelais, Rochelais, and inhabitants of Rennes wanted harsher treatment of colonists who took advantage of laws that prevented seizure of their property for debt. The Third Estate of Nantes produced the sole demand in any of the cahiers for a measure favoring slavery: It asked for better naval protection of slave ships visiting the coast of Africa.[87] The remarkable silence of the centers of colonial trade on both slavery and colonial representation certainly does not indicate a lack of concern about these issues. Taken together with what was clearly a coordinated campaign against the edict of 30 August 1784, it strongly suggests a concerted decision to keep these potentially explosive questions out of the cahiers. It also indicates the danger of judging the extent of concern with these questions only on the basis of the small number of cahiers that explicitly mention them.

While the interest groups concerned with colonial issues maneuvered to gain support for their positions in the electoral assemblies, they also continued to appeal to the public through pamphlets and articles in the press. Ignoring the reservations voiced by the Comité colonial, Malouet published his *Mémoire sur l'esclavage des nègres*, inspiring several responses by members of the Amis des Noirs. In addition to rehearsing the group's objections to the institution of slavery, these pamphlets explicitly opposed the idea of the white slaveholders being granted seats in the Estates General. "Would one dare to try to establish the rules of servitude and despotism in an assembly which excites the enthusiasm of the Nation only because it realizes in advance that justice and, above all, *equality*, must be the bases of its deliberations?" an anonymous member wrote.[88]

Responding to his critics in the *Journal de Paris*, Malouet warned that the campaign against slavery was threatening to "light the torch that will burn down the ports and the colonies." The demands of the abolitionists, he claimed, were setting a dangerous precedent for the discussion of all of the country's problems. "I invite the censors and reformers to be wary of the perfection of theories, and of the triumphant march of an ardent zeal," he wrote, anticipating the arguments he would make against the abolition of long-standing institutions in his role as one of the leaders of the conservative *monarchien* faction in the National Assembly. Recognizing the appeal of the arguments for natural rights that were being heard on all sides in France, he did not hesitate to evoke the realities of a slave society. "Five hundred thousand men with no property, and spread over a territory divided among 80,000 owners, must necessarily be kept under strict discipline and cannot, without immediate danger, be treated as free men. . . . It is therefore not permitted for any citizen to stir up those five hundred thousand men and to call on them to think about and exercise the rights of free men," he insisted.[89]

The heated exchanges between Malouet and his critics in the columns of the paper prefigured a new form of debate about slavery: In addition to substantial treatises like Frossard's book or Malouet's pamphlet, the arguments of both sides would henceforth be expressed in the newspaper press. Brissot and Mirabeau, the two most articulate members of the Société des Amis des Noirs, were also the two publicists most determined to set off the "media revolution" that would become an integral part of the French Revolution as a whole. In mid-April, Brissot circulated the prospectus for a newspaper to be called the *Patriote françois*, arguing that both the nation and the Estates General needed an outlet for the public discussion of the issues that assembly was supposed to discuss. When the government banned his planned paper, he responded with an impassioned pamphlet "on the necessity of making the press free immediately, and above all for political journals." Mirabeau, as an elected deputy to the Estates General, was in a stronger position to defend his right to publish. When the newspaper he announced was banned, he responded by retitling it "Letters to My Constituents," insisting that he had to be able to communicate with the voters who had elected him.[90]

By the time the Estates General finally convened in Versailles on 3 May 1789, the stage was set for a dramatic revolution that would transform every aspect of French society, including the long-running debate about slavery. The advocates of abolition and the various groups opposed to it both realized that they were no longer engaged in an abstract debate; instead, there was a real prospect that the assembly would take actions that could decisively change the government of the colonies and the institution around which their economies had been built. The struggle over slavery would now be conducted with an unprecedented degree of publicity: Even though Brissot's first effort to create his newspaper was blocked, it would be only a matter of weeks before the restrictions on the press were blown away. Above all, the debate about colonial slavery would now take place in the context of a revolutionary movement to base all of French life on the principles of liberty and equality—principles that were clearly antithetical to slavery and racial discrimination.

CHAPTER FOUR

Slavery and the Colonies

FROM THE ESTATES GENERAL TO THE DECLARATION OF THE RIGHTS OF MAN

AFTER MONTHS OF anticipation, the Estates General finally convened on 3 May 1789. For the first time in 175 years, an assembly chosen by the people of France—or at least the male half of the population—prepared to debate the great issues facing the country. In less than four months, between the opening of the Estates General and the passage of the Declaration of the Rights of Man and Citizen in late August, the twelve hundred deputies—three hundred Catholic clergy, three hundred nobles, and six hundred commoners from the Third Estate—would completely overturn the centuries-old absolutist monarchical government and the elaborate system of privileges that had made it seem natural to think that some individuals had rights that others did not enjoy. In the process, they would engage in a major debate about the relationship between France's slave colonies and a country that was about to adopt the axiom that "men are born and remain free and equal in rights" as its guiding principle.

Both the advocates of the reform or the abolition of slavery and the slave trade and the defenders of colonial interests had made a determined effort to get their representatives elected and their concerns incorporated into the *cahiers de doléances*. Neither side achieved as much success as they had hoped for. Seventeen members of the Société des Amis des Noirs were elected as deputies, but Jacques-Pierre Brissot and Condorcet, the group's two main leaders, were not chosen and Honoré Gabriel Mirabeau, the most prominent deputy affiliated with the group, was clearly more concerned to be seen as the champion of the French commoners of the Third Estate than with the issue of slavery. The white plantation owners from the colonies had failed to gain authorization to elect deputies of their own. Some metropolitan deputies were colonial slave owners, although the exact number is unclear: Conventional estimates have put the figure at around 150, but a careful study finds only 17 deputies who definitely owned property in Saint-Domingue in their own name, with an additional 24 who had family relations in the colony.[1] Some of these slave-owning deputies, such as Lafayette and the three Lameth brothers, were also members of the Amis des Noirs, testimony to the blurry line between advocates of the "reform" of slavery and those who aspired to do away with the institution altogether. Whereas the colonists had been denied the right to choose deputies, the populations of the port cities had participated actively in the elections and several merchants had gained seats in the assembly. Although they had strong economic reasons to support the system of slavery that made trade with the colonies profitable, the merchant communities were at odds with the colonists on many other issues, particularly the question of trade regulations, and initially at least some of their representatives sided with the Amis des Noirs in opposing the seating of colonial deputies.

On 5 May 1789, the royal minister Jacques Necker opened the first working session of the Estates General with a report on the state of the kingdom, and particularly of its finances. His speech took so long to deliver that his voice gave out; a secretary had to read the last parts of it. Necker's presentation gave no indication of what kinds of reform measures the king might accept, and he avoided taking a position on the crucial question that had dominated debate in France for months: whether the Estates General were to meet as three separate chambers, one for each of the three traditional "orders" of French society, with each one having a veto over any proposed reform measures, or whether they were to form a single assembly in which the majority would rule, presumably giving an advantage to the Third Estate because of its larger numbers.

Necker also said nothing about whether deputies from the colonies should be admitted to the Estates General.

Necker did, however, make two important references to slavery in his speech. The first was a proposal to diminish the subsidies the government provided to French slave traders, which amounted to 2.4 million livres per year. "There is reason to believe that this . . . expense can be cut in half, by adopting a measure which humanity alone should have recommended," he said.[2] Toward the end of his discourse, Necker made a longer reference to slavery. Listeners could have been forgiven for thinking that the king's first minister had joined the Amis des Noirs: He drew the deputies' attention to "this unfortunate people who have been made the object of a barbarous trade . . . these men like us in their capacity to think and above all by their ability to suffer; these men who . . . we stuff into the hold of a vessel in order to proceed under full sail to deliver them to the chains that await them." He expressed admiration for the "enlightened compassion" being displayed across the Channel, where the House of Commons was about to take up William Wilberforce's motion to ban the slave trade. In his speech, Wilberforce cited the call for the abolition of the slave trade that Necker had made in his 1784 treatise on the workings of the French government. Necker warned of the shame France would suffer "if she does not seek to show herself worthy, and if such an ambition is too much for her."[3]

Necker's remarks about slavery, made in the name of the king, were unprecedented: For the first time, an official spokesman for the French government openly condemned the cruelty of the slave trade and expressed the hope that it might be abolished. Nevertheless, Necker was careful not to translate his sentiments into a concrete proposal. The slavery problem, he insisted, was one for some future assembly, not for the Estates General in which the colonies were not represented.[4] In private, Brissot composed a sharp critique of the minister's speech. Echoing Louis de Jaucourt's 1765 article in the *Encyclopédie*, he wrote, "Let the riches of our colonies perish, if they have to be purchased at the price of human blood, by the violation of every natural right, by ignoring pure morality!"[5] To the colonists, on the other hand, Necker's speech was a warning of the dangers the assembly might pose for them if they did not win their battle for representation.

The Estates General immediately ground to a halt when the deputies of the Third Estate, at Mirabeau's urging, refused to deliberate until the other two orders agreed to meet and vote in common, thereby abandoning their right to veto proposed reforms. Meanwhile, Louis-Marthe Gouy d'Arsy's group continued their campaign for representation in the assembly. On 8 June 1789, after the overall proceedings of the Estates General had been at a standstill for a month, they formally presented their request to the three orders. Since none of their members were clergy, the members of that order simply ignored them, and the nobility rejected their petition: Although many colonial proprietors had noble titles in France, noble status and privileges had never been recognized in Saint-Domingue. The issue was thus left to the deputies of the Third Estate.[6] Because the Third Estate deputies were still refusing to take any actions before their conflict with the other orders was resolved, the Gouy group was told that no decision would be taken on their request, but they were provisionally allowed to attend the assembly.[7] The day after the appearance of Gouy's group, the Third Estate deputies began their momentous discussion of the abbé Emmanuel Sieyès's proposal to declare themselves a "national assembly" with the right to act without the consent of the other estates. The colonial-representation question resurfaced on 14 June, after the completion of the reading of the roll call of Third Estates deputies, when Gouy's group renewed its request to be included. This time, their petition was referred to a committee established to settle credentials disputes.[8]

The Gouy group's petition unleashed a public debate that went well beyond the bounds of the assembly. In contrast to the situation in the British Parliament, however, where Wilberforce focused his colleagues' attention on the "wickedness of the slave trade," which he insisted was "so enormous, so dreadful and so irremediable, that he could stop at no alternative short of its abolition," the French debate was ostensibly limited to the question of whether the slave colonies were entitled to representation in the Estates General.[9] Even if they did not say so, however, both sides understood that this question involved the issue of slavery. The admission of deputies for the colonies would constitute a decision to treat their white inhabitants as full citizens of the French nation and consequently to endorse the legitimacy of their claim to their properties, including their enslaved labor force. Since the organizers of the movement for colonial representation had excluded free people of color from their proceedings, granting their demands would also amount to endorsing their claim that only whites were entitled to such status.

Metropolitan public opinion accepted the Gouy group's claim to speak for the whites in the colony, although the *Journal de Paris* reported that there was actually a division among the colonists about the wisdom of seeking representation in the assembly.[10] Etienne Clavière told the Amis des Noirs that the admission of colonial deputies would endanger their cause and "that there was no time to waste in taking up the defense of the Blacks in the Estates General."[11] Condorcet dismissed the planters' appeal to "the natural right of every man to be subjected only to laws to whose formation he has contributed. We reply that any man who violates one of the natural rights of humanity, immediately loses the right to invoke this principle in his own favor."[12] Condorcet's formulation anticipated one of Abraham Lincoln's most famous lines—"Those who deny freedom to others deserve it not for themselves"—but it was Brissot who made the most emphatic refutation of the planters' arguments, first in an appendix to his lengthy tract on the Estates General, which he had presented to the Amis des Noirs in mid-May 1789, and then in a separately published pamphlet, *Réflexions sur l'admission, aux Etats-Généraux, des députés de Saint-Domingue*, which he completed in late June.[13]

In both his publications on this issue, Brissot, echoing an argument for American independence from Thomas Paine's *Common Sense*, was ready to concede the autonomy of the colonies—"It is impossible that, in this whirlwind that pushes everything toward liberty, substantial colonies can remain attached to bodies that are 2000 leagues away from them"—but he rejected the Gouy group's claim to a right to seats in the French assembly. The colonists' electoral assemblies were illegitimate, since they had excluded free people of color from participation, and if the economic importance of the colonies was to be considered a justification for granting them representation, then "the Black slaves have a much better right to deputies than the colonists," since it was their labor that made the colonies a source of wealth.[14] The basic issue was simply the injustice of slavery and racial discrimination. In the appendix to his *Plan of Conduct*, he thundered,

> Let the planters publicly acknowledge that all men are born free and equal in rights; that the Blacks are brothers of the whites; that they have the same rights; that no power on earth can take those rights away . . . let them acknowledge the iniquity of the slave trade, the iniquity of slavery, the necessity of abolishing both of them; let them swear not to put any obstacle in the way of this abolition . . . and then I will believe in the purity of their intentions, and then we will demand their admission [to the Estates General], the aid of their knowledge to carry out, with all possible prudence, this great operation.[15]

If the colonists were allowed to have representatives without making these commitments, Brissot warned, they would introduce into the upcoming assembly "these disgusting ideas of inequality and servitude, to which they have a dangerous and ineradicable attachment." Like the southerners in the United States, the colonists were demanding a number of deputies based on the population of the colonies, including enslaved Blacks. Perhaps aware that one of the participants in the American Constitutional Convention had opposed the clause that allowed the southerners to count the Blacks as three-fifths of whites by remarking that, if enslaved people were regarded as their owners' property, they should no more be counted than the "cattle and horses of the North," Brissot pointed out that, in allocating deputies in France, "we have not given a greater number of representatives to those who own more horses or oxen." Mirabeau, who recognized a memorable phrase when he heard one, appropriated this line in one of his editorials and has received the credit for it ever since.[16]

Brissot concluded his *Refléxions* with a justification of the efforts intellectuals like himself were making on behalf of the Blacks and a stark message to the plantation owners. In words that evoked the famous passage from the *Histoire des deux Indes*, Brissot warned that unless the evils of slavery and racism were confronted, the Blacks, "unwilling to bear an insupportable yoke . . . will revolt and will have avenged with blood the torments of two centuries. Reform will forestall this massacre, by attaching the Blacks to the whites, who will have restored to them all their rights." Brissot then followed the familiar pattern of abolitionist literature by conceding that "the time is not yet ripe for the admission of representatives of the Black slaves, for the restitution of all of their civil and political rights." In the meantime, however, the National Assembly should recognize the Amis des Noirs as the official representatives of the antislavery cause and prepare to abolish the slave trade.[17]

Even as Brissot was arguing against the admission of colonial deputies to the National Assembly, the cascade of events that were plunging France into a full-fledged revolution offered his opponents an opportunity to win their case. On 19 June, two days after the creation of the National Assembly, the credentials committee heard their request to join that body. The government's control over the press was quickly breaking down, and, in his newly created newspaper, the *Point du jour*, Bertrand Barère, one of the committee members and a future member of the Committee of Public Safety during the Terror, praised Gouy d'Arsy for the "noble and energetic manner" in which he had presented the argument for colonial representation, and summarized his remarks:

> The colony of Saint-Domingue, French in origin, French by choice, French in its administration and by the tribute with which it enriches the treasury of the mother country, deserves to be admitted to explain its important interests in the most admirable assembly that the French monarchy has ever had. Even if natural right were not to be consulted in this century of enlightenment, political right and what is called *raison d'état* should dictate the admission of this colonial deputation. We know what it cost England to debate this question with its colonies with arms, rather than according to the invariable laws of reason and natural equity.[18]

Barère was clearly impressed, but not to the point of complete agreement. "Before presenting to the national assembly this question of public law, the most important that can arise in a great empire," he commented, "it would be desirable to . . . reconcile the rights of humanity with the calculations of politics, in order to improve in our American provinces the condition of so many unfortunates condemned to slavery and debilitating labor in a burning climate."[19]

Meanwhile, in response to the Third Estate's defiant decision to declare itself a "National Assembly" on 17 June, the king announced the scheduling of a "royal session" of what he still called the Estates General, at which he hoped to regain the initiative by announcing his own program of constitutional reform while putting the Third Estate back in its place. In preparation for this meeting, on 20 June royal officials locked the deputies out of the large hall in which the National Assembly had been meeting. Fearing that this move signaled a plan to dissolve the assembly altogether, the deputies broke into the royal indoor tennis court, where they swore a solemn oath not to let themselves be dispersed until they had enacted a new constitution of their own. Gouy d'Arsy and his group, who had been attending the assembly's meetings as observers, seized the opportunity: They asked to be allowed to join in the oath, thus tying their fate to that of the rest of the group, with Gouy d'Arsy announcing that the colony "puts itself under the protection of the National Assembly, and declares that from now on, it will be called a national colony." Jean-Sylvain Bailly, the assembly's president, told the body that the credentials committee had recommended that the colony of Saint-Domingue be given twelve seats, fewer than the twenty Gouy's group had originally sought, but twice as many as the six Mirabeau had been prepared to concede them a week earlier.[20] Since the credentials committee had not yet made its report, the admission of the Saint-Domingue deputies was still declared provisional, but their willingness to voluntarily join the assembly at a moment of danger clearly made it difficult to reject their demand.

Three days later, on 23 June, Louis XVI presided over the previously announced royal session. He was prepared to make some significant reforms to the structure of the French monarchy, but he adamantly rejected the National Assembly's demand for an end to the privileges of the clergy and the nobility, and in particular to their right to meet and vote separately from the Third Estate. After the king's speech had been read to the deputies, the royal master of ceremonies ordered them to disperse. The clergy and nobles left the hall, but the Third Estate members remained in their seats. Mirabeau rose and addressed the royal official, telling him that "we will only be driven from our places by bayonets." In defiance of the king, the assembly continued to deliberate. On the following day, a majority of the clergy deputies, many of whom were parish priests from commoner backgrounds, joined the assembly, lending momentum to what was now clearly an open revolt against the king and the more intransigent members of the privileged orders.

With the king and his ministers seemingly paralyzed in the face of the National Assembly's defiance, the deputies prepared to deal with the question of the colonial deputies, which needed to be resolved before they could move to other matters. On 27 June, Pierre-Louis Prieur de la Marne, a future member of the Committee of Public Safety, delivered the credentials committee's report, opening three days of extended debate on the topic, during which at least twenty-six deputies intervened.[21] The speakers included Mirabeau, Pierre-Victor Malouet, and many other deputies who would become major figures in the assembly's proceedings. Although the majority of the speakers expressed opposition to the Saint-Domingue delegation's demands, only two of them—Mirabeau and La Rochefoucauld—were members of the Société des Amis des Noirs, and only one can be clearly identified as a spokesman for the colonial merchants who opposed colonial representation on economic, rather than moral, grounds. Hardly any of the antislavery deputies came from *bailliages* that had mentioned the topic in their cahiers, a further indication that concern with the issue was more widespread than the cahiers themselves show. Gouy d'Arsy was largely responsible for presenting the colonists' case: Aside from the committee's spokesman Prieur, those who spoke in his support usually made only short comments endorsing an award of twelve seats for Saint-Domingue or else simply urging that the debate be concluded.

Prieur began by repeating Gouy d'Arsy's arguments about the economic importance of Saint-Domingue and the need to "give it a good constitution that will finally free it from the oppressive regime that holds back its industry and discourages the spirits of the colonists." He made no mention of the slavery issue. Instead, he asked the assembly to decide three questions: Should the colony have representatives in the National Assembly? Had the delegation led by Gouy d'Arsy been legitimately elected? And finally, how many deputies should the colony be awarded? In the committee's view, the answer to the first question was obvious: The colonists paid taxes, they served in the French military, so they were therefore French citizens. Although the election procedure that had resulted in the nomination of Gouy d'Arsy and his colleagues had never been officially authorized, Prieur claimed misleadingly that they had followed the procedures used in choosing deputies in the rest of France. This left only the question of numbers. If the colony's representation were to be based only on its population of forty thousand whites, it would receive six seats, the minimum given to metropolitan France's smallest provinces. Accepting the colonists' claim that Saint-Domingue paid 60 million livres a year in taxes, Prieur maintained that such a decision would be "an injustice": The province of Dauphiné, which paid only 5 million livres, had twenty-four deputies. The committee had agreed that Saint-Domingue deserved more than six deputies but had split down the middle on the appropriate figure, with eighteen of its thirty-six members opting for the twenty deputies Gouy d'Arsy had sought and the remaining eighteen preferring twelve.[22]

Although the deputies quickly endorsed the importance of maintaining the colonies and the principle of colonial representation—"If the British Parliament had admitted colonial deputies, America would still be English," the marquis de Sillery asserted—a number of them seized the opportunity to insist that the whites alone did not represent the whole of the Saint-Domingue population. Six deputies declared that their cahiers obligated them to insist on a discussion of slavery, and one raised the question of the rights of the island's free people of color, who, "although free men, had no voice in the assemblies." Finally, after reminding the assembly that the British Parliament was debating the slave-trade issue—he was apparently still unaware of the House of Commons' vote on 23 June to refer the issue to a committee for further study, thereby killing the momentum on which the French abolitionists had counted—La Rochefoucauld made a specific motion "that the assembly take up the freedom of the Blacks before it separates."[23]

Rather than discussing La Rochefoucauld's motion, the assembly voted to approve the principle of colonial representation and to declare the Saint-Domingue elections valid. The decision to grant any seats at all to Saint-Domingue was a major one: For the first time, a European empire granted its colonies a voice not only in their own affairs but in those of the metropole as well. Wanting to avoid the experience of the British in North America, the French revolutionaries committed themselves to a radical experiment whose consequences were to be felt throughout the coming years. Before they settled the final issue of numbers, however, the deputies took a break. While most of them were outside the hall, metropolitan revolutionary history made a dramatic intervention in the colonial discussion: Following new instructions from the king, the deputies from the two privileged orders who had been holding out against joining the National Assembly arrived, and La Rochefoucauld himself took the lead in welcoming them. The great question that had paralyzed the meeting of the Estates General for almost two months was finally settled, and Bailly, the assembly's president, decided to adjourn the discussion of Saint-Domingue's representation so that the deputies could "abandon themselves to the joy that a so ardently desired reunion . . . must produce in the heart of all the French."[24]

When the steering committee of the Amis des Noirs met on 30 June, Condorcet, although he had shortly before written a pamphlet suggesting that Saint-Domingue be given at most a derisory one or two deputies, recommended that the group accept what he regarded as a fait accompli. Saint-Domingue was going to get at least twelve deputies, he said, and any further opposition, "far from being useful to the Society, might on the contrary work against its interests."[25] Others were not as willing to give in, however. In his newspaper, Mirabeau complained that there had been no discussion of the implications of granting the colonies representation and, falling back on an argument made by his father three decades earlier, expressed doubts about whether they really were an economic asset. As for the validity of the Saint-Domingue deputies' election, if it was justified because they were taxpayers, how was it that "the free men of color, property owners who pay taxes, weren't electors and weren't represented?" Since the colonists were citing the enslaved Blacks as part of the population, Mirabeau demanded "to know . . . if they intend to count their Negroes in the class of men or in that of beasts of burden. . . . If the colonists want the Negroes considered as men, let them free them, let them give them the right to vote and to be elected. In the contrary case, we wish to remind them that in setting the number of deputies in proportion to the population of France, we have not taken into consideration the number of our horses or our mules," a variation on the memorable line that Brissot had used in one of his tracts on the subject.[26]

Equally indignant about the proposal to admit colonial deputies, although for very different reasons, was the merchant deputy from Bordeaux, Pierre-Paul Nairac, who kept a voluminous chronicle of the Third Estate's proceedings. What concerned Nairac was not any violation of the rights of man but the danger to the privileges of France's colonial merchants. The colonies could not be assimilated to the metropole, "by reason of their climate, of their distance, of the nature of the soil, their tax system, the things they produce, the slavery of the Negroes, the population, [and] all the other differences that the prohibitive trade regime, necessarily admitted for the administration of colonies, has established between them and the mother country," he wrote. The interruption that had led to the postponing of the debate was, in Nairac's view, "a very lucky event."[27]

For various reasons, then, when debate about seating the Saint-Domingue delegation resumed on 3 July, a number of deputies had concluded, as Barère put it in his newspaper, that the discussion six days earlier had failed to take into account "all the considerations of politics and legislation, the careful examination of which should have preceded such an important deliberation."[28] Once again, Mirabeau led the attack, repeating his denunciation of the white colonists' claim to represent the entire population of Saint-Domingue, and the momentum in the debate appeared to have shifted decisively in favor of the critics of slavery. Several pro-colonial speakers tried to end the debate by insisting that the credentials committee's report had already committed the assembly to accepting at least twelve deputies,[29] but Anne-Pierre, marquis de Montesquiou-Fézensac undercut their efforts by moving that the Saint-Domingue delegation be limited to four deputies. At this moment, the deputy Dominique-Joseph Garat delivered a long speech examining the implications of the decision to give slaveholding colonists parliamentary representation.[30] Garat had identified himself with the abolitionist cause ten years earlier, when he composed notes to a literary work denouncing slavery. His speech on 3 July, which borrowed heavily from Brissot's pamphlets, was the most wide-ranging consideration of the issue delivered in the Constituent Assembly during the entire two years of its existence.

Garat began by praising the assembly for having "unanimously pronounced that a colony is a province, which not only resolves, but ends all further discussion of these questions about metropoles and colonies." Having said this, however, Garat immediately backtracked, wondering whether the legitimate interests of a colony could be adequately represented in an assembly where its representatives' voices would inevitably be drowned out by metropolitan deputies. He therefore suggested that the colonists might be better off with an assembly of their own, a proposition that was in fact part of the program presented in their own cahier as well as in Brissot's pamphlets. After having shown that there was a major question as to whether the colonists belonged to the same political community as the metropole, Garat turned to the question actually facing the assembly. Like Mirabeau, he objected to the idea that deputies chosen only by the island's white population could be considered representatives of the free people of color and the Blacks. The enslaved population "ought to have representatives to oppose their tyrants, and it is their tyrants who pretend to represent them!"[31] he exclaimed. By this logic, Garat arrived at the conclusion that the white Saint-Domingue colonists deserved only a minimal number of representatives.

Garat promptly muddled this argument, however, by reflecting that the result of his own reasoning would be that the colonial deputies would be outvoted by representatives of metropolitan interest groups. "The colonists have slaves, and they themselves are the slaves of metropolitan commerce," he declared. Having thus put the injustice to the white colonists on the same moral level as the injustice of plantation slavery, Garat returned to the latter issue. He concluded by suggesting that the admission of the Saint-Domingue deputies be made conditional on their acceptance of the principle that "the enslavement of the Blacks is a crime . . . that no political interest can justify" and that they be required to promise "that they will never oppose any effort that the assembly may make to find ways to end this crime as soon as possible; that they promise also that every time this subject is discussed, they will have no vote in the National Assembly."[32] By suggesting that the colonies be given deputies only if they agreed to forgo the defense of their most important special interest, Garat inadvertently underlined the impossibility of reconciling the arguments for colonial representation and the abolition of slavery.

The assembly was just about to vote on Montesquiou's motion to give the colonists four deputies when La Rochefoucauld proposed referring the question to its *bureaux*, the thirty-member subgroups into which it was at that point dividing to facilitate discussions.[33] In view of La Rochefoucauld's principled opposition to slavery, the sense of his motion is hard to interpret. Was he hoping to get a vote against any colonial representation at all, or perhaps to get Garat's conditions attached to the motion? In any event, when debate in the full assembly resumed on the following day, opinions seemed more confused than ever. Gouy d'Arsy went on the offensive, repeating his arguments about the colony's economic importance and reviving his demand for a delegation of at least eighteen seats. He tried to finesse the issue of slavery by promising that "if the assembly, in its wisdom, finds a way to combine the conservation of the colonies, the colonists' properties, and the maintenance of their work force, with the abolition of slavery and the slave trade, there is no colonist who would not enthusiastically give proof of his humanity and his patriotism."[34]

In contrast to the previous day, however, several speakers now rose to oppose the very idea of colonial representation. Nairac, reflecting the view of the port cities, objected to allowing the colonies to participate in metropolitan politics. No other European empire had granted its colonies such representation, Nairac reminded his colleagues.[35] Gouy d'Arsy's position was also challenged by a rival group of Saint-Domingue colonists, whose letter protesting the illegality of the process by which the putative deputies had been chosen and the very idea that the interests of slave-owning colonies could be reconciled with those of a metropole bent on promoting liberty was read to the assembly. "What could colonists think of cahiers that say, 'you will call for the admission of deputies for Saint-Domingue,' and, next to that article, 'you will call for the emancipation of the Negroes,'" these dissenters asked.

Whereas the Gouy group had been careful to avoid explicit references to slavery, these rivals made no secret of their conviction that what mattered most to the colonies "is the maintenance of Negro slavery."[36] Although the deputies chose to ignore this objection—the deputy Jacques-Antoine Creuzé-Latouche thought it might be a maneuver by the royal ministers to justify their opposition to colonial representation—at least one newspaper publicized the document.[37]

To settle the issue, the assembly proceeded to take its first roll-call vote on a parliamentary motion. (The fact that the deputies from the privileged orders voted as individuals was taken as evidence that they had finally accepted voting by head rather than by order.)[38] Not a single vote was cast in favor of the twenty deputies that half the members of the credentials committee had been willing to recommend on 27 June. Two hundred twenty-three deputies voted for a twelve-member delegation and one for giving the colony eight seats, but the majority—523 voters—approved only six Saint-Domingue deputies, with an additional nine favoring the even smaller total of four. On the surface, this appeared to be a defeat for colonial and proslavery interests: The assembly had clearly listened to the arguments about the injustice of endorsing elections in which only whites had voted. In contrast to subsequent assembly debates, opponents of slavery had been allowed to openly denounce the institution without interruption, and the tone of the press reports on the proceedings suggests that the assembly had been sympathetic to these speeches. Sieyès, for one, didn't see that the decision made any difference; as he wrote to Brissot, the colonial deputies would be heavily outnumbered in the assembly, and when the "affair of the Blacks" finally came up for debate, "no matter how things turn out, you will be heard."[39]

Nevertheless, what might have appeared as a defeat for the proslavery colonists disguised a more complicated situation. "The deed had been done without recall," the early twentieth-century American historian Mitchell Garrett wrote. "Colonial deputies had been definitively admitted to the Parliament of the nation, and Santo Domingo [*sic*] had been drawn into the Revolution."[40] As Mirabeau and others had warned, by accepting a delegation chosen exclusively by colonial slave owners, even if it was a smaller one than Gouy d'Arsy and his allies had sought and even if they had had to listen to some harsh words about slavery from their opponents, the assembly foreclosed any possibility of taking immediate action against that institution or the racial status quo in Saint-Domingue. In the daily newspaper he founded at the end of July 1789, the *Patriote françois*, Brissot lamented the baleful influence he expected the colonial deputies to exercise.[41]

Future discussions of colonial issues would be stymied by the assembly's unwillingness to impose its will on the slave owners unless they voluntarily made concessions. This is why slavery survived the celebrated orgy of renunciations of privileges on the night of 4 August 1789, when representatives of the nobility, the clergy, the provinces, and the kingdom's cities voluntarily surrendered their special rights. The issue was brought up by the indefatigable La Rochefoucauld, but the spirit of the occasion required that any motion to abolish slavery would have had to be proposed by a slave owner. The best La Rochefoucauld could do, according to Mirabeau, was to "ask the Assembly to take up this matter before it ends its sessions," a suggestion that was ignored.[42]

After the three days of heated debate leading up to the vote on 4 July, partisans on both sides looked forward to a breathing spell to prepare for future confrontations. Meanwhile, however, a new stage of the revolutionary crisis was unfolding. The court's diehard supporters of absolutism had not given up hope of stopping the erosion of the king's powers. They persuaded Louis XVI to summon dependable troops from the frontiers, and by 9 July, Mirabeau was publicly demanding to know why "the capital is surrounded." Two days later, on 11 July, the minister Necker was abruptly dismissed, signaling the start of an outright confrontation between the government and the revolutionary movement. In response, the population of Paris began the insurrection that culminated on 14 July with the storming of the Bastille. Both the advocates of abolition and the defenders of slavery were swept up in the rapidly unfolding drama, and colonial issues were forgotten. The Amis des Noirs did not hold another meeting for a month and a half.

Many of the men who had been at the forefront of the campaign to put abolition on the National Assembly's agenda played major roles in the mid-July crisis. Mirabeau urged his fellow deputies to stand firm against any attempt to divide or disperse them. Lafayette became the commander of the National Guard, the improvised citizen militia organized in Paris during the crisis, and Brissot helped organize the militia in his Paris neighborhood. Leaders of the proslavery movement, such as Malouet and Gouy d'Arsy, joined their opponents in trying to ward off the danger of a resurgence of the absolutist regime they also regarded as an enemy. Médéric Louis Élie Moreau de Saint-Méry found himself thrust into a prominent role as chairman of the assembly of the Paris electors, who had reconvened as an emergency committee to try to maintain order in the city. In that capacity, he worked closely with Lafayette and with the other electors, who "swore to have a single goal: to consolidate true liberty, to restore order in the capital . . . and to perish, if necessary, in striving for that purpose." On 17 July 1789, when Louis XVI visited Paris's Hôtel de Ville, the site of the municipal government, to demonstrate that he accepted the result of the storming of the Bastille, Moreau was the first to address him, expressing confidence that "your reign will be the epoch of liberty," and at the beginning of August, when Necker resumed his post as minister, it was Moreau who officially welcomed him to the Hôtel de Ville.[43]

Once the storming of the Bastille had cleared the way for the National Assembly to pursue its self-proclaimed task of giving France a new constitution, the deputies turned their attention to another issue with weighty implications for the issue of slavery. Already before the mid-July crisis, many of them had been pressing for the drafting of a declaration of rights, a statement of principles that would serve as a guide for the constitution. During the American Revolution, most states had issued such documents, enumerating the basic rights of their citizens and indicating how the governments they were establishing would protect them. With the exception of the 1777 constitution of the independent state of Vermont, none of the American state bills of rights explicitly abolished slavery, but the idea of proclaiming individual natural rights as the basis of the social and political order obviously raised serious questions about its legitimacy. The idea of a declaration of rights had been widely discussed from the start of the French revolutionary crisis, and leading members of the Amis des Noirs had been among the earliest to offer draft proposals. In early 1788 Mirabeau outlined "the tableau of the rights that belong to you by virtue of being men . . . these inalienable and imprescriptible rights . . . without which it is impossible for the human species, in any climate, to preserve its dignity, to perfect itself, to enjoy the favors of nature in peace."[44]

As one reads through the versions of a declaration of rights put forward in 1789 by authors who were also members of the Amis des Noirs, one is struck by their reluctance to confront the issue of slavery. The instructions Sieyès drafted on behalf of the duc d'Orléans, for example, which were supposed to guide the duke's representatives in the electoral assemblies in districts where he held property, called for the Estates General to abolish "everything that is opposed to full individual liberty, considered in all its aspects," but there was no mention of whether this applied to the enslaved Blacks on the duke's colonial properties. Condorcet produced a draft with a long and detailed section on "personal freedom," covering freedom of enterprise, freedom of movement, freedom of religion, and freedom of thought. He did insist that "no man can be obliged to perform any kind of personal service, whether for an individual or for the public, whether civil or military, except voluntarily or as a result of a freely agreed upon engagement made for a limited time," a formulation that a clever lawyer might have interpreted as outlawing slavery, but not one whose application to the institution was immediately obvious.[45]

Brissot, when he presented his own proposal for a declaration, which he must have written at almost the same time as the vehement denunciation of slavery appended to his *Plan de conduite*, declared that "this declaration can be contained in this line: 'All men are born free and equal in rights.'" Having made that statement, he evidently saw no need to make any explicit mention of slavery.[46] Pierre-Samuel du Pont de Nemours, who had published articles critical of slavery nearly twenty years before the Revolution, drafted a lengthy declaration of rights that asserted that "no authority can oblige a man to work without pay, or for pay that seems insufficient to him," but he did not address the question of whether this implied the abolition of slavery.[47]

By the summer of 1789, after the question of colonial representation had been raised, a few proposed rights declarations contained wording that had a clearer relationship to the issue of slavery. In the long disquisition on rights that Sieyès published in mid-July, he stated explicitly that "the property of one's *person* is the first of all rights," a formulation rooted in John Locke's theory of property that could easily be interpreted as a condemnation of the idea of slavery.[48] Guy-Jean-Baptiste Target, a prominent legal expert, opined that "the right of property only exists with regard to things. Any power that a man exercises over other men, to the prejudice of their natural rights, is a usurpation based on force and cannot constitute a property; it is not a right, but a crime."[49] Several authors restated the venerable "freedom principle" that "any slave regains his liberty upon entering the lands under French domination" and that "France is a land of liberty . . . it suffices to live there to be free."[50] Others argued that no one could sell himself into slavery, a formulation that would be incorporated into the declarations of rights of the French constitutions of 1793 and 1795, but one that did not address the status of individuals enslaved against their will.[51]

Among the dozens of authors who proposed declarations of rights in 1788 and 1789, the only one who explicitly and unequivocally called for an end to slavery in the French colonies was the Protestant minister Jean-Paul Rabaut Saint-Etienne. Before the Revolution, he had been one of the most outspoken representatives of France's Protestant minority; for him, the issue of natural rights was not an abstraction but a concrete concern. In a pamphlet published early in 1789, he argued that society did not require its members to give up their natural rights, and that "if slavery exists, it is only due to a complete forgetting of principles and of these eternal rights that can never be denied." He asserted that the National Assembly should seize the opportunity to consecrate "the immortal maxims of the liberty of all men, without exception." Among the propositions he wanted to see included in the declaration was the statement that "the enslavement of people is forbidden forever, even with respect to foreigners who may be brought into the empire."[52] This formulation, unlike those of every other participant in the debate about rights in 1789, left no room for ambiguity: When Rabaut declared liberty to be universal, he meant his statement to apply not only to the white population of the metropole but to the Blacks who had been brought to the colonies from Africa.

Although the vast majority of the rights declarations proposed in 1789 contained at best implicit criticisms of slavery, the defenders of colonial interests recognized that the widespread discussion of natural rights inspired by the revolutionary movement constituted a threat. Unsurprisingly, Malouet, the veteran defender of slavery, was one of the most outspoken opponents of the very idea of a declaration of rights. The idea might be appropriate in America, he told his colleagues, because "American society, newly formed, is composed in its totality of landowners already accustomed to equality," a description that glossed over the existence of slavery there, but in France, "we have for fellow citizens an immense multitude of men without property." The poor, he agreed, had "an equal right to liberty," but it was necessary for "men placed by circumstances in a dependent condition to see the just limits [of their freedom] rather than the breadth of natural liberty. . . . In such circumstances, an explicit declaration of the general and absolute principles of natural liberty and equality could rupture necessary bonds."[53]

In his speech, Malouet spoke in general terms and made no reference to the colonies or slavery. His warning about the dangers in proclaiming abstract principles of liberty has made some historians treat him as a French equivalent of Edmund Burke, the father of modern conservatism. Malouet may have been prescient about some of the difficulties the Revolution would encounter, but it is worth bearing in mind that until 1789, his whole career had been devoted to the colonies, and there is little doubt that his concern for maintaining social order in France reflected his experience as a plantation owner and colonial official. The power of Burke's conservative vision came from his evocation of society as an organic whole whose institutions benefited all its members and that endured through time, "a partnership not only between those who are living, but between those who are living, those who are dead, and those who are to be born." No bonds of tradition or mutual obligation sustained the colonial slave societies that shaped Malouet's thinking; as he knew full well, they were maintained solely by naked force. In the atmosphere prevailing in France in the summer of 1789, such arguments could hardly stand up against the generally shared enthusiasm for liberty.

The defenders of slavery were not the only ones who had reservations about the idea of drafting a declaration of rights before any of the other practical aspects of the new constitution had been settled. Many of the clergy in the National Assembly feared that a declaration would inevitably undermine the position of the Catholic Church, and nobles foresaw that it would threaten their special status. Nevertheless, on 4 August 1789, a few hours before the start of the famous evening session at which the assembly would abolish all special privileges, the deputies voted to proceed immediately with the elaboration of such a document. Various drafts were put forward, and for a full week, between 21 and 27 August, the assembly debated the precise wording of the preamble and the seventeen articles that became the historic Declaration of the Rights of Man and Citizen.

The Declaration of Rights was clearer and more concise than any of the American bills of rights. Written in the eighteenth century's most widely known language, it remains the most powerful and eloquent summation of the meaning of the era's ideals of liberty and equality.[54] It is incorporated in France's present-day constitution, and it served as a model for the 1948 Universal Declaration of Human Rights. As we have seen, numerous members of the Amis des Noirs participated in the polemical exchanges, inside and outside the National Assembly, that led to the elaboration of the final document. It is therefore remarkable that the issue of slavery went unmentioned in almost all of those debates, and in particular in the heated discussions held from 21 to 27 August.

The deputies such as Malouet, who might have wished to make sure that some kind of protection for slavery was included in any declaration, probably decided that they could not take the risk of bringing up the subject. A letter written at the time by a member of the colonists' group in Paris to their correspondents in Saint-Domingue and later published in Brissot's *Patriote françois* explains the predicament in which the proslavery lobby found itself. The letter writer warned that the Parisian revolutionaries "are drunk with liberty . . . a society of enthusiasts, who call themselves the *Friends of the Blacks,* openly denounce us; they are waiting for the best moment to set off an explosion against slavery; all it might take is for us to have the misfortune of pronouncing the word for them to seize the opportunity to demand the freeing of our Negroes. Our fear has reduced us, against our will, to silence." Fortunately, according to the letter writer, "the National Assembly is too occupied with domestic affairs of the kingdom to think about us."[55]

Although slavery was not explicitly mentioned in the debates about the declaration, the colonists' fears that its consecration of liberty and equality might have drastic consequences for them were not unfounded. After the assembly had approved the first article of the declaration, announcing that "men are born and remain free and equal in rights," Mirabeau took a victory lap in his newspaper, now called the *Courier de Provence*. "This is not one of those sudden decrees, passed without reflection, that often emanate from the wisest assemblies; it is a great and important truth . . . which is found, in approximately the same terms, in fifty different projects of declarations proposed by various members of the Assembly," he told his readers. The declaration "is the law for the Assembly itself; it is the law for every province awarded representatives there; consequently, it is the law for this colony of Saint-Domingue, which has demanded so insistently and so cleverly obtained a significant representation."[56]

Fulfilling the colonists' worst fears, Mirabeau drew the logical consequence of the wording of the declaration's first article:

> After having loudly posed the principle, the National Assembly will not shrink from the most just, the most legitimate consequence. It will not, undoubtedly, say to these Negroes . . . to these unfortunates born into slavery, shackled with iron collars, and bloodied under the whip of pitiless overseers, *that they are born free*. . . . It will not say to these pitiable victims of our ferocious avarice, that they *are equal in rights* to those who buy them, resell them, mistreat them. . . . But what it will say to the Negroes, what it will say to the planters, what it will teach the whole of Europe, is that there are not, that there cannot be, either in France, or in any other territory under France's laws, any men except *free men*, except *men equal to one another*; that any man who keeps another in involuntary servitude violates the law, injures the great national charter, and cannot hope for either support or protection from it.[57]

This great achievement, Mirabeau claimed, was due to the "generous *Amis des Noirs*." They had feared that the colonists would oppose a broad statement about liberty, but among the colonial deputies,

> not a single one of them has objected to a principle of which the emancipation of their slaves is an immediate consequence; not one of them has proposed an amendment to declare that *only white men* are born and remain free; not one of them has proposed the insertion of this clause for the Africans: *Black men are born and remain slaves*; the distinction of color destroys the equality of rights. . . . Not a single one of these deputies has spoken such sinful words, none of them has given the slightest hint of any reservations about his adhesion to the Assembly's decree. It is therefore not only the vow of the National Assembly, but that of the planters themselves, that every man, regardless of his color, has an equal right to liberty.

In words dripping with sarcasm, Mirabeau concluded that "we have no doubt that the representatives of Saint-Domingue will hurry to post up, in every part of their island, this memorable decree of an assembly to which they so badly wanted to be admitted."[58]

This article in Mirabeau's widely circulated newspaper stated in the clearest possible terms the logical consequence of the French revolutionaries' axiom that "men are born and remain free and equal in rights" and foreshadowed the sweeping abolition decree that the National Convention would pass in February 1794. In 1789, however, it had no immediate impact. The radicalism of Mirabeau's statement was too much even for his allies in the Amis des Noirs. In his own newspaper, the *Patriote françois*, Brissot was careful to emphasize that "the Blacks are not yet ready for freedom; they need to be prepared; that is the doctrine of our Society." In line with the strategy of their British ally Thomas Clarkson, who was then in Paris, Brissot insisted that the only immediate measure the group advocated was the abolition of the slave trade.[59]

Once they realized that there would be no attempt to put Mirabeau's suggestions into practice, some supporters of slavery began to see that they might even be able to turn certain provisions of the Declaration of Rights to their own advantage. Articles 2 and 17 of the declaration explicitly protected the right of property, allowing them to argue that the enslaved captives they had purchased deserved the same legal status as their land and livestock. A clause in article 6 stating that "all citizens have the right to participate personally, or through their representatives," in the making of laws gave them an opening to insist that no legislation affecting the colonies' interests should be passed without the consent of their white citizens. Although local officials in Saint-Domingue banned the publication of the Declaration of Rights in the colony, a Port-au-Prince newspaper actually printed a redacted version of the document, omitting articles that "do not seem suitable for a country organized the way Saint-Domingue is," such as the assertion that "men are born and remain equal in rights," but praising those that promised to "guarantee forever all those who live under the government of the French empire from the tyrannical abuses of arbitrary power."[60]

In less than four months, the movement that had begun with the convocation of the Estates General had swept away the absolute monarchy, installed a representative assembly in power, made its overseas colonies full parts of the nation, abolished a centuries-old system of social privileges, and distilled decades of theorizing about the natural rights of man into a succinct declaration of rights. However, the Revolution had only begun to confront the flagrant contradiction between its declared principles of liberty and equality and the reality of colonial conditions. For the next two years, that struggle would rage in the National Assembly, in the press, in France's trading ports, and in the country's culture. It would affect the development of all the Revolution's major factions and the careers of most of its prominent leaders. At the moment when news of a massive slave uprising in France's most important colony, Saint-Domingue, arrived in the fall of 1791, France's revolutionaries would still find themselves bitterly divided about whether their principles required them to promote the end of slavery and racial discrimination, or whether the national interest required them to maintain those institutions.

CHAPTER FIVE

The Struggle for the Soul of the New France

ONCE THEY HAD passed the Declaration of the Rights of Man and Citizen, the deputies of the National Assembly turned to the task they had sworn to complete when they took the Oath of the Tennis Court two months earlier: the drafting of a national constitution based on the principles of liberty and equality. As they debated the myriad issues the constitution-making process raised, the deputies quickly found themselves confronting the conundrum that Honoré Gabriel Mirabeau had raised so forcefully in his newspaper commentary on the first article of the Declaration of Rights: Could a constitution based on the natural rights of liberty and equality be reconciled with the existence of Black slavery? As Jacques-Pierre Brissot would repeat over and over again in his newspaper, "If the National Assembly wants the principles it has consecrated to be respected," it had to answer the question, "Why should France be freer than Saint-Domingue?"[1] The contest over the answer to the slavery question would become a struggle to define the soul of France's new order.

Because the French constitution completed in September 1791 did not even survive for a year, the work of the National Assembly has never attracted the attention that the American constitution of 1787 continues to receive.[2] At the time, of course, the French deputies had no idea that their efforts would prove so ephemeral.

They were conscious that they faced many issues with which the members of the American Constitutional Convention had not had to contend. There had been no need to debate the place of a monarch in the American constitution, nor had America had a privileged noble class or an established church. The idea of remaking the governments of the thirteen states, whose institutions shaped most of their citizens' ordinary lives, never came up in the national constitutional debates. Slavery was, of course, a central issue in the American constitution-making project, but it was not linked to the question of maintaining a colonial empire.

Not only did the French constitution makers face complexities that the Americans had not needed to consider, but they also had to do their work under very different conditions. The fifty-five delegates who drafted the American constitution in 1787 met in private, which facilitated the working out of compromises. The National Assembly's debates were held in public, before audiences that never hesitated to express their reactions to the speakers, and they were reported in a contentious newspaper press that sprang up just as those debates were getting underway. Especially after the popular uprising of the "October Days" at the beginning of that month in 1789, which forced the king and the assembly to relocate from Versailles to Paris, crowds often gathered around the assembly's meeting place, pressuring the deputies to satisfy their demands. Slavery and the fate of the colonies were among the many issues capable of stirring angry passions and galvanizing outside groups to voice their views.

Like the French, the American constitution makers had also clashed over the issue of slavery. Historians continue to debate whether the outcome of their work should be viewed as "slavery's constitution," entrenching the institution in the new national order, or whether the delegates' refusal to explicitly protect "property in man" or to use the word "slavery" in the document indicated a desire to leave the door open for its eventual abolition.[3] The constitution makers in Philadelphia finally settled for a compromise that left it up to the individual states to decide on slavery's legality, while allowing the slave states to count three-fifths of their enslaved population as part of the basis for their representation in Congress and postponing for twenty years any ban on the importation of new captives. Had the French Revolution proceeded as the proslavery advocate Louis-Marthe Gouy d'Arsy had anticipated in the fall of 1788, with the different provinces of the kingdom allying to protect their historical rights against encroachment from the central government, the French colonies might have been able to claim the equivalent of "states' rights" to justify maintaining slavery. Once the representatives of the provinces had renounced all their special privileges on the night of 4 August 1789, however, the French movement took a very different direction. The decrees of 4 August and the Declaration of Rights left no room for regional differences: All parts of the country were now to be governed according to a single set of principles.

To the advocates of abolition, such as the members of the Société des Amis des Noirs, the breathtaking speed with which the revolutionary movement was dismantling France's old regime seemed to put the end of slavery within reach (figure 3). In the wake of the decrees of 4 August, Condorcet wrote optimistically to Brissot, "One has reason to hope, no doubt, that the National Assembly, which allowed itself . . . to attack properties much more legitimate than those of the planters over their slaves, will hear us favorably."[4] The conclusion that Mirabeau stated in his article a few days later seemed ineluctable: Any territory governed by French laws would necessarily have to grant freedom to all its inhabitants. This possibility was what drove a group of Saint-Domingue plantation owners in Paris to hold a meeting on 20 August 1789, just as the National Assembly was starting to draft the Declaration of Rights, "to confer about the pressing interest of the colony which is under threat."[5] The group named itself the Société correspondante des Colons (Colonists' Corresponding Society), but it quickly became known as the Club Massiac, because its meetings were held in the residence of one of its wealthy members, the chevalier de Massiac. The Club Massiac rapidly became the main center for the discussion on colonial interests. The number of its members eclipsed that of the Société des Amis des Noirs, and its sessions were held daily. At a time when counterrevolutionary opposition to the Revolution was just beginning to take shape, the club was the first organization formed to openly contest demands for liberty and equality.[6]

FIGURES 3A, B, C, D (grouped portraits): Leading figures in the fight against slavery and the slave trade during the early years of the French Revolution included Jacques-Pierre Brissot (1754–1793); Marie Jean Antoine Nicolas de Caritat, the marquis de Condorcet (1743–1794); Honoré Gabriel Riqueti, count Mirabeau (1749–1791); and Henri Grégoire (1750–1831). *Credit:* Bibliothèque nationale de France.

At the same time as the colonists were creating the Club Massiac, another group with a vital interest in the fate of the colonies and the slave trade was also organizing itself to lobby on those issues. Merchants invested in these branches of commerce had become increasingly frustrated by what they saw as a lack of attention to their concerns. When Saint-Domingue governor Marie-Charles du Chilleau opened the island's ports to foreign ships, the French merchants saw themselves confronted with the prospect of losing the protections that guaranteed their prosperity.[7] Committees formed in the port cities agreed to send "extraordinary deputies of commerce" to Versailles to oppose "the efforts that the deputies from the colonies . . . will not fail to make to release them from the restrictive trade laws," as the Marseille merchant committee put it. By the end of August, the extraordinary deputies were meeting regularly, and on 17 October 1789, the National Assembly gave them official recognition, assigning them a reserved loge in its meeting hall.[8]

Contemporaries and historians have often described the debates about the colonies that punctuated the two years of the National Assembly's session as duels between the Club Massiac and the Société des Amis des Noirs. The abolitionists were sure that the members of the club were behind every obstacle they encountered, and the defenders of slavery imagined that the "philanthropists" of the Amis des Noirs were at the heart of a massive conspiracy to destroy the colonies and cripple the French economy. In reality, neither group had the influence that its enemies attributed to it. The meetings of the Amis des Noirs after the summer of 1789 rarely attracted more than a dozen members. Arriving in France in July 1789, the British abolitionist Thomas Clarkson quickly became frustrated by the group's inability to schedule a session with him: Its key members were either busy at the National Assembly or, like Lafayette, tied down by affairs involving the Paris municipal government.[9] Individual members of the Amis des Noirs welcomed Clarkson, but it was clear to him that the French group lacked any strategy for exploiting the opportunity created by the dramatic events of July 1789.

While the abolitionists were overwhelmed by the sudden success of the Revolution they supported, the defenders of slavery were uncertain about the prospects of their cause. As we have seen, in the letter that the colonial deputies admitted to the National Assembly wrote to their correspondents in Saint-Domingue after the passage of the 4 August decrees, they expressed their concern that even mentioning the word "slavery" might provoke a decree abolishing it. In addition to their fear of the abolitionists, however, the colonial deputies in the assembly often found themselves at odds with the plantation owners who dominated the Club Massiac and with the extraordinary deputies of commerce. The divisions among the various groups committed to the defense of slavery and the slave trade were obvious from the start. The La Rochelle commerce deputy Jean-Baptiste Nairac's letters described the conflict between the "reasonable Americans" he had met at the Club Massiac, who were willing to compromise with the merchants, and the colonial deputies admitted to the National Assembly, whom he suspected of wanting to do away with all restrictions on the islands' trade.[10]

The deputies admitted to the National Assembly to represent the colonies—Gouy d'Arsy and his five colleagues for Saint-Domingue and two each for Martinique, Guadeloupe, and the Mascarenes—were able to participate directly in debates without consulting other colonists. Many members of the Club Massiac resented this fact, and some argued that the deputies' presence in the assembly, where none of them had objected to the wording of the Declaration of Rights, made it appear as if they had committed the colonies to accepting its premises. "Since the principles that the National Assembly had laid down imply rigorous consequences so diametrically opposed to the interests, or, more precisely, to the existence of the colonies, and since there is everything to fear and nothing to hope from the presence of their deputies in that assembly, they should withdraw from it," the vehement defender of slavery David Duval-Sanadon insisted.[11]

In addition to the danger posed by the participation of the colonial deputies in the National Assembly, the Club Massiac also worried about the activities of the extraordinary deputies of commerce. Members of both groups were in agreement on the need to prevent any Blacks or free people of color in France from returning to the colonies and spreading word of the movement for liberty in France. Although the minister César Henri de La Luzerne told the

National Assembly deputies that he did not have the legal authority to impose a travel ban, he looked the other way when the port cities took their own measures to do so. Nevertheless, the colonists and the merchant community remained at odds over the issue of trade regulations. Through the fall of 1789, the number of pamphlets for and against free trade for the colonies exceeded those concerning issues related to slavery. The claim made by one of the colonial deputies, in advocating free trade, that the failure to open the colonial ports was condemning as many as twelve thousand enslaved Blacks per year to death from hunger particularly enraged French merchants, who accused their adversaries of giving support to the Amis des Noirs by confirming their accusations about the inhumanity of slavery. Some merchant spokesmen, such as the National Assembly deputy Jacques-François Begouën, suspected that the plantation owners might even welcome the abolition of the French slave trade, "in the belief that they wouldn't have to pay as much for Negroes that foreign traders would furnish them."[12]

From the time of their first meeting, the members of the Club Massiac were also aware of another group that was determined to be heard on colonial questions. At the club's inaugural session, a member announced that "a man of color from Saint-Domingue was charged with petitioning in favor of his peers, that this petition no doubt had the object of improving their civil status." The man referred to was Julien Raimond, who had come to France five years earlier to lobby for rights for the free men of color in the colonies. After the failure of his efforts, he had settled in the provincial town of Angoulême, but when the Revolution began, he returned to the capital. In late July 1789 he recruited a friendly white nobleman, the comte de Jarnac, to act as his group's official representative, with the mission of obtaining a "law that will grant persons of color of the second generation from legitimate marriages" the same rights as whites.[13] Jarnac never carried out his mission, so on 26 August 1789, as the National Assembly was concluding debate on the Declaration of Rights, Raimond himself appeared at the Club Massiac, where he was allowed to lay out his demand for "civil and political prerogatives from the second generation for quarterons," or, in other words, for persons like himself with only one Black grandparent.[14]

Raimond was not the only free man of color who thought the colonial planters of the club might be willing to listen to their case. Two weeks later, Vincent Ogé, a wealthy businessman from the Saint-Domingue port city of Le Cap, offered to share his "plan for the regeneration of the colony" with the club's members. He was told that they would examine his document and reply to him. On 9 September, a white lawyer, Hector de Joly, and a delegation of six men of color were allowed to present a set of demands including "all the rights attached to liberty . . . which they have a right to demand, and which they intend to seek from the National Assembly." Had the club listened to the free men of color, as a few of its members seem to have wanted, the racial politics of the Revolution might have taken a very different course. Instead, the club members decided to tell de Joly that only an assembly of white representatives in the colonies could decide whether to grant such demands.[15]

Spurned by the white colonists, the men of color took a revolutionary step: They formed their own organization, the Colons américains, identified as "the free citizens and property owners of color of the French islands and colonies." "They understand what they are: the Declaration of the Rights of man had told them what they are worth; and their views have immediately turned . . . toward this precious freedom that the laws promise them," they wrote in their first manifesto.[16] The Colons américains were the first political group of nonwhites created anywhere in the Atlantic world, and the program they initially laid out was a radical one. They were careful not to challenge the institution of slavery; many of them were themselves slave owners. But they cited the Declaration of Rights to insist that all "Créoles of color, whether free Blacks, Mulattos, Quarterons or others," were entitled to the same rights as white colonists. To end the sexual exploitation of enslaved Black women, their cahier called for any free man who "cohabited, in any manner," with one of them to be fined and for the woman to be granted her freedom. Mixed marriages were to be legalized, and the restrictions imposed by the *police des noirs* of 1777 that barred people of color from France done away with.[17] In order to prove their loyalty to France and their enthusiasm for the Revolution, the Colons américains pledged to contribute a fourth of their annual income as a "patriotic gift" to the country.[18]

Even though the Colons américains skirted the issue of slavery, their appearance made it clear that the Revolution was now going to have to confront the issue of racial privilege. Just as there were differences of opinion among the white colonists, however, there were also different views among the free people of color. Julien Raimond's name did not appear among the signatories of the radical set of demand the Colons américains published at the end of September 1789. When he did join the group in October, the language of its pamphlets became tamer and more focused on obtaining deputies in the National Assembly.[19] The encouraging response the group received from the assembly's presiding officer—"No part of the nation will seek its rights in vain from the Assembly and its representatives: those who seem to be outside of its field of vision because of the expanse of the seas or the prejudices concerning a difference in origin will be included because of the sentiments of humanity that guide all its efforts"—alarmed the white colonists.[20]

Throughout the remaining two years of the National Assembly's session, which lasted until September 1791, the issue of rights for free people of color constantly resurfaced in revolutionary debates, culminating in May 1791 in a furious weeklong confrontation as explosive as any of the many clashes that marked the deputies' tortuous constitution-making efforts. Although the supporters of the free men of color repeatedly insisted that their demands had nothing to do with the abolition of slavery, all participants in these debates understood that the two issues were linked. If the assembly decided that any group of people of African descent deserved the same rights as whites, a path would be opened for demands to extend those rights to all Blacks. Fear of that possibility drove the colonists to oppose concessions to the free men of color, even as they realized that their stubbornness risked alienating metropolitan opinion. The issue mattered less to the French merchants. Nairac, La Rochelle's "extraordinary deputy," thought that "the colonists were wrong to exclude [the men of color] from their assemblies."[21]

Although the Société des Amis des Noirs hardly met during the fall of 1789, its leader Brissot found another and more effective tool to promote the antislavery campaign: his daily newspaper, the *Patriote françois*, whose first issue appeared on 28 July 1789, just two weeks after the storming of the Bastille. Brissot's paper quickly became essential reading for France's new political class, and especially for those concerned with the issue of slavery. The members of the Club Massiac cited it in their debates more often than any other publication. Unlike his one-time friend Jean-Paul Marat, whose *Ami du Peuple* began to appear in September and who quickly distinguished himself by his tirades against the National Assembly, Brissot spoke the deputies' language. His strategy was to pose as their conscience, constantly reminding them of the promises contained in the Declaration of Rights and the importance of creating a constitution that embodied its ideals.

Determined to have his say on everything the assembly did, Brissot editorialized about many issues during the hectic months of the summer and fall of 1789, but he seized every opportunity to mention the issues of race and slavery and to promote the program of the Amis des Noirs. On 12 August, Brissot lamented the admission of representatives from Guadeloupe to the assembly and offered his homage "to the virtuous La Rochefoucauld, who did not forget [the Blacks] in the middle of the intoxication of the night of 4 August, and who had appealed to the sentiments of the Assembly in their favor." A rival journalist had commented that the British Parliament's decision to put off any action regarding the slave trade seemed to show that support for abolition across the Channel was cooling. Brissot insisted that "the conviction of the English has neither diminished nor changed"; the issue, he was sure, would be brought up again in the next parliamentary session.[22]

Even though the Amis des Noirs rarely managed to hold meetings in the fall of 1789, Brissot's paper gave the impression that the abolitionists were still active. On August 24, after the group held its first session since early July, Brissot repeated the society's mantra that it was seeking only the ending of the slave trade, not the abolition of slavery, and he indignantly denied rumors that the society was amassing weapons to send to the colonies. Nevertheless, he insisted, "If the planters understood their interests, they would see that they need to unite with this Society. It is impossible that such an infamous business should not be abolished. It is possible that, if it is not, the Blacks will rise up."[23] By this time, the British abolitionist Clarkson had established himself in Paris, and Brissot let him use the paper to answer critics of the movement.[24] Clarkson's zeal alarmed Brissot's ally Condorcet, who feared that the British reformer was making it sound as though the Amis des Noirs wanted to end the slave trade immediately, a position that risked alienating the seaport cities at a moment when critical aspects of the new French constitution were being debated. "The Blacks cannot become free and have a tolerable situation unless France is free," Condorcet told Brissot, adding that "if the colonists and the Blacks fight in America, let's not do anything that could get us accused of being partly responsible for the horrors that would take place there."[25]

Although Brissot printed his articles, Clarkson was unable to prod the Amis des Noirs into taking any public initiative as a group. He concluded that "the revolution was of more importance to Frenchmen, than the abolition of the Slave-trade."[26] Then Etienne Dumont, one of Mirabeau's political team, contacted him in mid-November, suggesting that Mirabeau might be willing to put forward a motion to abolish the trade. Clarkson responded immediately, arguing, as he had in the British debates, that the question of the slave trade should be separated from that of slavery itself, since the latter issue would arouse too much opposition. For the next month and a half, he wrote to Mirabeau almost daily, providing details about the conduct of the trade, descriptions of the conditions of life for Blacks in Africa, and answers to all the possible objections defenders of the slave trade might put forward. Among other things, Clarkson provided Mirabeau with a copy of the celebrated engraving of the slave ship *Brooks* that was one of the British abolitionists' most powerful pieces of propaganda. Mirabeau was so struck by the force of this visual demonstration of the cruelty of the Middle Passage that he had a scale model of the ship constructed; it is still preserved in a Paris library (figure 4).[27]

Rumors that Mirabeau was preparing a speech on the slave trade that "would bring about the complete ruin of our commerce, our port cities, the loss of our colonies, bankruptcy, an uprising against the decrees of the National Assembly, anarchy, and all the horrors that would naturally follow," as one resident of Nantes wrote to the Club Massiac, spread quickly.[28] "Mirabeau is much to be feared, because of his talents, his party in the assembly and that of the Amis des Noirs," the La Rochelle deputy Nairac warned.[29]

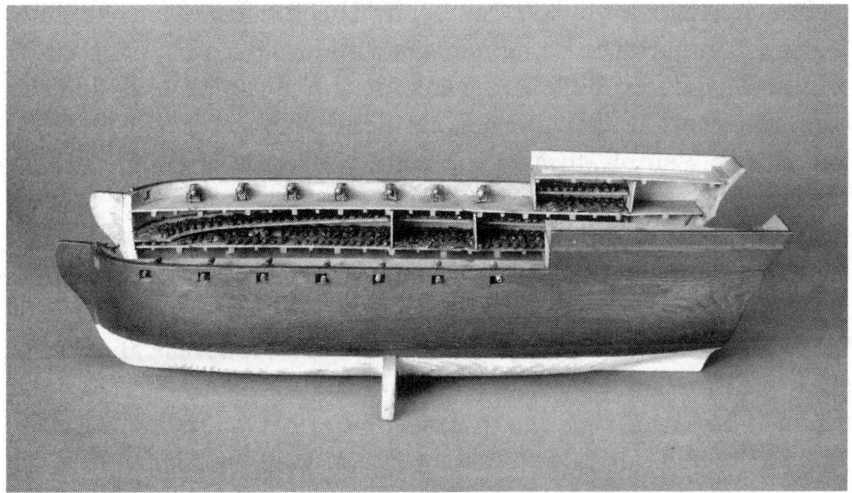

FIGURE 4: To reinforce his arguments against the slave trade, Mirabeau commissioned a model of a slave ship, based on information provided to him by the British abolitionist Thomas Clarkson. *Credit:* Bibliotheque de l'Arsenal and Bibliothèque nationale de France. Maquette de bateau négrier, commandée par Mirabeau et donnée par lui à la Société des Amis des Noirs.

Nevertheless, the opponents of abolition were so divided among themselves that they had trouble organizing a coherent response to this threat. A letter from the Club Massiac to the colonists and merchants in Bordeaux in early October reflected the delicate dance going on between the various groups involved with colonial issues. The club, the letter writer explained, was making every effort to avoid an open clash with "our so-called deputies" in the National Assembly. In addition, they did not want to get drawn into "their debates with the merchants about the prohibitive [trade] laws."[30]

At the end of October, the king's ministers sent the National Assembly a memorandum pointing out that since that body now claimed the power to set government policies, it needed to clarify whether its measures applied to the colonies. "A number of its decisions . . . might produce a sudden and unfortunate revolution in countries where ten elevenths of the inhabitants, if they were no longer slaves, would be left without any property or any means of subsistence," the memorandum warned.[31] The petition presented by free men of color in late October had been referred to a committee for examination; its opponents had managed to delay its consideration repeatedly, but there was widespread expectation that the committee would ultimately recommend that they be given deputies to the assembly, forcing the body as a whole to take a vote on the matter.

Brissot had at first failed to appreciate the significance of the campaign launched by the free men of color, but after the appearance of their delegation at the National Assembly on 22 October, he suddenly made it one of his main themes. Whereas abolishing slavery or the slave trade meant challenging powerful economic interests, granting rights to free men of color appeared to be a cost-free way to demonstrate the assembly's devotion to the principle of equality. After a lapse of almost three months, the Amis des Noirs met on 24 November. Brissot introduced Raimond, Ogé, and three of their colleagues, along with their white spokesman de Joly. Two days later, Brissot editorialized that "one must believe, according to the Declaration of Rights, that the free Blacks will succeed. The National Assembly would contradict itself, dishonor itself, would overturn the principle of equality among all men, if it judged otherwise."[32] All through the last months of 1789, rumors that Mirabeau was readying a speech that would electrify the assembly continued to circulate. In the middle of November, one of the extraordinary deputies of commerce from Nantes reported that once Mirabeau's motion was introduced, he and his supporters were "ready for anything, that they would meet reasons with reasons, arguments with arguments, fury with fury, in short, that it would be hand-to-hand combat . . . and that to prevent any trouble that the American [colonists] or others might incite, there would be 18,000 men under arms on that day."[33]

Up to this point, the strategy of the pro-colonial interest groups had been to try to avoid any open debate in the National Assembly about the issues that concerned them, which they feared might lead to some impulsive action against slavery. But on 26 November 1789, the Guadeloupe deputy Louis de Curt suddenly proposed the creation of a colonial committee charged to examine any legislative proposals concerning the islands. His motion set off the first extended assembly debate concerning the colonies since the arguments in July about the admission of colonial deputies. Pierre-François Blin, a representative from the slaving port of Nantes, smelled a rat: If a colonial committee was established, the assembly would implicitly be asserting its right to pass laws for the colonies, which would be a "usurpation" of the colonists' rights. Médéric Louis Élie Moreau de Saint-Méry seized the occasion to deliver a lengthy disquisition on the impossibility of applying the principles of liberty and equality in the colonies.[34]

In response, a new champion came to the fore on behalf of the abolitionists: the deputy and Catholic priest Henri Grégoire. The curé of a small town in the northeastern province of Lorraine, Grégoire had drawn national attention in 1787, when he won a prize for his essay proposing the granting of rights to France's Jews. One of a number of parish clergy elected to the Estates General, he had eagerly embraced the patriotic movement. In October, in his first public statement concerning the issues of race and slavery, Grégoire had spoken in support of the petition from the free men of color, and he would remain concerned with the issues of race and slavery for more than forty years, until his death in 1831. His fifty-two-page *Mémoire en faveur des gens de couleur ou sang-mêlés de St. Domingue* (Statement in favor of the men of color or mixed-bloods of Saint-Domingue), published just a week after Curt raised the issue of a colonial committee, was his first major intervention on these subjects.[35]

Grégoire countered Curt's motion by insisting that the National Assembly needed to admit deputies representing the free men of color before it made any other decision regarding the colonies. He angrily denounced the treatment they had suffered from colonial governments and the "refined malignity" of the white colonists. "Ah! Celebrate your triumph, respectable curé, who has been the first to defend the cause of the unfortunate Blacks in the National Assembly," Brissot wrote. Grégoire received surprising support from Charles Lameth, a wealthy plantation owner who was also a member of the Amis des Noirs. "God forbid that a vile concern for my interests should shape my opinions, that it should make me sacrifice the great principles of humanity, of equity, of liberty, that I have sworn to defend," he proclaimed, before carefully noting that, while he supported the granting of rights to free men of color, it was much too soon to consider the emancipation of the enslaved Blacks.[36]

The momentum Grégoire's speech gave to the cause of the men of color was halted by the intervention of another of the clerical deputies, Jean-Siffrein Maury. Like Grégoire, Maury was a man from a modest social background whose intelligence had allowed him to make a career in the Church, but, unlike Grégoire, he established himself as a diehard defender of royal authority and social order. Brushing aside the caution that led most of the proslavery deputies to avoid naming the institution they were determined to protect, he stressed that "some men are slaves in the islands" and insisted that the assembly not do anything that might threaten the existing colonial system. Maury persuaded the assembly to table Curt's motion, thereby leaving unresolved the questions of what powers it would claim over the colonies and how it might use them.[37] Nevertheless, the clash over the creation of a colonial committee had demonstrated that whatever the assembly decided to do about colonial issues would generate fierce reactions. If Curt had not put forward his motion, the members of the Club Massiac wrote to the colonists in Bordeaux, "the mulattos would not have had an opportunity to show themselves, [and] the abolition of slavery itself would not have been demanded!"[38]

The proposal for the admission of deputies of the free men of color remained stalled, but the campaign for their rights now became a major public issue. At a meeting of the Amis des Noirs on the day after the end of the debate, the group welcomed Grégoire as a member. When he urged them to lobby the National Assembly more actively, both on behalf of the men of color and for the abolition of the slave trade, Raimond, now the recognized spokesman for the free men of color, worked to temper his zeal. "Having made them understand that making two demands at the same time could hurt the chances of both of them," according to the group's minutes, Raimond persuaded them to give priority to his group's cause.[39] Grégoire's *Mémoire* appeared a few days later, providing the arguments for the rights of free men of color a degree of publicity they had not previously achieved. Whereas French readers could easily imagine the cruelty of slavery and of the slave trade, the injustices that free people of color suffered in the colonies were less familiar.

Drawing on information supplied by Raimond, Grégoire explained how members of the group were forced to perform militia service from which whites were excused, how they were excluded from public office and prestigious professions, how their racial status was noted on official documents, how they were confined to separate sections of theaters and churches, and how white men who married women of color were discriminated against. Grégoire pointed out that the militia in which free men of color served was "a sure protection against slave insurrections." Whereas colonial prejudices looked down on people of mixed racial ancestry, Grégoire praised the "robust constitution" they enjoyed, "because the crossing of races improves the species."[40]

Although Grégoire was ostensibly writing only to demand full citizenship rights for free people of color, he could not restrain himself from also raising the issues of the slave trade and of slavery itself. "Freedom for men is a right as well as a need in all climates," he announced. Having warned that the free men of color might resort to force if their demands were not granted, since "resistance to oppression is a right that comes from God, and is recognized by the National Assembly," he added that "it needs only an Othello, a Padrejean, to awaken in the soul of the Negroes the sentiment of their inalienable rights." If the enslaved Blacks did rise up, "which of us would dare condemn them, if he imagined himself in their place?" he asked. For good measure, Grégoire added that the overthrow of kings throughout the world could not be far off.[41]

Grégoire was not the only Catholic priest to speak out in favor of the abolition of slavery. His friend Sébastien-André Sibire issued an even more strongly worded denunciation of the institution. Sibire was one of the rare abolition advocates who had witnessed the cruelty of slavery with his own eyes: He had been a missionary in Angola and then a priest in Saint-Domingue before returning to France.[42] Leaving aside entirely the issue of the rights of free men of color, Sibire denounced slavery as being equally opposed to reason and to the teaching of the Gospels. If God had created men of different colors, "this random diversity of external appearances doesn't affect their inner nature." Like the other French abolitionists, he abruptly ended his pamphlet by conceding that the Blacks were not ready for immediate freedom, but he nevertheless urged the deputies of the National Assembly to "break the fetters of the world as soon as you can. . . . Then the earth, renewed in all its parts, will gradually become, under the reign of Louis XVI and in accordance with your wise constitution, another heaven."[43]

To the opponents of abolition, publications like those of Grégoire and Sibire revealed the real agenda of the Amis des Noirs: Even their proposals for modest reforms were part of a grand scheme that would culminate in an assault on slavery. The energy that had been going into the pamphlet campaign for the opening of colonial ports to free trade was diverted to publications denouncing Brissot's group and opposing the granting of rights to free men of color. Colonists probably inspired an anonymous publication claiming to express the "protests of the free Negroes, American colonists," which exalted the Blacks who "came from a pure blood," as opposed to "the mulatto . . . a melange of Black and white . . . a bastard species."[44] A more substantial response came from Moreau de Saint-Méry. Although he was living in Paris with his own mixed-race daughter, to whom he was deeply devoted, he insisted that colonial society could not survive if free people of color were made the equals of the whites. "It is impossible that beings, who were enslaved yesterday, would today be in the first ranks of society, charged with positions that require education, morals, and general acceptance," he wrote.[45]

The passions aroused by the issues of race and slavery were evident not only in National Assembly debates but in other arenas as well. The Revolution had freed Paris's theaters from the strict regulations imposed under the ancien régime. Olympe de Gouges, an ambitious playwright who had protested that "it is an injustice on the part of men to not allow women to participate in public matters," was finally able to get her views heard when the play she had written several years earlier, *Black Slavery, or the Fortunate Shipwreck*, was performed at the end of December 1789. De Gouges claimed that she had sympathized with the fate of the Blacks from childhood on. "Several men had taken an interest in them and worked to lighten their burden; but none of them had thought of presenting them on stage in their costume and their color as I would have tried, if the Comédie-Française had not been against it," she wrote.[46] Rumors about the play and the reactions it might provoke circulated in Paris even before it was put on. "The slave traders seem to fear a drama that will soon be presented," wrote a member of the Amis des Noirs. "One of them said in front of me, the other day, that the act where the slave trade is portrayed will create the greatest sensation." The counterrevolutionary *Actes des Apôtres* warned that "a female who has never been outside of Paris, and who has read some bad novels, is going to give us a rhapsody about the Congo."[47]

The opening-night performance of de Gouges's play did indeed provoke furious reactions. The *Moniteur universel* told readers, "One cannot think of many theater performances as stormy as this one. . . . In view of the fervor with which both sides were animated, one would have thought that the great issue of slavery and of the freedom of the Negroes was going to be thrashed out by the parties whose opposing interests drove them to attack or defend it."[48] De Gouges was convinced that her plot, in which an enslaved Black man who has killed a white plantation overseer who has attempted to rape the woman the Black man loves voluntarily submits himself to be judged by the white authorities, would convey the injustice of slavery. At the same time, if her play was performed in the colonies, it would persuade Blacks to remain submissive, "while waiting for the colonists and the French nation to abolish the slave trade, and [give them] a happier situation."[49]

De Gouges's play was firmly in the tradition of sentimental literature about slavery that went back to Jean-François Saint-Lambert's *Ziméo*. That tradition reached its apogee in 1789 with the publication of the two longest French novels on the subject, Jean Lecointe-Marsillac's *Le More-Lack* and Joseph Lavallée's three-volume *Le Nègre comme il y a peu de blancs* (The Negro equaled by few whites). *Le More-Lack*, which purported to express the thoughts of a Black who had gained his freedom and then embarked as a sailor on a British slave ship in the hope of finding his family in Africa, praised the "philanthropic societies" that had just been founded in Britain and France to promote the cause. The program the work put forth called for better treatment of enslaved Blacks and an eventual end to the slave trade, but only after enough African women had been shipped to the Americas to ensure the growth of the population. To encourage the others, one enslaved

Black out of twenty would be freed every year, but even these freedmen would still be subject to forced labor for twelve hours a day.[50]

Lavallée's much longer novel avoided explicitly political comments, although one of the twists in its convoluted plot involved its virtuous Black hero, Itanoko, being freed in Saint-Domingue and becoming the owner of a plantation, where he grants the Blacks their freedom, abolishes the punishment of whipping, and nevertheless succeeds in doubling the amount of work accomplished. As befits the genre of the sentimental novel, love—for the mixed-race daughter of a Frenchman he had known in Africa—drives Itanoko to leave the Caribbean for Europe, where he marries and cherishes the hope that progress will overcome "the vilest of all the passions of the human heart, avarice," and make it possible for whites to recognize that prejudice has kept them from recognizing the Blacks' humanity.[51] Despite its length and its improbable plot, Lavallée's novel was reprinted several times during the revolutionary decade and also translated into English.

While de Gouges's play and the novels of Lecointe-Marsillac and Lavallée sought to stir up a generalized sympathy for the enslaved Blacks, pamphlets and newspapers purveyed news from the colonies and debated specific measures concerning the slave trade and the rights of the men of color. The number of books and pamphlets devoted to colonial issues peaked in 1790, with 108 titles.[52] No other prorevolutionary paper devoted as much attention to these subjects as the *Patriote françois*, but readers could find articles supporting the antislavery cause in Jean-Louis Carra's *Annales patriotiques et littéraires*, which had a wide audience among provincial supporters of the Revolution, and in the weekly *Révolutions de Paris*. The opponents of abolition could count on the *Gazette universelle*, noted for the extent of its coverage of foreign and colonial events and edited, ironically, by Antoine-Marie Cerisier, one of the early members of the Amis des Noirs. In April 1790 a lengthy article defended the Club Massiac, which had "interested all the districts of Paris, and consequently all the people of this capital in defense of the colonies." The *Gazette de Paris* boasted that "the committee of the deputies from Saint-Domingue has named us to be its interpreter for the entire colony."[53] The ultraroyalist *Actes des Apôtres*, which expressed the fear that "as far as the colonies are concerned . . . Mirabeau and his band, with their diabolic philosophy, will have landed us in a pickle," was edited by Jean-Gabriel Peltier, who had just returned from a slave-trading voyage to Saint-Domingue when the Revolution broke out.[54]

Paris was not the only place in France where colonial issues were hotly debated as the Revolution proceeded. In Bordeaux, local colonists under the leadership of the wealthy Jewish merchant David Gradis organized themselves into a club with some two hundred members. Their Société des Colons de Bordeaux carried on a regular correspondence with the Club Massiac in Paris and drafted addresses to the National Assembly. In September 1789 one of their addresses asserted that "our properties in the Blacks are legal, and . . . no one could take them from us without injustice, or without reimbursement."[55] Like the shippers in other port cities, the Bordeaux merchants made sure that Blacks and other people of color could not book passage on ships heading for the colonies, where it was feared that they would spread revolutionary ideas. Among the lower classes of the city, however, some wanted to do just the opposite: White domestic servants held several gatherings to demand that all the Black men and women who competed with them for jobs in wealthy households be returned to the Caribbean.[56] Not everyone in Bordeaux was in favor of slavery or hostile to the Blacks. Alexandre Deleyre, a local notable and former contributor to Guillaume Thomas François Raynal's *Histoire des deux Indes*, succeeded in getting a local civic committee to send an address to the National Assembly supporting the "freedom of the Blacks." That proposition had "scandalized our merchants," the local chronicler Pierre Bernadeu noted, and the local authorities had dissolved the committee that had endorsed it. Bernadeu himself corresponded with Brissot, "to give him the necessary information for the war that he is going to wage against the idiocies here."[57]

The slaving port of Nantes was another hotbed of agitation about the slavery question. In mid-November 1789 rumors about Mirabeau's intention to introduce a motion to abolish the slave trade sent the city into an uproar, according to a letter sent to the Club Massiac. "The commerce of slaves is the most essential branch of trade with our colonies; it is the base of it; it employs around 140 ships built for this trade, and which could not be used for any other," the Nantais protested. Throughout 1790, colonial issues were the main preoccupation of the city's local commercial council; they were on the agenda of twenty-six out of the group's fifty-four meetings.[58] Bordeaux and Nantes had unusually strong reasons to be concerned with the colonies, but between December 1789 and the beginning of March 1790, at least thirty-three cities sent addresses on colonial issues to the National Assembly, in the name of the local government, the local merchants, or a local revolutionary committee. Writing to Clarkson after the latter's return to England in early 1790, Brissot described these expressions of opinion from the provinces as "a violent storm against us."[59]

The dramatic news of the Revolution in France sparked upheavals in the colonies. In Saint-Domingue, white colonists determined to free themselves from the "despotic" rule of the French administration forced the royal intendant François Barbé-Marbois to flee, and a false report that Moreau de Saint-Méry had called for the abolition of slavery led to physical assaults on several of his relatives. In Martinique, according to the governor, enslaved Blacks had circulated letters announcing that they were a nation ready "to spill its last drop of blood rather than support the yoke of slavery."[60] News of these disturbances in the colonies began to reach France in December 1789, when the *Gazette universelle* reported the troubles in Martinique. The news of Barbé-Marbois's ouster was published at the end of that month, and at the beginning of January, the paper carried a letter claiming that a slave revolt had broken out in Saint-Domingue's South Province and that the colony was in a state of "complete anarchy."[61] The drumbeat of alarming reports from the colonies, many of them false or exaggerated—the *Patriote françois* reassured readers that the celebrated chevalier de Saint-George, said to have been hanged in Guadeloupe, was actually giving concerts in London—contributed to the sense that the National Assembly urgently needed to take some kind of action regarding them.[62]

Despite these widespread expressions of concern with the issues of race and slavery, the National Assembly did not return to these subjects for nearly three months after the abortive November 1789 debate about the colonial committee. On 1 February 1790 the lawyer de Joly and a delegation of free men of color appeared at a meeting of the Commune, Paris's municipal assembly, to ask that body to lobby the National Assembly on their behalf. Brissot, a member of the Commune, "was the first to mount the tribune and wanted the matter to be taken up immediately, in the rush of the moment," a pro-colonial deputy reported, but the discussion was adjourned. When the Commune returned to the issue on 11 February, Brissot gave an inflammatory speech, calling the colonial planters descendants of brigands. Among the Commune deputies whom Brissot listed as supporting the men of color, one name stands out: that of Georges Danton, a lawyer who was already attracting notice for his embrace of radical populist positions. Although he took little part in debates about slavery in the next four years, Danton would play a decisive role in getting the 1794 decree abolishing slavery passed. Despite Brissot's efforts, the Commune tabled his motion.[63]

Twelve days after the free men of color failed to win the support of the Commune, a delegation from Bordeaux appeared before that body and obtained a more positive response. Calling themselves "the patriotic army of Bordeaux," the group sought the Paris assembly's support in getting the National Assembly to pass a decree promising to maintain slavery and the slave trade. The address of the "patriotic army" repeated the arguments that proslavery groups had been making for months to the effect that slavery was necessary to the survival of the colonies and that the colonies were essential to the prosperity of France.[64] The arrival of the Bordeaux "army" in Paris precipitated two weeks of frenzied activity culminating in the passage of a decree that killed the reformers' hope that the National Assembly would support any steps toward abolition.

Even before the Bordeaux delegates arrived, the National Assembly's agriculture and commerce committee had approved a draft decree stating the assembly "did not intend to make any changes in the bases of the colonial regime" and that the colonies' "commerce, along with all the branches that depend on it, will continue to be conducted as they have been in the past." The committee carefully avoided using the words "slavery" and "slave trade," but its meaning was unmistakable. From the colonists' point of view, however, this proposal was still unsatisfactory in one major regard: It went on to promise that the assembly would proceed to "draft rules for the colonies whose special purpose would be to improve the condition of all the individuals there." What upset the colonists was the idea that the National Assembly would assert its authority to make laws for the colonies, conceding to the colonists only the power to raise objections after those laws were proposed, and that those laws might affect "all individuals" in the colonies, including the enslaved population.[65]

At this point, Mirabeau finally made up his mind to deliver his long-awaited speech. By this time, he was no longer the irresistible force he had been in the early months of the Revolution. The great tribune had hoped that the National Assembly would create a parliamentary system similar to Britain's, in which a deputy could simultaneously serve as prime minister, directing the government, but in early November 1789, in a vote clearly directed against their ambitious colleague, Mirabeau's colleagues rejected the idea. (Pierre-François Blin, the deputy who introduced the motion that dashed Mirabeau's hopes, represented the slaving port of Nantes. Whether Mirabeau's association with the abolitionist cause had anything to do with Blin's role on this occasion is unknown.)[66] Mirabeau and other leading supporters of the Revolution had come together to form the Jacobin Club, where they could plan strategy to influence the debates in the assembly. At this point, the club was not yet the hotbed of radicalism it would become later in the Revolution. The members included several prominent slave owners, such as the Mosneron brothers from Nantes, one of whom had addressed the Jacobins just a few days earlier, telling them that "it is the question of the freeing of the Blacks and the abolition of the slave trade that has been one of the largest pretexts of the troubles" affecting the country's trade.[67] Nevertheless, Mirabeau decided to deliver his speech to the Jacobins first, presumably hoping to ensure their support before he addressed the National Assembly.

To read Mirabeau's speech, which French scholar Marcel Dorigny pieced together in 1999 from a partial printed version and manuscript fragments, is to experience what made his contemporaries regard him as the greatest of the period's orators. Even his opponents felt the impact of Mirabeau's words, which took three and a half hours to deliver. "This speech is full of passages of the greatest eloquence," Jean-Baptiste Nairac wrote. "There are powerful images, designed to produce the most powerful effect, the moral issues are treated in a superior fashion."[68] In his opening sentences, Mirabeau confronted his listeners with the full horror of the institution of slavery and its incompatibility with the principles of the Revolution:

> I undertake to plead before you the cause of a race of men who . . . live, suffer, and die as slaves of the most detestable tyranny whose crimes history has transmitted to us. You already know that I speak of the slaves in America. I will not dishonor either this assembly or myself by undertaking to prove to you that the Negroes have a right to freedom! You have settled this question, because you have declared that all men *are born and remain free and equal in rights*; and it is not on this side of the Atlantic that corrupt sophists would dare to claim that the Negroes are not men![69]

(This thrust may have aimed at Mirabeau's own brother, André-Boniface-Louis, vicomte de Mirabeau, a leading figure of the counterrevolutionary opposition in the assembly, who had drafted a speech of his own in which he said that "the intelligence of the Negro is terribly limited . . . I would not place him on the level of men of a race superior to his.")[70]

After conceding that the immediate liberation of the enslaved Blacks in the colonies would leave them subject to the "tyranny of passions," Mirabeau returned to his main theme. Reminding his audience that the French Revolution's Declaration of Rights "had been heard in all parts of the globe," he asked whether the enslaved Blacks would be the only ones who did not benefit from it. The whites in the colonies could not possibly maintain their domination forever. The United States, he was sure, was moving toward abolition. The French colonists themselves were undermining slavery by creating the class of free people of color and then alienating them by denying them full rights. Reform, he insisted, was opposed only by groups with selfish interests. Drawing on the lessons he had learned from Clarkson, Mirabeau refuted claims that slavery and the slave trade were indispensable to the prosperity of the colonies and of metropolitan France. Even if it could be proved that slavery was profitable, "to contend that it is appropriate for a free and generous nation to authorize crimes because they are a source of wealth is to expose oneself in advance to the contempt and the indignation of the men who have the honor of representing the French people."[71]

The colonists did not need to worry about an immediate effort to do away with slavery, Mirabeau assured them, but "it cannot be the same with the slave trade; it cannot be too rapidly abolished." He defended the Amis des Noirs and the rights of the free men of color in the colonies, "the natural friends of our constitution." In a ringing peroration, he called on the National Assembly, "which, with so much courage, has destroyed the aristocracy whose yoke humiliated France," to show that it was true to its principles. "Do not let the sacred fire go out in your hands! . . . Show all the nations what the true spirit of our Revolution is. . . . Be the protectors of suffering humanity. . . . Like the gods, answer all just prayers; spread at once in all regions the regenerating influence of peace and freedom, and may the restorers of France free the whole world!"[72]

Coming after such a torrent of powerful rhetoric, the motion that Mirabeau proposed struck his hearers at the Jacobin Club as an anticlimax. It called on Louis XVI to invite Britain's George III to join in formulating a plan "to carry out in a peaceful and lasting manner the complete abolition of the slave trade" and for the National Assembly to appoint a committee to study the best way to govern the colonies and to "prepare the freedom of the Blacks," without any specific guidelines or a deadline for the completion of its work.[73] In the *Patriote françois*, Brissot wrote that Mirabeau's speech "had caused the strongest possible impression and had received the liveliest applause." Not everyone was so impressed, however. In his diary, the moderate deputy Adrien Duquesnoy described "long declamations on the condition of the Negroes, an overdrawn portrait of the evils they suffer; fifty pages to repeat what the abbé Raynal said in four." The timidity of Mirabeau's proposed motion reassured Duquesnoy, who concluded that "this idea seems impractical to me at the moment; it would cause too much panic among our merchants, who must be reassured and encouraged."[74]

The day after Mirabeau's performance at the Jacobin Club, "everyone expected an important debate about a question that concerns philosophy as much as commerce" at the National Assembly, the *Gazette universelle* reported. "An immense crowd filled the tribunes and the galleries, when it was learned that the work of

M. de Mirabeau was not sufficiently perfected to be presented."[75] On 2 March, the vacuum left by Mirabeau's unexpected silence was filled by what that newspaper described as a long and boring report on the troubles plaguing Martinique and Saint-Domingue. At this point, Alexandre Lameth, a one-time member of the Amis des Noirs who had by this time become an ally of the abolitionists' opponents and a leader in the Jacobin Club, revived the proposal to create a colonial committee that would consider all the issues concerning them and return to the assembly with a concrete motion for its consideration.

The proposal to create a colonial committee was a relief to many assembly members with little interest in these issues, because the deputies were in the middle of a multiday debate about the legislation meant to carry out the promise made at the session of 4 August 1789 to abolish feudal dues, a matter that affected the interests of every property owner in France and every member of the country's peasantry. Nevertheless, Lameth's motion set off "a tumult that lasted for almost the entire session and which prolonged it until 7 o'clock," the *Patriote françois* informed its readers. Sensing that, after the misfire of Mirabeau's speech, the tide of opinion was running in his party's favor, the colonial deputy Nicolas Cocherel wanted the assembly to immediately pass a resolution maintaining the colonial status quo. As he had in the earlier debate about the creation of a colonial committee, the ultraconservative provocateur Maury insisted on reminding the deputies of the real issue behind the various euphemisms that most of them preferred. "There is a serious question, and here it is: will we abolish the slave trade, yes or no. . . . The assembly has no choice but to take a position on this question."[76]

This time, in contrast to the situation during the earlier debate about creating such a committee, the proslavery faction in the assembly was well prepared and made sure that not a single advocate of reform was named to it. Behind the scenes, there had been efforts to promote some kind of negotiation between them and the Amis des Noirs that might have led to a more balanced committee, but, the Mosneron brothers wrote, "we have rejected this proposition with horror. We said that we were not sent to bargain about the interests of France with its enemies, that we did not want to have any communication with those inspired by Clarkson, Thornton, Frossard . . . that we feared being put into quarantine when we went home, as having frequented contagious individuals."[77] "One regrets not seeing on this list celebrated men, known for having delved into the question of the slave trade, such as the count Mirabeau, the duke de la Rochefoucauld, Pétion de Villeneuve, Grégoire," Brissot commented.[78] The member who received the largest number of votes was Begouën, described by Duquesnoy as a "very skillful and very rich slave trader from Havre," who had laid out the standard arguments for the indispensability of colonial slavery and the slave trade in a pamphlet in 1789. Other committee members included two of the colonial deputies and others involved with colonial trade. The member elected with the smallest number of votes—less than half those cast for Begouën—was Antoine Barnave (figure 5).[79]

The selection of Barnave as a member of the colonial committee proved fateful, both for the outcome of the March 1790 debate and for Barnave himself. One of the youngest deputies in the National Assembly, he had been regarded as a revolutionary firebrand, notorious for excusing the lynching of two royal officials during a riot a week after the storming of the Bastille. Although he had an uncle, Jean-Jacques Bacon de la Chevalerie, who was a leader of the white colonists in Saint-Domingue, it is not clear that the two men had ever met, and Barnave had no personal connections with the colonies. By early 1790, however, he had become close friends with a number of figures in Paris who had colonial interests, including the Lameth brothers, with whom he shared a house. He and the Lameths had made themselves leaders of the Jacobin Club and encouraged the admission of a number of other men supportive of the colonies.[80] Barnave quickly emerged as the spokesman for the colonial committee, and from that point on he was seen as the assembly's most influential defender of colonial interests. It was an involvement that would derail his political career and that would form part of the indictment that led to his execution in 1793.

Behind the scenes, the interest groups concerned with the colonies had already hammered out most of the details of the decree the colonial committee was to present. "The only problem is the language of the decree. We want to find a way of preserving

FIGURES 5A, B, C, D: Defenders of slavery and the slave trade in the National Assembly included Médéric Louis Élie Moreau de Saint-Méry (1750–1819), Pierre-Victor Malouet (1740–1814), Louis-Marthe Gouy d'Arsy (1753–1794), and Antoine Barnave (1761–1793). *Credit:* Bibliothèque nationale de France.

everything that currently exists while avoiding the words 'slave trade' and 'slaves,'" the La Rochelle representative Nairac told his colleagues at home.[81] The colonial committee worked quickly, and the debate on its proposal was announced for 8 March. "So much importance was attached to this decision," the *Gazette universelle* reported, "that the hall of the assembly was occupied that day, early in the morning, by those who had been able to obtain tickets, and by noon, the Tuileries gardens were full of a select crowd, all the creoles, all the colonists in Paris, waiting impatiently for what would be pronounced."[82]

Brissot had expressed the hope that Barnave would prevent a complete victory for the pro-colonial party, but the proposal presented to the assembly on 8 March 1790 incorporated all of their demands. "The French nation's interest in maintaining its trade, in conserving its colonies, in favoring their prosperity . . . has struck us, from every point of view, as an incontestable truth," Barnave began. As the proslavery colonists had insisted since the passage of the Declaration of Rights, the colonies needed a constitution of their own that would not incorporate that document's principles, even as it recognized France's ultimate sovereignty. In a rough draft of the committee report, Barnave had written that "all the freemen paying taxes and domiciled for over a year in the parish without distinction of color" should have the right to vote in those assemblies, but he had evidently been persuaded to omit this concession to the free men of color; the draft presented to the assembly made no mention of the issue. According to the motion Barnave put forward, "The National Assembly declares that it has never intended to make any innovations in any of the branches of commerce, whether direct or indirect, of France with its colonies; [it] places the colonists and their properties under the special protection of the nation; [and it] declares criminal to the nation anyone who works to incite insurrections against them."[83]

Despite its coded language, the colonial committee's proposal gave the colonists and the French merchant community the assurances they had been demanding. The abolitionist deputies Jérôme Pétion and Mirabeau rushed to the front of the meeting hall, demanding the right to speak, but months of antiabolitionist propaganda had had its effect. "Their voices were stifled by the general impatience," the *Gazette universelle* reported; "the discussion was closed without having been opened."[84] In his diary, Duquesnoy wrote, "I cannot express the fury that drove the count Mirabeau. . . . It was all over his face, and I heard him say to those around him, 'What cowardly villains you are!' Nevertheless, from every corner of the chamber, one heard: 'He wants to ruin everything.—What does it matter to him if France is destroyed?'"[85]

The crowd in the Tuileries gardens "replied with cheers to the applause from the hall; everyone congratulated each other, as at the news of a victory," the *Gazette universelle* said, adding that the deputies of commerce had dispatched special couriers to carry the news to their home cities. The colonists and the overseas merchants were ecstatic. "The slave trade is implicitly continued. The colonists and their properties are expressly under the special protection of the metropole," the Club Massiac wrote to the members of the assemblies formed in the colonies, and the La Rochelle deputy Nairac rejoiced that "without naming things by their true name, it preserves the slave trade, slavery, the exclusive [trade] regime." He ended his first letter on the matter with the words, "Thanks be to God."[86]

As he saw nearly a year of his efforts reduced to nothing, all Brissot could do was use the columns of his newspaper to deplore the assembly's precipitous action and the "stain imposed on the [nation], in the very cradle of liberty." The decree amounted to an endorsement of the slave trade, "a commerce recognized as infamous, even by those engaged in it." The accusation that abolitionists were traitors to the nation left the Amis des Noirs "threatened by the blade of slander." All he could do was hope that the assembly "will return to those great principles, that have been too strongly immortalized in the declaration for it to ignore for long. This hope should encourage the good friends of the Blacks; they must prepare materials to enlighten the next legislature." In Bordeaux, Brissot's ally Bernadeu, observing the "joy" with which the news of the assembly's action was welcomed, also tried to maintain his conviction that "one day, the assembly, guided by its principles, must declare the Negroes free." For the time being, however, even Brissot admitted that "the decree is passed, it must be obeyed."[87]

As the American scholar Lauren Clay has written, "Lawmakers themselves grudgingly recognized the March 8 decree as a fundamental act of the Revolution. In officially condoning the slave trade, they crossed a line."[88] Barnave had done his best to tie all the threads of the debates concerning the colonies together into a tight knot that could not easily be undone. He had left only one loose strand: He had completely elided the question of rights for the free men of color. If they met all the other qualifications for political rights, would they be allowed to participate in the assemblies in the colonies and to hold office? A pamphlet published by the free men of color demanded that the assembly explicitly state that they would be allowed to do so. Putting their finger on an issue that continues to echo in both France and the United States down to the present, they argued that discrimination on the basis of skin color could only be eliminated by addressing the issue explicitly. "Color is a reality: one must therefore have the courage to name it, and, either to recognize it or to prohibit it, the dignity of the National Assembly needs to explain itself so clearly that no one can misunderstand it," they wrote. They proposed language specifying that "all citizens in the colonies, whether white or of color, will enjoy the rights and prerogatives of citizens."[89]

The assembly discussed the question three weeks later, when Barnave sought approval for instructions on the implementation of the decree of 8 March. Article 4 of that document stated that "all persons twenty-five years of age, owners of real property, or residents of a parish for two years who pay taxes" would be eligible to participate in their local assembly. The wording said nothing about race, and Grégoire seized on the omission. "I fear that article 4 leaves some ambiguity on an important issue," he said, "but the deputies from the colonies assure me that they do not intend to deprive the men of color of their eligibility, and I will give up the floor, on condition that they give up the aristocracy of color." The Saint-Domingue deputy Cocherel immediately objected, and when Grégoire tried to push the issue, the assembly cut off discussion of his "indiscreet proposition," without explicitly taking a position on it.[90] In subsequent debates, Grégoire would continue to insist that he had been assured orally, by Barnave and others, that free men of color who met the other conditions for political participation would be allowed to vote and participate in colonial assemblies. At every opportunity, Brissot and his allies repeated the argument that since the language of the law said nothing about race, free men of color were necessarily included in its purview. In the colonies, however, the ambiguity of the wording of the instructions was ignored and free men of color were firmly excluded from political participation. For more than a year, the abolitionists tugged at this thread that Barnave had left dangling. Finally, their efforts began to unravel the defense of the colonial order that their enemies had so skillfully put together.

CHAPTER SIX

The Storms Before the Hurricane

WITH THE PASSAGE of the decrees of 8 and 28 March 1790, the National Assembly thought it had settled the questions about the future of slavery, the slave trade, and the government of France's overseas colonies that had hung in the air since the start of the Revolution. Like the American revolutionaries, the French had decided to tolerate the glaring contradiction between their assertions about natural rights and the reality of slavery. It was a severe defeat for the Société des Amis des Noirs. In a letter, Jacques-Pierre Brissot wrote, "I am no good to anyone . . . not even to these unfortunate Blacks who, in spite of all my efforts, have been so cruelly abandoned to their torturers."[1] The assembly's ambiguous silence on the issue of rights for free people of color, the one issue Antoine Barnave had not managed to include in his otherwise comprehensive legislative package, left that issue unsettled, but the deputies had made it clear that they were not in a mood to do anything further about it. They had more than enough other matters to deal with, such as debating the extent of the king's war powers, drafting a controversial reform of the Catholic Church, and dealing with outbreaks of violence in different parts of the kingdom.

Meanwhile, in the wake of the 8 March decree, colonial trade revived and French slavers broke all their previous records. During 1790, which enthusiasts for the Revolution liked to call "the Year

2 of Liberty," ships sailing under the French flag made 155 slaving voyages and delivered at least 43,463 African captives across the Atlantic, mostly to Saint-Domingue.[2] Slave traders even continued to receive their customary subsidy payments from the royal treasury. While the slave ships were negotiating the often turbulent weather of the Atlantic, however, new storms that threatened the beneficiaries of the March decrees were taking shape on both sides of the Atlantic. In France, the opponents of slavery refused to concede that their cause was lost. In Saint-Domingue, both white colonists intoxicated with visions of complete autonomy and free people of color unwilling to accept their second-class status prepared to challenge the arrangements the National Assembly had endorsed. And building up into a menacing cloudbank that would overwhelm all these smaller tempests was the potential for a slave revolt that might draw on the newly imported Africans, many of them experienced fighters taken as prisoners in a recent war in the Kongo region of the continent. Barely a year and a half later, this force would hit France's prized colony like a hurricane, compelling all the other groups involved in the empire's conflicts over race and slavery to reckon with it.

In the first weeks after the debates of March 1790, any prospect of such a drastic change seemed remote to the members of the Amis des Noirs in Paris. On 22 March, Honoré Gabriel Mirabeau read them the speech he had wanted to give in the National Assembly. Instead of hundreds of deputies and spectators, his audience consisted of a dozen other members of the group, and the speech was never printed. It was Mirabeau's last expression of support for the cause his colleagues had hoped he might lead to victory in the National Assembly. Brissot, Condorcet, and the other members of the Amis des Noirs were unaware that the great tribune was about to embark on a risky gambit: he was secretly plying the king with advice on how to restore his authority while publicly appearing to support the Revolution. For Mirabeau, it was a repetition of the double game he had played in the fall of 1788, when he negotiated privately with the white Saint-Domingue colonists about representing them even while participating actively in the antislavery group. His surprising proposal to urge the king to take the lead on the antislavery issue in his speech to the Jacobins may even have been one of his ideas for promoting Louis XVI's popularity. Seeing no prospect of any immediate action on the issues that concerned them after the debacle of Mirabeau's speech, the Amis des Noirs decided to put their efforts into a long-term project to compile information about Africa and the slave trade. In an address to the National Assembly, they repeated their hope for a peaceful abolition of the slave trade and of slavery, but in the meantime, their only concrete request was that the assembly protect them from being prosecuted for its activities, as the wording of Barnave's decree had threatened.[3]

Discouraging as the situation looked to the abolitionists after March 1790, the triumph of their opponents was less solid than it appeared. The decree of 8 March was only a promise about the future nature of the relationship between the metropole and the colonies that still needed to be translated into legislation. To the disappointment of the proslavery forces, nothing was done to silence the Amis des Noirs. Just a month after the passage of the 8 March decree, the deputy Jérôme Pétion published the seventy-one-page speech he had wanted to deliver during the debate. Once again readers were confronted with the grim details of the slave trade and the sufferings of enslaved Blacks on the plantations, and once again they were assured that, if the National Assembly adhered to the principles it had adopted in 1789, "a day will come, one cannot doubt it, when the Africans' chains will be broken, when liberty will spread its gifts over the whole world." To the merchants of the slave-trading port of Le Havre, it appeared as if the decree of 8 March had had no effect, since, as they complained to the National Assembly, "this destructive system justly proscribed by your decrees is reborn and multiplies."[4]

On 19 June 1790 the issue of slavery surfaced at a celebration for the anniversary of the Oath of the Tennis Court. In honor of the event, a number of revolutionary politicians held a rustic banquet in Paris's Bois de Boulogne. Among them were Barnave, who had steered the decrees of 8 and 28 March through the National Assembly, and his friend Charles Lameth, a Saint-Domingue plantation owner. The two may not have had any objection to the first toast, "To the freedom and the union of all the peoples of the universe," proposed by Georges Danton, or to the final one, from

Maximilien Robespierre, "To all the courageous writers who wrote and suffered for liberty," but one wonders how Barnave and Lameth reacted to the second one: "To the freedom of the Blacks and of all oppressed men."[5] Three years later, almost to the day, Léger-Félicité Sonthonax, the obscure provincial lawyer who made this toast, acting as a representative of the French revolutionary government in Saint-Domingue, would issue a decree offering freedom to any Black man willing to fight for the French Republic, beginning the sequence of events that culminated, on 4 February 1794, with the National Convention's decree abolishing slavery throughout the French empire.

The free men of color in Paris also continued their campaign, and one of them, Vincent Ogé, was preparing to take direct action in Saint-Domingue to press the issue of their rights. Already in the previous fall, when the National Assembly had kept postponing consideration of the petitions from the free men of color, Ogé had told Thomas Clarkson that their patience would not last forever: "Dispatches shall go directly to St. Domingo; and we will soon follow them. . . . Our own arms shall make us independent and respectable." Now, passing through England and the United States to avoid the travel ban on people of color, Ogé made his way to the Spanish colony of Santo Domingo, which shared the island of Hispaniola with French Saint-Domingue, and prepared to enter French territory. While Ogé was making his lengthy journey, other men of color in Paris continued to protest that their rights were being violated in the colonies and even in France itself.[6]

The biggest colonial crisis facing the metropolitan government during the summer of 1790, however, was caused not by the Amis des Noirs or the free men of color but by the fractious whites in Saint-Domingue. As the authority of the royal government in the island disintegrated in the wake of the news of the storming of the Bastille, the colonists formed local assemblies in the island's three provinces and then a general assembly for the whole colony. By the end of April, this assembly had begun its sessions in the city of Saint-Marc, on the colony's west coast.[7] News of the French National Assembly's decree of 8 March reached Saint-Domingue just as the Saint-Marc assembly was beginning its sessions. Encouraged by the decree, the Saint-Marc assembly immediately asserted its authority, insisting that the local military commander take an oath to obey its orders, demanding that the governor do likewise, and passing laws freeing trade and reshaping the colony's judicial system. It also took measures against the colony's free men of color, accusing them of "manifesting intentions contrary to public tranquility."[8]

On 28 May 1790 the Saint-Marc assembly passed a constitution for the colony. The document's preamble announced that the inhabitants of the colony had the sole right to make laws governing their affairs, "because of the difference in climate, in the nature of the population, of morals and customs," the traditional euphemistic justifications of slavery and racial discrimination. Under the proposed constitution, the colony would notify the king of its decrees, but it denied that the French National Assembly or the appointed royal governor had any right to oppose them.[9] The Saint-Marc assembly's decrees made no overt mention of slavery or the rights of free people of color, but it was an open secret that they were intended to "preserve the rights of its constituents and all the plantation owners of French Saint-Domingue against the disposition in article 4 of the [instructions of 28 March 1790], by which . . . it appears that [the National Assembly] meant that the free people of color as well as the Negroes, should enjoy all the rights of active citizens," as the members of the local colonists' committee in Port-au-Prince put it.[10]

The Saint-Marc assembly's defiant actions were strongly opposed by the royal governor Antoine Thomassin de Peinier and by the provincial assembly of Saint-Domingue's North Province, located in Cap Français, where merchant interests tied to France had more influence. At the end of July, the governor sent troops to disperse the Saint-Marc assembly, accusing its members of intending to declare the colony independent.[11] Eighty-five of the more intransigent assembly members managed to board the French warship *Léopard*, whose crew had mutinied rather than obey orders to participate in the military operation, and set sail for France.[12] The eighty-five "Léopardins," as these deputies became known when they reached France in October 1790, added to the number of disparate pro-colonial and proslavery groups active in the metropole.

By the time the Léopardins reached France, news of the Saint-Marc assembly's decree of 28 May had already stirred strong reactions there. The Club Massiac, which received a copy of the document on 24 July, was thrown into confusion. To endorse the Saint-Marc assembly's actions would amount to abetting a revolt against metropolitan authority, but to condemn them would undermine the proslavery group's interpretation of the March decrees. The club members threw up their hands and decided to let matters run their course.[13] Whether or not the decree amounted to a declaration of colonial independence, it was certainly a challenge to the authority of the National Assembly. Barnave, the spokesman of the assembly's colonial committee, had no choice but to denounce the Saint-Marc assembly's actions, "and he did not spare their authors," the *Gazette universelle* reported.[14]

By its clumsy overreach, the Saint-Marc assembly gave the French antislavery movement a new lease on life. Expressing "sadness, or rather our indignation," at the white colonists' actions, the free men of color seized the chance to depict themselves as the colony's most loyal supporters of the National Assembly.[15] A vehement denunciation of the colonists appeared in the weekly *Révolutions de Paris*, the first of a number of lengthy articles that made that publication one of the major organs of the abolitionist cause. Published anonymously but written by Sonthonax, the radical who had called for the freedom of the Blacks at the celebration for the anniversary of the Tennis Court Oath, the article lambasted the colonists' "system of rebellion against the decrees of the National Assembly." The colonists wanted "liberty for themselves; but they refuse to grant citizenship to the men of color; but they want to perpetuate slavery and the slave trade." Their efforts, the author insisted, would be in vain: "The governments of Europe will not be able to resist the cries of philosophy, the principles of universal liberty that have sprouted and spread among the nations." In a conclusion that made the article a cause célèbre, the author predicted that "a time will come, and the day is not far off, when one will see a woolly-headed African, with no recommendation other than good sense and virtue, come to participate in making laws in our national assemblies."[16]

On 2 October, the eighty-five Léopardins presented themselves at the bar of the National Assembly, precipitating an awkward discussion about where they should stand, since the space allotted for people addressing the body could not accommodate so large a group. Their spokesman, Valentin de Cullion, made an intransigent defense of the Saint-Marc assembly's conduct.[17] Privately, Barnave assured the Léopardins that they would not be punished for their actions, but he was firm in defending the prerogatives of the National Assembly. His report concluded that the Saint-Marc assembly had had no authority to pass legislation and nullified its decrees. Nevertheless, Barnave admitted that the colonists had reason to be concerned about the implications of the Declaration of Rights, and he suggested that their complaints about the trade laws deserved consideration. Above all, he called on the National Assembly to make an explicit statement of its "firm intention to include, as a constitutional article . . . that no laws regarding the status of persons will be passed except in response to a precise formal request from the colonial assemblies." Such a declaration would "end the disquiet that it would have been impossible to calm as long as the colonists have seen that their most cherished interests were at the mercy of the first change of opinion" in France.[18]

Pétion, Henri Grégoire, and Mirabeau rushed to the podium, but, as in March, the assembly blocked any debate about Barnave's motion, which was passed by an overwhelming majority. Once again, Barnave had managed to obtain support for a measure consecrating the institution of slavery without using the word, and this time, it was clear that the rights of the free people of color were also being left to the discretion of the white colonists. The decree of 12 October 1790 committed the assembly to making the final document a French version of "slavery's constitution." Brissot was predictably outraged. The decree was "a cowardly abandonment of all the principles of humanity, of liberty, of justice and of policy," he lamented. Brissot's faithful ally Pétion rushed into print with the forty-four-page speech he had intended to deliver, and Grégoire followed with a *Letter to Philanthropists*, asking Barnave and his supporters "whether you dare to say that only whites are born and remain free and equal in rights?"[19] In the weekly *Révolutions de Paris*, Sonthonax protested even more vehemently: "Thus the Negroes are abandoned to the furor, to the discretion of the colonial plantation-owners! . . . The Negroes will never be free!

But what do we say? They will be in spite of their tyrants, in spite of the National Assembly itself, but their freedom will cost blood, and their barbaric oppressors will be cruelly punished for having rejected the cry of nature and of humanity."[20]

Whereas Pétion, Grégoire, and Sonthonax set out to destroy Barnave's arguments, Brissot went to work to destroy his political career. In a lengthy *Letter to M. Barnave*, published in November 1790, Brissot wrote that at one time, Barnave had appeared to be a supporter of liberty, but now, "seduced by the planters" and "the love of fame," he had abandoned his principles. "On the one hand, you declare that the rights of man are universal, inalienable, unchangeable, and on the other, you maintain that the extension of these rights to Africans is a false and blamable measure." Echoing the phrase from Louis de Jaucourt's article in the *Encyclopédie* that would become notorious when Robespierre employed it six months later, Brissot concluded, "Ah! Let us rather lose our colonies . . . rather than ourselves making them an impious laboratory in which open or disguised aristocrats constantly generate the poisons most apt to infect the soil of liberty."[21] Publicized in the pages of the *Patriote françois* and handed out to attendees heading for the Jacobin Club, Brissot's *Letter* devastated its target. In a private note, Barnave reflected that at one point, he and his ally Charles Lameth had enjoyed more popularity than any of the other revolutionary leaders, but "we lost it over the colonial business." It was "Brissot who took it from us," he conceded.[22]

After the passage of the decree of 12 October 1790, the National Assembly was able to put colonial issues aside for several months. On 29 November 1790, with little discussion, it passed a measure authorizing the dispatch of "civil commissioners" to the colonies to try to calm the ongoing disputes disrupting them. This was the first time the assembly had asserted its authority to bypass the traditional chain of authority extending from the king through his ministers to the appointed officials in the colonies, and it would eventually become the mechanism by which the racial order in the colony of Saint-Domingue would be overturned. At the time, however, no one suggested that the commissioners would have powers to do anything affecting slavery or the rights of nonwhites. The proslavery lobby nevertheless feared the possibility and succeeded in blocking the nomination of Daniel Lescallier as a commissioner because he was a member of the Amis des Noirs.[23]

Meanwhile, several new elements were introduced into metropolitan debates on colonial issues. In the course of Grégoire's and Brissot's attacks on Barnave, they had both taken notice of a new argument in favor of slavery and racial discrimination that neither Barnave nor any of the other prominent defenders of the institution in France had previously employed. Although the idea that Blacks were a separate species or race from whites had surfaced in some prerevolutionary writings, it had not yet been voiced openly in the public debates in revolutionary France. In 1790, however, a pamphlet originally published in Saint-Domingue by the baron de Beauvois, a former member of the Conseil supérieur du Cap, began to circulate in France. Beauvois's pamphlet proposed legislation for the colonies based on the recognition that "in Saint-Domingue . . . men are of two different species." Furthermore, Beauvois claimed, these two different racial groups had "given birth to a third *hybrid* species, which one can call unnatural, since it did not exist at the creation of the world," namely the mixed-race population. "These men are not equal to each other in the natural order," he continued, "and cannot and should not be so according to social conventions." If Blacks were given the same rights as whites, it would also be necessary to give rights to "the orangutan, which is also a man." As for the members of the hybrid race created by intercourse between whites and Blacks, they should be confined to a "sphere halfway between the whites and the Negroes," and strictly forbidden to own landed property. To prevent any further increase in their numbers, Beauvois wanted to prohibit interracial marriages and inflict severe punishments on any whites who entered into them.[24]

In early 1791 another Saint-Domingue colonist, Guillaume-François de Mahy de Corméré, joined Beauvois in advancing an overtly racist argument for denying that universal rights applied to Blacks. Citing Thomas Jefferson's *Notes on Virginia*, he argued that even if members of all races could become educated, a multiracial society was inconceivable. "We . . . can conclude that the mixture of races in the human species, must be one of the most obvious causes of disorganization in any society, and that these unpleasant effects are rooted in nature itself," he wrote.[25] In 1790 and 1791 these racist tropes remained marginal in the ongoing debates about slavery, but they were destined to become far more common after Napoleon's seizure of power in 1799.

Meanwhile, thanks to the radical priest Claude Fauchet, the antislavery cause was gaining a powerful new voice and a new locus of organizational support. Fauchet turned a club he had helped found, the Cercle social, into a platform for the campaign against slavery. Originally known as the Confédération des Amis de la Vérite (Confederation of the Friends of Truth), the organization brought together many of the more radical participants in Paris municipal politics, including Brissot and Condorcet, as well as a number of others attracted to the idea of creating a purified Christianity or a new religion of humanity. It would become a center for, among other things, agitation in support of rights for women. Nicolas Bonneville, a political radical and religious mystic who cofounded the group with Fauchet, established its printing shop, which published a succession of newspapers and numerous abolitionist tracts in the following years.[26]

Unlike the Amis des Noirs, the Cercle social held large public meetings in an amphitheater at the Palais-Royal, sometimes attracting crowds that numbered in the thousands. Fauchet, who had been the preacher in the royal chapel at Versailles for several years before the Revolution, had the voice and the experience to address such large audiences.[27] In November 1790 he delivered a lengthy oration on Jean-Jacques Rousseau's *Social Contract*. The audience for Fauchet's passionate antislavery sermon was probably the largest gathering to listen to a talk on the subject in the entire course of the Revolution, in either France or any other country of the time. Fauchet turned his commentary on Rousseau into an attack on slave owners, slave traders, and "theologians, obvious adversaries of the Evangel in the interest of servitude" who wanted to "perpetuate the slave trade, the warehousing, the imprisonment, the chaining up, the infamous tortures, the infernal vexations, the profound degradation to a level below that of brutes and the sweeping depopulation of a part of the human species."[28]

Like the other French abolitionists, Fauchet admitted that the enslaved Blacks could not be freed overnight, but, he insisted, the Amis des Noirs "have demonstrated . . . with irresistible force and invincible evidence, that the interest of commerce, as well as the equity of principles and the sanctity of nature, require an immediate cessation of the slave trade. . . . Slavery destroyed throughout the world, and annihilated in all its forms, there is the first step toward universal regeneration: we must resolutely will it, and success is assured." In Fauchet's concluding enumeration of nine basic principles underlying human society, the first four propositions concerned slavery, "a violation of nature, the epitome of social disorder . . . the greatest of crimes and the ultimate excess of which men have ever rendered themselves guilty."[29]

The spokesman for the free men of color Julien Raimond added another new element to French debates with his *Observations sur l'origine et les progrès du préjugé des colons blancs contre les hommes de couleur* (Observations on the origin and development of the white colonists' prejudice against the men of color), published in January 1791. In contrast to Fauchet, Raimond was careful not to touch on the question of slavery. The white colonists, he asserted, "have deceptively confused the issue of the people of color with that of the slaves." Raimond limited his focus to the question of race. Whereas Beauvois and Mahy de Corméré had argued that racial differences were rooted in biology, Raimond contended that they were social constructions. As he noted, in the early days of Caribbean colonization, white men had shown no reluctance about marrying Black women and recognizing their children. Prejudice against free people of color in the colonies was, he claimed, "no more than thirty years old," dating to the introduction of harsher racial policies after the Seven Years' War. "It is due entirely to the jealousy of white women, and to the impolitic and tyrannical ordinances by which, since 1768, it has been attempted to abase the men of color," he wrote.[30] Unsurprisingly, since Brissot contributed an introduction to his pamphlet, Raimond embraced the arguments that his white allies had made to show that the granting of rights to his group would benefit both the colony and the metropole. A single, united class of free people would be better able to maintain its domination over the more numerous enslaved Blacks. Furthermore, rendering justice to the free people of color would resolve the contradiction between the National Assembly's stated principle of equality and the reality of discrimination in the colonies.[31]

While Fauchet and Raimond were adding to the arsenal of arguments in favor of the abolitionist cause, their efforts came under attack from an unexpected quarter. Anacharsis Cloots, a Prussian nobleman who proclaimed himself "the orator of the human race" when he led an international delegation that addressed the National Assembly on 19 June 1790, surprised his revolutionary allies by denouncing "the indiscreet friends of the Blacks." "A precipitous action would ruin France, cause a bankruptcy, overturn the constitution, and, in wanting to free 500 thousand Blacks, one would have turned 25 million whites into slaves," he wrote.[32] Although Cloots added that he hoped it would eventually be possible to end slavery, his paradoxical argument that spreading the universal principles of the French Revolution to the world required the maintenance of slavery, an argument that he would repeat on numerous occasions, jolted Brissot and other reformers. It raised the specter of opposition to abolition coming from the revolutionary left, a specter that would become very real a few years later.

At the same time as new ideas were being injected into public discussion of the issues of slavery and race, the National Assembly's colonial committee was holding secret meetings to discuss how to carry out the promise made in the decree of 12 October 1790 that the constitution would protect colonial interests. Along with the assembly deputies who were officially members of the committee, a number of others participated in these sessions, including some of the Léopardins who were still officially waiting to hear whether they would be punished for participating in the Saint-Marc assembly. For the first several months after the committee began meeting in late October, its discussions, diligently recorded by the omnipresent Médéric Louis Élie Moreau de Saint-Méry, focused on the details of how the colonial government would function. There was no dissent about maintaining slavery; several of the colonial representatives warned that extending the revolutionary reform of the Church to the colonies might be dangerous because reform-minded priests could "stir up our slaves."[33]

Just as Raimond was putting forward his argument about the social construction of racial prejudice, and just as the colonial committee was hammering out its proposed colonial constitution, the metropole was jolted by news that at the end of October 1790,

Raimond's one-time associate in the Parisian campaign for rights for free men of color, Vincent Ogé, had raised the banner of revolt in Saint-Domingue. After landing in the Spanish half of Hispaniola, Ogé had crossed over to the French colony, where he had joined forces with a group of local free men of color. Dressed in a National Guard uniform he had brought with him from France, Ogé appeared to be the leader of the group, and he drafted several letters to the white colonists insisting that the decrees of 8 and 28 March 1790 were meant to guarantee the men of color representation in the colonial assemblies.[34] White troops quickly dispersed Ogé's group and forced him to flee back to the Spanish colony, where he was arrested several months later, but the news of the insurrection sent a shock throughout the colony that echoed across the ocean.[35]

News of what came to be called "Ogé's rebellion" reached France at the end of December 1790. For the first time, French abolitionists were forced to decide whether to endorse the use of violence by the victims of racial injustice whose cause they had espoused. In Bordeaux, the chronicler Pierre Bernadeu rejoiced that the men of color "had armed themselves against the despotism of the whites, who certainly deserve to be punished for the insults they have showered on dark-skinned humanity for centuries." Emphasizing that Ogé had "not demanded anything regarding slavery, that he was far from wanting to raise up the Negroes," Brissot insisted that he "conducted himself, in his insurrection, with all the loyalty and moderation that one had no right to expect from men inflamed by long resentments." Ogé's actions were "an act of virtue, a duty, a sacred duty. The conquerors of the Bastille are heroes, and for the same act of heroism, Ogé will be punished!" In the *Révolutions de Paris*, Sonthonax, anticipating Ogé's probable fate, promised him that "the sacrifice of your life will not be in vain, your memory will be revered in free countries . . . a new Spartacus will be born from your ashes."[36] The French defenders of the colonial regime took a very different view of Ogé's rebellion. Moreau de Saint-Méry called Ogé and his followers brigands and assassins whose actions had "placed a great colony in danger." A virulent pamphlet published in Nantes claimed that "as soon as Ogé arrived in these peaceful and happy lands, fires, murders and ravages carried out by capable and conspiratorial leaders broke out everywhere . . . women of color added poisons within homes to the bloody daggers."[37]

The colonial committee's private discussions about the rights of men of color were more nuanced than the polemics in the press. In a lengthy session at the beginning of February, Barnave warned the committee members that, if the issue was not settled, it might be left to a future legislative assembly in which Brissot was likely to be a member. Even some of the most intransigent colonists agreed that it would be advantageous to increase the number of white citizens by giving some men of color that status. However, they argued, it was essential to leave the matter up to the whites in the colonies. If instructions on the issue were imposed by the metropole, "all the spirits will revolt." The men of color would think that Ogé's rebellion had driven the assembly to act. In a pamphlet, Moreau de Saint-Méry put the matter even more forcefully. "If the National Assembly has the misfortune to pass a decree about the men of color, everything is lost. . . . If our slaves come to suspect that there is an instance that has the power to rule on their condition, apart from their masters; above all, if they see the evidence that the mulattos were able to make use of this power; . . . if they see that without our participation, the mulattos have become our equals . . . France has no hope of keeping its colonies."[38]

As they waited for news of Ogé's fate in Saint-Domingue, the free men of color and their supporters in France kept up their own campaign. In the provincial city of Angers, up the Loire River from the slaving port of Nantes, a powerful new voice on their behalf emerged: that of Claude Milscent de Mussy, a white plantation owner from Saint-Domingue who had had to flee the colony in June 1790 because of his support for rights for men of color. By mid-1792, he would replace Brissot as the most active journalist devoted to the cause, and he would become the first metropolitan advocate of the immediate and unconditional emancipation of the enslaved population. In early 1791, however, his attention was still focused exclusively on the cause of the free men of color. For Milscent, although he was white, the issue was personal: The mother of his children was a free Black woman, and as one of his mixed-race sons would write in an article published in Haiti in 1818, "his love for her inspired in part the great interest that he had for the men of color and which attracted the hatred of the colonists, who called him the 'Negro-lover.'"[39]

Despite his "misalliance," Milscent had been very much part of white colonial society. He owned a substantial plantation and commanded a unit of men of color used to hunt down enslaved Blacks who had escaped from their owners. In 1789 he took part in the unauthorized movement to elect deputies to the Estates General and participated in the assembly of the colony's North Province. In his collection of documents about events in the colony, Moreau de Saint-Méry preserved a copy of a motion written by Milscent congratulating the colonial deputies in the National Assembly for having warded off any attempt to ban the slave trade.[40] However, when other colonists discovered that he had also written a pamphlet under the pseudonym "Michel Mina, mulatto," demanding rights for that group, Milscent realized that his life was in danger and fled to France.[41]

Although he had been born in Saint-Domingue, Milscent had relatives in Angers, including one of the city's deputies to the National Assembly. After his arrival there, he quickly became active in the local Jacobin club. In early March 1791 a local Angers newspaper published several addresses and petitions approved by the Jacobin Club on behalf of "a very numerous class of free men, who hold in their hands a third of the French possessions, which they work with slave labor. These rich landowners, for the sole reason that they are mulattos, men of color, are treated by the whites with total disdain, to the point where they are denied the rights of active citizens." Ogé, the Angers Jacobins declared, had been wrong to take up arms, but his demands were fully justified. Although these documents were signed by others, there was no doubt that they were the work of the man the paper described as "a generous defender of the colony" who had been forced to leave Saint-Domingue, and who was identified as "M. D. M., prop[riétaire] am[éricain]"—that is, Milscent de Mussy.[42]

Brissot reprinted the Angers Jacobin Club's address in the *Patriote françois*, and it was circulated to the network of Jacobin clubs all across the nation.[43] This was the first time the Jacobins as a whole were challenged to take a position on an issue related to colonial affairs. In late April one observer claimed that "all the clubs of friends of the constitution excepting those of the maritime cities" had endorsed the demands of the free men of color. A pamphlet published by the Amis des Noirs included nearly two dozen statements of support from clubs in cities throughout the country.[44] In Paris, the antislavery movement was given new vigor by the merger of the Amis des Noirs and the Cercle social. "Your principles about the means of gradually elevating the Negro slaves to natural and civic freedom, as well as the absolute necessity of abolishing the slave trade, have long been recognized by all members of our confederation as social dogmas that can only be opposed by enemies of reason and morality," Fauchet and his colleagues told the members of the Amis des Noirs.[45]

Milscent, although still residing in Angers, soon started to contribute to the Cercle social's journal, the *Bouche de fer*. For the French abolitionist movement, Milscent was an important recruit. As the abolitionists' opponents regularly pointed out, Brissot, Condorcet, and Grégoire had never seen the French islands in the Caribbean, but Milscent could speak with the authority that came from having lived in Saint-Domingue and participated in every aspect of its affairs. Milscent's early articles repeated the arguments that had already been made by Brissot and Julien Raimond: Free men and property owners, the men of color met all the requirements for the status of active citizens. They were indispensable contributors to the functioning of the slavery system in the colonies, and the whites' prejudices against them were "without foundation."[46]

The campaign on behalf of the free men of color took on a new intensity with the arrival of the news that Ogé had been condemned to death in Cap Français and broken on the wheel, a cruel punishment already outlawed in revolutionary France. Brissot exploded with fury, going further than he ever had before in justifying violence on behalf of his cause. Ogé's uprising was more legitimate than the French revolt of 1789, he claimed. "If . . . Ogé was obliged to spill blood, to burn some houses, to demand compensation from his enemies, didn't blood also color our revolution?" The whites in the colonies should be forewarned: "You cannot deny nature, it is she who now prepares the punishment of the whites, who will avenge innocent blood, who will avenge the mulattos subject to the most odious despotism."[47]

As the opponents of slavery and racial injustice were ramping up their efforts and their rhetoric in the wake of Ogé's execution, the National Assembly's colonial committee was finally preparing to present its proposal for the integration of the colonies into the constitution. The group's sense that something drastic needed to be done to prevent chaos in the colonies was strengthened by the latest news from Saint-Domingue, where troops and sailors newly arrived from France had caused a new crisis by lynching Thomas Mauduit, the colonel of the army regiment stationed in Port-au-Prince and a staunch opponent of the most extreme white colonists.[48] Had Brissot been privy to the debates within the enlarged committee, he might have been surprised to discover that his bitter enemy Barnave was making strenuous efforts to persuade the white colonists to make some gesture in favor of the free men of color. Barnave's argument was based on a pragmatic and, as events would prove, accurate assessment of the balance of opinions in the National Assembly. "There are two very distinct issues," he told his colleagues. "One is slavery, the other the exercise of rights by the men of color. The National Assembly will leave the first one alone, but with regard to the second, it will want to take some action." If the committee did not put forward some provision in favor of that group, he warned, the assembly would decide the matter on its own and would probably endorse legislation more favorable to their cause than the colonists wanted. Moreau de Saint-Méry and others kept insisting that any decision on the issue had to be left to the future all-white assemblies that would be elected in the colonies, but Barnave feared that "the colonies . . . will make an impolitic decision, contrary to their interest, because at this moment prejudice speaks more powerfully than reason."[49]

As far as Moreau de Saint-Méry was concerned, Barnave was threatening to nullify the assurances made to the colonists in the decrees of 8 March and 12 October 1790 that no change would be made in "the status of persons" unless representatives of the white colonists proposed them. Did Barnave mean that the National Assembly "will thus examine our constitution before we have even discussed it?" If that was the case, "who will reassure the colonists against the danger of a subsequent [French] legislature on whose opinion or the composition the so-called philanthropists, the so-called friends of the Blacks might have . . . an influence that we know they haven't acquired in the present National Assembly?" Pierre-Victor Malouet came to Barnave's defense, telling Moreau de Saint-Méry that "the political situation demands that something be done for the men of color." The colonial deputy Louis de Curt remained unconvinced, however, arguing that "once you have given something to the men of color, they will want to have more," and in the end, Barnave was forced to give way. The proposal voted out of the committee said nothing about the rights of free people of color.[50]

The stage was now set for the longest and most heated of the National Assembly's debates on the issues of race and slavery. As the *Gazette universelle* wrote, the question to be decided "concerns both Europe and America. The decision of the assembly could decide on life or death, slavery or freedom for millions of men, and signal either prosperity or decline for our commerce and our national wealth."[51] In contrast to the confrontations in November 1789, March 1790, and October 1790, this time both sides succeeded in laying out their arguments at length. Mirabeau was no longer there to deploy his oratorical skills on behalf of the abolitionist cause—he had died unexpectedly a month earlier—and Brissot, because he was not a deputy, had to cheer his colleagues on from the sidelines, but the antislavery movement could count on its dedicated advocates Grégoire and Pétion; on Pierre-Samuel Dupont de Nemours, whose 1771 article on the cost of slave labor had made him one of the earliest French abolitionists; and on Maximilien Robespierre, who involved himself seriously with these issues for the first time. Opposing them were the most prominent spokesmen for the colonial lobby: Moreau de Saint-Méry, Malouet, Louis-Marthe Gouy d'Arsy, Barnave, and Jean-Siffrein Maury.

As the deputies battled back and forth, they were cheered and jeered by their colleagues and by the spectators in the galleries, whose applause and "murmurs" were noted in transcriptions of the debates. A witness described the proslavery faction: "Barnave at the tribune, Alexandre Lameth at his feet giving orders to speak or to be quiet according to the circumstances . . . while the infamous Gouy acted as their aide de camp from one end of the chamber to the other."[52] The Paris Jacobin Club became another center of debate. Brissot suddenly emerged as its dominant figure, challenging Barnave on what had long been his home turf. The debates were commented on and transmitted to the country by the full range of the Paris press. For a tumultuous week, the "affair of the colonies" was unquestionably the major subject in the French news.

The great debate of May 1791 began with an opening skirmish on 7 May, when the deputy François-Pascal Delattre presented the motion worked out by the combined committees. In its final form, the proposal had two main provisions. In the first place, it called for the National Assembly to incorporate into the constitution the promise made in the decree of 12 October 1790 that no change would be made in the "status of persons" in the colonies except in response to an explicit request from the colonists themselves. Second, the committees proposed to have the French Caribbean colonies elect delegates to a "congress" that would meet on the small island of Saint-Martin. That body would be obliged to come up with a proposal regarding the status of free people of color, which would then be submitted to the metropolitan legislature. This complicated arrangement was the committee's effort to square the circle: It was meant to reassure the colonies that nothing concerning slavery or racial hierarchy would be done without their consent, while giving the free men of color "the assurance of being treated with justice."[53]

The committee had hoped that, as on 8 March and 12 October 1790, it could get its proposal approved without debate, but instead the motion was greeted with a storm of objections. Grégoire and Pétion denounced the "horrible project" as an attempt to perpetuate the oppression of the free men of color. Even though he had been involved in the drafting of the proposal, the colonial deputy Moreau de Saint-Méry also rejected it. Instead of the pan-colonial congress in Saint-Martin, which he feared might be favorable to the pretentions of the free men of color, he wanted each colony to be able to decide for itself on their status. And in case anyone failed to recognize what was at stake, he allowed himself to outrage the audience by remarking, "I have heard mention here of the declaration of the rights of man. Very well! If you want the declaration of rights, as far as we are concerned, there will be no more colonies." According to the record of the proceedings, this attack on the National Assembly's proudest achievement excited "violent murmurs."[54]

On 7 May the assembly voted to postpone discussion for two days, an interval that grew to four because of other urgent business. This gave the Amis des Noirs time to prepare a pamphlet that they handed out to all the deputies as they entered the hall on 11 May to resume the debate. As a result of the group's campaign, they claimed, public opinion was now on the side of the free men of color. Furthermore, they optimistically predicted, the British Parliament was on the verge of voting to ban the slave trade. In short, the die was cast, and there was really no choice for the deputies. "The latest events have proved to it that there is only one way to save the colonies: that of putting into effect the rights of man and citizen."[55]

Grégoire led off the debate on 11 May with a powerful statement of the abolitionists' arguments. "You should not any longer allow the declaration of the rights of man and justice to be violated to the detriment of a class of citizens who are free, property owners, taxpayers and native sons of the soil of the colonies," he insisted. The supporters of the colonists had unfairly tried to link the issue of rights for the free men of color with slavery. An obscure deputy not affiliated with the Amis des Noirs, Jean-Louis Viefville des Essarts, had in fact wanted to outline a plan for the abolition of slavery, which would have been the first such proposal presented to the French legislature, but he was never allowed to speak. Instead, as the Amis des Noirs had consistently done from the start of their campaign, Grégoire separated the two questions and conceded that the enslaved Blacks were not ready for freedom. But why, he asked, would the granting of rights to free men of color compromise the institution of slavery? After evoking the martyrdom of Ogé, he concluded by calling on the assembly to reject the committee proposal and instead confirm that the decree of 28 March 1790 had been meant to give free men of color political rights in the colonies.[56]

Grégoire's broadside began five days of all-out warfare. Stanislas Clermont-Tonnerre, a moderate remembered best for his argument in favor of rights for the Jews, a topic on which he found himself in agreement with Grégoire, was the first to speak against the men of color. Among other things, he pointed out that the

British Parliament had just made "a decision quite the opposite of what philosophy expected" by refusing to ban the slave trade. To the surprise of many, Clermont-Tonnerre was followed by Jean-Louis Monneron, a representative of the slave colonies in the Indian Ocean, who sided with Grégoire and cited Montesquieu on the Roman practice of granting citizenship to freedmen. In his account of the debates, Gouy d'Arsy explained Monneron's unexpected intervention as a consequence of the fact that he was married to a woman of color, so that he was "speaking for himself and his children."[57]

Gouy d'Arsy himself provided the most outspoken answer to Grégoire. Whereas the committee proposal scrupulously avoided any mention of the word "slavery," Gouy d'Arsy made sure that the deputies understood that it was the fundamental issue at stake. The Amis des Noirs pretended to be moderates, but they had "published and signed at the origin of their society, 'We seek the complete and prompt abolition of slavery.'" The three issues they raised—the rights of free men of color, the abolition of the slave trade, and the abolition of slavery itself—were "inseparable; they are the consequences of the same principle." Any change in colonial institutions would bring the whole system down. Lest anyone ignore the nature of that system, Gouy d'Arsy spelled it out for them: "The colonial regime is entirely based on the system of slavery. The system of slavery depends on the continuation of the slave trade and of this ancient prejudice that positions the men of color as a necessary barrier between the Blacks and the whites."[58]

Gouy d'Arsy's frankness put his opponents in the awkward position of having to state openly that they were not trying to make any change in the institution of slavery. Antoine Destutt de Tracy acknowledged that the very word was an embarrassment. "In this assembly, you have never wanted to pronounce the word 'slave.' You have recognized that you could not destroy slavery. You have been reluctant to consecrate it, and in order to designate the slaves, you have talked of 'the status of persons,'" he remarked. In that case, Malouet responded, the assembly should be honest with itself. Slavery might indeed be unjustifiable "in law and in principle: no intelligent man with a sense of morality would say otherwise." But that was not the question. "The issue is whether it is possible, without unleashing an avalanche of crimes and misfortunes that would terrify you, to change such a state of things in your colonies."[59]

Barnave was evidently unhappy about the direction the debate was taking. Repeatedly forcing the deputies to recognize that they were being asked to provide constitutional protection for slavery risked provoking a backlash. He insisted that slavery and the rights of the free men of color were two separate issues, and that only the latter was under debate. Everyone recognized, he maintained, that the colonies would never consent to any proposition hostile to slavery, and the question was, "Do you want to have colonies? Or do you not?" Referring to the arguments in the colonial committee, he said that he now found himself forced to oppose propositions that he had "strongly supported in discussions where they were, strictly speaking, possible." But, he went on, "there is, I would say, some merit to putting forward, when great interests require it, some modifications to principles. He who courageously takes on this unpopular task, has some patriotism, some daring in his character, some love for his country in his heart."[60] It was an unusually personal statement for Barnave, who normally kept his feelings carefully concealed.

Barnave's intervention brought the first day of debate in the assembly to a close, but he still had to face another confrontation that evening. At the meeting of the Jacobin Club, Brissot was lying in wait for him. Up until now, Brissot announced, he had avoided speaking to the Jacobins, but the cause of the free men of color was too important for him to remain silent. To deny them equal rights was to "declare that skin color can make a difference between a man and another man," he protested. "It is not a question here of the Black slaves, they are unfortunate orphans whose situation might occupy us after our constitution," he conceded. Clearly exasperated, Barnave replied that he had never wanted to get involved with the colonial issue, but that he had proposed the decrees of 8 March and 12 October 1790 "with the conviction that I was doing everything for my country. I knew that I would have public opinion against me; I knew that after having usefully served my country, I would be blamed." Whether or not the country had turned against him, it was clear that he could no longer depend on the support of the Jacobins.[61]

The tumult in the National Assembly continued for four more days, frequently driving its presiding officer to complain that he could not maintain order because deputies were interrupting each other and spectators were making noise in the galleries. Speaking out on a colonial issue for the first time, Robespierre demanded to know "if it makes political sense to let the menaces of a faction make us yield up the rights of men, of justice, and humanity!" Barnave countered with a baldly utilitarian argument: "It is absurd, once one has consented, because of national interests, because of public benefit, to leave 600,000 men in slavery, to not be willing to suspend for a time . . . the exercise of political rights for a small number of men." After hours of impassioned argument on 12 May, the assembly took a roll-call vote about whether to set aside the committee proposal. Three hundred seventy-eight deputies voted to continue discussing it, while 276 sided with the abolitionists in trying to table the motion. By the next day, supporters of the colonists were circulating a list of those "who voted for England against France, on the question of whether the National Assembly would sacrifice its colonies."[62]

After the second day of debate, the advocates of slavery held an evening meeting. Confident that they had the support of a majority in the assembly, they decided, according to Gouy d'Arsy, "to deliver the final blow to our adversaries, by proposing to the National Assembly on the next day to recognize and categorically consecrate the slavery of the Negroes."[63] Moreau de Saint-Méry was chosen to speak on their behalf, and on the following morning, he introduced the proposition the group had approved the night before: "The National Assembly decrees, as a constitutional article, that no law on the status of slaves in the American colonies can be made by the legislature except in response to a formal and spontaneous request from their colonial assemblies."[64]

This challenge was too much for the antislavery deputies. The economist du Pont enraged the colonial party by asserting that "the Negro slaves are the true people of the country, since it is they who cultivate the soil, with the labor of their arms." He then invoked the famous line from the chevalier de Jaucourt's 1765 *Encyclopédie* article, telling the assembly that "your interest, that of Europe, that of the world would demand that you not hesitate to sacrifice a colony rather than a principle." This provoked the colonists as much as the call to constitutionalize slavery had enraged the abolitionists. Maury gave another lengthy argument for the necessity of racial hierarchy as a defense of slavery, and Moreau de Saint-Méry doubled down on his proposition: "We must explain ourselves clearly, in a manner that leaves no doubts. Let us not talk any more of unfree persons; let's simply say slaves, that is the accurate term."[65]

Now Robespierre rose to speak. He had never previously shown any particular interest in the issue of colonial slavery and had never joined the Amis des Noirs, but he was the assembly's most consistent defender of the principle of universal natural rights.[66] "From the moment when, in one of your decrees, you will have pronounced the word 'slaves,' you will have pronounced your own dishonor," he told his colleagues. "Ah! perish the colonies, if that is the price of preserving them." Like du Pont, Robespierre borrowed this rhetorical figure from Jaucourt, but the context in which he deployed it, in direct response to Moreau de Saint-Méry, and the concision of his formulation caught the public's attention. For the next several years, until he became a member of the National Convention's Committee of Public Safety, "Perish the colonies!" became the phrase most intimately associated with Robespierre. To his supporters, such as the journalist Camille Desmoulins, Robespierre's defense of principles was "one of the most admirable successes than any member has had in the assembly." The royalist newsman Barnabé Farmian Du Rozoi, however, told Robespierre that "you are committing, by your system, a parricide," sacrificing the fatherland to uphold "your sublime declaration of the rights of man." In fact, however, Robespierre knew he had no chance of prevailing on the underlying issue. As the Jacobin journalist Jean-Louis Carra put it, "Robespierre fought a war over words since he could not fight it about substance."[67]

Despite Robespierre's impassioned intervention, the proslavery forces were sure that they had forced the abolitionists into an impossible position. "Their embarrassment was extreme," Gouy d'Arsy concluded. "They were afraid to oppose [the motion] for fear of justifying the suspicion that I had raised"—namely, the accusation that their real aim was to obtain a vote against slavery.

Satisfied that the assembly was not going to embrace Robespierre's appeal, Moreau de Saint-Méry made a clever tactical retreat. "It is not worth fighting over words; since I am persuaded that things are well understood, in the sense that I mean them, I withdraw my amendment with the word 'slave,'" he said. The final version of the decree stated that the colonists would have the prerogative to decide on the status of "unfree persons" in the colonies.[68] With their victory on the issue of slavery ensured, the pro-colonial deputies wanted to force through the other parts of the decree, but their opponents finally brought the stormy session to an end by leaving the hall. The question of whether any provision about the rights of free men of color would be passed remained unsettled.

From the assembly, a number of deputies moved to the Jacobin Club, where that question was definitely on the agenda. For the first time, Julien Raimond, a "métis" or "mixed-blood," as one hostile reporter put it, spoke to the members. Challenging a white Saint-Domingue plantation owner to acknowledge that men of color owned many of the slaves in the colony, he asked, "If it is shown that the browns have at least a third of the slaves, isn't it impossible that they would join with the slaves to rise up against the whites?" For other speakers, the symbolic importance of Raimond's appearance was more important than what he actually said. He was followed at the podium by a speaker variously described as an "Arab," a "Turk," or an "Armenian," who announced, "It is with the rights of man in my hands that I ascend this tribune," and concluded that "the colonists' demand, that the others should not have the same right as they do, is the demand of despotism." Adding his voice to the defense of the free men of color, Robespierre said, "Because it has pleased the Supreme Being to give their faces a different color, you have deprived them of their natural rights."[69]

When the National Assembly reconvened on the morning of 14 May, the first order of business was a request from the representatives of the free men of color in Paris to address the body. Their spokesman Raimond was accorded the privilege of being the first person of acknowledged African descent to address a national legislative body anywhere in the Western world. As he had at the Jacobins' meeting the night before, Raimond depicted the free men of color as respectable owners of property and dismissed the notion that granting them rights might in any way affect the system of slavery. "What concept could a slave form of the dignity of an active citizen?" he asked. "I can assure you, Messieurs, that anyone who knows this unhappy class of men would say that for them, it would be an unintelligible idea."[70] The debate dragged on through the afternoon, with the usual adversaries squaring off and other deputies expressing increasing impatience with the amount of time it was consuming.

Raimond and his group were frustrated by the assembly's lack of reaction to his speech. By the morning of 15 May, they had drafted a plaintive letter that was read to the deputies, in which they begged to at least be given a guarantee that they could sell their properties and leave the colonies if their demands were ignored. "This address had a lot of impact," Gouy d'Arsy conceded. At this point, the Alsatian representative Jean-François Rewbell, known primarily for his ferocious opposition to the granting of rights to the Jews of his native province, put forward an amendment to the committee proposal that, he claimed, would cut the Gordian knot confronting the assembly. It was obvious, he said, that left to themselves, the white colonists would never approve any concessions to the free men of color, but it was dangerous not to do anything on behalf of that group. Asserting that the National Assembly did have the right to legislate on the issue, he proposed granting rights to free men of color who had been born to free parents. Having taken that step, the assembly would guarantee the whites that it would not do anything more on the issue, and, since the number of individuals affected would be small, his proposal would ensure the whites a "perpetual preponderance" in the colonies. At the same time, however, it would appease the free men of color, because they would know that at least their children would qualify as full citizens.[71]

Michel Regnault de Saint-Jean d'Angély, a deputy who had spoken several times on behalf of the free men of color, called the proposal "a means to reconcile all the friends of France, of the constitution and of humanity."[72] Sentiment in the assembly was so strong in favor of the amendment that Rewbell had to intervene personally to beg his colleagues to let Barnave speak in opposition to it. Although the proposal resembled ideas he himself had floated in the colonial committee, Barnave's experience with the colonists' representatives had taught him that they would react violently to any measure on "the status of persons" passed by the National Assembly. The proposal contradicted the assurance that had just been given to the colonies that no such law would be passed unless it had their prior approval, he said. If the amendment was adopted, he warned, white resistance in the colonies would prevent its implementation, and "your decree will destroy the trust between you and the colonies."[73]

In response to Barnave, Robespierre had a rare opportunity to voice sentiments he sensed that the majority of the deputies shared. By consenting to protect slavery in the constitution, he said, "we have certainly gained the right to demand the price of such a great sacrifice." He himself was not going to vote for the amendment, since it still violated the principle of the universality of natural rights, but he understood his colleagues' determination to do something for "men who were not already deprived of freedom . . . whom you should keep free." To give in to the threat that the colonies might rebel would be "to overturn with your own hands the bases of your authority." Despite his own refusal to vote for it, he gave his colleagues an argument for supporting Rewbell's amendment: "I think that every member of this assembly recognizes that he has already done too much by giving constitutional consecration to slavery in the colonies."[74]

After rejecting a last-ditch effort by Maury to restrict the number of beneficiaries of the amendment by requiring that rights be limited to free men of color whose parents had been both free and legally married, the assembly passed Rewbell's proposal on a voice vote, with Grégoire and Pétion joining Robespierre in voting no on the grounds that it should have included all free people of color. The result was another demonstration of the price Barnave was paying because of his involvement with the colonies, made all the more painful because he had been forced into defending a position that he did not really support. "Mr. Barnave, who has, for some time past, taken upon himself to act as Minister for the Colonies, has, by so doing, contrived to destroy, or at least very much to diminish, his ill deserved popularity," the British ambassador Earl Gower noted.[75] Meanwhile, Robespierre benefited tremendously from his speeches on the issue. For the first time in his legislative career, he succeeded in rallying a majority in the assembly, a triumph that was followed by an even more striking one just a day later, when his colleagues endorsed his motion that deputies to the National Assembly should be ineligible to sit in the legislature that was going to succeed it. This "self-denying ordinance" was another stinging repudiation of Barnave, who, according to one of his colleagues, "want[ed] re-election with incredible passion." As Robespierre's former schoolmate the journalist Camille Desmoulins put it, these two votes left Barnave isolated and gave Robespierre a new credibility that would help him lead France "to the freedom toward which we are all marching."[76]

Limited as it was, what came to be known as the law of 15 May 1791 had a revolutionary significance. For the first time in the Western world, some people of African descent were officially promised the same civil and political rights as whites. The decree provoked widespread public reactions. Visual artists used their medium to celebrate the struggle for racial justice. In an image captioned, "Mortals are equal. It is not birth, it is only virtue that makes a difference," an anonymous engraver showed the goddess of Reason holding a level above the heads of a white man in the uniform of the French National Guard and a dark-skinned figure, naked from the waist up and dressed in a *pagne* or wrap, something no self-respecting free man of color in the colonies would ever have worn (figure 6).

Because the Black figure is dressed like a field laborer, it has often been assumed that this image refers to the abolition of slavery in 1794, but the scroll in his hand reads "decree of 15 May," making it clear that the artist was celebrating that law. A far more elaborate depiction of the "discussion on the men of color" shows Barnave holding the ends of a chain that surrounds a group of men of color while a group of colonists, including Moreau de Saint-Méry, Gouy d'Arsy, and Malouet, cheer him on. Facing Barnave, Julien Raimond, dressed in European clothes, holds up a mutilated copy of the Declaration of Rights and says, "In tearing it from my hands, cruel one, do you think you can tear it from all the hearts in which it is inscribed, this immortal declaration?" Behind Raimond, dark-skinned men of various complexions express distress. Above the realistically depicted figures in the foreground, three allegorical figures representing "humanity, justice, and reason" and who may also

FIGURE 6: *Mortals Are Equal.* An allegorical image celebrating the National Assembly's decree of 15 May 1791 emphasizes the granting of equality to Blacks in the French colonies. The Black figure in the image holds a copy of the decree. In reality, the decree only granted rights to a small number of Blacks who were already legally free. *Credit:* Bibliothèque nationale de France.

stand for Robespierre, Pétion, and Grégoire gesture toward the fracas below (figure 7).[77]

Like the creators of these two images, Brissot decided to present the decree of 15 May as a victory for his cause, even though its provisions fell short of what he had long advocated. "This decree certainly does not fulfill the hopes of the rigid patriots, . . . but it is a step in the direction of a return to principles," he wrote.[78] At the Jacobin Club meeting on 16 May, Raimond assured the members that "my fellow citizens in America will be full of sentiment when they learn how much the Friends of the Constitution have done for the decree that the National Assembly has just passed in their favor."[79] Grégoire, who, like Robespierre, had actually voted against the Rewbell amendment, went beyond Brissot in praising the law after it was passed. In an open letter to the free men of color in Saint-Domingue, he wrote, "Friends, you were men, you were

FIGURE 7: *Discussion About the Men of Color*. An elaborate engraving shows the leading participants in the May 1791 debate about slavery and the rights of free people of color. The image includes the only known depiction of Julien Raimond, the first man of African descent to address a legislative body in the Western world. *Credit:* Bibliothèque nationale de France.

citizens, and, given back the full extent of your rights, you will now participate in the sovereignty of the people." Echoing the prophecy that the radical Sonthonax had made in the *Révolutions de Paris*, he foresaw the day when "deputies of color will cross the ocean to sit in the national parliament, and swear along with us to live and die under our laws." As usual, Grégoire could not restrain himself from going further and anticipating the abolition of slavery. "Do not forget," he told the free men of color, "that, like you, they are born and remain free and equal. It is part of the irresistible march of events . . . that all the peoples who have been deprived of liberty will finally recover this property."[80]

In Angers, the Jacobin Club welcomed one of Milscent's mixed-race sons, who told them, "It is from your town that the first electric spark in favor of the men of color in our American colonies appeared." Later in the summer, Milscent began publishing his own newspaper, in which he touted the decree of 15 May as having "raised the French people above all others."[81] Julien Raimond wrote to the colonies in a more sober tone, urging the free men of color to prove themselves worthy of citizenship by obeying the law, promoting education, treating their slaves humanely, and showing respect for the whites, even though they were now their legal equals. As for the free men of color who were still excluded from full citizenship by the law of 15 May, they should console themselves with the knowledge that "the time of their political regeneration is not far off, that they can accelerate it by good behavior, education, by the progress of their industry and their attachment to France."[82] In Saint-Domingue, the free men of color celebrated the decree. One of Raimond's correspondents wrote to him that he would have liked to send him his copy of the local newspaper that had published the text of the decree, but "my brothers take such pleasure in seeing it" that he could not part with it.[83]

The supporters of the white colonists were correspondingly furious, both about the granting of rights to even a small number of nonwhites and about the National Assembly's violation of the promise contained in its vote on 13 May to leave questions about the "status of persons" to the colonies. On 16 May the deputies from the Caribbean colonies announced that they were withdrawing from the National Assembly in protest. Du Pont commented that, in 1789, the deputies of the nobility and the clergy had not quit the assembly when their privileges were curtailed: "Those from the colonies . . . show less patriotism."[84] On the day after the vote, the American diplomatic representative Gouverneur Morris described the Guadeloupe deputy Curt as "outrageous about the Decree," and the British ambassador reported that the French colonists would soon be sending a representative to London to seek backing for a plan to declare themselves independent.[85]

The Club Massiac called an emergency meeting of all those concerned with the colonies. "Your properties are in danger . . . no one can yet know the extent of the incalculable consequences of a decree that resulted from the most blamable intrigues," their president told them. After one meeting of the National Assembly's colonial committee, which he and the other colonial deputies continued to attend even as they boycotted the National Assembly, Moreau de Saint-Méry was so angry that he burned the notes he had taken. Malouet insisted that they had to find some way to prevent the decree's implementation. He evoked the possibility that a free man of color who had enslaved relatives might now be elected as a local justice of the peace, with responsibility for maintaining discipline on the plantations. "Subordination would cease to exist," he grumbled. Even more alarmed, Gouy d'Arsy warned that the vote for Rewbell's amendment "silently predicts the outcome on the terrible question of the emancipation of the slaves."[86]

In contrast to the situation in March 1790, when the port cities had provided overwhelming support for the colonial lobby, in May 1791 their reactions were divided. A letter from "merchants, ships' captains and citizens" of the slaving port of Havre warned that "the strength of this prejudice" against the men of color in the colonies was so great that any attempt to implement the new law was bound to lead to disorder that would in turn cause a collapse in France's economy, but a printed address from the "commerce of Havre" called the decree "the savior of our colonies."[87] In Marseille, the chamber of commerce denounced the decree, but the mayor and the city council applauded it, and in Nantes, the chamber of commerce decided not to take an official position on it.[88]

The biggest shock to the colonial lobby came from Bordeaux. In February 1790 the arrival of that city's "patriotic army" in Paris had precipitated the passage of the decree of 8 March with its assurance that the colonial order would be left unchanged. This time, however, the merchants, city officials, and political activists of France's largest trading port not only endorsed the decree of 15 May but even offered to send members of their National Guard to enforce it. An address from the directory of the department of the Gironde, the administrative unit of which Bordeaux was now the capital, praised the decree, "since it reconsecrates the rights of every free man, and if these rights had been violated in any part of the empire, liberty itself would have been in danger." A jubilant Brissot concluded that the attitude of the Bordelais "should show the friends of liberty that, under its reign, there is no prejudice that can long resist the efforts of reason."[89]

Aside from ideological arguments, there were several reasons for the strong support for the decree in a city so tied to colonial interests. A letter from Bordeaux published in the *Chronique de Paris* claimed that "it is plain to see that the American [colonists] want to make themselves independent, and turn their trade over to foreigners." The *Feuille du Jour*, a royalist paper sympathetic to the colonists, took quite a different view of the Bordeaux proposal: "I ask you if there was ever conceived a more barbarous plan of crusade. . . . The decree or bloodshed: that is the alternative at the heart of the expedition proposed by the Bordelais."[90] While most criticism of the decree of 15 May came from the colonists and their supporters, Anacharsis Cloots again expressed dissent from the left. Challenged by spokesmen for the free men of color to explain "by what strange aberration of principles you have criticized the decree of the French legislators that gave us back the eternal rights of liberty that you demand for all inhabitants of the earth," Cloots replied by reminding them that they were themselves slave owners. Furthermore, he added, "I do not in any way deny my principles when I oppose to the tactic of tyrants, another tactic without which the hopes of the human race would disappear along with the French constitution."[91]

Since the deputies from the colonies had withdrawn from the National Assembly, supporters of the decree of 15 May had the upper hand in framing the instructions for its implementation. A draft drawn up by a committee chaired by the veteran abolitionist La Rochefoucauld on 29 May 1791 argued that the white colonists had no reason to complain, since the National Assembly had guaranteed "the conservation of the means on which property owners depend to exploit their [lands]." The assembly had been justified in maintaining slavery because "this only involves individuals from a foreign nation, who, because of their profound ignorance, the misfortunes linked to their expatriation, the consideration of their own interests, the imperious law of necessity, can only hope for a change of condition from time [and] the progress of the public spirit." With regard to the free men of color, however, "reason, good sense, the text of the laws say that the colonies are composed of all the free citizens who inhabit them," and there was therefore no excuse for denying them their rights. The final instructions approved by the National Assembly on 15 June 1791 firmly reminded the colonists that it was their duty to implement the decree "whose execution they can neither halt nor suspend."[92]

Just as the National Assembly was preparing to send these instructions to the colonies, the deputies were suddenly confronted with an urgent crisis that diverted their attention from all other issues. On the night of 20 June 1791, Louis XVI, Marie-Antoinette, and their children escaped from Paris, trying to reach a location near the frontier where they could, if needed, call on the queen's brother, the Habsburg emperor Leopold, to send troops to protect them. The king left behind a manifesto denouncing the changes the revolutionaries had made since the start of the movement. Colonial issues were forgotten as the deputies scrambled to decide how to react to the king's flight, and then to the news that the royal party had been stopped in the small town of Varennes and were being brought back to the capital. The National Assembly was now confronted with questions about the whole future of the Revolution and the country. Would the king be allowed to stay on the throne? If not, should the country follow the example of the United States and declare itself a republic?

The crisis caused by the king's flight provided the colonial deputies with an excuse to rejoin the National Assembly. Meanwhile, the leading members of the antislavery campaign became swept up in the arguments about the king's fate. Condorcet and his American friend Thomas Paine, who had moved to Paris, formed a small group to argue that France had no further need of a monarch. Brissot, Pétion, and Etienne Clavière participated in discussions about the idea, but Brissot hesitated to go that far. At the Jacobin Club, on 10 July 1791, he gave a vehement speech denouncing the idea that the king could not be judged for his actions: It was the first time he elevated himself to the top rank of revolutionary orators. His friend Madame Roland wrote that "he convinced people's minds, he electrified their souls."[93] As he looked forward to obtaining a seat in the new legislative assembly—the election process had begun on 16 June, just before the king's flight—Brissot could suddenly imagine himself as the man who might determine the destinies of France.

While Brissot and Milscent were speaking out for the abolitionist cause, the members of the Club Massiac cast around for some way to reverse the decision made on 15 May. At the end of June, the club president met with Barnave, who assured him that "he would continue to give the colonies his full attention."[94] Along with Pétion, Barnave had been one of the three assembly deputies dispatched to accompany the king and queen on their return journey from Varennes to Paris. During the carriage ride, he and the queen had reached an understanding that Barnave would use all his influence to convince the assembly to keep Louis on the throne, in exchange for his promise to accept the new constitution. Barnave also promised to work to modify features of that constitution that the king found particularly objectionable. Barnave's central argument was that an independent sovereign formed an essential counterweight to the power of an elected assembly that might be too susceptible to public opinion. On 15 July 1791 the National Assembly, swayed by Barnave's argument that the alternative was to "start the Revolution anew," voted to restore the king to the throne. In protest, both the Paris radicals of the Cordeliers Club and the more moderate members of the Jacobin Club drew up petitions; Brissot was the author of the Jacobins' document. On 17 July 1791 a large crowd gathered at the Champ de Mars, the present-day site of the Eiffel Tower, to sign the Cordeliers' petition. In response, the mayor of Paris, Jean-Sylvain Bailly, and Lafayette, the commander of the National Guard, sent in troops who fired on the crowd, killing at least sixty people.

The trauma of this "massacre of the Champ de Mars" transformed revolutionary politics. All but a handful of the National Assembly deputies withdrew from the Jacobin Club and formed a new grouping, the Feuillants, committed to following Barnave's conservative course. Lafayette, who had made one of his rare appearances at the National Assembly to support the cause of the free men of color in May, joined Barnave and separated himself from his former colleagues from the Amis des Noirs. Robespierre, who had carefully avoided endorsing the radical opposition to the restoration of the king, now emerged as the dominant figure in the Jacobins; unlike Brissot, he was a longtime member of the club and understood how to keep its network of provincial affiliates intact. Brissot's influence was growing rapidly, however, and he was determined to use it to promote the cause to which he had devoted so much of the previous three years.

While France was convulsed by the crisis precipitated by the king's flight, another crisis was unfolding in the Caribbean colonies. News of the 15 May 1791 decree reached Saint-Domingue on 30 June 1791, quickly followed by the resolutions from Bordeaux promising to help enforce it. In Cap Français, a furious crowd surrounded the meeting hall of the provincial assembly, applauding an address that promised that "the province of which we are the representatives, will never consent to receive laws from the grandsons of slaves." Grégoire was hanged in effigy, and there were threats to cut off all commerce with Bordeaux. Faced with the boiling anger of the colonists, governor Philibert François Rouxel de Blanchelande realized that he would not be able to put the decree into effect.[95] News of the "unanimous vow of the white colonists and the troops . . . against the decree of 15 May" in Saint-Domingue reached Paris at the end of August 1791. By this time, Barnave's effort to "revise" the constitution in a conservative direction was in full swing, and the colonists' violent opposition to the decree strengthened his hand. Always loyal to the colonists, the *Gazette universelle* published articles publicizing the colonists' resolve that "all the armies of the world will not be able to force the seating of a man of color in the colonial assembly of Saint-Domingue."[96] Alarmed by the disruption of trade with the colonies, even Bordeaux, which had so resoundingly embraced the decree of 15 May when it was passed, now sent addresses calling for its revocation. In Paris, the Jacobin Club, whose leadership now consisted largely of Brissot's closest associates from the Amis des Noirs, prepared for another confrontation with Barnave and his supporters. Brissot himself rushed to print a speech "on the necessity of maintaining the decree voted on 15 May," and Grégoire published an impassioned article denouncing the claim that the decree's supporters had any intention of advocating the immediate abolition of slavery.[97]

Finally, on 23 September, with the end of the National Assembly's session just a week away, Barnave made his move, giving what proved to be the final major oration of his career and setting off the last of the National Assembly's fiery debates on colonial issues, a debate that consumed two of the precious last days of that body's time. In his speeches in the May debate, Barnave had carefully avoided using the words "slaves" and "slavery," but he now abandoned that precaution. He admitted that the regime of the colonies was "contrary to nature," but this was, he argued, what made it necessary to rely on "prejudices" to sustain it. Otherwise, "the small number of whites could not control a great number of men of color. . . . This regime is oppressive," he continued, "but it allows several million men in France to live; this regime is barbarous, but sudden and violent efforts to end it would be even more barbarous."[98]

The speech Robespierre gave in response to Barnave was, like his adversary's, his last important intervention in the National Assembly. For the only time in his career, Robespierre gave a concrete description of the condition of the enslaved Blacks rather than referring to them in purely abstract terms, but the portrait he traced was not a sympathetic one. They would not be affected by debates about liberty because they were "men reduced to brutes by slavery, who have very few ideas, or only ideas entirely divorced from those we are discussing at the moment," and there was no danger that they would, "all at once, break with their old habits and their chains."[99] Having dismissed the possibility that the granting of rights to free men of color could undermine slavery, Robespierre deployed all his rhetorical skill on behalf of the intended beneficiaries of the decree of 15 May. "What is a man deprived of the rights of active citizenship in the colonies, under the dominion of the whites?" he asked. "He is a man humiliated, whose destiny is at the mercy of the caprices, the passions, the interests of a superior caste."[100] Robespierre received support from Grégoire, Pétion, and Dupont, but, as Carra's report put it, "the anti-Negro party counted on its forces and the exhaustion of the members who didn't have a firm view." On 24 September, the assembly voted to repeal the decree of 15 May. The only consolation the supporters of the abolitionist cause received came on 28 September, when the body voted to affirm the prerevolutionary "liberty principle" that "any individual is free as soon as he has entered France. Any man, regardless of color, enjoys all the rights of a citizen in France, if he meets the constitutional requirements for exercising them."[101]

After more than two years of repeated clashes about the issues of slavery and race, the National Assembly ended by leaving the prerevolutionary colonial order intact. The word "slavery" was kept out of the constitution, but the institution received explicit protection. The slave trade survived untouched, and the question of granting rights to free people of color beyond what they had enjoyed under the old regime was left to the discretion of the white colonists.

The deputies had acknowledged the contradiction between these decisions and the principles of the Declaration of the Rights of Man, but they had concluded that it was better to abandon a principle than to let the colonies perish. In a secret letter to Marie-Antoinette, Barnave presented the outcome as a great victory for the cause of the monarchy. Not only did the assembly's decision "go directly against the hopes of the republicans," but it would "give the king one more means to defeat them, by the influence it will give him with all of [our] commerce, whose relations with the colonies, put partly under the exclusive authority of the king, are immense." Barnave's enemy Brissot was left to lament the "dishonor that has been imprinted on the French Revolution."[102]

Even as Barnave celebrated and Brissot mourned, however, the storm cloud that had loomed over France's prized colony of Saint-Domingue since the start of the Revolution had unleashed its fury. Although the news would not reach France for nearly two months, the uprising that would become the largest slave revolt in recorded history began in the island's North Province on the night of 22–23 August 1791. Almost simultaneously, free men of color in the colony's West and South Provinces launched their own insurrection against the whites who had refused them even the slightest political concessions. When the news of these rebellions reached France in the last week of October, it completely changed the nature of the Revolution's confrontation with the issues the National Assembly had debated with such intensity.

CHAPTER SEVEN

Black Insurrection and Girondin Victory

ON 20 OCTOBER 1791 the merchant ship *Triton* docked in the northern French port of Le Havre bearing "terrible news." As the *Triton* was leaving Saint-Domingue two months earlier, it had encountered a small corvette whose captain reported the outbreak of a violent slave uprising in the northern part of the island, in which "ten thousand Negroes had been killed and that they had set fire to all the plantations on the plain" near the colony's major city, Cap Français. This was the first word received in France of the event that would transform the country's and the world's debates about race and slavery: the Black insurrection now called the Haitian Revolution. The municipal authorities in Havre hastily forwarded the news to Paris. "There may be some exaggeration in the report from the *Triton*," they wrote, "but certainly something bad has happened and it must be serious since the corvette was carrying orders for an embargo on shipping. There is the result of the letters of Bishop [Henri] Grégoire," the prominent critic of slavery, they concluded.[1]

Until the arrival of the news of the uprising that began on the night of 22–23 August 1791, the participants in the French debates, whether they opposed slavery or defended the colonial regime, had all shared the assumption that it would be decisions made in France, and not the actions of those whom Maximilien Robespierre, in his speech on the decree of 24 September 1791, had called "men reduced to brutes by slavery," that would determine the institution's future. Through the report from the *Triton*, the participants in the slave uprising suddenly made themselves what one modern scholar has called "invisible players" in metropolitan debates, a virtual presence that could not be ignored.[2] Already in the early reports that were printed in the French press in the last months of 1791, several of the movement's leaders—Boukman Dutty, Jean-François Papillon, Jeannot Bullet—were mentioned by name. For the next two years, until the French revolutionaries finally decided to decree the abolition of slavery and declare the inhabitants of Saint-Domingue to be free French citizens, the question of how to confront this unexpected challenge from the Blacks dominated metropolitan struggles over race and slavery.

The letter from Havre containing the report from the *Triton* was delivered to the ministry of the navy on 21 October, and on the following day, a member brought a copy of it to the Club Massiac. Just three weeks earlier, club members had been preparing a packet of Paris newspapers to send to Saint-Domingue with the good news of the repeal of the decree of 15 May granting political rights to free men of color. Now they suddenly confronted reports that evoked the fictional depictions of violence familiar from the pages of Jean-François Saint-Lambert's *Ziméo* and the *Histoire des deux Indes*. A delegation from the club met with the navy minister Bertrand de Molleville and the king on 23 October. Like the municipal authorities in Havre, Louis XVI immediately concluded that the uprising was inspired by "the indiscreet and incendiary letters that they say were sent to the colony." The *Gazette universelle* made the *Triton* captain's report public on 24 October, although it expressed doubt about the claim that ten thousand Blacks could have assembled so quickly, let alone have been killed so rapidly.[3]

The first actual letter from Saint-Domingue, sent from the southern city of Cayes on 31 August 1791, arrived in Bordeaux on 22 October. "We are about to be slaughtered by our Negroes," the writer lamented. Instead of blaming the French abolitionists, this author connected the uprising to the free men of color: He was sure that "it is the mulattos who are stirring up the Blacks in order to make themselves the masters."[4] Along with his own letter, the correspondent in Cayes attached a copy of a document from the new colonial legislative assembly that had just begun meeting in Le Cap a week earlier. This was the first actual account to reach France from the region affected by the insurrection. "A large number of the Negro slaves have gathered in the past few days. Wherever they go, they set fire and burn everything, and slaughter all the whites they encounter," it reported. A few days later, an English merchant passed along information sent by a well-known Jamaican plantation owner, Bryan Edwards, that confirmed these details and, from the French point of view, raised the question of whether the British would try to profit from their troubles.[5]

Within two weeks, Médéric Louis Élie Moreau de Saint-Méry had compiled a dossier of nearly twenty letters and reports from Saint-Domingue about the insurrection. The details they offered varied widely. One source estimated the number of participants at fifty thousand, while another said that only six thousand were involved. According to one letter, no whites had been killed; another gave an estimate of three hundred deaths. The revolt was spreading out of control, or it had already been defeated. The free men of color were fighting alongside the enslaved Blacks, or they were allying themselves with the whites. To compound the confusion and anxiety in Paris, no word came from General Philibert François Rouxel de Blanchelande, the colony's governor and the person who should have been the first to report such a serious event.[6]

The news of the insurrection was a shock for the colonists, many of whom realized that their own properties had been devastated, but it was also a shock for the French abolitionists. Their assumption that the enslaved Blacks would suffer in silence until their self-proclaimed allies in France could bring about a change in their condition was no longer tenable. As the first reactions to the news from Saint-Domingue showed, the reformers risked being blamed for the uprising, despite their caution about explicitly advocating the abolition of slavery. Brissot and Grégoire had been prepared to justify Ogé's resort to force on behalf of the free men of color in 1790, but they hesitated to extend that argument to the more numerous slave population. Just a month prior to the arrival in France of the news of the slave uprising, Grégoire had asserted that "morality forbids putting a kind of knife in the hands of a child who could use it to injure himself or others. The negroes are, so to speak, big children. Left to themselves, they will perish or kill others."[7]

The news of the Saint-Domingue insurrection arrived in France just as the new constitution drawn up by the National Assembly was being put into effect. On 30 September 1791, after more than two exhausting years of debates, the National Assembly gave way to its successor. The transition was supposed to mark the end of the revolutionary interval and the beginning of an era of political stability. The changeover also meant a turnover in political personnel. Because of Robespierre's self-denying ordinance, the figures who had dominated the scene since 1789—Robespierre himself, as well as Emmanuel Sieyès, Antoine Barnave, Grégoire, Moreau de Saint-Méry, Pierre-Victor Malouet, and Jean-Siffrein Maury—were now replaced by an entirely different cast of characters. Few of the 745 newly elected deputies arrived in Paris with national reputations. Jacques-Pierre Brissot was an exception: Thanks to his newspaper, his name was already familiar to the public and to his new colleagues.

Compared with the two "great" assemblies of the French Revolution, the National Assembly of 1789–91 that began the Revolution and the National Convention of 1792–95 whose dramatic decisions created the Republic and the Terror, the Legislative Assembly of 1791–92 has never attracted much attention from historians. Elected under a law that limited the right to vote to men paying a certain level of taxes, it lost legitimacy as radical democratic ideas spread in the country. The legislators immediately found themselves in conflict with Louis XVI, whose attempt to flee the country in June 1791 had shown his hostility to the new ideas introduced since 1789. After just eleven months, in August 1792, both the king and the Legislative Assembly were swept away by a popular uprising and replaced by a National Convention chosen by universal manhood suffrage. During its short life, however, the Legislative Assembly made important decisions on a number of critical issues. Its measures intensified the religious conflict stemming from the Civil Constitution of the Clergy, and it was responsible for the decision to plunge France into a war that would last almost without interruption until the final defeat of Napoleon in 1815. It also fell to the Legislative Assembly to confront the outbreak of the Haitian

Revolution. The assembly's one modern historian has claimed that its members "were glad to forget so awkward a problem," but in fact, they took up "the affair of the colonies" repeatedly, in sessions that were just as stormy as the debates in the National Assembly, and the decree on behalf of free men of color that they passed on 24 March 1792 was as significant as any of the measures about race and slavery passed in the French Revolution's first two years.[8]

Brissot had missed his chance to participate in the National Assembly. Now he finally had his opportunity not just to comment on great national issues but to influence decisions on them directly. His growing prominence in revolutionary politics in the spring and summer of 1791, due largely to his campaign for racial justice, had won him numerous admirers but also a number of increasingly vocal enemies. Brissot's opponents were sufficiently numerous to see that he was only the fourteenth deputy elected to represent Paris, but the crucial thing, from his point of view, was that he did finally win a seat. Condorcet, his faithful ally from the Amis des Noirs, joined him, and the department of the Gironde, the district of the port city of Bordeaux, sent several deputies, including Sylvain Vergniaud, Arnaud Gensonné, and Marguerite-Elie Guadet, who had already shown their abolitionist sympathies in local debates about colonial policy. They would become so closely identified with Brissot that the group around him became known as the Girondins. Jean-Philippe Garran-Coulon, a close ally of Brissot in Paris municipal politics, who would survive to become one of the strongest defenders of abolition after the Terror, and Jean-François Delacroix, from Brissot's home town of Chartres, who would play a crucial role in the passage of the decree of 16 pluviôse, were also elected, and a number of other deputies proved to have abolitionist sympathies.

Initially, moderates associated with the Feuillants Club that Barnave had founded in July 1791 outnumbered members of the more radical Jacobins in the Legislative Assembly, although sympathy for the Feuillants did not necessarily imply opposition to abolitionist ideas.[9] The supporters of the colonial cause were probably not happy about the makeup of the new assembly. Robespierre's self-denying ordinance had banished their most effective advocates, and the new constitution did not allot seats to the colonies.

The new legislature did include some deputies with strong loyalties to the colonial regime, such as Vincent-Marie Viénot de Vaublanc; Charles Tarbé, who became the regular spokesman for the colonial committee; and Salvador-Paul Leremboure, son of the mayor of Port-au-Prince, but they proved less effective than their predecessors in the National Assembly.

Outside the assembly, the balance of forces was more favorable to the abolitionists. In the aftermath of the struggle over the rights of free men of color during the spring and summer of 1791 and the controversies following the king's flight to Varennes, moderates had quit the Jacobin clubs. Brissot was loudly cheered by the other members of the Paris club when he was elected to the Legislative Assembly, and numerous provincial clubs sent protests after the passage of the decree of 24 September 1791 revoking the rights of free men of color in the colonies.[10] In order to devote himself to his legislative duties, Brissot turned over much of the day-to-day running of the *Patriote françois* to his associate, Jean-Marie Girey-Dupré, but the paper continued to follow his line on racial issues. Although he rarely spoke in the assembly, Condorcet published daily accounts of the debates in the *Chronique de Paris* in which he promoted the abolitionist cause. Other titles that had already embraced abolitionist positions, such as the *Annales patriotiques* and the *Révolutions de Paris*, remained steadfast in their principles. The radical activist Jean-Marie Collot d'Herbois's pamphlet *L'Almanach du Père Gérard*, aimed at the peasant population, used folksy language to warn the common people against "the orators who plead so strongly for the despotism of the whites."[11]

Whereas the Jacobin Club recovered quickly from the effects of the split with the Feuillants in July 1791, the new rival club was unable to build an equivalent network of supporters. Newspapers sympathetic to the colonial cause, such as the *Gazette universelle*, were more successful. The royal government provided that paper with a secret subsidy, enlarging its circulation to the point where the editors had to apologize to readers about their difficulties in producing enough copies for all of them.[12] The colonists could count on the sympathies of Louis XVI. On 2 November 1791 a delegation from the Club Massiac was received by the king and his family. The king "tried to console the colonists with judicious reflections and the most touching expressions," the delegates reported, and the queen was so overcome with emotion at hearing their stories that she broke into tears.[13]

Under the new constitution, however, it was the Legislative Assembly more than the king that determined the country's reaction to the Saint-Domingue insurrection. Debates on the matter quickly turned as vitriolic as the confrontations on colonial issues in the National Assembly. Along with equally violent disagreements about the enforcement of the controversial reform of the Catholic Church and the proper response to the growing threat from counterrevolutionary émigrés who were gathering in the German principalities across the Rhine, these debates contributed to the triumph of Brissot and the more radical faction in the assembly. History has remembered Brissot above all for his campaign in favor of launching an offensive war against the foreign powers whose toleration of the émigrés constituted, in his view, an existential threat to the Revolution. With his characteristic optimism, Brissot was sure that the patriotic spirit of France's troops would guarantee victory and the overturning of monarchies throughout Europe. Brissot's campaign was supported by most of the Jacobins, with the exception of Robespierre, who warned prophetically that "no one likes armed missionaries." Brissot's split with Robespierre would have serious repercussions for the abolitionist movement that both men had earlier supported.

Even as Brissot plunged into the campaign for war, he remained committed to remaking the racial order in the colonies. On 27 October 1791, just days after the arrival of the first reports about the slave uprising in Saint-Domingue, he gave his first speech on the matter. Other deputies had already made it clear that the issue would be a divisive one. No doubt anticipating what Brissot would say, one warned that, even in the face of the revolt, it would never be possible to force the whites in the colony to accept full equality with the free men of color. Another speaker, however, reminded his colleagues that "we have declared, in the Rights of Man, that insurrection against slavery and servitude is the most sacred of duties. In consequence, we should not condemn men to that condition."[14]

Despite his high-flying rhetoric about natural rights, Brissot was not ready to go that far. He was, however, determined to make any aid to the colony conditional on the granting of the demands of the free men of color that he had supported so vehemently for the previous two years. Earlier in his career, Brissot had written a lengthy treatise on philosophical skepticism; now he applied skeptical reasoning to the reports about the Saint-Domingue uprising. “You should never forget that all the news that reaches you from the colonies should be regarded with suspicion,” he insisted. Surely the movement could not be as extensive as the most lurid accounts claimed. Why had the news reached London before it arrived in Paris? Why hadn’t Governor Blanchelande sent an official dispatch? “How was it possible to assemble 50,000 Blacks in a few days? Could a revolt grow so large in a few days in a country where the plantations are dispersed?” And was it not suspicious that “the news of this catastrophe arrives precisely at a moment when emigration is increasing so strikingly[?] . . . Isn’t this one part of a large plan that will no doubt fail like all the others?” In any event, there was only one remedy for the crisis: the granting of citizenship rights to the free men of color, “the true defense of Saint-Domingue.”[15]

In casting doubt on the seriousness of the uprising and in insisting that it proved the necessity of relying on the free men of color in the colony, Brissot drew heavily on arguments furnished by Claude Milscent, the white colonist whose firsthand experience allowed him to play the role of oracle on these issues. In a pamphlet written at the end of October 1791 and republished in the *Patriote françois* and also in the leading London newspaper of the day, the *Morning Chronicle*, Milscent traced the history of slave revolts in Saint-Domingue. They had always been nothing more than “the project that some determined Negroes have formed several times . . . to throw off the yoke of slavery, and to take refuge in the woods.” In the present case, he thought it likely that “what is deliberately labeled, in order to scare the assembly, as a general uprising, is only one of the incidents of which I have spoken, blown up, according to the custom always followed in the colony, and in accordance with the colonial spirit.”[16]

By the middle of November, after official dispatches from Governor Blanchelande had finally arrived, it was no longer possible to deny the seriousness of the uprising. When the government requested 10 million livres to cover the expenses of sending ships and troops to Saint-Domingue, however, a number of deputies raised objections to giving the king's agents such a large sum without conditions. Some wanted to insist that only patriotic National Guards, rather than professional soldiers from the royal army, should be sent to the Caribbean. The deputy Merlin de Thionville, one of a small group of legislators representing the most radical fringe of the Jacobin movement, raised a more fundamental objection that hinted at the possibility of a left-wing position more radical than Brissot's. "It is indecent that the farmer and the agricultural worker, that the people . . . should have to suffer from excessive expenses from which it does not profit," he complained. "If anyone benefits from the alleged profits that are made from the colonies, it is the privileged classes . . . the rich." He proposed that the Saint-Domingue colonists be required to repay the money being spent to defend them.[17]

Merlin's populist outburst drew applause from the spectators' gallery, but the majority of the deputies were not ready to abandon the colonies to their fate. Meanwhile, another element entered the discussion. Governor Blanchelande's official letters explained that the colony was experiencing not just one insurrection but two. In the colony's West Province, free men of color, more numerous in that region than in the north, had not only taken up arms but had defeated the whites and forced them to sign a peace treaty, or "concordat," that granted them rights even more extensive than those promised by the National Assembly decree of 15 May 1791. The concordat, which the Jacobin Club in Bordeaux applauded as "the triumph of reason and philosophy over pride and prejudice," was the realization of the program for racial equality among free people in the colonies that Brissot and his allies had been advocating for the previous two years. They seized on this development to insist that any troops and government commissioners sent to Saint-Domingue be instructed not to enforce the decree of 24 September 1791, since it would conflict with the concordat and prevent the union of whites and free men of color that they had long advocated as the only way to defend against a slave insurrection.[18] In Saint-Domingue itself, the concordat split the white population. Some large landowners accepted it as a way to build an alliance to prevent a slave revolt in their region, but other whites vehemently rejected the dismantling of racial hierarchy. By the time the deputies in Paris were hailing the concordat as the key to restoring peace in the colony, renewed conflict between intransigent whites and free men of color had boiled over into a melée that destroyed most of the colonial capital of Port-au-Prince, a demonstration of how far removed the debates in Paris were from the reality in Saint-Domingue.[19]

By the end of November, the Legislative Assembly had still not reached agreement on what conditions should be set on the assistance being prepared for Saint-Domingue. At this point, a delegation of members from the colony's General Assembly arrived in Paris, where they immediately met with the members of the Club Massiac to plan their strategy.[20] On 30 November 1791 they were allowed to speak to the Legislative Assembly, setting up the first direct confrontation between Caribbean slaveholders and Brissot. For decades, opponents of slavery had used emotionally charged stories about the atrocities inflicted on the Blacks to stir up sympathy for their cause. Now the colonists' spokesman, J.-B. Millet, employed the same strategy to evoke support for the white colonists. The litany of cruelties he recited, beginning with the claim that the Black insurgents "had for a banner the corpse of a white child, impaled on the point of a pike," was destined to be repeated endlessly in subsequent accounts of the Haitian Revolution. The cause of insurrection had nothing to do with the treatment of the enslaved Blacks, Millet insisted. Instead, it was entirely the fault of the Amis des Noirs. In his version of events, that organization "seizes on the Declaration of the Rights of Man, an immortal work and excellent for enlightened men, but inapplicable and therefore dangerous in our regime. It distributes it with profusion in the colonies; the newspapers that it subsidizes or seduces make sure the declaration is heard among our slave gangs."[21] Engravings published in Paris gave visual form to the colonists' descriptions of the uprising (figure 8).

At the end of his speech, Millet demanded not only the rapid dispatch of troops to put down the uprising but measures against the abolitionists. The colonists wanted to see "the firmness with which you will punish the authors of our disasters, and repress their new efforts." The abolitionist deputies were outraged by this

FIGURE 8: *The Slave Uprising in Saint-Domingue.* News of the slave uprising that began in Saint-Domingue in August 1791 reached France in late October of that year. Colonists' letters emphasized violence against whites, although the number of Blacks killed in the fighting was far higher. *Credit:* Bibliothèque nationale de France.

vehement attack. Claude Basire, another of the assembly's far-left firebrands, challenged the body's presiding officer: "How can you allow men who have outraged philosophy and freedom to join the session?" Nevertheless, as Carra's *Annales patriotiques* admitted, "initially the legislators . . . let themselves be moved by pity."[22] The Saint-Domingue colonists circulated their version of events to cities all across France, asking for expressions of support. "The hideous tableau that you have painted of these monstrosities shocks reason and stuns our intellectual faculties," the mayor and municipal officers of Tonneins replied.[23]

On the next day, Brissot occupied the podium for nearly four hours, delivering the longest oration about colonial issues ever given in any of the revolutionary legislatures. The passion with which he denounced the white colonists was every bit as intense as that with which Millet had attacked the Amis des Noirs. For Brissot, the debate between the two sides was "a battle between liberty and despotism, a battle conducted in the very temple of liberty." The deputies needed to understand that "it is not only a revolt by Blacks that you need to punish, it is a revolt by whites. The revolt of these Blacks has been only a means, an instrument in the hands of these whites who want to free themselves from dependence on France in order to free themselves from laws that humiliate their vanity, and from these debts that interfere with their taste for dissipation." Why, he demanded, had Governor Blanchelande and the colonial assembly invited foreign intervention by sending appeals for aid to the neighboring British and Spanish colonies and to the United States before they notified the French government of the situation? Why had Blanchelande not immediately sent his troops to disperse the Blacks, instead of giving the revolt time to spread? "Wasn't it to give the rebels the time and the means to enlarge their forces, and to ravage all the plantations?" Why had he not called on the free men of color, the only dependably patriotic element of the population, whose cause, Brissot insisted, was "the cause of the patriots, of the former Third Estate, in short, of the people"? And why, he wanted to know, had the colonists' spokesman not mentioned "this sublime concordat, of which Locke and Montesquieu would have been proud, this concordat . . . which is the only thing that can protect the whites from the insurrections of the Blacks?"[24]

Brissot recognized the emotional impact of the horror stories told by the colonists. But if the Blacks committed brutalities, it was because they themselves had been brutalized by the whites, who had thrown Blacks into roaring furnaces, separated infants from their mothers, and even, he claimed, forced enslaved captives to eat their own flesh. The Black insurrection needed to be brought under control, he agreed, but the most urgent measure required to maintain French authority in Saint-Domingue was the suspension and indictment of the entire membership of the colonial assembly and Governor Blanchelande and their replacement by a newly elected colonial legislature in which free men of color would be represented, together with the dispatch of commissioners and troops from France to see that the metropole's decisions were enforced. As for the colonists' demand for measures against the Amis des Noirs, Brissot replied, "Accuse so many philosophers who wrote before it existed, and who wrote the same truths as it did; accuse the Constituent Assembly itself, which approved these truths; accuse the Declaration of Rights, the most philosophical work and the one most capable, thanks to its concision and its character, of electrifying minds."[25]

Although they had avoided the issue of slavery, Millet and Brissot injected a new level of anger and hostility into debates about "the affair of the colonies." Neither was willing to concede, as the obscure deputy Jean-François Michon-Dumarais put it, "that it is much more natural to think that the sentiment of liberty . . . has awakened with energy in the soul of some proud and courageous Negroes, . . . and that the spark from their mind, which, although it is covered by a Negro's woolly hair, is capable of powerful thoughts, has inspired all those who have broken their chains."[26] Instead, Millet and Brissot both propounded elaborate conspiracy theories that blamed their white opponents for plotting to destroy the country. By demanding judicial proceedings against those he blamed for committing treason, Brissot, in particular, foreshadowed the lethal politics of what would come to be called the Reign of Terror.

Throughout the week following Millet's and Brissot's speeches, angry debate about the crisis in Saint-Domingue continued. At one point, the assembly became so chaotic that the body's president shouted at his colleagues, "In the name of the fatherland, shut up!" Brissot and his allies insisted that no troops be sent to the colony unless it was specified that they would not be used to put down the movement of the free men of color. The deputy Jacques Brival, who said that his wife owned property in Saint-Domingue, went even further. He demanded that the military officers sent to the colony be instructed that they could not "in any circumstances . . . employ their forces, either to maintain slavery, or to deprive the free men of color of their status as active citizens." To counter the clamor to link aid to the colony to the granting of rights to the free men of color, pro-colonial deputies found themselves arguing to delay any decision until the assembly's colonial committee was able to make a full report on the situation. Since an initial contingent of soldiers and the three members of the civil commission originally authorized the previous February had left the port of Brest en route to the colony in September, the Legislative Assembly set the issue aside, finding one excuse after another not to make any further decisions on policy despite periodic alarming reports from its colonial committee.[27]

Although it did not immediately provoke any action from the Legislative Assembly, the slave uprising in Saint-Domingue provoked some new thinking about racial issues in metropolitan France. At the beginning of 1791, when news of the short-lived revolt of free men of color led by Vincent Ogé had reached France, Brissot had justified their resort to violent means to defend their rights, but he had been careful to point out that Ogé was not seeking to overthrow the system of slavery. In response to the much larger slave uprising that had now broken out, Brissot and his allies continued to insist that the policy exemplified by the concordat in Saint-Domingue was the only way of maintaining slavery. Jean-Paul Marat, the fire-breathing journalist who called himself the "Ami du Peuple" (Friend of the People), saw things otherwise. Unlike Brissot, Marat had little real concern for the Black population in the colonies, and he fully embraced the idea that the uprising was part of a conspiracy on the part of the king's ministers and the moderate party in France "to use secret agents to push the peoples to insurrection, to oblige the Assembly to authorize them to constantly employ armed force to restore calm." But he was happy to contrast the apathy of "men degraded by their long servitude, weakness and addiction to pleasures, such as the Parisians and the majority of the French," with the behavior of Saint-Domingue's men of color and Blacks.[28]

While Marat was openly praising the Saint-Domingue insurgents' resort to violence, Camille Desmoulins, another journalist with a reputation as a revolutionary firebrand, seized on the same violence to blame Brissot for damaging the cause of liberty. Writing just as the issue of declaring war against Austria was dividing the Jacobin movement and turning Desmoulins's friend Robespierre against Brissot, Desmoulins did to his target what Brissot had done to Barnave a year earlier, portraying him as a traitor to the Revolution because of his involvement with the issue of slavery.

By threatening the interests of the port cities, Desmoulins charged, Brissot had turned their populations against the Revolution, and by stirring up the enslaved Blacks, he had made himself responsible for the Saint-Domingue uprising. "Yes, if so many plantations are reduced to ashes, if women have been disemboweled, if an infant carried at the end of a pike has served as a banner for the Blacks, if the Blacks themselves have perished by the thousands, it is you, you wretch, who has been the cause of so many evils. Would you have behaved otherwise, if you had been colluding with Coblentz and the Austrian committee [the agents of the counterrevolution]?" he asked. Desmoulins's explosive polemic foreshadowed the alliance that many radical Jacobins would later make with proslavery advocates in order to destroy their common enemy, Brissot's Girondin faction.[29]

Olympe de Gouges, the advocate of women's rights who had proudly proclaimed herself one of the earliest opponents of colonial slavery, also condemned the violence of the Black uprising. Just a few months earlier, in September 1791, she had published her historic "Declaration of the Rights of Women," a landmark in the history of feminism. In February 1792, however, in a preface to the published version of her play *The Slavery of the Blacks, or, the Fortunate Shipwreck*, whose performance at the end of 1789 had outraged the colonial party, she told the enslaved Blacks and the men of color that "by imitating the cruelty of tyrants, you vindicate them. . . . In your blind rage you do not distinguish innocent victims from your persecutors. Men were not born to be in chains, yet you prove that they are necessary." The oppressed populations in the colonies needed to recognize that they had to submit to the law. "If the savage, ferocious man does not recognize it, he is made to be loaded with chains and broken like a beast."[30]

In between the two extremes represented by Marat's eager embrace of Black violence and Desmoulins's and de Gouges's condemnations of it, two members of the new political class associated with the Legislative Assembly, the deputy Mathieu Blanc-Gilli and the "substitute deputy" Armand-Guy Kersaint, reacted to the situation created by the Saint-Domingue insurrection by concluding that slavery as it had existed in the colony could not be restored and offering detailed proposals for its gradual abolition. In the speeches by the white colonists from Saint-Domingue and Brissot, Blanc-Gilli wrote, the sufferings of the whites and the free men of color had been amply depicted, but no one had spoken for "the most numerous, the most mistreated of the three classes" of the colonial population. The news of the Declaration of Rights had given the Blacks "the hope . . . of seeing [their] irons, if not broken, at least made less oppressive. Imagine the pain in their hearts, when they saw all eyes turn away from them. Then they have calculated the chances of revolt . . . in the initial convulsions of their despair, they were heard speaking these words that the legislators must take seriously: 'This land belongs to us . . . we have watered it enough with our blood and our tears to make it our property.'" Kersaint, a naval administrator with property in Saint-Domingue, saw no reason why France should spend lives and treasure to defend a social system "which can only be a state of war, of sedition, of rebellion and of crime. . . . Will she deploy the efforts of free citizens to place new chains on the unfortunate Africans?"[31]

Both Blanc-Gilli and Kersaint stopped short of calling for the immediate abolition of slavery, but their proposals broke new ground in the abolition debate by acknowledging that the Saint-Domingue revolt made it impossible to maintain the colonial status quo with regard to slavery. Both rejected the notion that the uprising proved the inherent savagery of the Blacks. Both also endorsed the demands of the free men of color, but, unlike Brissot and the mainstream abolitionists, they did not do so for the purpose of enrolling them to force the Blacks back into submission. Among the slave owners alarmed by the radicalism of Kersaint's proposal was the Paris spokesman for the free men of color, Julien Raimond. Acting as the editor of Kersaint's pamphlet, which was published by the Cercle social, Raimond inserted a lengthy footnote into the text, insisting that "the first thing that must be done is to get the slaves back to the plantations and their daily tasks."[32]

Like Raimond, Claude Milscent, who would eventually become the first French abolitionist to conclude that the Saint-Domingue revolt made it necessary to accept the immediate end of slavery, was still far from adopting positions as radical as those of Blanc-Gilli and Kersaint at the end of 1791. In a lengthy pamphlet, he postulated that slaves were needed to work the colony's plantations, and that if they were abruptly declared free, they would harbor so much resentment against their former masters that they would never agree to continue working for them as paid laborers. In addition, he wrote, "one could not deprive the master of his slave without paying him its value." Nevertheless, he agreed, something had to be done to improve the slaves' lot. Milscent proposed to offer enslaved people the opportunity to earn a certain amount of money that they could eventually use to purchase their freedom. He was careful to explain, however, that his system would be calculated to ensure that they could only accumulate the necessary funds through many decades of steady effort and that most of them would no doubt be at the end of their working lives before they succeeded. He saw this as an advantage of his scheme from the master's point of view: "Thanks to his slave's almost illusory hope, he will have gained doubly, from his work and his loyalty; the slave will have been kept happy for a long time by a far-off and often imaginary perspective."[33]

While journalists and legislators debated the legitimacy of armed revolt against the colonial racial order and put forward plans for the gradual abolition of slavery, common people in Paris reacted violently to the Saint-Domingue insurrection's most direct impact on their lives: the sudden increase in the price of sugar. Disturbances at grocers' shops put the abolitionists in an awkward position, since they seemed to vindicate the claim that the defenders of the institution regularly made about the importance of the colonial regime to the lives of ordinary French people. In his newspaper, Brissot offered a contorted response, claiming that the impact of the Saint-Domingue uprising on sugar production had been exaggerated, that "fear, the daughter of ignorance," was driving speculators to buy up supplies, and that colonial sugar would soon be replaced by maple syrup from North America and new supplies raised by free laborers in Africa and Asia. The sugar shortage, he added, "will no doubt have a good effect, that of making us realize the absurdity of making our existence dependent on foreign plants, and of making us return to the native products of our own country."[34] The embarrassment with which he and other "patriots" who saw themselves as defenders of the people reacted to the sugar riots reflected their fear that a populist movement in the metropole might not work to their advantage.

The various proposals for the eventual ending of slavery put forward in response to the news of the Saint-Domingue uprising were all premised on the notion that the insurrection could be brought under control and the Black population persuaded or forced to accept a gradual and orderly process of abolition. At the time, this notion did not seem entirely unrealistic: In December 1791, after the arrival of the first French civil commission, the leaders of the insurrection made a proposal to end the violence and urge their followers to return to work in exchange for freedom for themselves and an amnesty for the other participants in the uprising.[35] The colonial assembly insisted on the insurgents' unconditional surrender, however, and negotiations were broken off. Meanwhile, in France, the colonists' representatives realized that the price of military assistance from the metropole was going to be the granting of equality to the free people of color.[36]

While the colonial debate remained stalled, Brissot engineered a political revolution in Paris. On 14 March 1792 he forced the resignation of the ministers appointed by the king and their replacement by figures ready to back his demand for a declaration of war against Austria. As a member of the assembly, Brissot could not himself take a ministerial post, but the men chosen were close allies of the Girondins and Brissot was now regarded as the real leader of the government. Louis XVI accepted this unnatural alliance with one of his most outspoken enemies because he and Marie-Antoinette had decided "force and foreign help" were their only remaining chances to defeat the Revolution.[37]

Preoccupied as he was with remaking the ministry and pushing France into war, Brissot had not forgotten the cause that had first brought him to political prominence. On 21 March 1792, while the new ministry was still being put together, he strode to the Legislative Assembly's rostrum and delivered another version of his by-now-familiar argument denouncing the decree of 24 September 1791 that had repealed the measure adopted the previous May in favor of the free men of color. If their rights had been recognized, he insisted, the slave uprising would never have broken out. Rather than abandon their racial prejudices, he claimed, the whites in the colony's assembly "contemplate the burning of the plantations with indifference." The Black insurrection "is not completely put down," he acknowledged, but the slaves were "tranquil wherever the men of color are the masters, turbulent and seditious wherever the whites triumph."[38]

Brissot's tirade was the opening shot in another of the Revolution's lengthy debates about race and slavery. For four days, advocates and critics of equality for free men of color exchanged rhetorical blows and heckled and interrupted their opponents, just as their predecessors in the National Assembly had done in May 1791. Brissot was ably seconded by his allies from Bordeaux, Gensonné and Guadet. According to the *Patriote françois*, Guadet's speech on 23 March "offered an incredible abundance of new arguments. Sentiment, energy, logic, and irony, he managed to combine all these colors with the most delicate artistry. . . . He was powerfully moving when he responded to those who wanted to leave the fate of the mulattos up to the whites, as he enumerated all the excesses, all the betrayals, all the crimes of the latter."[39]

The defenders of colonial interests did their best to fight back, but they knew that they were at a disadvantage. Writing to their counterparts in Saint-Domingue after the final vote, the delegates of the colony's assembly sadly reported that "not only the members of the national assembly, but also the public galleries, were exalted to the point where there would have been danger to anyone who expressed a contrary opinion." Nevertheless, several speakers, notably Mathieu Dumas and Vaublanc, did their best. Both conceded that slavery was a bad thing but, as the defenders of the colonial regime had always done, they emphasized the danger of trying to abolish it abruptly. Given the disproportion between the small number of whites and the large population of enslaved Blacks, Dumas argued, the belief in white racial superiority, while irrational, was necessary to maintain social order. In his speech, Vaublanc artfully wove in references to Guillaume Thomas François Raynal, Jean-Jacques Rousseau, Sieyès, and the reforming old regime minister Etienne-François Turgot to defend the proposition that reforms needed to be made gradually and cautiously. He admitted that it would have been sensible for the whites in Saint-Domingue to "have the wisdom to make a fraternal alliance with the men of color." Nevertheless, he insisted that the white colonists deserved the privilege of making this decision for themselves, rather than having it imposed on them, and he tried to embarrass Brissot by reminding him that in 1789, he himself had said that the colonies should be allowed to make their own laws.[40]

At the end of the fourth day of debate, Gensonné offered a motion to repeal the decree of 24 September 1791. Any opposition to his position, he said, was the sign of an "odious conspiracy." To give teeth to the message, Gensonné's motion called for the naming of a new civil commission, a new colonial governor, and the dispatch of a significant military force.[41] Although Brissot and his allies hewed to the position enunciated by the Amis des Noirs from its inception by denying that they had any intention of raising the question of slavery—Guadet had insisted "that is not I who wants to violently destroy the slavery of the Blacks in our islands. If my conscience could reproach me with anything, it is rather that I am assuring its survival with my proposal"—the debate about the decree of 24 March 1792 showed that some people hoped that its passage was a first step in that direction. The Girondin deputy Jean-François Ducos sought to add a provision to the decree declaring that all mixed-race children born in the colonies should be declared free and that the tax imposed on masters who freed their slaves should be abolished. In the *Patriote françois*, Brissot's close ally Garran-Coulon took the colonist Milscent to task, even though Milscent was an outspoken advocate of rights for the free men of color. Milscent had argued that if slavery was abolished, the slave owners would have a right to compensation. Garran-Coulon replied that a fundamental legal principle opposed the payment of compensation to anyone who purchased stolen goods, and that "this denial of a claim is even more justified when it concerns the most precious good of all, the only genuinely natural form of property, that of one's person."[42]

Louis XVI signed the law on 4 April 1792, and it became known as the law of that date. The king presumably regarded his approval as part of the price for the assembly's consent to the declaration of war against Austria that he requested on 20 April. The law of 4 April was in no sense an attack on the institution of slavery. The constitutional law of 13 May 1791, which promised that any changes in that institution would have to emanate from the colonies themselves, remained intact and, as Brissot and Guadet made clear in their speeches, one of the main justifications for the law of 4 April was the claim that it would strengthen the forces struggling to put down the Black insurrection in Saint-Domingue. Nor did it affect the slave trade, which may explain why opposition in the port cities was limited. Nevertheless, the new law marked a significant step in the direction of racial equality. In contrast to the decree of 15 May 1791, which applied only to a small minority of the free population of color, the new law promised rights to all of them. At a time when free Blacks in the American states that had adopted gradual emancipation laws still did not enjoy anything like equal rights of citizenship, the French law went beyond anything that had been enacted in any other part of the Atlantic world. Reviewing the Legislative Assembly's accomplishments in the first half of 1792, Condorcet wrote that 24 March 1792, the date on which the decree was passed, deserved to be included among the "glorious dates for French liberty."[43]

For a brief moment, the coincidence between the passage of the law of 4 April and a vote in the British House of Commons to abolish the slave trade raised hopes that there might be an opening for action on that matter as well. The British abolitionist Lord Stanhope wrote to Condorcet, "We have arrived at the glorious moment when philosophy and reason are making justice triumph everywhere."[44] On 10 April 1792 Emmanuel Pastoret, who had been a member of the Amis des Noirs in its early days, said that France should follow the British example, so that "there should no longer be any rivalry between the two nations other than to work together for the welfare of the human race." The proslavery colonists were sure the British vote was a trick meant to lure the French into making a hasty decision, and their supporters in the Legislative Assembly, anticipating correctly that the House of Lords would kill the British bill, sent Pastoret's suggestion to the colonial committee, where it was buried.[45]

Although Pastoret's motion failed to galvanize any action by the French legislature, it did inspire an outspoken article denouncing slavery and the slave trade in the *Révolutions de Paris*, an article noteworthy because its author, Pierre Chaumette, was destined to play a central role in abolitionist campaigns in 1793 and 1794. As a young man, Chaumette had been a crew member on naval ships sailing to the Caribbean, where he had come face-to-face with the reality of slavery. By 1790 he was in Paris, where he eventually became a regular contributor to the radical weekly. "The most fervent friends of the Blacks have, up to now, maintained a painful silence, both about the slave trade and slavery," he complained. There could be no further hesitation about abolishing "this cannibalistic commerce." As far as slavery itself was concerned, everyone in France was still claiming "that the Negroes aren't ready for freedom . . . but the insurrection in the colonies, the de facto emancipation of the Negroes, has taught them more in six months than a constitutional and metaphysical catechism would have done in six years. The slaves in America have seen their masters tremble; and when a master has trembled, there are no more slaves."[46]

Chaumette's article foreshadowed the radical measures that would be taken in 1793 and 1794, but in the spring of 1792, things had not yet reached that point. Unbeknownst to the politicians in Paris as they debated the law of 4 April, however, events in Saint-Domingue were already turning to the advantage of the cause of the free men of color there. Frustrated by the intransigence of the white colonists, two of the three members of the First Civil Commission had left the island. Their remaining colleague, Philippe Roume, although he could not have known of the debates taking place in Paris, then joined forces with Pierre Pinchinat, the leader of the armed free men of color in the colony's West Province. In the spring of 1792, Pinchinat created the biracial Council of Peace and Union to challenge the authority of the all-white colonial assembly in Cap Français. Acting on his own, Roume decided to give Pinchinat's council his backing. "One sees this league start by vigorously denouncing both the Provincial Assembly of the West and the Colonial Assembly as responsible for all public misfortunes, and then sees a national civil commissioner applaud this insurrection and keep it going," Roume wrote to the French government. "Either the Colonial Assembly is guilty of the charges against it, or the commissioner deserves the ultimate punishment."[47] Since many whites had fled the colony after the outbreak of the insurrections, there was now a realistic prospect that the free men of color could gain control of the colony's institutions.

Brissot was too busy with other issues to spend much time celebrating the victory of the free men of color. Julien Raimond, the chief spokesman for the free men of color in Paris, took a larger role in underlining the law's significance. On 30 March, even before the king had approved it, he led a delegation of free men of color to congratulate the Legislative Assembly for what it had done. "It was given to you, Messieurs, to look with benevolence on the colonies, and to destroy in them the last and the most disastrous of prejudices," Raimond said.[48] Press commentaries on the new law after it was passed were limited, although the Bordeaux *Courier de la Gironde* published a lengthy article denouncing its opponents. Bordeaux was not the only place outside Paris where its significance was recognized. At least ten National Guard units, representing widely scattered parts of the country, wrote to the Legislative Assembly volunteering to be sent to the Caribbean to enforce the law.[49]

Thanking the Legislative Assembly was only one of Raimond's concerns in the wake of the passage of the law of 4 April. There was the question of who would be named as members of the new civil commission that would be sent to implement the law. The white colonists in Paris feared that, in order to underline the change in the status of free men of color, Raimond himself might be selected as one of them. The pro-colonial deputy Tarbé succeeded in getting the assembly to stipulate that no one who owned property in the colonies could be named as a commissioner. Raimond was disappointed to be excluded, but he was satisfied with the nominations that were finally made. Brissot had undoubtedly weighed in on the decision, making sure that two of the three commissioners, Léger-Félicité Sonthonax and Etienne Polverel, were committed Jacobins. Like Sonthonax, Polverel had published proabolition articles in the press, writing in one of them that "no man has received from nature the right to command other men or sell them."[50] The fact that neither Sonthonax nor Polverel had been a member of the Amis des Noirs served to shield them from an all-out assault by the colonial lobby. The third member of the civil commission, Jean-Antoine Ailhaud, was the only one with experience in the colonial world, having been an official in the Mascarene Islands. Whereas Sonthonax and Polverel would pursue their mission in Saint-Domingue with heroic determination, Ailhaud was so traumatized by the situation facing them after their arrival that he fled back to France at the first opportunity.[51]

Together with Brissot, Raimond met with the newly named commissioners before their departure to discuss the details of their mission. Brissot had no doubt that the free men of color in the colonies not only would welcome the law of 4 April 1792 but would now take the initiative in proposing measures to phase out slavery. In a draft of a letter to them, he wrote, "It is up to you to embarrass the whites first by improving the situation of the Blacks. It is with this hope that the friends of liberty have supported your cause here. It will be simple, once you reflect on the matter, to reconcile the interests of the owners with what humanity requires of you."[52] Raimond knew that the issue was more complicated. In his own letter to the men of color, he first worked to convince the fellow members of his group that they had nothing to fear from the revolutionary "popular government" in France. In Saint-Domingue, the free men of color had good reason to be wary of the elected assemblies and political clubs that the self-proclaimed white "patriots" had founded in imitation of the revolutionaries in France. Since 1789, those institutions had regularly opposed the granting of rights to nonwhites. Raimond assured them that there was no inherent contradiction between democratic institutions and slavery: "Athens had slavery and there was never a more popular government than theirs." Once all free men in Saint-Domingue were represented in its political institutions, their shared interest in keeping the slaves under control would deter any resistance from the latter.[53]

Raimond took pains to refute rumors circulated by other free men of color that he favored the immediate end of slavery, a charge made by two representatives of the free men of color from Saint-Domingue in a letter published in Milscent's newspaper.[54] "One could not imagine that I would want to ruin at one stroke my whole family, which owns property worth between seven and eight million livres," Raimond responded. The first priority, he insisted, had to be putting down the slave insurrection; only then could there be consideration of measures to "improve their situation without doing too much damage to the interests of the owners and the whole society." To end the insurrection, he urged the commissioners to issue a proclamation offering amnesty and personal freedom to its leaders if they would get the rest of the Black population to return to work on the plantations.[55]

Raimond's cautious ideas were similar to those of the white ex-colonist Milscent, who had now moved to Paris. At the beginning of June 1792, Milscent launched a daily newspaper, initially called *La Revue du Patriote* but soon renamed the *Créole patriote*, a title that emphasized its editor's dual identity as a supporter of the French Revolution and a man from the colonies. The early issues of Milscent's paper gave little hint of the remarkable evolution in his own thinking about slavery that would take place over the next nine months. A letter from Cap Français, published on 7 June 1792, combined familiar depictions of the "furious Africans" who had "risen up, fire in one hand, the blade in the other, and assaulted their proud masters" with an unsympathetic portrayal of the whites, "most of them enriched by thefts from the free men of color, fattened on the sweat of their slaves." In subsequent articles, Milscent expressed his high hopes for the civil commissioners, who "are going to cover themselves with pure glory, by regenerating one of the most precious portions of the French empire."[56] As preparations for the departure of the civil commissioners and the troops went forward, the best the representatives of the Saint-Domingue colonists could do to limit the mission's impact was to get the navy minister to order the soldiers to change the motto on their units' flags from "Live free or die" to "The nation, the law and the king."[57]

Within a few weeks of its debut, Milscent's newspaper showed the impact of a crisis in French domestic politics that was about to divert the attention of nearly all the other participants in the abolitionist movement and ultimately lead to the death of Brissot and most of his closest associates. The war that Brissot had worked so hard to launch did not go as he had expected. Instead of winning easy victories and inspiring revolutions in the countries bordering France, the poorly organized French troops suffered humiliating defeats. The Jacobins blamed Louis XVI, whom they accused of protecting disloyal aristocratic army officers. When the interior minister Jean-Marie Roland de la Platière, one of Brissot's closest associates, published a letter upbraiding the king for his conduct,

Louis retaliated by dismissing the "Brissotin" ministers he had appointed three months earlier. Milscent, along with the other pro-revolutionary journalists, was furious. "Oh, Louis XVI! Louis XVI!" he expostulated. "One would think that an evil spirit presides over all of your actions."[58]

Matters quickly escalated in Paris. On 20 June 1792 a crowd estimated at more than twenty thousand, many of them armed with pikes and other weapons, invaded the royal palace in the Tuileries. Angry "sans-culottes," as the capital's revolutionary militants were now called, surrounded the king, forcing him to don a red "liberty cap" that had become a symbol of their cause. Despite this pressure, the king refused to recall the ministers he had just removed. Brissot and the other Jacobin deputies responded by having the Legislative Assembly declare "the country in danger," and sans-culotte leaders openly threatened to stage a popular uprising if the deputies did not force the king from the throne. In mid-July Austrian and Prussian troops began to advance toward Paris. On 25 July 1792 their commanding general, the duke of Brunswick, issued a manifesto warning of drastic reprisals if the king and the royal family were harmed. Finally, on 10 August 1792, the storm broke: At dawn, armed sans-culotte battalions converged on the Tuileries. Louis XVI and his family took refuge in the Legislative Assembly's meeting hall while the king's loyal Swiss Guards were overwhelmed by the attackers in what became the bloodiest of Paris's revolutionary *journées*, or days of violence.

The uprising of 10 August, often called a "second revolution," sent France in a new, more radical direction. The Legislative Assembly declared that Louis XVI had forfeited the throne, and, since the 1791 constitution had been based on the assumption that France would remain a monarchy, the deputies called for the election of a "national convention" to replace it. In place of the wealth-based election system established in 1789, they decreed universal manhood suffrage, thus enfranchising the Parisian sans-culottes who had brought the monarchy down. The Legislative Assembly continued to meet, but real power was in the hands of a provisional council of ministers, dominated by the radical firebrand Georges Danton, and the municipal assembly, the Commune, where the sans-culottes held sway.

Colonial issues played no role in the crisis of the summer of 1792, but all those who had been involved in them were drawn into the maelstrom that brought down the constitutional monarchy. Brissot and his Girondin supporters had been among the loudest voices denouncing the king at the start of the crisis, but as tension mounted in late July and early August, their behavior aroused suspicions that their real aim was to make a deal with the king that would return their allies to their ministerial positions. A more radical revolutionary faction, known as the Montagnards, or "men of the Mountain," because they sat in the highest rows of seats in the Legislative Assembly's meeting hall, accused the Girondins of abandoning the patriotic cause. Robespierre and the journalist Marat were among the most prominent of the Montagnards. As the cleavage between the two revolutionary factions became deeper, the decision to grant rights to the free men of color began to appear as a Brissotin policy, and some Montagnards began to embrace conspiracy theories that portrayed it as an attempt to cripple the French economy in order to favor a counterrevolution.

The journée of 10 August 1792 had an even more drastic effect on the proslavery lobby. In the purge of counterrevolutionary suspects that followed the uprising, the Club Massiac was denounced as a nest of aristocrats and closed down, and monarchist newspapers such as the *Gazette universelle* that had opposed the abolitionists disappeared. The proslavery priest Maury had already emigrated from France following the end of the National Assembly's session in 1791. After 10 August 1792, other prominent pro-colonial figures also fled. Moreau de Saint-Méry spent more than a year in hiding before escaping to the United States, and Malouet made his way to England, where he entered into contact with the British government.[59] Only a few other colonists noticed the arrival in Paris of two new deputies from the island's colonial assembly, Pierre-François Page and Augustin Brulley. Sent to seek metropolitan endorsement of a decree passed by the colonial assembly declaring slavery an immutable institution, these two men would become the most ruthless and effective opponents of the abolition movement during the next phase of the Revolution.[60]

Even as the Austro-Prussian army continued its advance toward Paris in the hectic weeks that followed the journée of 10

August 1792, the distant colonies were not entirely forgotten. Although half its members had fled, the Legislative Assembly continued its sessions. The deputies even took some important actions, such as passing a progressive divorce law that gave women equal rights in marriage. On 18 August 1792 the colonial committee's spokesman Jean-François Merlet put forward a measure to determine how many deputies each French colony would have in future national legislatures. Like the American constitution makers who had decided that enslaved people would be counted as three-fifths of a person for the purpose of apportioning seats in their national legislature, Merlet said that the enslaved population should be included in population figures. His justification for this proposal was curious, however: "We thought that unfree persons should be part of our enumeration, because, although their enjoyment of their rights is suspended or undetermined . . . it is possible that they might even become active citizens. . . . Even if the powerful interest and the conservation of the colonies require that they be deprived of their freedom, at least they will have the small consolation of learning that the legislators of France count them as men." Since Merlet was raising the possibility of a future emancipation of the slaves, the Montagnard deputy François Chabot tried to open a discussion about abolishing the slave trade, but that idea was quickly tabled.[61]

After that discussion, the Legislative Assembly abandoned the fate of the colonies to its successor, the National Convention. During the eleven months of the Legislative Assembly's session, Brissot and his allies, aided by the sense of crisis caused by news of the Saint-Domingue uprising, had succeeded in defeating the colonial lobby in the metropole and imposing a policy that they believed would ultimately bring about the end of racial hierarchy and slavery. The chances of that policy's success now depended on two things: the ability of the Second Civil Commission, whose members were halfway across the Atlantic and completely unaware of the events of 10 August 1792 in France, to implement the law of 4 April and end the slave revolt, and the ability of revolutionary France to defeat the foreign armies steadily advancing toward Paris.

CHAPTER EIGHT

The Abolitionist Cause in Jeopardy

AS THE LEGISLATIVE assembly in which Jacques-Pierre Brissot had achieved his greatest victories—the law of 4 April 1792 and the declaration of war—prepared to dissolve itself, elections were underway for its successor, the National Convention. The three years of the Convention's session, from September 1792 to October 1795, were the most tumultuous period of the Revolution. They saw the trial and execution of Louis XVI, the creation of a dictatorial "revolutionary government" that took drastic measures to combat the Revolution's enemies, wild swings in the fortunes of war, radical measures to promote social equality, and then a drastic reaction to what came to be stigmatized as the "excesses" of "the reign of terror." Like all other stages of the Revolution, the years of the Convention were also marked by dramatic decisions on the issues of race and slavery. After initially embracing Brissot's colonial policies, the Convention turned against him and the abolition movement. By the fall of 1793, the Montagnards were in power and Brissot and his allies were facing the guillotine. A revived colonial lobby managed to win Montagnard support for its cause, only to be stunned when the Convention suddenly voted to abolish slavery, a decision that that assembly stuck to even when it reversed many of the other radical measures adopted during the Terror.

The six weeks between the overthrow of the monarchy on 10 August 1792 and the opening session of the National Convention on 20 September were more tense and chaotic than any other comparable period of the Revolution. Until the French army's victory at the battle of Valmy in northeastern France on 20 September, it was by no means certain that the movement would survive. During these critical weeks, the revolutionaries who had been involved in the abolition movement were completely occupied with the war and with domestic politics. The closing of the Club Massiac after 10 August and the emigration of many of its members left the Saint-Domingue colonial commissioners Pierre-François Page and Augustin Brulley as the main representatives of their cause in France. The provisional government created on 10 August 1792 had issued a proclamation announcing that France's new constitution would be based on the principles of liberty and equality. Page and Brulley wangled two meetings with Gaspard Monge, the new navy minister, and got him to promise that the government "did not intend the decree on liberty and equality to extend to the unfree Negroes." On 28 August, as he was rallying the country to fend off the foreign invasion, Georges Danton, the provisional ministry's central figure, took the time to meet with them. They came away convinced that "he took the liveliest interest in the misfortunes of Saint-Domingue."[1]

Whether Monge's and Danton's promises would have any meaning depended on the outcome of the war and the political situation in France. Just as elections for the National Convention were beginning, news reached Paris that the fortress of Verdun, the last major obstacle to the enemy advance, had surrendered. In response, sans-culotte militants invaded the Paris prisons, which were filled with suspected counterrevolutionaries arrested after the journée of 10 August, and massacred many of the inmates. As this "September massacre" was unfolding across the city, officials from the insurrectional Commune issued an arrest warrant for Brissot, whose *Patriote françois* had criticized sans-culotte violence after the overthrow of the monarchy. The full story behind the attempt to arrest Brissot has never been clarified, but he and his friends were convinced that Maximilien Robespierre and Jean-Paul Marat were behind it, a suspicion that made relations between Brissot's faction and the Montagnards more hostile than ever.[2]

The Montagnards dominated the elections to the Convention in Paris, with Robespierre making a triumphant return to national politics as the first deputy chosen in the capital and Marat gaining office for the first time. Ironically, the last of the twenty-four deputies chosen in Paris was Brissot's one-time patron, Louis XVI's cousin the duc d'Orléans, whose vast wealth included plantations in Saint-Domingue. Now calling himself Philippe-Egalité, the duke had embraced the Revolution and joined the Jacobin Club. He was one of the few members of the Convention who was also a colonial slave owner. Despite being rejected in Paris, Brissot was elected as a deputy in three provincial departments; he chose to represent his native Eure-et-Loir. Not only was Brissot reelected, but so were nearly all of his proabolitionist allies from the Legislative Assembly, including Condorcet, Sylvain Vergniaud, Arnaud Gensonné, Marguerite-Elie Guadet, Jean-Philippe Garran-Coulon, Jean-François Delacroix, and Claude Fauchet. In addition, a number of like-minded figures from the National Assembly, such as Henri Grégoire, Jérôme Pétion, and Jean-Paul Rabaut Saint-Etienne, gained seats.

Most of the Convention deputies who had a record of support for the abolition movement were associated with the Girondins, and the fate of that cause became linked to the fortunes of Brissot's party. There were fewer outspoken advocates of abolition in the rival Montagnard faction. Robespierre had vigorously defended the rights of free men of color in the great debates of May and September 1791, but once he came to regard Brissot as an enemy of the Revolution, he was no longer willing to associate himself with his rival's trademark cause. One Montagnard deputy, Joseph Lequinio, did include a vigorous denunciation of slavery in his *Les Préjugés détruits* (Prejudices destroyed), a lengthy tract addressed to the country's peasant population. The main thrust of his work, which foreshadowed the de-Christianization campaign that would break out in October and November 1793, was its denunciation of religious beliefs. His chapter on slavery ended with a call for European countries to invade the Muslim world and do away with Islam, which he claimed "consecrates ignorance by law."[3] Other

Montagnard deputies' opinions on colonial issues varied from indifference to outright hostility toward a cause they came to regard as a mask for foreign influence in France.

Despite the presence of so many committed reformers and the absence of outspoken defenders of colonial interests, the National Convention paid less attention to these matters than its predecessors. Its members were overwhelmed by more immediate issues: organizing the war effort, restoring some kind of stability after the journée of 10 August 1792 and the September massacres, deciding the fate of the king, drafting a new republican constitution, keeping the economy from collapsing, fighting counterrevolutionary opponents at home, and battling each other. Initially, Brissot's Girondin faction was more successful in winning support from the undecided Convention deputies of the "plain" or the "swamp," but the Montagnards had the upper hand in the Jacobin Club. Brissot did not even bother to appear there in mid-October, when he was ousted from membership. When the Girondins appeared indecisive about supporting the execution of the king, they lost further support. Meanwhile, after the dispatch of Léger-Félicité Sonthonax and Etienne Polverel to Saint-Domingue, there did not seem to be much more that the metropole could do to affect events in the Caribbean. Once France found itself at war with Britain and Spain in February 1793, news of events in the colonies arrived only sporadically and after long delays.

The only individuals who devoted themselves seriously to colonial affairs during the fall of 1792 and most of 1793 were those who had personal connections overseas. Julien Raimond and Claude Milscent were the most outspoken of these on the reformist side. In order to make sure that the free men of color who had benefited from the decree of 4 April were seen as firm supporters of the Revolution, Raimond and his allies appeared at the Legislative Assembly on 7 September to ask for authorization to form an armed "legion" to join in the defense effort. "Although nature, so rich in its varieties, has set us apart from the French by exterior appearances . . . it has made us perfectly like them, by giving us, like them, a heart that burns to fight the enemies of the country," Raimond announced. Milscent, who had commanded a unit of free men of color during the 1779 Savannah expedition, hailed the proposal, telling the men of color that "one will see memorable heroes rise from the companies you will form." The Legion of Americans, commanded by the chevalier de Saint-George, eventually saw combat against the Austrians and later against the counterrevolutionary rebels in the Vendée.[4]

The most active opponents of the abolitionist cause were the proslavery colonists who had avoided identification with the Club Massiac, particularly the duo of Page and Brulley. The colonial assembly in Saint-Domingue had appointed the two men as "commissioners" in June 1792, with the mission of obtaining the Legislative Assembly's approval of that body's resolution stating that "the colony of Saint-Domingue cannot exist without slavery" and that "the slave is the master's property; no authority can restrict this property." They arrived in France to find a political landscape completely different from what they had expected. With startling speed, the two men adapted themselves to the new circumstances. On 11 August 1792 Page wrote to a colleague in Saint-Domingue denouncing the now-banned Club Massiac. The best way to counter the abolitionist threat was to claim that the troubles in the colony were the fault of "the counterrevolutionary aristocracy," Page insisted.[5]

Page and Brulley's optimism that the interests of colonial slaveholders could still be defended in the midst of the new phase of the Revolution contrasted sharply with the strategy of almost all of those who had tried to defend slavery and racial hierarchy during the previous three years. Many of the earlier opponents of abolition had been conservatives, the majority of whom had now fled France and pinned their hopes on the country's foreign enemies. Colonial émigrés who had joined the king's brother, the comte de Provence, at his court in exile put their hopes in the Spanish, who were in a position to invade the French half of Hispaniola from their own colony of Santo Domingo in the east of the island. In London, Pierre-Victor Malouet joined other French exiles to negotiate a treaty by which they promised to support a British takeover of the Caribbean colonies in exchange for the maintenance of slavery. Some of them were even willing to envisage a permanent British annexation of the French islands.[6]

The two men who now became the backbone of the "patriotic" colonial lobby in Paris had both been active participants in the white colonists' resistance to metropolitan authority in Saint-Domingue. Both were plantation owners, and Brulley even arrived in Paris with one of his enslaved Black domestics.[7] As Milscent complained, the two men quickly established their authority over the other exiles from the colony by arrogating to themselves the right to issue the official certificates needed to receive the relief payments the French government had promised to those whose plantations had been destroyed.[8] In addition to issuing refugee certificates, Page, Brulley, and their secretary Jean-Baptiste-Bernard Legrand met daily to discuss the best ways of carrying out their campaign. The detailed record Legrand kept in his nearly illegible handwriting is an invaluable source for documenting their activities.[9] As Brulley wrote to his mother in November 1792, the Convention was considering legislation about the colonies, but "there are divisions of opinion on this subject [and] none of them are favorable to us." He and his colleagues were setting up meetings with government officials and legislators and preparing publicity materials.[10] By the end of the year, he and Page had each written a substantial pamphlet denouncing the "counterrevolutionary maneuvers" that they blamed for the troubles in the colonies. Brulley affected a calm tone, whereas Page denounced a long list of "traitors," especially Governor Philibert François Rouxel de Blanchelande, whom he held responsible for deliberately letting the slave insurrection spread.[11]

In addition to writing propaganda, Page and Brulley made it their business to meet regularly with the members of the Convention's colonial committee and with the navy minister and any other officials who would listen to them. They were always ready to provide any information their interlocutors requested about Saint-Domingue, and many revolutionary politicians and officials came to rely on their assistance. As they made their rounds, Page and Brulley concluded that they needed to avoid openly lobbying for a decree protecting slavery in Saint-Domingue. Nevertheless, they were optimistic that they were gaining the confidence of the public and the politicians they talked to. In early February, they were pleased to learn that a fellow Saint-Domingue plantation owner, François-Thomas Galbaud, had been named as the new governor of the colony. For once, they were in agreement with Julien Raimond, who assured Sonthonax that Galbaud, a hero of the campaign against the Austro-Prussians, was "absolutely in line with the Revolution." Neither Page and Brulley nor Raimond could have imagined that the man they both praised would inadvertently precipitate the freeing of the enslaved Blacks in Saint-Domingue.[12]

As Page and Brulley were insinuating their way into the good graces of the new republican political establishment in Paris, Claude Milscent was working to make his newspaper, the *Créole patriote*, a major feature of the capital's journalistic scene. On 15 August, Milscent announced that he was going to challenge the *Moniteur universel*, the Revolution's "newspaper of record," by producing two separate editions a day of the *Créole patriote*: Their combined content would almost equal that of the large-format *Moniteur*. Jacobin militants, who considered the *Moniteur*'s politics too equivocal, welcomed Milscent's initiative, especially after he publicly renounced his friendship with Brissot. "O! Brissot! O! Guadet! . . . I worshipped you, and you force me to silence, if not because of the conduct for which you are reproached, at least by a nullity which snuffs out even paternal love," he wrote in October 1792 when the Girondins were expelled from the Jacobin Club. Milscent's change of allegiances paid off. A few days later, he announced that the club had designated his paper the official outlet for its correspondence. At the beginning of January 1793, a club member called the *Créole patriote* "an excellent journal, admirable, the only one that the Jacobins should recognize."[13]

Even though he separated himself from Brissot, Milscent continued to pay close attention to colonial issues. In the first issue of his paper to appear after the opening session of the National Convention, he called slavery a crime "which nothing can excuse," although he still did not see any immediate prospect of abolishing it. In the months that followed, Milscent's ideas on the subject began to change. At the end of November, he posed a series of pointed questions to the members of the Convention: "1. Is it really true that Saint-Domingue cannot exist without the maintenance of slavery? . . . 3. Is there a family of men whom nature has condemned to be the property of another? 4. Does domination over another man give one the right to treat him as property? . . . 6. If it is shown that ownership of one man by another is a violation, can the usurper remain an owner?"[14]

Milscent was moving in a more radical direction than Julien Raimond, the major spokesman for the free men of color in France. In his *Réflexions sur les véritables causes des troubles et des désastres de nos colonies*, published in early 1793, Raimond was still searching for a way to "considerably ameliorate" the condition of the enslaved Blacks "without destroying our commerce, or injuring private fortunes." He proposed issuing a proclamation to the Black insurgents that would begin by ordering those "misled men" to "return promptly to order . . . and wait in respectful silence, for the laws which will regenerate you." The Blacks needed to learn the rules of civilized society, including respect for property, "the love and habit of work," and good morals. Raimond proposed to set prices for which enslaved people could buy their freedom: 3,000 livres for men up to the age of forty, 2,600 livres for women, and 4,000 livres for those whose masters had taught them special skills. Black women had to learn "modesty" and stop going out in public "without being decently covered."[15]

While Raimond was setting out this condescending program, Milscent was defending a new play, *Zabeau et Courville, ou la révolte des Nègres*, which brought scenes from the Saint-Domingue uprising alive for Paris spectators. Milscent praised the drama and especially the white actor who played the part of the "chief of the rebels" because "his expressions speak to the eyes the electrifying language of great passions." Page and Brulley also attended the production. In an example of their skill at working behind the scenes to counter abolitionist propaganda, they pressured the theater manager to change the show's content. They were especially upset that the play showed the Black insurgents fighting under a flag bearing the French revolutionary motto, "Live free or die." After their first meeting with the theater manager, they returned the next day and showed him a flag that they claimed had been captured in Saint-Domingue and that was inscribed in Arabic characters. According to Page and Brulley, the flag said nothing about liberty. Instead, they claimed, "one sees only invocations of God, of Mohammed, of the king and of their generals."[16] Some modern historians have cited this story as evidence of the influence of Islam among the Blacks of Saint-Domingue, but it is also possible that Page and Brulley had manufactured the flag to support their case.

A few weeks later, in the aftermath of the king's execution on 21 January 1793, France declared war on Britain, signaling that hostilities were about to spread to the Caribbean. At this point, Milscent began a lengthy series of articles in which he argued that it would now be impossible to force the Blacks back into slavery. The "Negro army . . . grows every day, while our forces diminish," he wrote. Furthermore, the Black fighters were now definitely demanding their freedom, in a letter "that bears the stamp of the Rights of Man."[17] The letter to which Milscent was referring, which he was about to publish in his paper, was the first extended political statement issued by the Black insurgent leaders themselves to appear in France. This "Letter of Jean-François, Biassou and Belair," written in Saint-Domingue and addressed to Philippe Roume at the time when he was forging his alliance with the free men of color there, had been brought back to France by a royalist military officer, Joseph Cambefort, who included it in his justification of his own conduct, published in January 1793. Milscent was one of the few people who recognized the letter's significance. "For too long, I say, we have been the victims of your lust for money and your avarice," the letter began. "You made a business out of us, you traded men for horses. . . . We are Blacks, it is true, but tell us, Sirs, you who are so learned, what law says that Black men should belong to and be the property of the white man? . . . Placed on earth like you, being all of us children of the same father created in the same image we are therefore your equals according to natural law and if it pleases nature to diversify the colors of the human race it is no crime to be black nor any advantage to be white."[18]

Continuing its reproaches of the white slave owners, the letter writers asked, "Have you forgotten that you have explicitly sworn the Declaration of the Rights of Man which says that men are born free and equal in rights?" If the colonists truly wanted to end the insurrection, they would have to agree to "freedom for all men held in slavery" and a "general amnesty for everything that has taken place." Commenting on the letter, Milscent remarked that "if its French language is not pure, one does at least recognize energetic sentiments, and one can judge whether it is possible to defeat 94,000 men, oh! true sans-culottes if ever there were any, who think and express themselves this way."[19]

Milscent was clearly strongly affected by the "Letter of Jean-François, Biassou and Belair." Between the first week of February 1793 and the middle of March, he published some thirty substantial articles, first in the *Créole patriote* and then, when financial problems forced him to suspend its publication, in the Cercle social's *Bulletin des Amis de la Vérité*, arguing that slavery could not be maintained in Saint-Domingue and that its abolition would be in France's interests. Taken as a whole, Milscent's articles made the strongest and most coherent case for the immediate abolition of slavery published not just in France but anywhere in the Atlantic world during the revolutionary era. "Anyone who has not closed his soul to every sentiment of justice, of humanity, and even of political interest, properly understood, cannot fail to see the justice and the moderation of the Negroes' demands," he wrote. French merchants must surely understand that it was in their interests to get the plantations back into production, Milscent argued, and this could only be done by granting the Blacks their freedom. The government would have to provide some compensation for the plantation owners, but the colonists needed to realize that slavery was doomed. If the whites attempted to reinstate it, the Blacks would have every right to respond, "Our aim is to regain our rights, which have been stolen but not extinguished. And you, in whose name do you give us orders contrary to the same law that forms the basis of your authority? . . . Here are the constitutional decrees; they tell us that the law authorizes us to break our chains."[20]

Becoming ever more outspoken, Milscent went on to ask, "Should slavery even exist in lands inhabited by Frenchmen? It is said that we should improve their condition. How would you do that? There is no compromise possible between slavery and the state of freedom." In any event, the cost of an "unending war that one would have to wage against them" would surely exceed "all the temporary sacrifices that the planters would be making if they consented to their immediate emancipation."[21] He denounced the sexual exploitation of enslaved women by their white masters, and he explicitly justified the violence that the Blacks in Saint-Domingue had used to free themselves.[22] If Milscent's articles, which appeared in two journals that were widely circulated at the time, had been put together as a pamphlet, they would undoubtedly be remembered as one of the most detailed and eloquent presentations of the abolitionist case in the entire period.

Even though Milscent's newspaper was a semiofficial organ of the Jacobin Club, it did not have as much impact on the deputies in the Convention as the lobbying efforts of Page and Brulley. Initially, the two lobbyists, as well as their allies in Saint-Domingue, pretended to accept the law of 4 April establishing equality between whites and free people of color. In return, the colonists in Saint-Domingue wanted a clear statement of the revolutionary government's acceptance of slavery and measures against the remaining royal officials and army officers in Saint-Domingue. Upon their arrival in Cap Français in September 1792, the civil commissioners Sonthonax and Polverel satisfied the local whites by publicly swearing to maintain slavery, and in October they ordered over a hundred military officers and administrators to return to France. Sonthonax soon realized, however, that the self-proclaimed white "patriots" in the colony had no intention of accepting real equality with the free men of color. When whites in Cap Français rioted to prevent the appointment of men of color as officers in the local garrison, he had several of the leading agitators arrested and deported to France. "They have fought to the last ditch against the rights of free men, they have covered the earth with human blood in the interest of their pride and to maintain the most absurd of aristocracies," Sonthonax told the navy minister.[23]

At a meeting with the navy minister Monge on 19 January 1793, Page and Brulley learned about the arrest of their Saint-Domingue allies. From that moment on, the two men concentrated all their efforts on denouncing Sonthonax and Polverel and getting them recalled from Saint-Domingue. As the white colonists had done since the beginning of the Revolution, Page and Brulley insisted that the colonies had to be assured of their "inalienable and imprescriptible right to decide on their domestic regime," or, in other words, of the continuation of slavery.[24] In the early months of 1793, while Brissot still exercised influence in the Convention, Page and Brulley's efforts were countered by Julien Raimond, who urged the Convention's colonial committee to approve Sonthonax's arrest of the white agitators in Cap Français and his creation of a militia made up of free men of color. Even as they took measures against the white colonists and cemented an alliance with the free men of color, Sonthonax and Polverel were still faithfully carrying out the mandate they had been given, which was to end the slave insurrection, not to abolish slavery. In January 1793 they launched a major military offensive against the insurgents. Sonthonax did write to Milscent in February 1793, urging him to "get the Convention to do something for the slaves," but the most radical step the commissioners took on their own authority was to have Louis XIV's Code Noir translated into the Creole language spoken by the Black population, so that they would be able to claim the protections it was supposed to give them.[25]

The conflict between Raimond on one side and Page and Brulley on the other reached the floor of the Convention on 5 March 1793, when the deputy Simon Camboulas, who may have developed abolitionist sympathies when he served as secretary to his great-uncle, the famous abbé Guillaume Thomas Raynal, presented a decree authorizing the free colored militia units the civil commissioners Sonthonax and Polverel had formed in Saint-Domingue.[26] This was a measure proposed by Raimond, but the colonial lobbyists' influence was evident in the language Camboulas used about the insurgent Blacks. He repeated familiar claims that these "stupid men" seemed bent on the "destruction of all free men" and that "they know the word 'freedom,' but it is, for them a word without meaning." The decree, which was voted with almost no discussion, gave the civil commissioners in Saint-Domingue authority to "make whatever provisional alternations they judge necessary to the police regulations and the discipline of the slave gangs [*ateliers*] for the maintenance of domestic peace in the colonies." Since Raimond was the main influence behind the drafting of the decree, it is unlikely that this wording was meant to lead to the abolition of slavery. When the two commissioners did decide to take that step three months later, however, they cited this clause as justification for their action.[27]

The decree of 5 March 1793 infuriated the white colonists in Paris, whose number was steadily growing as Sonthonax deported more of them from Saint-Domingue. Page and Brulley accused Sonthonax and Polverel of reverse racism because they had, "in violation of the law of 4 April, formed corporations of citizens of color, excluding white citizens." On 19 March 1793 the Convention voted to suspend the dispatch of the decree it had passed two weeks earlier until its committees on the navy and the colonies had debated the matter. Raimond, Page, and Brulley were invited to address the combined committees at hearings held toward the end of the month. Camboulas, exasperated by the colonists' attacks on Sonthonax and Polverel, said that if there was going to be a debate about the colonies, they should discuss "the great question of whether it was important for France to have colonies, and whether it could let slavery continue to exist there." Page and Brulley understood that the word "slavery" was considered too "blasphemous" to be uttered in the Convention. In the confines of the committee room, however, they left no doubt that it was slavery that they were defending. They objected vehemently to the clause in the 5 March decree that authorized Sonthonax and Polverel to make provisional changes in the slave code. "No Negro would be able to understand what 'provisional' meant, and the interpretation he would give to these changes . . . would destroy, absolutely and forever, the order and subordination without which slave work teams cannot exist," they insisted.[28] As the meetings of the Convention became increasingly contentious, further sessions of the joint committees were postponed until mid-May.

In the meantime, the white colonists scored a victory with dangerous implications for anyone who fell afoul of them. In March 1793 the National Convention voted to create a special "revolutionary tribunal" to conduct speedy trials of suspects accused of political crimes. On 11 April 1793 the tribunal took up its first important case: the accusations against Blanchelande, the disgraced governor of Saint-Domingue, who had been sent back to France by Sonthonax and Polverel soon after their arrival in the colony. Blanchelande was an easy target: He had been unable to put down the slave uprising, and he had failed to prevent conflict between the whites and the free men of color. Brissot had already accused him of counterrevolutionary actions in his speech of 1 December 1791, and he had no political supporters in France.

The witnesses against Blanchelande were all white colonists from Saint-Domingue, led by Brulley, who claimed that the governor "had always wanted to carry out a counterrevolution in the island of Saint-Domingue, that for this purpose he had on different occasions stirred up and armed the Negroes." The only testimony on Blanchelande's behalf came from the three members of the First Civil Commission, two of whom—Philippe Roume and Edmond de Saint-Léger—were themselves under indictment. Saint-Léger told Blanchelande, "I have always considered the job you had, not just too great for your strength, but for that of any human being," but the jury accepted the white colonists' unsubstantiated accusations and condemned him to death. "He was taken to the place of execution in the midst of an immense crowd, who cried out that the guillotine was too light a punishment for him," the *Nouvelles politiques*, a continuation of the pro-colonial *Gazette universelle*, reported.[29]

Blanchelande's conviction made the white colonists the first group to demonstrate how political factions could manipulate the institutions of the nascent revolutionary government that was taking shape in the spring of 1793 to destroy their enemies. Elated by their success, Page, Brulley, and their associates targeted numerous other victims during the period that came to be known as the Reign of Terror. Even when they did not succeed in sending their enemies to the guillotine, they often managed to get them imprisoned. The conviction of Blanchelande also allowed them to claim that their increasingly fantastical conspiracy theory about the causes of the "troubles and disasters" in Saint-Domingue had been upheld in court. In the longest of their pamphlets, issued in early June 1793, they maintained that Blanchelande had been just one part of an immense counterrevolutionary plot that involved all the colonial officials of the old regime, together with the "monster" Brissot, the members of the First Civil Commission, Julien Raimond and the free men of color in the colony, French merchant interests, Catholic priests in Saint-Domingue, and the Spanish and British governments.[30]

When the Convention's colonial committee resumed its hearings in mid-May 1793, Raimond presented his own explanation of the causes of the slave revolt. Like the white colonists, he refused to admit that the Blacks might have acted on their own, claiming instead that the Blacks had been "led to rise up . . . as a result of the calculations of various parties," although they had now "gone much further than those who stirred them up had expected." To end their insurrection, "it would suffice to improve the treatment of the slaves and to give them a way to buy their freedom" and to grant them a general amnesty. In response, Page asserted that he "shuddered at the degradation of the enslaved man" but said that freeing the slaves would be a "harmful gift" that would "import to the colonies all the horrors of Africa." In any event, he said, the task of making laws about slavery needed to be left to the colonists themselves. His arguments persuaded the committee, which maintained the decision to suspend the decree of 5 March. This news never reached Sonthonax and Polverel, who continued to assume that they had the authority it had bestowed on them.[31]

While Raimond and the Saint-Domingue colonists confronted each other in committee meetings, the National Convention encountered the subject of slavery when it tried to formulate a new declaration of rights to replace the document adopted in August 1789. The longtime abolitionist Condorcet chaired a committee charged with drafting a new republican constitution to replace the constitutional monarchist plan adopted in 1791. The declaration of rights in this draft, published in mid-February 1793, included, as part of a series of articles defining the rights of property and contract, the statement that "any man can hire out his services, his time; but he cannot sell himself: his person is not an alienable property."[32] This formulation echoed earlier statements by John Locke and Jean-Jacques Rousseau, but no one in 1793 interpreted it as a ban on slavery. The Blacks in the French colonies had not sold themselves into slavery: They had been seized by force and kept in captivity against their will.

Denounced by the Montagnards as a "Girondin" constitution, Condorcet's plan was never enacted. Two months later, the Montagnard leader Robespierre presented his own ideas about how the declaration of rights should be revised. In arguing that the right of property should be limited by moral considerations, he gave three examples of what he considered illegitimate property claims: that of the "merchant of human flesh" who, "pointing at this long coffin that he calls a ship, in which he has loaded and packed together men who appear alive," says, "there are my properties, I bought them at so much a head," as well as those of the feudal lord who claimed to own land and vassals and of the members of the Bourbon dynasty, who claimed their right to rule over France. He then proposed a declaration of rights stating that the right of any individual to own property "may not prejudice either the safety, or the freedom, or the existence, or the property of our fellow men," a provision that might perhaps have been interpreted as outlawing slavery. Whether Robespierre meant this to apply to slavery in the French colonies is impossible to determine; he did not address the question.[33] The declaration of rights actually included in the Constitution of 1793, adopted by the Convention after the expulsion of Condorcet and the Girondins, ignored Robespierre's suggestions, incorporating instead an article much closer to Condorcet's wording: "Every man can hire out his services, his time; but he cannot sell himself, or be sold; his person is not an alienable property."[34] Although the addition of the words "or be sold" should have signaled the end of the slave trade, no one drew this conclusion.

By the time the "Jacobin" constitution was adopted in June 1793, revolutionary France had gone through yet another political convulsion with serious consequences for the abolitionist cause. Throughout the spring of 1793, the Convention confronted one crisis after another. In mid-March, a counterrevolutionary peasant rebellion broke out in the southwestern department of the Vendée. At the same time, the Austrians inflicted a crushing defeat on the French Army in Belgium, and the French general in chief, Charles-François Dumouriez, defected to the enemy. Dumouriez had been linked to the Girondins, and his treason gave the Montagnards a new weapon against their rivals. Meanwhile, food prices were rising rapidly, and the sans-culottes in Paris demanded the imposition of price controls, which the Girondins opposed in the name of economic freedom. In several major provincial cities, violence erupted between local factions aligned with the Girondins and the Montagnards. The Convention remained hopelessly divided, with power swinging back and forth between the two rival factions. In late May, Robespierre and other Montagnard leaders forged an alliance with radical sans-culotte militants who had been demanding the expulsion of the leading Girondin deputies from the Convention. For three days, from 31 May to 2 June 1793, sans-culotte battalions armed with pikes and loaded cannons surrounded the assembly's meeting hall. Seeing no other way to avoid bloodshed, the majority of the deputies voted to suspend twenty-nine Girondin deputies and two ministers allied with them.

The targets of the journée of 31 May–2 June 1793 included almost all of the prominent supporters of abolition in the Convention, with the exception of Grégoire, who had managed to steer clear of factional disputes. Brissot was at the top of the list, along with Guadet, Gensonné, Vergniaud, Pétion, Fauchet, Rabaut Saint-Etienne, and Brissot's longtime ally Etienne Clavière, the finance minister. Condorcet was added a few weeks later, after he signed a protest against the arrest of his colleagues. Fearing arrest, most of them fled Paris or went into hiding. When revolts against the Convention broke out in several provincial cities, the Girondins were accused of being "federalists" trying to break up the country. By midsummer, a majority of the group, including Brissot, had been captured. Robespierre and the Montagnards emerged with clear control of the Convention, although they now had to keep a wary eye on the sans-culotte militants who had made their triumph possible.

The defeat of the Girondins posed a serious threat to the abolitionist cause. Brissot, the founder of the Société des Amis des Noirs, was now singled out as the Revolution's greatest enemy, and anyone who had been associated with him was now vulnerable. In this critical situation, some slavery opponents did see an opportunity. Two weeks before the ouster of the Girondins, a group of free men of color had submitted an "address . . . for the Negroes held in slavery in the French colonies in America" to the Convention. At a moment when Julien Raimond was calling for a slow process in which individual Blacks would have to purchase their freedom, the signatories to this address demanded a decree stating that "slavery is abolished for all the Negroes in the French colonies; that from now on, no master will have any right over these men, other than what shall be agreed between them for their salary and their work." This radical address bore the signature of a certain Julien Labuissonnière, followed by eighteen other names, six of them identified as members of the "American hussars," the military unit of free men of color authorized by the Convention in September 1792. One of the signatories, Saint-George Milscent, was a son of the journalist Claude Milscent. This group joined forces with the radical journalist Pierre Chaumette. The journée of 10 August 1792 had elevated him to a position of power in the Paris city government as the Paris Commune's procureur or chief legal officer, second in authority only to the mayor. Having been an active participant in the campaign against the Girondins, Chaumette was able to provide the Labuissonnière group a chance to promote their cause in the new environment resulting from the just-completed journée.[35]

Accompanied by Chaumette, the Labuissonnière group appeared at the Jacobin Club on 3 June 1793, just a day after the expulsion of the Girondins. They brought with them Jeannette Odo, a mixed-race woman said to be 114 years old, and a tricolor flag showing a Black, a white, and a man of mixed race, symbolizing the union of the three racial groups. The group's spokesman called on the French to make sure that the Blacks "do not suffer eternally in the darkness of despotism." François-Louis Bourdon de l'Oise, the Montagnard deputy presiding over the meeting, responded that "you will become free because you have sought the support of a society that wants freedom" and gave them a "fraternal embrace." There was a motion to immediately confer Jacobin membership on the group's members, but the Convention deputy Jeanbon Saint-André, who had ties to Page and Brulley, objected to giving them special treatment. Robespierre then spoke up to "remind the society that it has traitors to punish. Many patriots have been swallowed up in the colonies, and that is one more of Brissot's crimes," a formulation that echoed the white colonists' accusations, and the club moved on to other matters.[36]

The day after their visit to the Jacobin Club, Chaumette and the Labuissonnière group appeared at the Convention itself, accompanied again by Jeannette Odo and their symbolic flag. Grégoire, the only remaining abolitionist stalwart from the National Assembly, seized the moment to denounce the last remaining form of aristocracy, "that of skin color. . . . I certainly hope that the National Convention will apply the principles of equality to our brothers from the colonies, who only differ from us by their color. I hope that this petition . . . which is too long to read at the moment, will not be forgotten, like so many others, in a committee, and that you will quickly receive a report on the basis of which you will pronounce the freedom of the Blacks."[37]

Labuissonnière understood only too well what referral to a committee meant. In a letter to Chaumette written the next day, he complained that "the vile countrymen of the Convention managed to stifle our voice." Chaumette would later conclude that the Convention "was not itself" when it failed to endorse the petition's demands. Chaumette arranged for the group to be received by the Paris Commune assembly on 8 June, but their campaign to get the Montagnards to embrace the abolitionist cause came to a sudden halt three days later, when Labuissonnière was arrested on charges of stealing valuable objects from, among others, Julien Raimond and Claude Milscent. The French abolition scholar Yves Bénot wondered whether Labuissonnière was a compulsive kleptomaniac, or whether the charges against him were brought to sideline his effort to get the Convention to act on the slavery question. In any event, after his arrest, the Convention would not address that issue again until it passed its historic decree of 4 February 1794. The only immediate outcome of the flurry of public appearances he and Chaumette had staged was to provide a template for such events that Chaumette would revive, on a larger scale, when the passage of that decree finally gave him the opportunity.[38]

With the abolitionists in disarray, Page and Brulley set out to turn the machinery of the revolutionary government to their own purposes. They quickly realized that the Convention's Committee of Public Safety was now the center of power. One of its members, the Montagnard firebrand Louis-Antoine de Saint-Just, had been assigned to draft a report on the troubles in Saint-Domingue, and the two colonial lobbyists began meeting regularly with him. On 23 June they were able to do Saint-Just a big favor. Brissot had been arrested a few days earlier, and Saint-Just needed material for an indictment against him. In a matter of hours, Page and Brulley came back with the requested information. When they heard that Danton might be trying to get the two incarcerated members of the First Civil Commission, Roume and Saint-Léger, released from prison, they dashed off a letter to him, demanding that they be allowed to present evidence against them. When one of their fellow colonists complained that the Revolutionary Tribunal wasn't taking action in response to their denunciations, Page and Brulley wrote to Antoine Fouquier-Tinville, the court's chief prosecutor.[39]

Another of Page and Brulley's key contacts was Jeanbon Saint-André, a member of the Committee of Public Safety with special responsibility for naval and colonial affairs. On 15 July Page and Brulley sent him a lengthy denunciation of the civil commissioners Sonthonax and Polverel, whom they accused of persecuting the white colonists in Saint-Domingue. The explanation was simple, the lobbyists maintained: "Sonthonax and Polverel, creatures of Brissot, this disorganizer of the colonies," were agents of their patron's conspiracy. Their letter was read aloud at the Convention on the following day. The deputy Jean-Jacques Bréard, who had already called Sonthonax and Polverel "aristocrats and intriguers" two months earlier, moved that the two men be indicted immediately. He was seconded by Nicolas Billaud-Varennes, another Montagnard radical and future member of the Committee of Public Safety, and the motion was passed without debate. The procolonial *Nouvelles politiques* claimed that Polverel and Sonthonax "had decided to surrender Saint-Domingue to the naval forces of England and Spain."[40]

The decree of 16 July 1793 ended the two commissioners' mandate and ordered them to return to France to face the charges against them. Page and Brulley nagged Saint-Just and the Committee of Public Safety to get the decree dispatched to Saint-Domingue as rapidly as possible and suggested reliable men who could be sent to enforce it. Once Sonthonax and Polverel were replaced, the commissioners wanted to see all their actions and proclamations annulled, the military units of free men of color that they had created dissolved, and the mixed-race administrative bodies they had created dismissed. While Page and Brulley were imagining a return to white rule in the colony, Julien Raimond realized that his allies there might be in danger. He wrote to warn them not to expose themselves to the fate of the Girondins by resisting the Convention's decree against Sonthonax and Polverel. "Be careful, *frères et amis*, not to fall into the criminal errors of some of the departments who soon either recognized their mistakes or were punished for them."[41]

In the midst of all this bad news for the abolitionist cause, Grégoire achieved one small victory. On 27 July 1793 the interior minister Dominique-Joseph Garat asked the Convention whether he should continue to give out the subsidies to various branches of French commerce and industry that had been supported by the monarchy, including the payments meant to encourage the slave trade. Grégoire seized the moment, asking, "For how long, citizens, will you permit this infamous business? . . . Let it no longer be permitted to any Frenchman to go take men, who are like us although of a different color, to transport them to a foreign land where they are employed like beasts of burden." His words suggested a complete ban on the slave trade, but his actual motion was limited to demanding the end of government subsidies. The Convention endorsed that proposal, but when another deputy proposed a ban on the trade itself, the assembly tabled the motion. The significance of Grégoire's motion was further reduced two months later, when the Convention voted to pay the subsidies to slave traders whose ships had set sail before the vote to end them.[42]

Ironically, by the time Page and Brulley had achieved their victory over Sonthonax and Polverel in Paris, the two civil commissioners had done what none of the abolitionists in Paris had thought possible: They had begun dismantling slavery. Their decision was a response to an acute crisis. General Galbaud, the man whom both Page and Brulley and their opponent Raimond had endorsed for the position of colonial governor, had arrived in Saint-Domingue in May 1793. He quickly came into conflict with Sonthonax and Polverel, who ordered him to return to France. Instead, Galbaud rallied several thousand sailors from the numerous ships in the harbor of Cap Français. Together with white colonists hostile to Sonthonax and Polverel, they stormed ashore on 20 June 1793, bent on capturing or killing the commissioners. The armed men of color defended them, but they were outnumbered, and so Sonthonax and Polverel saw no alternative except to try to rally support from the Black population. On the evening of 20 June 1793, they issued the first emancipation proclamation in French history, offering freedom to any enslaved Black men who would fight on their side.[43]

Fighting in Cap Français continued for several more days, during which fire destroyed most of the city. Galbaud's improvised force was defeated, and all but a few whites fled to the ships in the harbor, which carried them to the United States. The destruction of Cap Français, the largest city in Saint-Domingue, set off a complicated sequence of events that corresponded neither to the French abolitionists' vision of grateful Blacks rallying around their liberators nor to the proslavery lobby's dire prediction of unrestrained mayhem and violence. The organized Black forces led by Jean-François, Biassou, and Toussaint Louverture stuck to the alliance they had made with the Spanish, in part because they had been persuaded that revolutionary France was facing defeat in Europe and that promises made by its officials would therefore prove to be worthless.

As they tried to win over the Blacks, Sonthonax and Polverel found themselves forced to expand the limited emancipation offer they had made on 20 June. They were unaware that their powers had been suspended by the Convention—that news would not reach them until November—and on 29 August 1793, Sonthonax issued a decree of general emancipation for the colony's North Province; Polverel soon followed suit in the West and South Provinces. Both men coupled the grant of freedom with elaborate labor regulations meant to keep the plantation economy functioning. This was not the freedom most Blacks sought. Anticipating the restrictions that he thought the commissioners were bound to add to their offer of freedom, Louverture wrote that "as long as God give us the force and the means, we will acquire another Liberty, different from that which you tyrants pretend to impose on us."[44]

Accounts of the destruction of Cap Français in June 1793 began to arrive in Paris at the end of August. "According to these reports, nothing was spared: men, women, children, old people, all have been massacred by the ferocious executors of the vengeances of Sonthonax and Polverel," Page and Brulley wrote in their register. As had happened with the first reports of the slave uprising in 1791, the news was at first met with incredulity. Saint-Just and the navy minister Jean Dalbarade dismissed the reports, and Claude Milscent, who had resumed publication of his newspaper at the end of July 1793, wrote that "the denunciations of the colonists against the national commissioners are those of nobles opposing sans-culottes. What importance should one give them?" The outraged colonists forwarded a copy of Milscent's paper to the authorities, complaining about his description of them, but for the moment they got no response.[45]

The news of the destruction of Cap Français and the flight of most of its white inhabitants was devastating for many colonists in France, but it served Page and Brulley's purposes perfectly. On 3 September 1793 they accompanied their ally Jeanbon Saint-André to the Convention, where he gave a report denouncing Sonthonax and Polverel as the instigators of the disaster. The Convention responded by renewing the decree ordering the arrest of the two commissioners. Two days later, Page and Brulley wrote a longer address to the Convention: "It is thus that the horrible project of the destruction of the most important colony will take place. Brissot and his accomplices have neglected nothing for the execution of this abominable plan. Sonthonax and Polverel, his creatures, have followed it only too well."[46] The day of 5 September was a particularly chaotic one: In addition to the news from Saint-Domingue, Paris had just learned that France's Mediterranean naval base of Toulon had surrendered to the British. Once again, as on 31 May, an angry crowd of sans-culottes surrounded the Convention, demanding that the deputies make "terror the order of the day" in order to defeat the country's enemies. Thanks to a clever speech by Danton, the Convention eluded that demand, but it took a number of radical measures, including adding Billaud-Varennes, who had spoken in favor of the decree against Sonthonax and Polverel on 16 July, to the Committee of Public Safety.[47]

Although the stage now seemed set for Page and Brulley to take revenge on their enemies, they suffered a temporary setback when the Convention's colonial committee resumed the hearings it had been holding with them and Raimond several months earlier. At a meeting on 11 September, Raimond presented proof that his opponents had falsified passages from his letters in order to make it appear that he was inciting trouble in the colony. When the committee held a follow-up session on 23 September, Page and Brulley refused to attend, and the committee unanimously agreed that Raimond's accusations were accurate. In the interval between the two committee meetings, Page and Brulley held the first of what would become nineteen meetings with another key figure in the revolutionary government: André Amar, a member of the Committee of General Security, which was in charge of tracking down enemies of the Revolution. At their request, Amar ordered the arrest of Raimond; he would remain in prison for the next fourteen months. Page and Brulley also denounced Milscent, and in early October Amar assured them that his imprisonment was imminent. While the abolitionists were coming under suspicion, the Convention's colonial committee handed Page and Brulley another victory, clearing the men Sonthonax had deported from Saint-Domingue of all charges and urging that they be given financial compensation.[48]

The arrest of Raimond and the looming trial of Brissot created an atmosphere of fear that affected even the one outspoken abolitionist who still seemed untouchable. On 6 October 1793 Page and Brulley noted in their register that Grégoire had come to see them, ostensibly to discuss methods for producing cochineal, a red dye that was one of Saint-Domingue's exports. According to their version of the meeting, Grégoire "expressed the pain that he feels about the disasters in Saint-Domingue; he excuses himself for what he wrote during the Constituent Assembly, admits that he was misled, and promises to make up for his unintentional faults by writing about the colonies in accordance with the more accurate information that has been given to him." As the Revolution turned increasingly hostile to the Catholic Church, Grégoire had more than enough reasons to worry about his safety, and it is plausible that he may have tried to protect himself from being denounced for his views on the colonies, although Brulley's account of their conversation is the only mention of this meeting.[49]

The first reports of the commissioners' general emancipation proclamations reached Paris in mid-October, but they were so garbled that no one seems to have realized what they meant. The *Moniteur universel*, the Revolution's "newspaper of record," reported that "the perfidious commissioners Polverel and Sonthonax have entirely unmasked themselves. The Negroes of Saint-Domingue seem to have proclaimed them kings. This infamous duumvirate is said to have seized the properties of the colonists whom they have forced to flee or else slaughtered."[50] Around the same time, the Convention also admitted a free man of color as a deputy for the first time. His name was Janvier Littée and he had been elected, along with several white men, to represent the colony of Martinique. Page and Brulley had no reason to be concerned about Littée: When he arrived in Paris, he sought them out and convinced them that he was a fellow slaveholder who shared their views. Littée rarely appeared at the Convention, and no one seems to have recognized the significance of his election.[51]

Having silenced Raimond, Page and Brulley now turned their attention to their most hated enemy: Brissot. In the run-up to the trial of the Girondins, Page and Brulley had a number of meetings with Saint-Just and Amar in which they made sure that their accusations were included in the general indictment against the Brissot group. Although they were disappointed that the issue was relegated to the end of the lengthy list of charges, they had the satisfaction of seeing their words incorporated in it: "[British prime minister William] Pitt wanted to destroy our colonies; they have destroyed our colonies. Brissot, Pétion, Guadet, Gensonné, Vergniaud, [Jean-François] Ducos, [Jean-Baptiste Boyer-] Fonfrède, have directed the operations concerning our colonies, and our colonies are reduced to the most terrible condition."[52]

Preparing himself for his day in court, Brissot filled some twenty manuscript pages with a review of all the arguments on colonial issues that he had made since the formation of the Amis des Noirs in 1788. Remembering the great debate of May 1791, he wrote "Ah! who does not recall with delight the day, the wonderful day on which the Legislative Assembly declared (for it would have thought it was outraging humanity if it did not do so) the rights of men of color? . . . Who has forgotten the holy fervor with which all the members, all the spectators rose up at the proposition of this declaration?" Looking back at his own efforts, he added, "Whatever happens to me, I will always take pride to have helped contribute to rescuing thousands of good citizens from oppression and degradation; whatever my fate, their tears will moisten my ashes, and I will take with me the sweet consolation that they will always cherish my name." The policy he had fought for had ensured the loyalty to the men of color and of "five hundred thousand Blacks, who, under the new French regime, could hope for the improvement of their condition." In a marginal insertion, he vented his anger at Robespierre, who in May 1791 had "made this energetic exclamation, so strongly condemned by the colonists he supports today: 'Perish the colonies, rather than sacrifice a single principle.'"[53]

The trial itself was a disappointment, both for Brissot and for the colonists. Brissot knew that his fate was sealed, but he was frustrated that the newspapers were not allowed to print the impassioned speech he had prepared. The *Nouvelles politiques*, for example, reduced his remarks about colonial issues to half a sentence, and the only comment Milscent made about the conviction of his one-time ally was that it marked "the end of the war of aristocracy, of federalism, of fanaticism, of moderantism against a great people which has sworn in its heart to be free or to die in the ruins of its freedom." Page and Brulley spent three days waiting for a chance to speak, but they were never called to testify. The most damaging testimony against the defendants that related to the colonies was delivered, ironically, by Chaumette, the procureur of the Commune who had arranged the demonstrations in favor of abolition in the days following the Girondins' exclusion from the Convention. He explained that he had declined an invitation to accompany Sonthonax and Polverel to Saint-Domingue in 1792 because he doubted their determination to abolish slavery and he accused the two of them of having "set up a throne on the bleeding skulls of the colony's inhabitants, from which you can judge the merits of those who named them for this mission and who have directed them."[54]

In the wake of the execution of the Girondins, Robespierre himself consecrated the accusation that they had plotted to ruin the colonies. Page and Brulley were in the audience at the Convention on 17 November, when the Incorruptible, now recognized as the dominant figure in the Committee of Public Safety, proclaimed that "the same faction which wanted to reduce the poor in France to the status of helots, and force the people to submit to the aristocracy of wealth, wanted to emancipate and arm all the Blacks over night to destroy our colonies." The two colonial lobbyists were surprised—they still thought of Robespierre as the man who had cried out "Perish the colonies!" in 1791—but their register recorded their "satisfaction" at hearing their accusations echoed by the leader of the revolutionary government.[55]

After seeing their Girondin enemies eliminated and their conspiracy theory embraced by Robespierre, Page and Brulley looked forward confidently to more triumphs. "Brissot is no more, Raimond his accomplice, now in prison, will be brought before the

Revolutionary Tribunal . . . other criminal agitators of our colonies will no doubt experience the same fate. [Antoine] Barnave himself will not escape the nation's vengeance," they gloated in their register.[56] The execution of the Girondins on 31 October 1793 was the prelude to a series of high-profile political trials whose victims included Marie-Antoinette and Brissot's close friend Madame Roland. Olympe de Gouges tried unsuccessfully to convince the jurors of her republican sentiments by reminding them of her play *The Slavery of the Blacks*. Page and Brulley were allowed to testify against Barnave, who fell victim to his efforts to save the monarchy in 1791. He was also accused of destroying the colonies, even after he pointed out to the court that if Brissot was guilty of that crime, he himself should be acquitted, since they had always advocated opposing policies.[57]

Although Raimond escaped trial in the fall of 1793, he was subjected to several grueling days of interrogation by the Committee of General Security. With the execution of Brissot and the Girondins still fresh in his mind, Raimond did his best to minimize his relations with the man who had long been his close ally. In testimony that makes painful reading, he claimed that "he had never been able to really understand Brissot" and that his relations with him "had no other purpose except that he thought he could see that Brissot, in accordance with his principles, was fighting for the same cause that he had embraced." The events of 31 May, Raimond claimed, had finally opened his eyes to Brissot's "perfidy." Brulley and Page were both allowed to submit extensive denunciations of Raimond. They claimed that he had always been "active in spreading falsehoods about the state of the colonies, that he had collaborated with Brissot and Milscent Créole in misleading public opinion . . . in order to induce the Legislative Assembly and the Convention to err and to render decrees destructive of Saint-Domingue."[58]

With victory for their cause seemingly at hand, Page and Brulley dared to dream of getting the Convention to endorse the program put forward by the Saint-Marc assembly in 1790 by passing "a positive decree to recognize the right of each colony to organize its interior regime, allowing the National Convention to decide only on their external political and commercial relations." They wanted the dispatch of a new governor to Saint-Domingue who would arrest Sonthonax, Polverel, and the leading whites and men of color who had supported them. "Two months would be enough to restore order in Saint-Domingue and destroy the revolt," they promised. Thinking in even more ambitious terms, they proposed the creation of an army of enslaved Blacks to conquer the Spanish colony of Cuba and the British island of Jamaica. During the month of December 1793, their register recorded upbeat meetings about their plan with Billaud-Varennes, Bertrand Barère, Georges Couthon, and Robert Lindet, all members of the Committee of Public Safety, as well as with deputies from the Committee of General Security about quashing the projects of "the men of color in Paris."[59]

Even the arrival in Paris of news that the whites in Saint-Domingue had welcomed the landing of British troops on the island's west coast, the beginning of a five-year effort to conquer the colony, did not faze Page and Brulley. Summoned to meet with the navy minister, they distanced themselves from what they called "a new maneuver of the island's aristocrats" and assured him that if the colony was given the help it deserved, the colonists would remain loyal to France. The minister sent them to meet with the Committee of Public Safety, which was holding one of its frequent late-night sessions. Facing Robespierre and his colleagues, they altered their approach somewhat. Rather than conceding that some whites in Saint-Domingue might have encouraged the British, they claimed that they must either have "yielded to *force majeur*, or else, seeing themselves threatened by inevitable death as a result of the actions of Sonthonax and Polverel, they acted out of an imperious necessity." After two and a half hours of discussion, ending at two o'clock in the morning, they left, confident that they could still count on government support even at a time when suspected collusion with the British enemy was enough to send anyone else to the guillotine.[60]

Knowing that they had nothing to fear from the Committee of Public Safety, Page and Brulley stepped up their campaign. On the last day of 1793, they led a delegation of colonists to the Convention, where Brulley read an address and his colleagues swore, "Long live the Republic! Long live the Mountain!" They made regular visits to the Revolutionary Tribunal and to their ally Amar to press for the prosecution of Raimond; for good measure, they also demanded the arrest of several other men of color who had signed a petition on Raimond's behalf. The issue of slavery rarely came up in their discussions, but on 2 January, barely a month before the day when the Convention would vote to abolish the institution, they did have a long conversation with the deputy Thomas Lindet. According to their register, "They worked to demonstrate to Citizen Lindet that the emancipation of the slaves is impossible, because . . . it is inevitable that if the Negroes were left to themselves, they would soon divide into ethnic groups and kill each other."[61]

Throughout these months, Page and Brulley faced hardly any visible opposition. Milscent's *Créole patriote* was the only newspaper that continued to comment on the rare items of news that arrived from the colonies and to combat the lobbyists' campaign for colonial autonomy. But Milscent was in increasing jeopardy himself. At the end of 1793, the Jacobin Club was subjecting its members to a process of scrutiny. On 28 December it was Milscent's turn to be questioned about his patriotism. An unnamed member demanded to know whether, during his time in Saint-Domingue, he had helped hunt down runaway Blacks and even killed some of them. Milscent acknowledged that he had been a militia commander in the colony and had "done his duty."[62] As the interrogation proceeded, Milscent warded off other accusations, including one from Committee of Public Safety member Jean-Marie Collot d'Herbois. Then Robespierre interrupted, claiming to recall that when he had shut down the *Créole patriote* in the spring, Milscent had directed an "infamous diatribe" at him. Not so, Milscent retorted: In reality, he had "invited Robespierre to keep standing firm against all the factions that were then tearing the Republic apart." Robespierre replied that "he now recalled that Milscent praised him at the time, but it was only to better conceal his perfidy," and he demanded the journalist's expulsion, which was duly voted. Just four days after his expulsion, Milscent found himself facing the Revolutionary Tribunal in connection with charges about an article he had published a month earlier. Fortunately for him, one of his printer's workers took responsibility for the insertion of the offending item and swore that "he had always seen and known [Milscent] for a good citizen who preached and practiced the principles of the purest patriotism."[63]

Despite Milscent's temporary escape from danger, the abolitionist movement's prospects in France at the end of 1793 appeared dismal. At the same time as the specter of French radicalism had led to a backlash against the abolitionist campaign in Britain, the specter of British-backed conspiracy served to justify the arrest and execution of abolitionists in France. From Robespierre on down, the leaders of the country's revolutionary government embraced the claims of the white colonists, and there was a serious question as to whether the emancipation decrees Sonthonax and Polverel had issued in Saint-Domingue would be upheld when news of them reached the metropole.

Perhaps only one man in France still remained convinced that slavery and racial prejudice were bound to disappear. Confined to a cramped hiding place throughout the last months of 1793 and anticipating that he would eventually suffer the fate of the other Girondins, the pioneering abolitionist Condorcet had devoted himself to compiling a comprehensive philosophical statement, his *Tableau of the Progress of the Human Mind*. In the work's final chapter, he contemplated a future in which the principles of natural rights would have triumphed throughout the world. Already, he noted, the British colony of Sierra Leone in West Africa was demonstrating that sugar could be produced without slave labor, a development that would "destroy the shameful brigandage" that had done so much damage to that continent. France could not fail to follow the British example, and the day could not be far off when "the sun will no longer shine, anywhere on earth, on any but free men."[64] The moment when slavery would vanish from the world was still distant, but Condorcet probably did learn of the Convention's decree of 16 pluviôse, which was passed a month and half before he took the risk of trying to escape from Paris. Arrested by the police in one of the capital's suburbs, he apparently committed suicide on 27 March 1794.

CHAPTER NINE

The Decree of 16 Pluviôse Year II

AS THE YEAR 1794 began, there was no sign that France's legislators were about to tackle the issue of slavery, which was still legal in the country's overseas colonies. The fact that the civil commissioners Léger-Félicité Sonthonax and Etienne Polverel had granted freedom to the Black population in Saint-Domingue was not yet really understood in Paris; in any event, during the journée of 5 September 1793, the National Convention had renewed its decree for their arrest and return to France, potentially nullifying the actions they had taken. The fate of Jacques-Pierre Brissot and his leading Girondin allies, tried and executed in October 1793, silenced the most prominent advocates for slavery's reform or abolition. Maximilien Robespierre and the other leaders of the revolutionary government were unanimous in blaming Brissot and France's foreign enemies for inciting the uprising in Saint-Domingue.

Pierre-François Page and Augustin Brulley, the indefatigable defenders of the proslavery cause, were confident that they had won the support of the Convention and the Committee of Public Safety. In the port cities, a network of white colonists, many of whom had managed to join local surveillance committees, watched for new arrivals from the Caribbean, ready to denounce anyone who contradicted the claim that Sonthonax and Polverel were the sole causes of the troubles in Saint-Domingue. On 29 January 1794, less than a week before everything changed, a member of this network from Bordeaux wrote to Brulley expressing confidence that "the National Convention will soon decree the reestablishment of order in Saint-Domingue; you will thus find yourselves rewarded for all the efforts that you have made to publicize the situation of our unfortunate colony, and the remedy it requires."[1]

Suddenly, in the last week of January 1794, the tone of the entries in Page and Brulley's register changed from optimism to panic. They had learned that "three emissaries sent by Sonthonax and Polverel, a white named Dufay, a mulatto named Mills, and a Negro, whose name isn't precisely known," had eluded their spies in the port of Lorient and arrived in Paris. Page and Brulley dashed to the offices of the Committee of Public Safety and then sought out their reliable ally André Amar from the Committee of General Security to demand that he have the three men arrested. Amar told them to draft a denunciation, which they brought to him on the following day, pointing out how dangerous it would be "if these men succeed in justifying the conduct of Polverel and Sonthonax and of having admitted into law the proclamation of 29 August relative to the general liberty of all the Negroes of Saint-Domingue." After that meeting, they went to the navy ministry, where an official, Pierre Adet, who would later play a major role in justifying the restoration of slavery under Napoleon, furnished them with the names of all six of the deputies whom Sonthonax had sent to France and told them "how much he hoped that they could ward off the blow that they proposed to inflict on the colony."[2]

The men whose arrival in Paris so agitated Page and Brulley had been chosen to represent Saint-Domingue in the National Convention, in accordance with the election law passed by the Legislative Assembly in August 1792. Sonthonax had supervised the election in the colony's North Province, and the white colonists in France were right in assuming that the deputies were supporters of his policies. Sonthonax had made sure that the delegation representing the colony was racially balanced: It included two Blacks, two men of mixed race, and two whites. Because of the British naval blockade, the deputies had to travel via the United States, where they were assaulted by white proslavery refugees. Fortunately for them, the French representative in America, Edmond Genet, was, like

Sonthonax and Polverel, an appointee of Brissot who sympathized with the civil commissioners. He intervened to ensure the deputies' safety and speed their departure for France; he also drafted a lengthy report to the ministry of foreign affairs justifying the commissioners' actions.[3]

At the moment when the Saint-Domingue deputies had left Saint-Domingue, the colony had been cut off from news from France for many months. During their stop in the United States, however, the men had had access to newspapers from France that gave them some idea of the situation that awaited them in Paris. In a letter to Sonthonax and Polverel, Louis Dufay, a white member of the group, summarized what he had deduced from these reports. He now knew that their once powerful patron Brissot and his supporters had been arrested and executed, and "it is natural enough that there should have been attempts to include you in their disgrace." Dufay was also able to report, however, that nothing had been done to implement the decree recalling the commissioners, and so he reassured them that the government probably did not mean to execute it.[4]

At the time when Sonthonax and Polverel had left France in July 1792, Louis XVI was still on the throne and the entire structure of the revolutionary government that existed in early 1794 was not yet dreamed of. Based on the newspaper accounts he read in America, Dufay tried to explain to Sonthonax and Polverel the importance of the Committee of Public Safety and how, under its leadership, "the country is coming together with a common desire to save itself." As he caught up on the events in France in the first half of 1793, Dufay was impressed by the role of Georges Danton, who had indeed occupied the limelight earlier in the year, and concluded that the great orator must be the most important revolutionary leader, with Robespierre "in second place." Danton had still been at center stage as recently as 5 September 1793, when he had successfully defused the political crisis sparked by the news of the surrender of Toulon; Dufay did not know that he had subsequently retreated to his country home in Champagne, leaving a vacuum that Robespierre quickly filled. By the time the Saint-Domingue deputies reached Paris, however, Danton had been back in the capital for two months, actively directing a campaign against the Terror that led to his followers being labeled "the Indulgents."[5]

Knowing that they risked being intercepted when they landed in France, the six Saint-Domingue deputies split into two groups of three so that at least some of them would have a chance to reach Paris. Dufay and his two colleagues reached the French port of Lorient in late January 1794. Victor Hugues, a white colonist who would soon be sent to the Caribbean, where he would enlist Black soldiers to drive the British out of the island of Guadeloupe, was at this point part of the proslavery network in the coastal ports and tried to get the Convention deputy Pierre-Louis Prieur de la Marne, who was on mission in the area, to have the three men arrested. After all, Hugues expostulated, "they have freed the Negroes and they are already fighting among themselves. That's what comes of a misunderstood freedom."[6] Despite Hugues's efforts, the three men managed to make their way to Paris, where they arrived on 26 January 1794.

The three Saint-Domingue deputies—Jean-Baptiste Belley, an African-born free Black man who had distinguished himself in the fighting in Cap Français in June 1793; James Mills, a man of mixed race; and Dufay—landed in the middle of a growing crisis in the ranks of the French revolutionary leaders. The harsh policies, often described as "the Terror," implemented under the direction of the Committee of Public Safety in the fall of 1793 had allowed the revolutionary government to beat off the invading foreign armies and to bring the peasant revolt in the Vendée under control. The drastic measures imposed to deal with inflation and food shortages had not succeeded, however, in relieving the population's complaints. As a result, Robespierre and his colleagues felt threatened by two rival political factions. One was a populist movement demanding even harsher measures that was led by the journalist and Paris Commune official Jacques-René Hébert, whose rabble-rousing pamphlet-journal, the *Père Duchêne*, enjoyed a broad audience. The second threat came from the Indulgents, the group formed by Danton and the journalist Camille Desmoulins, two former close associates of Robespierre who launched a campaign to end the Terror and free many of the prisoners arrested under the sweeping "law of suspects." In a major speech at the end of December 1793, Robespierre had condemned both factions, calling Hébert and his followers "ultras" who wanted to push the Revolution too far and labeling the Indulgents "citras" who were unwilling to support the measures necessary for its survival.

As soon as they arrived, the three Saint-Domingue deputies realized that they were going to have a hard time navigating these turbulent political waters. As Dufay would later recall, "On arriving in Paris, I asked questions; everyone was silent, or misled me, no one dared tell me the truth. . . . I saw those who I had known for their reputations as founders of liberty and its best defenders, held in irons and threatened with death, others already executed. . . . I didn't know what to think, what to do."[7] He also realized that everyone in France seemed to "be in the most profound ignorance" about what was happening in the colony. He and his colleagues were fearful of turning their cause into a partisan issue, however. In one letter he wrote, "We haven't wanted to appear yet at the Jacobin club or to see anyone in order to avoid being accused of trying to attract partisans, to win over support."

The situation facing the Saint-Domingue deputies was further complicated by rivalries within the ranks of the revolutionary government itself. Robespierre was generally regarded as the dominant figure within the Committee of Public Safety, but he was often at odds with his colleagues, some of whom resented his preeminence. In addition, there was tension between the Committee of Public Safety and the other "great" committee at the heart of the government, Amar's Committee of General Security. That tension proved fortunate for the newly arrived Saint-Domingue deputies. In response to Page and Brulley's complaints, on 26 January 1794, Amar made out arrest warrants accusing the three deputies of being accomplices in Sonthonax and Polverel's supposed plot to destroy Saint-Domingue, but it took three days before Dufay and Mills were actually imprisoned, and Belley remained free because of a confusion about his name. In the meantime, the Saint-Domingue deputies succeeded in contacting members of the Committee of Public Safety and convincing some of them that the generally accepted story about the situation in Saint-Domingue was completely wrong and that the Committee of General Security's arrest warrants were unjustified. Committee of Public Safety member Robert Lindet told Page and Brulley that he and his colleagues now recognized that the two civil commissioners, rather than deliberately setting out to sabotage the colony, might have acted because of "exaggerated principles of liberty, poorly applied," without being motivated by "views of royalism or counterrevolution."[8]

After their arrests, Dufay and Mills wrote to the Convention, claiming that they were victims of a plot to prevent the legislators from putting into effect the idealistic "principle of equality, of the fraternity of colors," that was the essence of the Revolution.[9] On 1 February 1794 the Committee of General Security reversed itself, probably under pressure from the Committee of Public Safety, and ordered them released from prison. Although the Saint-Domingue deputies did not realize it, they had benefited from a great stroke of luck: Robespierre, the Committee of Public Safety member most hostile to anyone identified with Brissot and his policies, was ill and was not attending the committee's meetings. On the following day, when Page and Brulley encountered Bertrand Barère, one of the Incorruptible's colleagues, he told them emphatically that the Committee of Public Safety was not happy with the lobbyists' efforts to have the Saint-Domingue deputies kept in prison. "It is well known that the whites are aristocrats in that colony and that the men of color and the Negroes are patriots," Barère informed them. Increasingly nervous, Page and Brulley turned for support to their friend Amar, who agreed with them that if the Saint-Domingue deputies were actually admitted to the Convention, "they would have general liberty decreed, which would lose all the colonies once and for all," but he could not promise to do anything further to stop them.[10]

On the following day, 3 February 1794, it became clear that Danton and his friends were ready to turn the abolition of slavery into a weapon in their struggle against Robespierre and the governing committees. Two days earlier, two of the three Saint-Domingue deputies had been in prison, fearing that they were about to be sent before the Revolutionary Tribunal; now the deputy Simon Monnel, speaking for the Convention's credentials committee, announced that the three of them had presented valid documents showing that they were entitled to seats in France's legislature. Simon Camboulas, who had defended Sonthonax and Polverel during the debate about the decree of 5 March 1793, celebrated their admission: "Liberty triumphs, equality is consecrated. A Black, a yellow and a white are going to be seated among you." Then Danton rose to speak. It was not one of the long and fiery speeches for which he was famous, but his words had an unmistakable significance in the context of his campaign against the revolutionary government. "We do not just owe homage to the equality of colors," he told the legislators. "The Convention, in the name of justice, needs to avenge the representatives of the nation, who have been outrageously treated in the person of the three deputies just admitted. There is no form of persecution they have not endured as a result of the maneuvers of the colonial aristocrats: they were even imprisoned to keep them from taking up their posts. I demand a report from the Committee of General Security on this subject."[11]

Translated into plain language, Danton accused the Committee of General Security, one of the pillars of the revolutionary government, of having been taken in by the colonial lobby. He called on the Convention, which had become accustomed to delegating its authority to that committee and the even more powerful Committee of Public Safety, to stand up for its own rights. Meanwhile, other deputies, conscious of the symbolic importance of what they were doing, focused their attention on their new colleagues. Jean-François Delacroix, an ally of Danton's who had spoken several times in favor of rights for free men of color in the Legislative Assembly, announced, "For a long time, the assembly wished to have in its midst some men of color, who were oppressed for so many years. Today it has two; I ask that their entry be marked by a fraternal accolade." As the other deputies applauded, Belley and Mills came forward and were solemnly embraced by the Convention's presiding officer.[12] Other than the almost-overlooked admission of Janvier Littée five months earlier, this was the first time that men of African descent were seated as members of a national legislature anywhere in the Atlantic world.

The Convention's admission of the Saint-Domingue deputies on 3 February was quickly overshadowed by what it did on the following day. After rendering homage to three "brave sans-culottes" who had rescued a man who had fallen into the Seine, the Convention gave the speaker's podium to Louis Dufay, the white Saint-Domingue deputy admitted the previous day, so that he could deliver a report on the events that had led up to Sonthonax and Polverel's grant of freedom to the enslaved Blacks in the colony.

There could hardly have been a more unlikely person to precipitate the abolition of slavery than Dufay. Born in Paris in 1752, he had gone to Saint-Domingue during the American Revolutionary War in hopes of making his fortune. Although he was legally a commoner, he claimed to be from a noble family and managed to marry a wealthy widow, which brought him ownership of a plantation with slaves. By 1785, however, the couple had separated and Dufay returned to France, where he was imprisoned for debt in 1788. By the time the Revolution began in 1789, he was free again, and his name appears on lists of attendees at meetings of the Saint-Domingue colonists' Club Massiac and the Jacobin Club. In late 1791 he went back to Saint-Domingue, perhaps to avoid responsibility for an illegitimate child he had fathered. Treated with disdain by most of his fellow colonists, he was one of the few whites willing to attach himself to Sonthonax and Polverel after they arrived in Saint-Domingue in September 1792.[13]

Not only had Dufay never shown any commitment to the cause of abolition, but nothing in his previous career had readied him for the challenge of addressing a legislative assembly on such a momentous occasion. He had certainly prepared himself carefully: His speech, which may have lasted as long as three hours, was skillfully constructed and was published in full less than forty-eight hours after he gave it, evidence that he must have provided journalists with a written version.[14] No doubt he had discussed what he would say with Sonthonax and Polverel before he left Saint-Domingue and with the ambassador Genet during his stop in New York. Danton may have seized on the arrival of the Saint-Domingue delegates for his own purposes, but Dufay was careful not to say anything that would tie him and his colleagues to the Indulgents or any other revolutionary faction. Reflecting back on his situation eighteen months later, Dufay recalled how nervous he had been, as he realized, "I had to say the same things about the colonies that the deputies of the Gironde had said. I had already been jailed for being a Girondin. I saw that the men who were responsible for the loss of the colonies, and who had accused the Girondin deputies of having lost them, were bound to pursue me."[15]

As a former slave owner, Dufay knew that his claim, "I had always carried the germs of liberty and equality in my heart," would sound dubious; he tried to sidestep that obstacle by claiming that the French Revolution itself, whose early stages he had witnessed in Paris, had taught him that slavery was a violation of natural rights, and that "a friend of liberty and equality had to also be a friend of humanity."[16] He was committed to justifying the actions that the commissioners Sonthonax and Polverel had taken in Saint-Domingue, but he was acutely conscious that his audience consisted of the same legislators who had voted, in July 1793, to have the two men arrested for abusing their powers, and he was now about to defend them for having even more dramatically exceeded their mandate. At a moment when the French population was being mobilized for all-out war against its foreign enemies, he had to explain actions that no less a figure than Robespierre, in his speech of 27 brumaire Year II, had blamed for giving Britain a major advantage in the struggle for control of the Caribbean. More fundamentally, Dufay knew he had to counter the pervasive belief that Blacks were, by nature, uncivilized beings who did not deserve the same rights as whites. In reality, this was a prejudice that he himself shared: A few weeks after his speech, he incautiously published a pamphlet in which he referred to the Blacks in Saint-Domingue as "these still savage peoples, of whom many even came from hordes of cannibals."[17]

Dufay's speech showed that he had managed to adapt the rhetorical strategies of the Terror to his purposes, or, as he later put it, "to use their language somewhat in order to get myself heard."[18] Rather than delivering a soaring speech about natural rights, he spent most of his time denouncing the Revolution's enemies. The published version of his speech omitted the names of Sonthonax and Polverel, whom the Convention had ordered arrested in July 1793, referring instead to "your commissioners" or "your delegates," even though the two had actually been appointed by the previous revolutionary legislature, not by the Convention. If they had taken seemingly extraordinary measures, it was because they had to ward off a counterrevolutionary attack led by General François-Thomas Galbaud and supported by "the gold of the Spanish Bourbons and the English," "the [colonial] whites," "the counterrevolutionaries who had arrived from France and Coblentz," the aristocratic officers of the naval ships sent to the colonies, and the "merchants of your principal commercial cities."[19] Dufay emphasized the patriotism of the colony's free people of color, who had been granted rights by the law of 4 April 1792. "The citizens of color . . . the people, the true sans-culottes in the colonies," had "immediately rallied around your commissioners," he said, proving that groups given rights would react with gratitude and eagerly join the French forces. The men of color had been "the first to sacrifice their slaves," he added, pointing dramatically to his two colleagues Mills and Belley, who, he claimed, "were the first to give the example," a remark that might have confused deputies who did not realize that free people of color in the colonies were often slave owners themselves.[20]

Rather than acting out of abolitionist zeal, Dufay insisted, the civil commissioners had conceded freedom to the Blacks out of necessity. He portrayed the Blacks who had joined the fight against Galbaud in June 1793 as having told the commissioners, "'We are going to fight for France, but as a reward, we ask for freedom.' They even added, 'the Rights of Man.'" The commissioners, in Dufay's telling, had no choice but to accept this offer: "The Blacks understood their strength; they might even have turned it against us if we had offended them." This was not entirely accurate: In fact, Sonthonax and Polverel had taken the initiative to reach out to the Black insurgents in the hills around Cap Français, offering them freedom in exchange for military assistance. Furthermore, at the moment when Dufay gave his speech, the majority of the armed Blacks in Saint-Domingue, including Toussaint Louverture, were still fighting against the French as part of the Spanish Army.[21]

After arguing that the commissioners' offer of freedom to the Blacks was "not spontaneous, that they were constrained to adopt it to save the sovereignty of the nation," Dufay emphasized how carefully limited Sonthonax's decree of general emancipation of 29 August 1793 was. "The proclamation, in declaring [the enslaved Blacks] free, assigned them to remain at their respective plantations, and subjected them to severe discipline as well as daily work, in return for a set salary; they are more or less attached to the estate," he explained, using terms that echoed many of the proposals for limited emancipation that had been put forward in prerevolutionary discussions of abolition. He assured his listeners that the freed Blacks would now be eager to work in order to earn money, and that they would spend that money on products from France. "You will see that your colony of Saint-Domingue, cultivated by free hands, will be more flourishing . . . that this new colony will produce more for the metropole than before, that your political influence is assured in Saint-Domingue and that soon it will dominate the entire archipelago of the Gulf of Mexico," he concluded, echoing similar promises in Genet's report to the foreign ministry.[22]

Dufay then tried to counter the familiar stereotypes of Blacks as lazy and violent. Referring to his own experience as a slave owner, he commented that these supposedly uncontrollable beings "allowed themselves to be ordered around by a single white man, and went along with all his whims." Parroting eighteenth-century commonplaces about unspoiled children of nature that had appeared in the *Encyclopédie*, he depicted the Blacks as "naturally sweet, charitable, hospitable, very devoted to their parents. . . . They love justice and have the greatest respect for their elders." Furthermore, he claimed, they were eager to embrace a new identity as French patriots. "The story of all that you have done for liberty enlightened, warmed, inflamed their hearts; the story of your victories raised their souls, and inspired in them sentiments of patriotism that had been previously unknown to them." Having assured the Convention deputies that granting freedom to the Blacks was both unavoidable and desirable from the point of view of ensuring the triumph of revolutionary France, that it would not harm the national economy, that the Blacks would be strictly controlled, and that they would happily embrace their new status, Dufay concluded by appealing to the legislators to seize the opportunity offered to them by the situation in Saint-Domingue. "You can . . . earn a consoling memory for yourselves in honoring humanity and carrying out the great act of justice it expects from you. Create a new world for the second time, or at least let it be remade thanks to you; be its benefactors; your names will be blessed like those of tutelary deities," he concluded.[23]

Newspaper reports give little sense of how Dufay spoke, although some mention that he was frequently interrupted by applause. But what action would the Convention take in response to his speech? Dufay himself offered no specific motion for debate. The Convention might simply have expressed approval for the measures

Sonthonax and Polverel had taken. Such a response would have defined emancipation as a pragmatic response to an emergency situation, rather than a fulfillment of the Revolution's supposed commitment to universal natural rights. It would have had no effect on France's other colonies, and it would have had only a limited impact on slavery anywhere else in the world.

In the early months of its existence, the National Convention had been the scene of stormy debates between deputies defending fundamentally opposing views. With the centralization of decision-making in the Committee of Public Safety, however, the deputies had learned to avoid expressing themselves until they knew what course that body wanted them to take. But on 4 February 1794, the members of the committee were conspicuous by their absence. On that day, Robespierre rejoined his colleagues on the Committee of Public Safety, but instead of coming to the Convention's hall, the seven members present in Paris convened in their own conference room for a private session.

Like the deputies listening to Dufay's speech, the Committee of Public Safety assembled to listen to representatives from Saint-Domingue and consider the colony's fate. The representatives the committee had agreed to meet with, however, were not there to advocate freedom for the enslaved Blacks. They were none other than Page and Brulley, the diehard defenders of the white slaveholders' interests. Desperate to overturn the decision made at Danton's behest the previous day, the two men argued that the Saint-Domingue deputies, whom they described as "a former marquis [Dufay], an Englishman [Mills, who had been born in one of the British colonies], and an African Bambara [Belley] have been presented to you as deputies of Saint-Domingue. . . . These men have been denounced as guilty of general and specific crimes that are attested to by eyewitnesses." According to Page and Brulley's notes, several committee members seemed swayed by their arguments, but the group as a whole was unwilling to take any immediate action. The proslavery lobbyists warned that if he wasn't stopped, Dufay was about to "immediately deliver a report whose result could be damaging for the entire regime of the colonies," but they were finally told to come back at a later date with a written memorandum. As the frustrated lobbyists stepped out of the meeting, they were met by other colonists who told them the bad news: The Convention had just voted to abolish slavery entirely.

The Convention had not taken this action without a certain amount of debate. The deputies might have expected Henri Grégoire, long identified with the abolitionist movement, to take the lead in supporting the idea. Once Dufay finished speaking, however, it was René Levasseur, a young deputy usually regarded as a loyal supporter of Robespierre, who stepped forward with a sweeping proposal that elevated the debate from the particularities of the situation in Saint-Domingue to the realm of universal principles. He urged the Convention, "not ceding to a movement of enthusiasm, but to the principles of justice, faithful to the Declaration of the Rights of Man," to "decree as of this moment that slavery is abolished throughout the territory of the Republic. . . . I want all men to be free, without distinction of color." Some deputies moved to refer the matter to the Committee of Public Safety, a disguised way of trying to sidetrack the assault on slavery, but in the absence of any of the committee's members, other legislators supported Levasseur.[24]

The Dantonist Delacroix, who had made the motion to admit the tricolor delegation of deputies from Saint-Domingue the day before, announced, "It is time to raise ourselves to the level of the principles of liberty and equality. . . . Proclaim the freedom of men of color. In carrying out this act of justice, you will give a great example to the enslaved men of color in the English and Spanish colonies. The men of color have, like us, wanted to break their chains; we have broken ours, we haven't wanted to be under the yoke of any master; let us give them the same benefit." Levasseur denounced "the aristocracy exercised in our colonies by some whites," and Delacroix chimed in again, calling on the presiding officer to "keep the Convention from dishonoring itself with a longer debate." He then proposed a motion that went even beyond what Levasseur had put forward. Levasseur's formulation promised legal freedom to the formerly enslaved Blacks; Delacroix's wording—"The National Convention decrees that slavery is abolished throughout the territory of the Republic; in consequence, all men, without distinction of color, will enjoy the rights of French citizens"—specified that they would also have full rights of citizenship.[25] The radicalism of the decree was underlined by the fact that, unlike the abolition law the British would pass in 1833 or the second French abolition law of 1848, it did not include any provision for compensation for the white slave owners.

According to newspaper accounts, Delacroix's sweeping motion brought the deputies and the spectators in the Convention's galleries to their feet, crying out, "Long live the Republic! Long live the Convention!" The official minutes of the session mention "a citizeness of color, named Marie Dupré," who was so overcome with excitement that she fainted. Dufay's colleagues Belley and Mills joined him on the speaker's platform and the presiding officer swept the three of them up in an embrace, after which they were congratulated by many of the other deputies. As the tumult died down, the deputies realized that there were still several details that had to be settled before their work was complete. One enthusiastic speaker moved that the navy minister be ordered to immediately send ships to the colonies to announce the news. At this point, Danton rose to give what would be his last significant public speech before his trial two months later. As he had at so many other crucial moments during the Revolution, he demonstrated the uncanny political talent described by one of his admirers: "He knew how to achieve at the same time his own goals and those of the opponents over whom he was triumphing."[26] Sensing the emotions the deputies were feeling, Danton managed to acknowledge the significance of what they had just done and, at the same time, restrain their impulsiveness and try to head off a confrontation with the Committee of Public Safety.

"Representatives of the French people," Danton announced, "until now we had only decreed freedom as egotists, just for ourselves. But today we proclaim, before the entire universe, and future generations will glory in this decree, we proclaim universal liberty. . . . But after having given the gift of liberty, we must be, so to speak, its moderators. Let us leave it to the Committee of Public Safety and the Colonial Committee to figure out the best way to make this decree useful to humanity without any danger to it." Having upheld the decree as proof of the French Revolution's idealism, he added that it would also be a valuable weapon in the ongoing war with Britain. "Today England is dead," he exclaimed, encouraging his audience to visualize revolts breaking out among the enslaved populations of the enemy's colonies. Thanks to the advantage the abolition of slavery would give it, "France will regain the rank and the influence promised by its energy, its resources and its population. . . . We can be sure of the blessings of the universe and of posterity." Lest anyone think he was trying to rehabilitate Brissot, he took the precaution of announcing, "We will defeat the tyrants, just as we smashed the perfidious men who wanted to make the Revolution go backward," before repeating his call to let the governing committees determine the details of the decree's application.[27]

In his speech, delivered, according to one journalist, with his customary "thunderous eloquence," Danton strove one last time to make himself the voice of the revolutionary movement.[28] Robespierre and his supporters were portraying the Indulgents as a faction concerned above all with saving imprisoned counterrevolutionaries; the debate of 4 February allowed Danton to put himself forward as the defender of the Revolution's true ideals and its universal mission. Armed with the force of its principles, his speech implied, revolutionary France had no need to fear its foreign foes and could therefore afford to be generous to those who had fallen under suspicion at home. Even as he challenged his opponents to return to the true spirit of the Revolution, however, Danton also showed himself a practical man of government. To simply send the decree to the colonies, without any plan for managing its consequences, would be irresponsible. By calling for the Convention to leave the measure's implementation to the Committee of Public Safety, Danton offered Robespierre and his colleagues an olive branch. If, instead of treating him as an enemy, they would recognize the value of his ability to galvanize the Convention in the cause of liberty while also restraining its impulsiveness, he in turn would uphold their authority to carry out the policies necessary for the Revolution's success.

Danton's motives in pushing through the law abolishing slavery were almost certainly more political than ideological: Nowhere in any of his previous speeches had he ever explicitly spoken out against the institution. The motivations of other deputies who supported the measure were varied. Many of them were no doubt persuaded by Dufay's argument that failure to endorse the actions of Sonthonax and Polverel would result in the loss of the Caribbean colonies, as well as by Danton's optimistic prophecy that the decree would set off revolts in the British and Spanish Caribbean. In his memoirs, Levasseur, the deputy who converted Dufay's plea for the acceptance of Sonthonax's limited emancipation plan into a motion to abolish slavery as a matter of principle, claimed that, for him, the abolition of slavery offered a chance to show that, in spite of the excesses of the Reign of Terror, the French Revolution was still a movement for liberty. Men like himself, he wrote, "could not see without shuddering the temporary results of our energetic measures and of the resistance they had excited." Evoking the debate on 4 February 1794 thirty-five years later, at a time when slavery had once again been made legal in the remaining French colonies, he wrote, "I never recall this session without an emotion that is both sweet and consoling." In his own memoirs, also written around 1830, the veteran abolitionist Grégoire was more reserved. He had been convinced at the time, he claimed, that "with regard to the slaves, it was necessary not to emancipate them suddenly, but to lead them gradually to the advantages of the social state." To him and his friends, "the sudden emancipation pronounced by the decree of 16 pluviôse, which Levasseur had provoked, seemed disastrous . . . it was the political equivalent of a volcano." Nevertheless, once the decree was passed, he saw no choice but to defend it.[29]

As the members of the Convention returned to their seats after the wave of applause, they realized there were still important questions about the decree to be decided. Some deputies proposed to modify the wording of Delacroix's motion in ways that would have made it possible to delay its implementation. After some back-and-forth, Delacroix offered a wordier version of his proposal that incorporated Danton's demand that the details of its implementation be left to the Committee of Public Safety: "The National Convention declares slavery abolished in all the colonies; as a consequence, it decrees that all men resident in the colonies, regardless of color, are French citizens, and will enjoy all the rights assured by the constitution. Referred to the Committee of Public Safety to present, as soon as possible, a report on the measures to be taken for the execution of this decree." François-Louis Bourdon de l'Oise then raised another question: Since the Convention had just voted to approve the measures taken by Sonthonax and Polverel in Saint-Domingue and even extend them to the other colonies, should it revoke the decree for the two commissioners' arrest that it had passed in July 1793? The deputies were not prepared to admit that their earlier vote had been a mistake and left the decision to the Committee of Public Safety.[30]

The extent of the opposition to the abolition decree became evident on the next day, when the Convention had to approve the minutes of the previous day's session. No one spoke openly against the measure, but several deputies wanted to alter its wording to remove the word "slavery," which one of them said "should not stain our decrees, or our minutes," an argument Robespierre had made during the debate of May 1791. Delacroix replied that the word "slavery" had to be included in order to make it clear to the Black population that "they are granted freedom." Grégoire made his one intervention in the debate, saying that "the word slavery must be included; otherwise, some will pretend that you meant something else, and you want all slavery to disappear." Furthermore, if the deputies wanted their decree to inspire the enslaved Blacks in the Spanish and British colonies, it was necessary to be explicit about the abolition of slavery.[31] The *Annales de la Révolution*, a newspaper published in Rouen, explained the issue to its readers: "The word *slavery* shocked some members, who, wanting to safeguard the honor of the Convention, did not want to admit that, in the Declaration of Rights, it had neglected a considerable portion of the men living in its territory; but the good spirits of the assembly thought that Convention could not equivocate; that when it had decreed the Declaration of the Rights of Man, it was aware that in reality slavery still existed in our colonies, and that in consequence it needed to declare explicitly that slavery is abolished."[32]

The Convention finally reaffirmed the wording proposed by Delacroix that had been approved the previous day. The deputy Jean-François Ducos, who had moved to declare all mixed-race children free at birth in the debate of 24 March 1792, proposed to increase the scope of the law by decreeing that "no French citizen can recognize the existence of slavery, no matter where on the globe he may have properties, on pain of being deprived of the honorable title of French citizen." Such a law would have penalized any French citizen who engaged in the slave trade or owned slaves in countries where slavery was legal, and it would certainly have antagonized foreign powers such as the United States. The Convention rejected the idea on the grounds that "we should no longer involve ourselves in the business of foreign governments." The deputy Jacques-Michel Coupé de l'Oise proposed another radical addition to the decree: He wanted the plantations belonging to white colonists who had fled Saint-Domingue to be broken up and sold in small pieces, "so that the new French citizens can acquire parts of them." This suggestion was sent to be buried in committee.[33]

The main business of the Convention on the day after the passage of the abolition decree was one of Robespierre's lengthy set-piece speeches, his oration on "the principles of political morality that must guide the Convention in the interior administration of the Republic." The Incorruptible had no doubt drafted his discourse well before the sudden passage of the abolition decree. In his speech, he hailed the French Revolution for making the country the first "to summon all men to equality and liberty, and to their full rights as citizens," but he did not see fit to add a single word about the extension of liberty and equality represented by the new law. The two instances of the word "slavery" in his speech were purely abstract and had no reference to conditions in the colonial world. In private, Robespierre left no doubt about his unhappiness with the Convention's action. He did not sign the official document with which the Committee of Public Safety approved the implementation of the abolition decree. Two months later, when his colleague Louis-Antoine de Saint-Just was drawing up the indictment against Danton, Robespierre urged him to include a charge claiming "that Danton and [De]Lacroix have had a decree passed whose likely result was the loss of our colonies."[34]

Robespierre was not the only person unhappy about the Convention's historic action. The white colonists in France were, unsurprisingly, furious. One of them wrote to Brulley lamenting that "so many injustices are reserved for republicans like us, who have sacrificed everything for the revolution," and anticipating that the members of their group might soon find themselves under arrest. Military men who had been sent to Saint-Domingue to fight the Black insurgents were confused to learn that their former enemies were now being admitted to their ranks. Four days after the passage of the abolition decree, an army captain addressed the Convention on behalf of "these soldiers who, in a bizarre situation contrary to that which animates us today, have had to fight these same men whose liberty you have just proclaimed. . . . We will, no doubt, fraternize with them . . . we'll teach them about your solemn decree, and we will fight together for the happiness and the freedom of all our fellow inhabitants of the earth." In fact, however, the second-ranking officer in the Saint-Domingue army had quit his post in protest of Sonthonax's emancipation policy, and the sailors and soldiers who had returned to France from the colony in the fall of 1793 were mostly hostile to the civil commissioners.[35]

While white colonists were working to sidetrack the abolition decree, other figures in Paris were moving to emphasize its significance. Administrative officials were instructed to identify Black people with first and last names, rather than only by their given names, as had previously been the case.[36] Public celebrations brought the decree's significance home to the general population. Dufay's speech to the Convention had precipitated the passage of the measure, but he had not provided the kind of soaring rhetoric that could be used for propaganda purposes; as the great twentieth-century Francophone author Aimé Césaire would write in 1961, Dufay's words "lacked grandeur." With Camille Desmoulins's newspaper, the *Vieux Cordelier*, shut down by the revolutionary government and its members expelled from the Jacobin Club, Danton's Indulgent group lacked any outlet to publicize its success. The Indulgents also had no contacts with the Blacks and other people of color residing in Paris. It was Pierre Chaumette, a leading member of the populist Hébertist faction that Robespierre and his allies had identified as their other enemy, who took the lead in commemorating what the Convention had done, together with the Saint-Domingue deputies themselves and some members of the capital's Caribbean community, with whom Chaumette already had ties dating back to the demonstrations that he had helped organize in early June 1793.

On the evening of 4 February 1794, just after the Convention's session, the three Saint-Domingue deputies appeared at the Jacobin Club, bringing with them the tricolor flag that had appeared in

June 1793, with figures representing a white, a Black, and a man of mixed race superimposed on its three stripes, symbolizing the unity of the three racial groups in the colonies. Two days later, Chaumette presided over a more organized celebration at the Paris Commune, the city's municipal assembly, which was under the Hébertists' control. "This decree is not the work of men," he proclaimed. "It is more the work of the Eternal . . . who wants all men henceforth to be nothing but a family of brothers."[37] On 8 February 1794 Chaumette and a group of Parisian men of color brought their tricolor flag to the Convention itself. "This sublime decree is going to give life and happiness to more than a million unfortunates," a spokesman for the men of color told the deputies. The assembly's presiding officer replied, "From now on, citizens, you will enjoy . . . all the advantages of a revolution which, in re-establishing the dignity of man and the sovereignty of the people, has signaled to all despots their coming overthrow."[38] Meanwhile, at the ceremony for the tenth day of the revolutionary week in the neighborhood assembly of the Tuileries district, a choir sang a newly composed hymn, "La liberté des nègres" (The freedom of the Negroes):

> You are Black, but good sense,
> Rejects an evil prejudice . . .
> In the eyes of white republicans
> Color is forgotten, and the man remains.[39]

On 9 February 1794 the three Saint-Domingue deputies joined Chaumette at another session of the Commune, where Chaumette reminded the audience that he had tried unsuccessfully to get the Convention to condemn slavery seven months earlier. Addressing himself to the Blacks in the French colonies, he exclaimed, "Oh you, unhappy mothers, obliged to curse your fecundity, take courage: your children will be citizens . . . you will bring them up to enjoy freedom, and to bless their liberators." The deputies Mills and Belley, who had not addressed the Convention during the decisive session on 4 February, proved that they were fully capable of speaking for themselves. Mills said that the word "slaves . . . would no longer stain the French dictionary," and his colleague Belley, after recounting how he had been taken captive in Africa and had earned his own freedom in Saint-Domingue, promised that "as long as a drop of blood remains in our veins, I swear to you, in the name of my brothers, that the [French flag] will always fly over our shores and our mountains."[40] Chaumette then announced that an even larger celebration would be held on 18 February 1794 at the former Notre-Dame Cathedral, where the Hébertist group had organized its widely publicized Festival of Reason during the radical de-Christianization campaign the previous fall.[41]

The Notre-Dame ceremony was certainly the most elaborate public event that had ever been staged anywhere in the world to condemn the evil of slavery and celebrate a blow against it (figure 9). Chaumette was once again at the center of things, delivering a lengthy peroration on the world-historical significance of the abolition decree. Evoking Jean-Jacques Rousseau's lament about how humanity had degenerated from the state of nature, he denounced slavery as "the worst of evils," called its abolition "the greatest of all goods," and assured the audience that a new era of human history had now begun.[42] As the diarist Célestin Guittard de Floriban noted, the event mobilized delegations from every significant institution in the city: "The revolutionary committees of the sections, the clubs sent deputations with their banners, along with women and drummers, the members of the city assembly, a deputation from the National Assembly accompanied by veterans and grenadiers of the Convention, the musicians from the opera and a procession of the Negroes and Negresses who live in Paris along with their three deputies who came from Saint-Domingue to obtain this decree. . . . Speeches were given, odes and appropriate songs sung." The deputies who represented the Convention at the ceremony returned to tell their colleagues that the legislators "had been showered with blessings for having restored dignity to thousands of long-oppressed men."[43]

Alongside Chaumette, one of those who spoke at the ceremony and composed a song for the occasion was Marie-Thérèse Lucidor Corbin, the daughter of a free Black resident of Paris who had married a white woman before the Revolution. Taking it upon herself to represent the newly enfranchised Blacks in the colonies, even though she had been born free and had never visited the Caribbean, Lucidor Corbin exclaimed, "The great day has arrived . . . , all our sufferings are at an end, the precious decree rendered by our

FIGURE 9: *Celebration of the Decree of 16 Pluviôse*. This allegorical engraving commemorates the ceremony held in Notre-Dame Cathedral, which had been renamed "the Temple of Reason," to celebrate the National Convention's decree of 16 pluviôse abolishing slavery. Black figures occupy a relatively marginal place in this image. *Credit:* Bibliothèque nationale de France.

legislators makes us equal to all other men, we are united by the bonds of fraternity, our chains are broken and we will never have to wear them again." Her "Hymn of the Citizens of Color," set to the rousing tune of "La Marseillaise," called on the "free people" who were to benefit from the abolition decree to "cover these heroes with flowers" and to "let your eyes, filled with tenderness, contemplate your friends and your benefactors."[44]

Paris was not alone in commemorating the Convention's decree. At least twenty-four other cities and towns staged official ceremonies, and the Convention received nearly six hundred resolutions, coming from all but three of the country's eighty-four departments, praising it. Bordeaux, the country's largest colonial port, held an elaborate celebration in which some two hundred men of color took part. After a reading of the Declaration of the Rights of Man, "these men who used to be treated like beasts . . . all cried out that they were French and that they would not accept any master other than the law." White members of the city's Jacobin Club marched through the streets, each one linking arms with a Black man or woman. Two delegations from the city addressed the National Convention, assuring the deputies of their determination "to die rather than allow any attack on the rights that philosophy has just rendered to this interesting portion of the human race." In Bourg-en-Bresse, several wagons traversed the town presenting tableaux vivants that illustrated racial harmony. On one of them, "several Negresses were nursing white infants, and whites were nursing Blacks." At Châlons-sur-Marne, two Black soldiers were promoted in rank and awarded red "liberty bonnets."[45]

By publicizing both the abolition decree and the public ceremonies held to celebrate it, the press communicated the importance of the event to the entire nation. Hébert, whose *Père Duchêne* was his faction's mouthpiece, was somewhat slow off the mark. Only after the Notre-Dame ceremony did he devote an issue to "the famous decree that abolishes the enslavement of the Negroes" and praise Chaumette, normally considered one of his allies but also, in the Byzantine world of revolutionary politics, something of a rival.[46] Newspapers identified with the official Montagnard regime, such as the *Feuille du Salut public* and the *Journal de la Montagne*, summarized the Convention debates and the various public ceremonies held in Paris, with occasional comments such as the *Feuille de Salut public*'s remark that the speeches on 4 February 1794 offered "the most touching tableau for humanity, liberty and equality."[47] The *Nouvelles politiques* limited itself to a neutral report about the decree itself. Its brief mention of the Notre-Dame ceremony reported that Chaumette had given "a speech that inspired the liveliest enthusiasm," but gave no details.[48]

Claude Milscent, the former Saint-Domingue plantation owner who had become converted to the antislavery cause, provided the most extensive journalistic commentary on the decree and the ceremonies it inspired. After summarizing the Convention's session of 4 February 1794, he wrote,

> Yes, representatives of the French people, you have done well for humanity, and consequently for the nation of free men. You have saved the colonies; you have broken the chains of more than ten million men, and not only of the 500,000 in Saint-Domingue; you have also freed the English and Spanish Negroes . . . you have drawn the consequences of the great principles of our constitution, and one recognizes in this decree the mark of the holy Mountain. . . . Oh my fatherland! I have lived long enough, I see you free! . . . I beg the reader to pardon these expressions of a heart that sees accomplished at last the wishes it formed since its birth, and sees triumph a cause that it has pleaded for five years. . . . Friend, you are a man; don't you share my satisfaction?[49]

Milscent's enthusiastic endorsement of the decree was echoed in what turned out to be the next-to-last issue of the *Révolutions de Paris*, the weekly that had published Sonthonax's and Chaumette's articles in support of abolition. "Our revolution needed this law," the magazine's editorialist admitted, adding that "it should not have been necessary to wait for the presence of two representatives of the people chosen from the caste of our brothers the Negroes, to restore to them all their original, natural and civil rights. But it is better to do good belatedly rather than never." Echoing Danton's reasoning, the *Révolutions de Paris* assured readers that the news of the Convention's action would galvanize a movement for liberty in Britain and "defeat the sinister projects of the cabinet of Saint-James."[50]

The decree of 4 February was celebrated in visual form as well as in words. Paris engravers produced numerous prints showing Black men and women wearing revolutionary "liberty caps" or jewelry in the form of a carpenter's level, a symbol of equality. The captions to these images sometimes echoed the Creole language of the Caribbean, announcing "Moi libre aussi" or "Moi égal à toi" ("Me also free" or "Me equal to you"); in other cases, the phrasing was in standard French, as in the case of a picture showing an attractive Black woman who told viewers that she was "in freedom like you. The French Republic, in accord with Nature, wants this: Am I not your sister?" Louis Simon Boizot, one of the artists who designed

FIGURE 10: *Decree of 16 Pluviôse.* In this elaborate drawing, attributed to Nicolas Monsiau, Black men and women celebrating the National Convention's decree abolishing slavery are prominently featured. *Credit:* Musée de la Ville de Paris, Musée Carnavalet, Paris, France / Bridgeman Images.

these images, created a porcelain sculpture of a Black couple with the inscription "Me equal to you. Me also free," and an unknown enthusiast emancipated the head from a prerevolutionary sculpture of an enslaved woman, putting it on a stand with a plaque celebrating the decree of 16 pluviôse.[51] Even as these images proclaimed the equality between Blacks and whites, however, they often depicted the new French citizens with exaggerated lips and frizzy hair, reflecting the persistence of racial stereotypes.

Among the most elaborate celebrations of the decree of 4 February 1794 was the artist Nicolas André Monsiau's pen-and-ink drawing of the decisive moment in the Convention's session (figure 10). Conserved today in the Musée Carnavalet, Paris's history museum, Monsiau's drawing resembles many other depictions of the Revolution's legislative assemblies, but it is unique in that the scene it portrays is dominated by Black men and women. Newspaper accounts agree that there were a few Black spectators in the public galleries, including the woman who reportedly fainted with emotion when the deputies took their crucial vote. Among the deputies, there were the two men of African descent, Jean-Baptiste Belley and James Mills, whom Monsiau showed ascending the steps to the podium to embrace the Convention's president.

In Monsiau's image, however, Black bodies are everywhere. The entire left side of the composition consists of a swirling mass of Black men and women, distinguished not only by their dark-skinned faces but by their headgear: scarves like those worn in the colonies for the women, fanciful hats more suggestive of the Middle East than the Caribbean for some of the men. In the upper right corner of the drawing, below a copy of the Declaration of the Rights of Man and Citizen, three female figures flank the president's desk: a standing woman wearing the towering turban of madras scarves made fashionable by colonial women of mixed race, a seated woman—perhaps Marie Dupré, the woman who had fainted when the decree was passed and who was invited, according to some accounts, to occupy the place of honor next to the president—and a young Black girl kneeling and clasping the seated woman's hands. Monsiau's decision to give these three female figures such a prominent position in his composition is exceptional, not only for its overturning of racial hierarchies but also for its disregard of gender norms.

In the lower right quadrant of the drawing, two pairs of male figures attract the viewer's eye. In the right-hand corner, a Black man, bare to the waist and shoeless despite the fact that the decree was passed on a cold Paris winter day, holds aloft a naked Black baby whose arm reaches out toward the Convention president. The two figures give visual representation to the promise Chaumette had made that the freed Blacks would know that their children would grow up in freedom. In the picture's foreground, an oddly costumed white figure with locks reminiscent of Jesus's, a Roman toga draped over his arm, and modern boots—one of which seems to have detached itself from the man's leg—raises a kneeling Black man to his feet. The Black man's pose is reminiscent of the most widely reproduced abolitionist image of the era, *Am I Not a Man and a Brother?*, created by the British ceramics manufacturer and opponent of slavery Josiah Wedgwood in 1787. Nowadays, it would be easy to read this element of the composition in particular and the picture as a whole as a conventional representation of white savior figures bestowing freedom on grateful Blacks. Whether he intended it or not, however, Monsiau's composition, in which Blacks are shown occupying the very center of revolutionary France's national legislative assembly, conveys more powerfully than the stilted rhetoric of the period the historic import of the decree of 4 February 1794.

Paradoxically, while the abolition of slavery was being celebrated in Europe, the decree evoked little immediate reaction in France's overseas colonies. At the moment when it was passed, the Black population of Saint-Domingue was already legally free, thanks to the edicts Sonthonax and Polverel had issued the previous year. In February 1794 the two other major French colonies in the Caribbean, Martinique and Guadeloupe, were under the control of the British, who maintained the slavery system there and in the parts of Saint-Domingue they had occupied. In the best of circumstances, it took four months for ships from France to reach the Mascarenes, France's two island colonies in the Indian Ocean. Under wartime conditions, with the British navy intercepting French shipping, the colonists there were able to ignore the law.[52] The only colony where enslaved Blacks gained their freedom as a direct result of the decree of 4 February 1794 was Guiana, or, as it was known at the time, Cayenne, the sole French possession on the South American mainland, whose Black population was only ten thousand.[53]

Although the pluviôse decree had little immediate effect on the situation in France's colonies, it did attract attention in other countries. In late February 1794, when the news reached London, British planters held a public meeting to demand the strengthening of defenses in the West Indies. The House of Commons was once again debating William Wilberforce's bill for the abolition of the slave trade, and speakers on both sides referred to the French decree. Robert Jenkinson, a defender of the slavers, said it demonstrated the dangers of making any changes to the existing system. William Pitt, the prime minister, came to the opposite conclusion, maintaining that the French decision demanded a pause in the importation of new slaves because they were the most likely to revolt. The colonial council in the colony of Tobago, which the British had seized from the French in 1793, reacted to the news of the pluviôse decree by passing an act designed to prevent the spread of the "spirit of anarchy and insubordination" resulting from the spread of "ideas of equality and liberty totally subversive of all order and good government" in the French colonies, and Admiral John Jervis, commander of the British fleet in the Windward Islands, complained that the French were circulating their "diabolical decree" in the region.[54]

Because of the extensive trade between the United States and the Caribbean, American newspaper readers were well informed about events in Saint-Domingue. Starting in mid-October 1793, at least seven newspapers in the northern states printed an "abstract of the proclamation issued by Léger Felicité Sonthonax" on 29 August 1793 explaining that in Saint-Domingue, "all negroes and persons of mixed blood now in slavery are declared free, to enjoy all the rights attached to the character of a French citizen, subject however to certain regulations."[55] Because of the British naval blockade, news from France itself was less regular. In late April and early May 1794, newspapers in New York and Philadelphia carried reports about the decree of 16 pluviôse and excerpts from the speeches in the Convention. The bilingual *American Star / Etoile américaine*, the voice of the white Saint-Domingue refugees in Philadelphia, commented that "Brissot has been guillotined—but all the negrophiles which he left at his death have not yet been so. And it appears, that they are now the very persons who govern the Convention."[56]

The *Gazette of the United States*, published in Philadelphia, the city with the largest population of free Blacks in the country, reported about the appearance of the delegation of people of color who had addressed the Convention on 20 pluviôse and told the deputies that "this decree . . . has restored to liberty, and consequently to happiness, one million of the human race, who have hitherto groaned under the chains of slavery." The paper also mentioned the Black deputy Belley's demand that the white colonists be arrested.[57] American abolitionists were inspired by the French action. At a national meeting in January 1795, the delegates passed a resolution noting that "by a decree of the National Convention of France, all the blacks and people of color, within the territories of the French Republic, are declared free, and entitled to an equal participation of the rights of citizens of France," and urging the American state governments to respect the rights of French Blacks in American territory.[58]

The law of 16 pluviôse Year II was undeniably a historic milestone. In Saint-Domingue, the most important of France's colonies, the decree gave the imprimatur of the national government to the local edicts the two civil commissioners Sonthonax and Polverel had issued on their own authority. Although it would be some months before the local Black population and the most talented of the insurgent commanders, Toussaint Louverture, decided to cast their lot with the French, in the long run, the decree gave republican France a decisive advantage over their British and Spanish enemies. As the deputies who voted for the law of 4 February 1794 recognized, the abolition of slavery was a logical consequence of the ideas about liberty and equality that had powered the French Revolution from its outset. Nevertheless, those ideas only triumphed in 1794 because of a peculiar constellation of political circumstances. The deadly conflict between Brissot's Girondin faction and its Montagnard enemies had resulted in the elimination of the major proponents of abolition in France; the passions aroused by the war with Britain had permitted the white colonists to forge an alliance with Robespierre and his supporters and to paint the abolitionists as traitors to the nation. Ironically, the decree abolishing slavery was passed primarily thanks to the intervention of Danton, a man who had never expressed any personal commitment to the abolitionist cause, and the ceremonies that celebrated it as a historic turning point were organized by Chaumette, one of Robespierre's populist rivals. Within two months, both men's heads fell under the guillotine, followed soon afterward by that of Claude Milscent, the most outspoken supporter of abolition among the Revolution's journalists. Enacted without the backing of a powerful political movement and left orphaned soon after its birth by the execution of its major promoters, the abolition decree of 4 February 1794 faced an uncertain future.

CHAPTER TEN

Thermidor and the Consolidation of Abolition

BY DECLARING ALL inhabitants of the French empire, regardless of their race, to be free and equal in rights, the decree of 16 pluviôse II fulfilled the promise of the Declaration of the Rights of Man and Citizen of 1789. But the decree was also one more in a series of often contradictory laws affecting race and slavery passed by the revolutionary assemblies, beginning with the National Assembly's admission of proslavery deputies on 4 July 1789 and including the decrees of 8 and 28 March 1790, 12 October 1790, 13 and 15 May 1791, 24 September 1791, and 24 March 1792. Many of those decrees had later been revoked. Would the abolition decree of 16 pluviôse, passed in haste during the most radical phase of the Revolution, actually be implemented, and would it survive if the revolutionary movement itself took a turn toward moderation? These questions hung over debates about colonial issues for a year and a half after the historic decree's passage.

Georges Danton's success in getting the Convention to let the Committee of Public Safety determine how the abolition decree would be implemented left the door open to efforts to delay its application or even repeal it. The Convention's colonial committee, which had been bypassed in the drafting of the decree, passed a resolution asking that the decree be carried out in such a way as to "assure its execution for the greater interest of the Republic and of the white men, without departing from constitutional principle." They also appointed Benoît Gouly, a slave-owning deputy from the Indian Ocean colonies, as one of their representatives to meet with the Committee of Public Safety.[1] The colonial lobbyists Pierre-François Page and Augustin Brulley redoubled their efforts, encouraged by André Amar, their ally on the Committee of General Security. The Convention's decision was "unheard of," Amar told them. "The Convention had done what [Jacques-Pierre] Brissot and his faction never dared to do . . . it was to go back on what it had decided, to contradict everything that had been done, to protest against the indictment of the Girondins and against justice." Amar singled out the role of Danton, for whose arrest he would vote two months later, saying that "it was astounding that Danton had lent himself to such a thing."[2]

In the days that followed, Page and Brulley had several less encouraging meetings with Bertrand Barère, the Committee of Public Safety member tasked with drawing up the report on measures to implement the decree. The Convention, he told them, could not afford to "give the appearance of trying to elude the principle" of abolition. When they tried to convince him that the application of the decree should be left up to the whites in the colony, he lost patience, telling them that "it is as if one had proposed to let the seigneurs in France decide how to abolish their feudal rights." All Page and Brulley could do was write to the white colonists who had taken refuge in the United States, promising them that they would keep up their efforts to make sure that their opponents would eventually join other revolutionary politicians "who have paid with their heads for the harm they did to our country." Meanwhile, four days after the enactment of the abolition decree, the newly seated Black deputy Jean-Baptiste Belley, in his maiden speech to the Convention, called for the arrest of the white colonists responsible for the brief incarceration of his two colleagues before its passage.[3]

A month after the passage of the pluviôse decree, an overzealous initiative of some of Page and Brulley's allies in the port city of Nantes triggered the response from the Convention that Belley had wanted. When rumors spread that Jean-Louis Gaspard Josnet, a military officer who had served in Saint-Domingue, was going to be named to command the French troops being sent to implement the pluviôse decree, two members of the revolutionary committee in Nantes denounced him and demanded his arrest. René Levasseur and Jean-François Delacroix, two of the main proponents of the abolition decree, seized on the affair to demand that the decree be implemented promptly. Delacroix wanted a broad measure against the colonists' network that would also be a strike against the system of denunciations that he and his fellow members of the Indulgents were opposing. "The reign of the slanderers must end," he said. "This denunciation comes from the rich colonists who want to destroy the beneficial effects of your decree. These gentlemen have intrigued even in the antechamber of the Committee of Public Safety."[4] After some debate, the Convention ordered the arrest of all the white colonists who had been members of any of the assemblies in Saint-Domingue or of the proslavery groups in Paris. When the deputies learned that Page and Brulley had been arrested, applause broke out.[5]

The proslavery lobbyists and the circle of white colonists around them now found themselves targets of the same revolutionary political apparatus they had so often invoked against their opponents. Although none of the white colonists seem to have fallen victim to the "Great Terror" of the summer of 1794, when the rate of executions reached its peak—Belley claimed that prosecutor Antoine Fouquier-Tinville had intervened when he saw their names on lists of suspects to be sent for trial—Page, Brulley, and many others spent months in Paris's overcrowded prisons, watching as inmates were dispatched to the Revolutionary Tribunal and then to the guillotine. César Duny, who had arrived in France as a representative of the Saint-Domingue colonists who had fled to the United States after the burning of Cap Français, expressed the bewilderment they felt. How could they have been arrested when they were the avowed enemies of "the Brissotins, the royalists, the Girondins, the Barnavists, the 'Anglicists'": in other words, of all the factions the Montagnards identified as the enemies of the Revolution? Duny even had the nerve to write directly to Maximilien Robespierre, asking for relief from "the horrible despotism of [Etienne] Polverel and [Léger-Félicité] Sonthonax" and their accomplices.[6]

Page and Brulley did not risk contacting Robespierre, but they wrote a lengthy letter to his Committee of Public Safety colleague Georges Couthon complaining that "[Louis] Dufay, this man of Danton's . . . has gotten a decree passed that mixed up the colonial assemblies and the Club Massiac, that is, water and fire, aristocracy and democracy, crime and virtue."[7]

Ironically, one of the colonists arrested as a consequence of the decree of 19 ventôse II was Page and Brulley's enemy, the abolitionist journalist Claude Milscent, who had been a member of the provincial assembly in Saint-Domingue's North Province in 1789. The deputies Belley and Jean-Baptiste Mills intervened on his behalf and he was freed after three days in prison, but the incident led him to stop publishing his *Créole patriote*. In spite of his own experience, Milscent was eager to see the law applied to the proslavery colonists. Immediately after his own release, he denounced two of them for having called the Saint-Domingue deputies "damned beasts" and objecting to the decree of 16 pluviôse. Other witnesses testified against these men at the Revolutionary Tribunal, but they were let off and Milscent was arrested on charges of having given false testimony against them. After a trial conducted by Pierre-André Coffinhal, a close ally of Robespierre's, he was convicted and executed on 7 prairial II.[8] Milscent was followed to the guillotine a month later by Louis-Marthe Gouy d'Arsy, the man who had ensured the admission of proslavery colonial deputies to the National Assembly in 1789, and then by Simon-Nicolas-Henri Linguet, the controversial prerevolutionary defender of slavery. Gouy was arrested primarily because of his involvement in financial speculations in the 1780s, but those who wrote the indictment against him did not forget to mention that he was the "author of the disasters of the colonies, which he wanted to deliver to the English despot." Linguet was accused of royalism.[9]

Between the passage of the decree of 19 ventôse II against the colonists and the executions of Milscent, Gouy d'Arsy, and Linguet, the political situation in France had undergone several more radical changes. First the members of the Hébertist faction and then the Dantonists were arrested, given hasty trials, and guillotined. Colonial issues did not figure in the accusations against Jacques-René Hébert and his followers, and when his one-time ally Pierre

Chaumette was tried several weeks later, his engagement on behalf of the abolitionist cause was not mentioned. When Louis-Antoine de Saint-Just was put in charge of drafting the indictment against Danton, however, Robespierre wrote to him that "Danton once said to me, 'It is too bad that we cannot propose to give our colonies to the Americans; it would be a way to seal an alliance with them.' Subsequently, Danton and [De]Lacroix have had a decree passed whose likely result was the loss of our colonies." Perhaps because he feared a mention of his own meetings with Page and Brulley, Saint-Just did not include these accusations in his report.[10] Although the slavery issue was not mentioned in these trials, the purge of the factions eliminated most of the key figures involved in the passage of the decree of 16 pluviôse, raising the question of who would be left to defend that measure if the political winds changed again.

The elimination of the Hébert and Danton factions silenced all public opposition to the Committee of Public Safety. On 22 prairial II, the Convention passed a law that virtually eliminated any protections for defendants sent to the Revolutionary Tribunal. The passage of this law marked the beginning of the Great Terror, during which the pace of executions reached unprecedented heights, with as many as sixty victims being tried as a group and beheaded in a single day. A decisive victory against the Austrians at the Battle of Fleurus in late June 1794 marked the end of any serious military threat to France in Europe. The politicians in Paris were unaware of a parallel development in Saint-Domingue, where the most effective of the Black generals, Toussaint Louverture, had switched his allegiance from the Spanish to the French in May 1794, greatly improving the prospects of warding off the Spanish and British invasions there. As the sense of crisis that had justified the harsh measures of the Terror faded, some Convention deputies and even some members of the Committee of Public Safety began to fear that Robespierre might be planning to turn the arbitrary procedures of the law of 22 prairial against them.

Political tensions within the Convention came to a head on 9 thermidor II (27 July 1794). The day before, Robespierre had given a rambling speech indicating that he might be about to demand the arrest of some of that body's members. Realizing that they could not wait any longer, deputies who feared that they might be on his list sprang into action as soon as the Convention's session opened. To shouts of "Down with the dictator!" the Incorruptible and his closest allies were declared "outlaws." After a tense day during which it briefly appeared that Paris sans-culottes might rally to their defense, Robespierre, Saint-Just, Couthon, and their supporters were overwhelmed; on the following day, they were hustled to the guillotine. The victorious "thermidorians," as they were soon labeled, now controlled the revolutionary government, opening a new phase of the Revolution that would, like all previous episodes of the movement, have major consequences for the issues of slavery and race.

By coincidence, 9 thermidor II was also the date on which a French warship carrying the two revolutionary civil commissioners from Saint-Domingue, Sonthonax and Polverel, arrived in Rochefort harbor. The two men's actions in freeing the enslaved Blacks in the colony had set the stage for the National Convention's historic decree of 16 pluviôse, but they returned to France as prisoners. Even as it had expanded their more pragmatic emancipation measures into a broader law, the Convention had maintained the arrest warrants for the two men voted on 16 July 1793 and reaffirmed on 5 September 1793. On 8 June 1794 the first French warship to reach Saint-Domingue in nearly a year brought official notification of both the abolition of slavery and the indictments of the two civil commissioners. Sonthonax was reduced to tears by the news; his older colleague assured him that "we have nothing on our consciences to reproach ourselves for, we can appear before the nation without having anything to fear."[11]

The two civil commissioners were fortunate that they did not arrive in France before the overthrow of Robespierre. Even though many of the white colonists whom they had deported to the metropole were in prison as a consequence of the decree of 19 ventôse, those who were free continued to work to punish anyone they could accuse of having violated the rights of whites in Saint-Domingue. On 2 thermidor, just a week before Robespierre's fall, the guillotine claimed the life of the twenty-year-old son of Governor Philibert François Rouxel de Blanchelande, who had accompanied his father to Saint-Domingue in 1790.[12] By the time Sonthonax and Polverel were transferred from Rochefort to Paris, however, the feverish atmosphere of the Great Terror was cooling and the two men were released, with orders to await the results of an inquiry into their conduct.[13]

The retreat from the policies of the Terror that led to the release of Sonthonax and Polverel was one of the first signs of what came to be known as the "thermidorian reaction" against the radicalism of the previous year and a half. Although the new atmosphere benefited the civil commissioners, it raised questions about the future of the abolition policy that they had helped promote. During the fifteen months between the fall of Robespierre and the end of the National Convention, many of the radical policies adopted by the Montagnards were overturned, especially if they were seen as threats to the rights of property owners. In the case of slave emancipation, however, the opposite proved to be the case. Rather than attempting to reverse the abolition of slavery, the thermidorian Convention upheld the measures adopted in 1793–94. Thanks to the thermidorians' actions, republican France was able to keep the loyalty of Toussaint Louverture, the Black commander who was rapidly emerging as the key figure in Saint-Domingue, and of his soldiers.

In the immediate aftermath of Robespierre's overthrow, most of the victorious thermidorians had little concern about colonial issues. The news of Toussaint Louverture's adherence to the French cause in Saint-Domingue had not yet reached France, and there did not seem to be anything more that the government could actually do to affect the situation in the Caribbean. One question required immediate attention, however: the fate of the numerous prisoners still being held in prison because of their involvement with colonial issues. The release of Sonthonax and Polverel led the white colonists who opposed them to demand their own freedom and an opportunity to present their accusations against the civil commissioners. In an "Adresse à la Convention" published on 2 fructidor An II, they showed their comprehension of the way in which thermidor had changed the political atmosphere. Now that he was dead, Robespierre became a convenient scapegoat, and from this point on, the abolition of slavery became one more of the "crimes" for which he was regularly blamed, even though the chief colonial lobbyists, Page and Brulley, knew perfectly well that he had been sitting across the table from them in the offices of the Committee of Public Safety on 16 pluviôse when the Convention passed its abolition decree. The colonists also put forward a demand that would lead to one of the most important thermidorian responses to the "affaire des colonies": the creation of a parliamentary commission to hear their charges against Sonthonax and Polverel.[14] Within a few weeks, the imprisoned colonists were freed, along with the free colored spokesman Julien Raimond, who had been incarcerated since late September 1793. Although he was freed, Raimond was not officially cleared of the accusations against him until mid-1795.[15] Seventy-three deputies arrested in October 1793 for protesting the execution of the Girondins regained their freedom and their Convention seats in December 1794. Some of them would play important roles in the renewed debates about the colonies.

The Convention, after several debates, gave formal approval to the idea of a Commission des colonies or parliamentary commission on colonial affairs on 9 vendémiaire III (30 September 1794).[16] The result was a long-running parliamentary hearing, beginning in late January 1795 and not concluded until six months later, during the last days of the thermidorian Convention.[17] It was clear from the start that the nine Convention deputies originally named to the commission were not sympathetic to the colonists. They included several who strongly associated with the campaign for abolition and racial equality, notably Henri Grégoire and the commission's chair, Jean-Philippe Garran-Coulon, one of Brissot's closest allies in the Legislative Assembly of 1791–92. Garran-Coulon dominated the commission's proceedings and eventually compiled a four-volume report that demonstrated the falsity of the claim that the violence in Saint-Domingue in the early years of the Revolution was the result of a conspiracy.[18] Another member was the prominent thermidorian Joseph Fouché. Fouché's views on slavery are unclear. He came originally from the slaving port of Nantes, and in February 1791, in his capacity as president of the city's Jacobin Club, he had signed a letter to Brissot disavowing the latter's campaign against the trade.[19] By 1795, however, Fouché seemed uninterested in defending colonial interests.

In drafting their charges against Sonthonax and Polverel, the colonists were constrained by the fact that they were not allowed to openly challenge the abolition of slavery, which had been consecrated by the Convention's decree of 16 pluviôse. They were therefore limited to attempting to prove that the civil commissioners had violated their instructions and the French constitution in their treatment of the white colonists. Presumably, the colonists hoped that if Sonthonax and Polverel were found guilty of the charges against them, the Convention might reconsider the policy of emancipation that it had adopted as a consequence of what the civil commissioners had done in Saint-Domingue. Among their accusations was the claim that the three Saint-Domingue deputies Sonthonax had sent to Paris, and whose appearance at the Convention had triggered the vote of the pluviôse decree, were "employees [of the commissioners] who presented themselves with illegitimate credentials."[20] Had the Commission des colonies accepted this assertion, it might have had to recommend that the Convention expel the Saint-Domingue deputies and repeal the decree it had passed in response to their appearance. Rather than resulting in any action by the Convention, however, the six-month hearing process served to keep the colonists tied up so that they would not have time to bother the deputies. The Paris press, although it generally supported the thermidorian reaction, paid little attention to the hearings, which droned on week after week but produced few newsworthy revelations.

The ailing Polverel was barely able to participate in the proceedings, even before he died midway through the hearings, but Sonthonax proved more than a match for the colonists. He was as wedded as they were to the notion that the events in Saint-Domingue were the result of a conspiracy, but in his view, the conspirators were the colonists themselves, together with the British, the Spanish, and General François-Thomas Galbaud, who had led the armed revolt against the two commissioners in June 1793 that had driven Sonthonax and Polverel to issue their first emancipation proclamation.[21] For all their efforts, the colonists failed to generate any real sympathy for their narrowly legalistic case against Sonthonax. They might have garnered more support if they had instead openly challenged the idea of racial equality and emancipation, as the Indian Ocean colonial deputy Benoît Gouly did in a lengthy pamphlet in November 1794 that marked the reentry into

French public discourse of the overtly racist arguments about Black inferiority that had been made by some proslavery writers in the first years of the Revolution. In addition to making the familiar claims about the economic and strategic importance of the colonies, Gouly, who had been an active Montagnard during the Terror, asserted that Black people were "very close to the orangutan" and that "no matter what you do, you will never raise this Black man to your level." Ironically, Gouly's pamphlet also included what may have been the first mention in France of Toussaint Louverture, a reference to his role in fending off the British in Saint-Domingue.[22]

Gouly's pamphlet alarmed Dufay, the white Saint-Domingue deputy whose speech had precipitated the pluviôse decree and who now showed that he had become an effective parliamentary brawler. He reminded his colleagues that the decree had been "translated into English, into Spanish, into Dutch, published everywhere with the greatest ceremony, received with the liveliest enthusiasm, with acclamations repeated a thousand times of 'Long live the National Convention! Long live the French Republic! Long live the French people!'" If the Blacks in the colonies became aware of Gouly's proposal, they might doubt France's determination to uphold their freedom. "Do you think that men, who have received an immense benefit from the hand of a great nation, would calmly see it taken away from them at the same moment?" But, Dufay warned, "it would be to try to do something impossible, yes, impossible even for all the forces of France; it would be to compromise the authority of the nation, to pervert morality, to destroy all principles."[23] It was a warning that the young army officer from Corsica, Napoleone Buonaparte, who was, in the fall of 1794, drifting around Paris without an assignment because he had been close to Robespierre's brother Augustin, would have done well to keep in mind when he became the master of France's destinies a few years later.

While the Commission des colonies was starting its hearings in late January 1795, the thermidorian Convention began to think seriously about its colonial policy. By this time, enough news had arrived from overseas, especially from Saint-Domingue, to make it clear that two of the most important French colonies had started to emerge from the crisis situation they had been in at the time of thermidor. Victor Hugues had retaken Guadeloupe from the British and was arming privateering vessels to wreak havoc with their shipping in the Caribbean. A letter in the *Moniteur*, written by a French ship's captain who reached Bordeaux in January 1795, gave encouraging news from Saint-Domingue and mentioned the Black leader who would take advantage of the thermidorians' policies to start his rise to power: "There is no doubt that the republicans, in Saint-Domingue, will wind up by driving out the enemy. . . . They fight with much more bravery since they have learned that the Convention has decreed their freedom. . . . Toussaint Bréda has taken Saint-Michel and Saint-Raphaël and others, the news is certain."[24]

The thermidorian Convention seized on these optimistic developments from the Caribbean to engage in a major debate on colonial policy. The importance of the issues at stake was underlined by the fact that the first anniversary of the decree of 16 pluviôse An II occurred during the discussion. A delegation of Blacks and men of color from the colonies visited the Convention and reminded the deputies that "on the 16 pluviôse, the day when, on the imperishable bases of the constitution, you recognized that those men whom a tyrannical force had made into slaves were free, you merited the true triumph of humanity."[25] Earlier in the month, the deputy Jean Pelet de la Lozère, speaking in the name of the Committee of Public Safety, had delivered a lengthy report on the colonies, culminating in a proposal to dispatch members of the Convention on mission to ensure their integration into the Republic. Pelet's own enthusiasm for the decision made a year earlier to abolish slavery was admittedly limited. "No doubt it would have been more useful to see that it was preceded by enlightenment brought about through education and suitable maturity; it might have been possible to avoid every kind of commotion, and to satisfy all political interests," he said, but he concluded "that it is pointless now to discuss a question that has been settled."[26]

Pelet's equivocation gave Gouly, the proslavery deputy from the Ile de France, an opening to try to protect slavery in the Mascarene Islands. He warned the deputies that trying to override the "prejudices" of their white colonists by force might drive them into the arms of the British, and added that "everything is lost in the Antilles, and everything is intact in the Ile de France, Réunion and the adjacent islands."[27] Gouly's transparent effort to defend the slave regime provoked a sharp response from Dufay. He demanded that any representatives sent to the colonies be given precise instructions not to "deviate from the fundamental bases of the republic, liberty and equality." Dufay was supported by several other speakers, particularly François-Xavier Lanthenas, one of the few surviving members of the original Société des Amis des Noirs, and the final resolution specified that any deputies or commissioners sent overseas "will not have the power to make any changes regarding the status of persons established by the law of 16 pluviôse."[28] Opponents of this motion succeeded in forcing a roll-call vote, in which 304 deputies voted yes, while 178 voted no. The thermidorian Convention thus put itself on record in explicit support of the emancipation policy adopted a year earlier, but the size of the "no" vote showed that emancipation remained controversial. Letters from the colonies published in conservative newspapers such as the *Nouvelles politiques* depicted the results of emancipation as catastrophic. One planter from Cayenne wrote that the Blacks "only obey the laws that favor them; they behave outrageously even to the best of masters. Ah . . . how hard it is, after 44 years in America, thinking that I would have an income for the rest of my days, to see myself completely ruined."[29]

In a narrow sense, the law of 26 pluviôse III turned out to be a dead letter, since no missions were sent to any of the colonies before the end of the thermidorian period, and the legislators did not specify what would happen in the Mascarenes, where the local authorities had never carried out the previous year's emancipation decree. In the wake of two massive sans-culotte protests against the high price of bread, the journées of germinal and prairial An III, the Convention decided to draw up a new constitution to replace the "Jacobin" document approved but never put into effect in 1793. As a result, the deputies had to consider the problems of the colonies' status and of slavery again. The draft constitution submitted by the Convention's Committee of Eleven made no mention of the colonies, a fact pointed out by Dufay. He stressed the continuing string of reports from the Caribbean showing that the emancipated free people of color and former slaves in Saint-Domingue were now loyal republicans and were fighting successfully to preserve French territory, whereas the white colonists had conspired to break away from the metropole since the start of the Revolution.[30]

The omission of the colonies from the draft constitution was not an indication that the thermidorian Convention was considering the reintroduction of slavery, as discussions of the new constitution's declaration of rights showed. Article 15 of the 1795 Declaration of Rights repeated, almost word for word, article 18 of the declaration from the "Montagnard" Constitution of June 1793, which had declared that men could not sell themselves or be sold. When the deputy Jean-Baptiste Mailhe proposed to delete the words "or be sold," on the grounds that they were redundant, Pierre Daunou, the most influential member of the committee that had drafted the new constitution, intervened personally to insist that the phrase be kept in. "It is not enough to say that a man cannot sell himself. One must also say that no one can sell him, otherwise it will appear that you are recognizing the right of the stronger, which has no legitimacy, and soon enough slavery will follow," he said.[31]

The issue of colonial slavery came up even more explicitly in a tense exchange that followed the presentation of the committee's proposed declaration of rights. Jacques Defermon, a former member of the National Assembly who had supported the rights of free men of color in 1791, objected that the new declaration omitted the famous phrase, "All men are born and remain free and equal in rights," which had appeared in the 1789 and 1793 declarations. Several deputies replied that its inclusion would raise troublesome questions about the definition of equality. In response, Garran-Coulon insisted that "there is certainly one part of the French empire where this declaration is of the greatest importance; it is in the colonies. . . . You have done well to say that a man cannot sell himself or be sold, but you have not done anything against the use of force to subjugate a man."[32] Garran-Coulon's intervention persuaded the deputies to approve Defermon's motion, and the constitutional committee was told to amend the declaration accordingly. Two days later, however, when Daunou tried to read the revised wording, the future member of the Executive Directory Louis-Marie Larevellière-Lépeaux cut him off with an impassioned speech against the inclusion in the constitution of any reference to abstract principles "about which men have argued since the beginning of the world."[33] Despite the Convention's earlier vote, Defermon's proposition was left out of the final version of the Constitution of 1795's Declaration of Rights, although article 15 prohibiting slavery remained.

Dufay's complaint that the constitution did not regulate the relationship between the colonies and the metropole had nevertheless not yet been addressed. The Convention took up the question in an extended debate on 5 thermidor An III (23 July 1795), in response to a report delivered by Defermon.[34] It was this debate that truly settled the policy that the thermidorians would bequeath to the Directory, the regime that would replace them in October 1795.[35] Defermon began by confirming what Dufay had said a month earlier about the success of the interracial French forces in Saint-Domingue. In praising the military commanders responsible for this success, Defermon became the first Convention deputy to make a detailed statement about Toussaint Louverture. According to Defermon, Louverture,

> African by origin, fought against us as long as he doubted the National Convention's intentions; he put himself under the banners of the Republic, along with his 5000 soldiers, as soon as he was convinced that we sincerely wanted to maintain the liberty of the Blacks. He is an intrepid soldier who accepts orders, and an enterprising leader. He knows how to gain the affection and respect of the Blacks, whites, and men of color who make up his little army. He knows how to make sure that properties are respected, and his conduct serves better than anything else to destroy the prejudices that exist against men of his color.[36]

More briefly, Defermon also mentioned the contributions of three officers of mixed race, Jean-Louis Villatte, Louis-Jacques Bauvais, and André Rigaud. The decree he presented proposed that all four be promoted to the rank of brigadier general, putting them just below the white governor Etienne Laveaux in the colony's military hierarchy.

Having dealt with the military situation, Defermon turned his attention to the state of the colony's economy. From the start of the Revolution, the defenders of slavery had insisted that the plantations that produced its wealth could not function without that institution. Defermon insisted that the results of the emancipation decrees of 1793 and 1794 disproved this claim. "Don't talk any more of the necessity of slavery for production. Several plantations have continued or resumed their work under the law of liberty, with no difference except in the division of the profits, of which the cultivators now receive a fourth, whereas previously their master gave them nothing in return for their efforts." Defermon admitted that one could not "compare the former riches of Saint-Domingue with the feeble product that this fertile soil yields at present." Nevertheless, once peace was secured, he predicted that the formerly enslaved Blacks, now working for their own benefit, would make the colony more productive than it had ever been.[37]

To ensure the success of the new arrangements, however, Defermon argued that the Convention had to make a firm commitment to maintain emancipation: "Remove all anxiety, all uncertainty about their situation; give the African . . . to whom you have promised the liberty that he courageously defends, a new assurance that you will maintain your decrees." Defermon's speech was not entirely devoid of traces of a kind of "republican racism" that viewed Blacks as not quite ready for complete freedom. He remarked that it would be necessary to "remind the Blacks of the necessity of work," and the decree he proposed required that "all the cultivators who are not called for army service will be obligated to continue to work on their plantations under the conditions and for the benefits determined by the regulations proclaimed by the governor and the chief civil administrator." Defermon's proposed decree also explicitly prohibited the creation of any local representative institutions in the colony. Although this closed off any possibility that the Black population might be consulted about the laws under which it lived, it was meant above all to prevent a resurgence of the movement for autonomy that white colonists had launched in the first years of the Revolution.[38]

Defermon thus outlined the principles that would be enshrined in the constitutional law on the colonies that would be presented a few weeks later by François Boissy d'Anglas. Before his proposals could be voted on, however, the Convention erupted into an angry debate that demonstrated the passions colonial policy, and especially the abolition of slavery, could still stir up. Although no one spoke explicitly in favor of slavery, the deputy Pierre Lecomte gave a vehement speech outlining the kind of policy the Convention might have adopted if the principles usually associated with "thermidorian reaction" had prevailed. "Let the bloody regime of Robespierre and his followers be solemnly banned in this unfortunate island," he began, thus tying the emancipation decrees to the execrated Montagnard leader. "The influence of the 9th of thermidor should extend to all French possessions, in spite of all the murderers of the human species. The handful of victims whom they have not yet sacrificed to their selfish rage should be freed. Make persons and property, or at least their ruins, sacred and respected in the future, after having been, for so long, the object of all possible crimes. . . . In maintaining the legal freedom of the Blacks and the yellows, let us finally put an end to the massacre of the whites."[39]

Lecomte was not alone in demanding a policy that would put whites first. Jean-Jacques Serres, Gouly's colleague from the Ile de France, joined in, insisting that "you surely do not want to let your brothers, who share your blood, be slaughtered in order to let the Africans triumph." His tirade was interrupted, according to the account in the *Moniteur*, by a Black deputy who called out, "What am I, a dog?" to which an unidentified speaker replied, "No, but you aren't French." Defermon did not lack for allies, however. The deputy Jacques-Charles Bailleul reminded his colleagues, many of them former supporters of the Girondins, of the role of the white colonial lobbyists in sending their friends to the guillotine. In the end, the Convention struck out two provisions of Defermon's proposal, the one authorizing the government to establish work rules on the plantations and another classifying plantation owners who had fled the island as émigrés, but it adopted the rest of his recommendations.

It was the decree of 5 thermidor III that effectively determined the thermidorian legacy on the issue of slavery. The better-known constitutional law of 22 thermidor An III (9 August 1795), put forward by Boissy d'Anglas on behalf of the committee that drafted the new constitution, did little more than restate the elements of Defermon's proposal. In the interval between the approval of Defermon's decree and Boissy d'Anglas's speech, one important event took place: On 22 July 1795 French and Spanish negotiators, meeting in the Swiss city of Basel, concluded a treaty that gave

France possession of the Spanish half of the island of Hispaniola, the colony of Santo Domingo.[40] Although the French did not actually occupy the territory, the Spanish withdrew their support for the Black armies of their supporters Jean-François Papillon and Georges Biassou, leaving the British invaders on the west coast of the island as the only remaining threat to French rule. At a moment when the thermidorians thought that the end of the war in Europe was almost within their grasp, this reinforced their optimism about the future of France's overseas empire.

It was in this context that Boissy d'Anglas, often considered the quintessential representative of the "thermidorian reaction," rose on 17 thermidor An III to propose a constitutional law governing the colonies. Boissy d'Anglas's speech stressed the reasons that, in his view, required France to maintain an overseas empire, but to also uphold the abolition of slavery. To ask whether France should have overseas colonies, Boissy d'Anglas began, amounted to asking "whether free France should still have a navy, commerce that regenerates it, active and brilliant industries . . . whether it should descend from the high rank of glory to which it has been raised by the centuries and by genius." Some argued, he continued, that it would cost less to let the colonies become independent, so that France could trade with them without having to pay for their defense and administration. The French islands, he replied, lacked the resources to maintain their independence; if they were not controlled by France, they would fall under the sway of a rival nation. Nor could France simply decide not to import colonial products: Commodities such as sugar and coffee had become necessities in people's lives.[41]

Like Defermon, Boissy d'Anglas remembered only too well the problems caused by the white colonists' autonomist pretensions. He therefore reaffirmed the Defermon decree's prohibition on the creation of local assemblies. The colonies needed to be assimilated to metropolitan France and governed by the same laws as the rest of the country. "There can only be one good form of administration, and if we have found it for European territories, why should those in America be deprived of it?" he asked. The colonies should be divided into French-style departments, although for the time being, in view of unspecified difficulties there, the metropolitan government should have the authority to send civil commissioners to govern them rather than letting them elect their own local officials.

At the end of his speech, Boissy d'Anglas turned to the subject of emancipation. His words were unequivocal:

> The status of citizens is determined by the constitution itself, and you will not make any exceptions. If it is permitted to make any in legislative provisions, it could only be in favor of the freedom of men. The abolition of slavery was solemnly decreed, and you would not want to change it; it was a consequence of your principles, one of the results of your revolution, and you could not fail to proclaim it forcefully. It is the one act of justice that tyranny had you pass; you would surely not want to seem less attached than it was to these eternal principles that it found so many ways to violate. To give to all the inhabitants of the colonies, without distinction, that liberty that could only have been taken from them by force and violence, is to make them not only free men, but also citizens. The exercise of political rights will thus be determined only by the constitutional laws that you have already decreed.[42]

Together with the decree of 16 pluviôse An II, Boissy d'Anglas's speech was the most clear-cut declaration the French revolutionary legislators would ever approve on the subject of slavery. It was far more eloquent than the final version of the constitution itself, in which the original draft's omission of any reference to the colonies was remedied by the inclusion of an article stating that they were to be "integral parts of the Republic, and are governed by the same constitutional laws," and specifying how many departments each colony was to be divided into.[43] Whereas Boissy d'Anglas had often been at the forefront of those denouncing the acts of the prethermidorian Convention, in this case he separated the content of the emancipation decree from the circumstances in which it had been passed and explicitly called it an "act of justice" that the new constitution could not repudiate. Boissy d'Anglas also tried to rule out one of the most insidious arguments advanced by the colonial lobby against the new regime in the colonies. By insisting that "all the inhabitants of the colonies, without distinction," were worthy of liberty and of the status of citizens, he denied the distinction that colonists repeatedly tried to make between "French" and "Africans" in the colonies.

In the days that followed the thermidorian Convention's endorsement of Boissy d'Anglas's constitutional proposal, the Saint-Domingue deputy Dufay, whose speech had provoked the decree of 16 pluviôse II, drafted an ambitious program to implement the integration of Saint-Domingue and the metropole. It was essential, he wrote, to convince the Black population that the promises being made to them would be fulfilled. "The Blacks are the basis of French power, it is on them that we must principally rely, they are the real people." He proposed appointing his Black colleague Belley as the commander of the French forces in the island, and he urged the dispatch of more than 20,000 printed copies of a Creole translation of the decree of 16 pluviôse, as well as the erection of bronze statues of liberty in the colony's cities. At the same time, however, he urged the implementation of the work regulations that Sonthonax and Polverel had incorporated in their emancipation decrees in 1793, so that the Blacks would understand that "liberty does not mean doing nothing, that without work there is neither leisure nor freedom." Just as metropolitan citizens served the *patrie* by fighting in the army, those in Saint-Domingue would serve by reviving the economy.[44]

The years that followed the installation of the Directory would show that, despite the strong words of the law of 22 thermidor An III, the rights of the colonies' Black inhabitants were by no means safely secured. Nevertheless, by emphatically reaffirming the emancipation decrees issued by Sonthonax and Polverel in 1793 and by the Montagnard Convention in 1794, the thermidorians gave the radical idea of extending citizenship to the formerly enslaved Blacks in the French Caribbean colonies a chance to take root in practice. In 1802 Napoleon would undo this achievement in Guadeloupe, but in Saint-Domingue, these Black citizens would successfully defend their freedom against his army, ultimately creating the independent nation of Haiti. The thermidorians also, however, created a justification for France's future republican empire. Whereas some of the propagandists of republicanism in the Atlantic world, such as Thomas Paine, had assumed that all overseas colonies would eventually become self-governing entities, the thermidorians, represented by Boissy d'Anglas, offered an alternative model in which colonies could, in theory, be fully integrated with their metropoles. The thermidorians were the first French leaders to set forth the principles of a republican "imperial nation-state." They thus anticipated the policies of French republican politicians of later eras such as Jules Ferry, Hubert Lyautey, Albert Sarraut, and the founders of the French Union of 1946.[45]

Along with the maintenance of the republican form of government, the "affaire des colonies" was one of the most important areas in which the thermidorians continued the policies adopted by the Montagnard Convention. Even though the abolition of slavery had involved a massive expropriation of private property, the thermidorians decided to maintain the principle that human beings could not be considered property. On this subject, at least, the distinction that French historian Florence Gauthier has drawn between a Jacobin Convention devoted to the doctrine of natural rights and a thermidorian and Directory period during which policies based on such rights were abandoned does not hold, any more than the assertion by an American scholar, Miranda Spieler, that there was no significant difference between the policies of 1794 and 1795 and those adopted by Napoleon.[46]

No doubt one reason even relatively conservative thermidorians such as Boissy d'Anglas defended the abolition of slavery was that they saw no practical alternative: To have put in question the freedom of the Black soldiers who made up the bulk of the French fighting forces in the Caribbean in 1795 would almost certainly have cost France its chance to retain Saint-Domingue and Guadeloupe. That there were pragmatic reasons for maintaining the decisions made in 1793 and 1794 does not mean that the thermidorians were simply hypocrites with no intention of fulfilling the promise of emancipation. The thermidorians' decisions concerning the colonies coincided with a period of optimism about the post-emancipation situation in the Caribbean. Military forces composed largely of freed Black men were enabling the French to hold off the British in Guadeloupe and Saint-Domingue, and reports reaching Paris claimed that production on the plantations was recovering. Only after a crisis in March 1796 in Saint-Domingue, in which the free colored general Villatte tried to depose Governor Laveaux and Toussaint Louverture, by rescuing Laveaux, demonstrated that he had become the most powerful figure there, would the French government realize that the populations to whom it had granted freedom and equality might have ambitions that conflicted with French plans for them.[47]

Although the thermidorians had pragmatic reasons for maintaining the emancipation policy embodied in the decree of 16 pluviôse, one should not entirely dismiss the notion that, on this issue, at least some of them were also expressing sincere convictions. When Boissy d'Anglas told the Convention that the abolition of slavery was "the one act of justice that tyranny had you pass," he may have remembered that, at the time of the National Assembly's great debate about granting rights to free people of color in 1791, he had defended his vote in favor of the decree of 15 May 1791 by saying that he was standing up for "the sacred and imprescriptible rights of universal liberty."[48] As they wrestled with the legacy of the other things they had done during the Terror, some of the thermidorians may well have recognized that the granting of freedom to the Black populations in France's colonies was tangible evidence that the Revolution's language of freedom did have real meaning.

CHAPTER ELEVEN

The Years of the Conservative Republic

AT THE BEGINNING of October 1795, the National Convention finally ended its session and the new constitution enacted a few months earlier went into effect. During the three years of the Convention's tumultuous existence, a sixth of its deputies had met their deaths, including most of those who had taken an active role in promoting the abolitionist cause. Nevertheless, the Convention left behind a remarkable legacy on these issues. It had not only maintained the law of 4 April 1792 granting citizenship to free people of color, but it had passed the decree of 16 pluviôse II that emancipated the enslaved populations of France's colonies and made them citizens as well. The Convention had admitted the first men of African descent to sit in the legislature of a predominantly white country, and it had promoted Black and mixed-race military officers to positions of command in its armies. Finally, the new constitution the Convention had drafted made the colonies integral parts of the French republic, governed by the same laws, and reaffirmed racial equality and the abolition of slavery.

The government established by the Constitution of 1795 was a republic, but it was designed to be a much more conservative regime than the Jacobin republic created in 1792. Universal manhood suffrage was maintained, but the new constitution's two-stage voting system restricted the right to participate in the electoral colleges that actually chose deputies to a small elite of wealthy citizens. To forestall hasty decisions, the legislative branch of government was made bicameral, with a Council of 500 and a smaller Council of Elders whose members had to be at least forty years old and married or widowed. Executive power was vested in a five-man Directory, from which the regime took its name.

The thermidorian deputies who had drawn up the Constitution of 1795 were haunted by two fears: that of a royalist restoration and that of a resurgence of the radicalism of Year II. Distrustful of an electorate that might be attracted by either of these two extremes, the thermidorian Convention decreed that two-thirds of the 750 deputies to be chosen for the two new legislative assemblies had to come from its own ranks. This "two-thirds decree" was highly unpopular, and on 13 vendémiaire Year IV (5 October 1795), right-wing activists mounted a counterrevolutionary insurrection against it. To put down this uprising, the thermidorian Convention called on loyal republican army officers, including Napoleon Bonaparte, who had been without an assignment for over a year because of suspicions about his political views. Bonaparte's services to the Convention on 13 vendémiaire relaunched his military career. Paul Barras, the Convention deputy who recruited him, became one of the five Directors and rewarded his young protégé with command of the Army of Italy on France's southeastern frontier. The assignment put Bonaparte on the path that would, four years later, enable him to seize power and, among other things, decide the fate of the laws respecting France's colonies.

In October 1795 even Napoleon Bonaparte could hardly have imagined that he would one day determine the destiny of France and its overseas empire. Decisions about the colonies were now in the hands of the five newly chosen members of the Executive Directory and the two legislative councils. Only one of the Directors, Jean-François Rewbell, had figured in any significant way in the debates about race and slavery earlier in the Revolution: He had introduced the proposition granting rights to free men of color that became the controversial decree of 15 May 1791. Among the deputies, Henri Grégoire was the most prominent abolitionist; he would continue to be engaged with colonial issues throughout the four years of the Directory's existence, but primarily through his participation in the Société des Amis des Noirs et des Colonies, a revival of the Société des Amis des Noirs that only began to meet regularly in the fall of 1797. He was joined by a few other veterans from earlier days, such as Jacques Defermon, Jean-Philippe Garran-Coulon, and Joseph Eschassériaux. The most active defenders of the new regime in the colonies, however, were the deputies from Saint-Domingue, notably Louis Dufay and Jean-Baptiste Belley. Although the two-thirds decree had guaranteed that the majority of the deputies in both legislative councils were men who had also sat in the Convention, conservatives hostile to the Revolution took most of the 250 open seats. Vincent-Marie Viénot de Vaublanc and Mathieu Dumas, the two deputies who had delivered the most substantial speeches opposing the decree of 24 March 1792 that granted rights to free men of color, and François Barbé-Marbois, the former royal intendant in Saint-Domingue, were elected, joining the deputies Benoît Gouly and Jean-Jacques Serres from the Mascarenes in defending the interests of white colonists.

Outside the legislative chambers, there did not seem to be much need for any further mobilization in favor of abolition and racial equality, which were now protected by law. The situation in the proslavery camp was very different. Although the most prominent opponents of abolition from the Revolution's early years were either in exile, like Médéric Louis Élie Moreau de Saint-Méry, Pierre-Victor Malouet, and Jean-Siffrein Maury, or else dead, like Louis-Marthe Gouy d'Arsy and Antoine Barnave, the upheavals in the colonies had driven a large number of white colonists to take refuge in France. A law passed by the thermidorian Convention in October 1794 set up a system of relief payments to support them until they could return to their properties in the colonies.[1] While they waited for that possibility to materialize, many of the colonists worked to turn public opinion against the abolition policy adopted by the Convention. The *Journal historique et politique de la marine et des colonies*, a daily newspaper founded by colonists, expressed the refugees' bitterness and anger at what they saw as a betrayal: "The colonists of Saint-Domingue, massacred, chased out, deported, are they not French? . . . And what are the Africans? . . . Are they not foreign with respect to all possible connections, of blood, of interest, of civilization and of color? Isn't it to surrender the colonies to foreigners, if they are given to Africans, in contempt of the rights of the nation itself, of French commerce, of the rights of protection and property?"[2]

In an official message to the two councils in January 1796, the Directory laid out the policies it intended to follow in the colonies. "The prosperity of the republic is too closely tied to that of the French colonies . . . for these precious territories not to become the object of the Directory's most lively concern," the message began. The colonies had been in danger of falling into the hands of France's enemies, but "the general freedom of the Blacks has changed the face of things, and already . . . these men to whom you have restored their natural rights have reconquered their homes, and inspired terror in our most implacable enemies." Having acknowledged the decree of 16 pluviôse and the military contributions the Blacks were making, the Directors then struck a more cautious note. It was necessary, they said, to get the Blacks to return to the agricultural tasks they had performed before the abolition of slavery. In order to achieve this result, the Directors concluded, they needed to establish "a powerful authority, imbued with patriotism, courage, and reason; an authority entrusted to agents who can, by inspiring security, also impose obedience, and who will be, to the Blacks, a guarantee of the good faith of the French and the eternal maintenance of your laws."[3]

In concrete terms, the Directors proposed to send new civil commissioners to the various colonies still under French control. The white Saint-Domingue deputy Dufay endorsed the plan, and the measure was rushed through the two councils. Privately, Dufay told Etienne Laveaux, the military commander in Saint-Domingue, not to take all the public rhetoric about respecting the freedom of the Black population at face value. In committee meetings, he said, he was "speaking in another manner."[4] The white colonists in France were concerned about another proposal from the Directory, which wanted to treat the plantations whose owners had fled the islands like the estates of émigrés from metropolitan France, by expropriating them and putting them up for sale. "Their goods, justly taken by the republic, would amount to two billions in solid money, once a wise and enlightened administration has restored them," the Directors optimistically predicted.[5]

The Directors' language about the necessity of establishing firm authority to get the Blacks in Saint-Domingue to resume work on the plantations indicated a recognition that the colony's new citizens were unlikely to go back to their old routines voluntarily. In Guadeloupe, Victor Hugues did not even pretend to implement the decree of 16 pluviôse. Although he recruited Black soldiers, he enforced a rigorous system of forced field labor for the rest of the population. Hugues had originally been sent to Guadeloupe by the Committee of Public Safety in early 1794, but the Directory made him one of the commissioners for the island under the law of 5 pluviôse Year IV, and he dominated the two new colleagues sent to join him. The five-man Third Civil Commission appointed for Saint-Domingue was more controversial. The white colonists in France were enraged to learn that Léger-Félicité Sonthonax, "whose name alone horrifies all those who didn't participate in his crimes," as one of them wrote, was being sent back to the colony. The republican deputy Antoine-François Fourcroy, on the other hand, urged the Directors to send not only Sonthonax but also Julien Raimond, predicting that the two would "form of the men in Saint-Domingue a bloc of good Frenchmen, united together, faithful to the metropole, and terrible to the English." In addition to Sonthonax and Raimond, the Directors named Philippe Roume, the member of the First Civil Commission who had allied himself with the free men of color in 1792, and two less controversial colleagues.[6]

One of the initiatives the members of the new civil commission promised to promote was the recruitment of children from the colonies to be sent to a school in France set up to educate a future elite of Black and mixed-race leaders for the colonies. Raimond and Grégoire took a particular interest in this project, and Jean-Baptiste Coesnon, an elderly Catholic priest loyal to Grégoire's "constitutional" church, was appointed to direct what came to be known as the Institut National des Colonies. The Saint-Domingue deputy Dufay wrote personally to Toussaint Louverture, urging him to send his two sons Isaac and Placide as students, and the Black deputy Belley's sons were also enrolled. Lobbying the Directory for support for the school, Dufay noted that the children of Black leaders would constitute "valuable hostages to assure us of the loyalty of certain men who hold important commands in

Saint-Domingue." By the fall of 1800, there were seventy-nine students in the school.[7]

The members of the Third Civil Commission landed in Saint-Domingue just days after an event that had threatened to overthrow French authority there. The mixed-race general Jean-Louis Villatte had staged a coup, imprisoning the white military governor, Etienne Laveaux, who had to be rescued by Louverture and his troops. In late July, the *Moniteur* published a letter from Louverture to the French representative in the United States, with an editorial note adding that "General Laveaux had thought that he had to express the nation's recognition of what it owed to the brave Toussaint Louverture by naming him as lieutenant to the general government of the colony, whose white population's existence he has preserved on two occasions."[8] A few months later, Louverture arranged to have Laveaux elected as a deputy to the French legislature, telling him that he could do more for the Blacks' cause in France than he could in Saint-Domingue.[9] Laveaux's departure left Louverture as the overall commander of the French military in the colony. It also set the stage for a power struggle between Sonthonax, the dominant member of the new civil commission, and the Black general, a struggle that would have important repercussions in France once Sonthonax returned there.

While events in Saint-Domingue were raising the question of whether the metropole could still maintain control over its most important Caribbean colony, events in the Indian Ocean were showing that its ability to enforce the abolition of slavery in the face of resistance was also tenuous. In accordance with the law of 5 pluviôse IV, two agents, René-Gaston Baco and Etienne-Laurent-Pierre Burnel, were sent to implement the two-year-old emancipation decree. After a three-month voyage, they reached the Ile-de-France (today's Mauritius) on 18 June 1796. They were prepared to negotiate with the local white authorities about a plan for the gradual phasing out of the slavery system and the introduction of labor regulations similar to those imposed by Victor Hugues in Guadeloupe. Instead, the whites, with the collusion of the military officers in the colony, forced the agents back onto their ship and ordered them sent to the Philippines. Baco and Burnel managed to return to France instead, but their mission was a failure: Slavery persisted in the two islands, and the Directory made no further effort to impose its authority on them. The standoff in the Indian Ocean raised questions about how determined the government was to implement abolition in territories where the slavery system was still intact.[10]

Back in France, conservatives hostile to the abolition of slavery faced a challenge that no defenders of that institution had ever previously confronted: How were they to make the case for bringing slavery back after it had been done away with? The most serious effort along these lines came from Jean-Baptiste Laplace, a Saint-Domingue colonist whose *Histoire des désastres de Saint-Domingue*, published in 1795, had recounted the convulsions in that colony before the freeing of the slaves. In 1796 Laplace published a two-volume work entitled *Réflexions sur la colonie de Saint-Domingue, ou Examen approfondi des causes de sa ruine, et des mesures adoptées pour la rétablir; terminées par l'exposé rapide d'un plan d'organisation propre à lui rendre son ancienne splendeur* (Reflections on the colony of Saint-Domingue, or, A thorough examination of the causes of its ruin, and of the measures adopted to restore it; followed by a rapid exposition of a plan of organization suited to bring back its former splendor).[11] Laplace's treatise was the most coherent and extensive argument in favor of the restoration of slavery published in the years between the passage of the decree of 16 pluviôse and the launching of Napoleon's expedition in 1802, and it essentially laid out the policy that inspired that fateful enterprise.

Unlike most of the other former Saint-Domingue colonists, Laplace did not waste time on futile denunciations of Jacques-Pierre Brissot, Grégoire, or Sonthonax, or on heart-wrenching depictions of the sufferings of the colonists during the slave uprising. His aim was to make a serious argument, supported by his fifteen years of experience in the colonies, that abolition could not succeed and that it would therefore be necessary to return to a system similar to what had existed before the Revolution. Laplace grudgingly admitted that Blacks were "variations of the human species," but he insisted that nature "has given them an unequal share of the gifts of intelligence, and that this race, perhaps the most handsome and the most vigorous . . . is inferior with regard to moral faculties" and had an "invincible aversion to work." Laplace pretended to regret his own observations, but only in order to underline the conclusion that slavery could not be done away with. "No doubt," he wrote, "slavery is a great evil in the eyes of nature and of humanity, but shouldn't it be categorized as one of those political evils that are, so to speak, necessary, in order to avoid greater ones, and that one should not even try to abolish?"[12]

Laplace began by putting his finger on a contradiction in republican colonial policy. The Blacks had been declared free, but at the same time, they were being told that they had to continue working on the same plantations where they had been enslaved before their emancipation. "This singular arrangement is contrary to the very spirit of freedom, which becomes an illusion, if those who should enjoy it are forced to act contrary to their wishes and their inclinations," he wrote.[13] After denouncing the hypocrisy of an such an emancipation policy, Laplace also denounced what he presented as the hypocrisy of measures that purported to uphold the property rights of the white colonists. "What white man would be brave enough to live, without protection and without any other guarantee, in the midst of these same individuals who have covered their hands with the blood of his fellows? . . . How would the Blacks accept among themselves and in charge of them their former master, a man of a race they detest, whose presence would constantly remind them of slavery and inspire them with the fear of being forced back into it!" In any event, Laplace continued, it was impossible to imagine that two races "that nature has made so different from one another, and that have no common beliefs, tastes, or habits," could live together peacefully.[14]

Having demonstrated the hypocrisy of the laws regarding abolition and the impossibility of a genuine coexistence between Blacks and whites, Laplace concluded, "Yes, I will have the courage to say it: better slavery, useful and well organized, as it existed for centuries, than this shapeless and anarchical chaos that has been substituted for it!"[15] But how was white authority to be restored in a territory where the Black population now dominated? All that was needed, Laplace claimed, was "the clear declaration of the national will, supported by a sudden and imposing deployment of its power."[16] What he proposed was essentially the strategy for the military expedition that Napoleon would launch five years later. "The direction of this expedition," he wrote, "should be entrusted to a well-intentioned, energetic leader. . . . He should be given vast power, but told to stick to a fixed plan worked out in the metropole by well-informed men with whom the government will have surrounded itself, and be given precise instructions from which he could not deviate. . . . Rigorous regulations would compel everyone to go back to his proper place, and one would expel without pity anyone, white, yellow, or Black, who could not justify his right to remain, by his ownership of property, his morals, his profession, or who could not obtain a testimonial from someone worthy of confidence." Putting forward a similar plan, another proslavery writer of the Directory period added that the decision to reestablish slavery should be kept secret until an armed force was in position to enforce it, a suggestion that the Napoleonic government would adopt in 1802.[17]

Once French authority had been restored, Laplace foresaw a situation in which "slavery, strictly speaking, is abolished," but where the Blacks would have the status of indentured servants. After twenty-four years of dutiful service, they would be given the possibility of purchasing their freedom and would be given ownership of a small plot of land. "Every form of arbitrary corporal punishment would be severely prohibited," he wrote, but landowners would still have the authority to put disobedient Blacks in chains. Runaways would be branded, as under the old colonial regime, and would be forced to work. In light of the population losses resulting from the conflicts in Saint-Domingue, Laplace called for the reopening of the slave trade, with rules to prevent the bad treatment of its victims. To achieve this goal, he suggested that some of the crews on slave ships should be Blacks, who could reassure the captives about their fate.[18]

When it was published in 1796, Laplace's book represented an extreme view, rooted in racism, that could only have been implemented if the ongoing war with Britain was successfully concluded and if the French government completely abandoned the policies adopted in 1794 and 1795. Another former colonist, Louis Rallier, put forward a more cautiously worded proposal, rooted more in a sociological and economic analysis of the situation in

Saint-Domingue than in outright racial prejudice. If Laplace's suggestions anticipated the policy Napoleon was to adopt in 1802, Rallier's ideas were significant because he made himself into an ally of Toussaint Louverture, who arranged for his election as a deputy from Saint-Domingue in 1797. Rallier acknowledged that there were differences between a society like France and the colonies that, in his view, made unrealistic the straightforward extension of French laws promised in the laws adopted in 1795. In France, virtually the whole population belonged to the same racial group and there was a general consensus regarding property rights and the relations between employers and workers. Colonial society, on the other hand, was divided into racial castes with strong reasons to distrust each other and the economy was based on the plantation system, which required a different framework for labor relations.

Rallier openly regretted the way in which freedom had been given to the Black population. "They should not have been freed from their former duties before they had been taught their new ones, nor should they have been entirely freed from forced labor before they had been given a taste for work performed voluntarily," he wrote. Nevertheless, it was now too late to reverse the decision made in 1794. Although the Blacks could no longer be made to return to their former plantations by force, he thought that most of them would be willing to do so, since they would want to live where they were known, had relations, and could continue to claim the personal plots most masters had allocated them under the slavery system. He strongly opposed the idea of breaking up the plantations into small properties, for fear that the Blacks would no longer be willing to work to raise export crops.[19]

The decree of 16 pluviôse had promised all Blacks in the colonies full French citizenship. Rallier wanted to limit rights to those who had been born in the colony or had performed military service. He warned that universal citizenship would "give one color . . . an immense majority which, for some time to come, could not fail to be very dangerous." Rallier urged the cultivation of an elite of enlightened Blacks who were "capable of understanding and practicing all the virtues" and who could serve as models for the rest of the population. The best way to do this, he thought, would be to take advantage of the Blacks' devotion to religion by sending them "wise and intelligent pastors, who . . . would teach them the love of work, the necessity of marriage, and the practice of domestic virtues." The program Rallier proposed anticipated in many ways the project of assimilation that French imperialists would seek to follow a century later, when the country acquired its vast empire in Africa. It was also not far removed from the ideas of Toussaint Louverture, who was equally concerned with maintaining labor discipline on the plantations and imposing adherence to religion and morality on the population.[20]

In differing ways, both Laplace and Rallier offered the *honnêtes hommes* (respectable men), the solid property owners to whom conservative politicians looked for support, coherent arguments against the official colonial policy of the Directory that the members of the Third Civil Commission were attempting to implement in Saint-Domingue. Journalists sympathetic to the colonists echoed these claims that emancipation had caused disorder in the colonies.[21] Legislative debate about that policy was renewed in March 1797, when the deputy Pierre Marec, speaking on behalf of the Council of 500's colonial committee, delivered the first detailed overview of the situation in Saint-Domingue that French legislators had been offered since July 1795.

Although the majority of the members of his committee, which included Brissot's former ally Garran-Coulon, were in favor of the policies adopted by the thermidorian Convention, Marec himself gave a largely pessimistic assessment of the situation. "I will have above all horrible circumstances, hideous images to put before your eyes," he told his colleagues. In addition to Villatte's unsuccessful coup attempt, he mentioned a massacre of whites in the southern city of Cayes, which the mixed-race general André Rigaud was accused of instigating. Marec spoke of the emancipation decrees issued by Sonthonax and Etienne Polverel in 1793 as "a risky, perilous, extreme measure" that the Convention, with its decree of 16 pluviôse, "had ratified, no doubt in a moment of enthusiasm." Marec nevertheless defended the actions of Sonthonax and the other members of the Third Civil Commission, but he added that their own letters contained "very painful reflections about the critical position of Europeans in the colony, about the hostility with which the Africans pursue them . . . with the commission's inability to halt so many disorders." In view of the litany of woes Marec recited, his conclusion, to the effect that the Directory needed to hasten the full application of the 1795 Constitution in the colony in order to end the "provisional government" that was, according to him, the cause of the disorders there, sounded less than convincing.[22]

In April 1797, eighteen months after the inauguration of the Directory, voters had their first chance to express themselves in elections to replace one-third of the deputies in the two legislative councils. The authors of the Constitution of 1795 had hoped that the electorate would support candidates who favored a conservative republican regime. Instead, the deputies chosen to make up the "new third" were mostly men who barely bothered to conceal their aspiration to bring back some form of monarchy. Among them were several veterans of the campaigns to defend colonial interests in the first years of the Revolution, such as Charles Tarbé, the main spokesman of the Legislative Assembly's colonial committee in 1791–92. Elections held in Saint-Domingue and Guadeloupe returned deputies supportive of the new colonial order, but even before the new conservatives were seated, metropolitan legislators nullified those results on procedural grounds.[23]

In spite of the election results, the majority of the Directory was at first determined not to change its colonial policy. On 3 floréal V (22 April 1797), the Director Rewbell announced to the councils that the Directory was ready to put the Constitution of 1795 into effect in Saint-Domingue "without any kind of modification." He called on the legislators to "once again remind themselves of the principle of the law of 16 pluviôse Year II on general liberty" and to never forget "that we are dealing here with new men, long oppressed, long unfortunate, suspicious because of their lack of instruction, because of the memory of all the evils they have suffered." The Blacks would be "calm once they will have read in the preambles to the various acts of the Legislature that their liberty is irrevocably assured, once they have seen the councils and the government speak out against the system of a return to slavery." Rewbell went on to propose that the properties of colonists classified as émigrés should be sold "in small portions, divided in such a way that a large number of men can bid on them," in order to create a class of Black landowners.[24]

Two weeks later, the Directory issued a veritable declaration of war against the white colonists who had come to France to escape the troubles in the colonies. The Directors wanted to suppress the payments authorized by a decree passed in September 1796 that had been meant to compensate the colonists for their losses. The Directory's message incorporated strong language from the *Républicain des colonies*, a proabolitionist newspaper, claiming that the colonists did not deserve aid since they had shown that they still wanted to be "able to degrade, torment and torture with impunity a man of color, buy and sell slaves, [and] obtain the return of the ancien régime and its privileges."[25] It was a bold assertion that all true French citizens necessarily had to embrace the principles embodied in the decree of 16 pluviôse II and the constitutional laws passed in 1795.

The Directory's provocative declarations in favor of the new egalitarian order in the colonies may explain why their conservative opponents, known as the Clichyens because they regularly met at one member's house on the rue de Clichy to discuss strategy, decided to make the colonies the first issue on which they openly challenged the republicans. The Clichyens launched their attack on 10 prairial Year V (30 May 1797). Their choice of the deputy Vaublanc, a prominent defender of colonial interests known for his royalist sympathies, as their spokesman was a deliberate provocation. Vaublanc lost no time in making it clear how he and his party saw the situation of the colonies: "Our shipping almost destroyed, our maritime commerce annihilated, the empire of the seas abandoned completely to the English, the balance of trade stolen from us, everything makes it our duty to finally do something about the colonies."[26]

According to Vaublanc, the Directory had lied to the councils when it claimed that things were going well in Saint-Domingue. In reality, he insisted, the colony was racked by racial conflict. "Everywhere the Negroes abandon fieldwork; they insist that the country belongs to them, that they don't want to see a single white man left." The cause of this deplorable situation was "the revolutionary fury, which, in precipitating the emancipation of the Negroes, rejected all the measures recommended by prudence and . . . infused into the measures adopted more hatred for the whites than concern for the Negroes." Vaublanc pretended to endorse the idea of abolishing slavery at some distant date in the future, but "to head toward this great goal like a tempest that uproots trees and destroys houses, without any concern for the men who are buried by the debris, to cause the death of two hundred thousand Negroes in order to free three hundred thousand Negroes, sacrifice for that ten thousand Frenchmen, ruin for that the trade of a great nation! Such an outcome is horrible."[27]

Vaublanc's speech set off what became the longest of all French revolutionary parliamentary debates about the colonies. On the following day, Tarbé, who had often tangled with Brissot in the Legislative Assembly five years earlier, went after Sonthonax, "the torturer of the whites, the enemy of the mulattos and the miserable sycophant of the Blacks." Admiral Louis-Thomas Villaret-Joyeuse, who would later command the French fleet in the expedition of 1802, insisted that the slaves had been "much better off than most of the peasants under the ancien régime" and called Saint-Domingue "a Vendée we need to reconquer."[28] The Clichyens' offensive resonated well beyond the walls of the council's chamber. Right-wing newspapers praised their speakers, and a police report noted that "all who appear interested in the colonial situation" were "let[ting] themselves run wild" in their denunciations of the government's policy.[29]

During the first few days of this debate, the Clichyens had the advantage, but on 15 prairial V (2 June 1797), Tarbé made a blunder that allowed the republicans to halt their adversaries' momentum. In the course of a violent sortie against Sonthonax, he said, "You know what evils France has suffered, for five years, because of atrocious decrees promoted by the same men who now seek to end [this] discussion." According to the *Moniteur universel*, "At these words, the indignation that had been held back for so long exploded with violence. A hundred members are on their feet, and crying for the speaker to be called to order." By speaking of five years of "atrocious" decrees, Tarbé was questioning everything that had been done since 10 August 1792, when the monarchy had been overthrown. Antoine Thibaudeau, a moderate republican who had tried to negotiate with the Clichyens, spoke in the name of "men who are proud to have founded the republic and who, let no one doubt it, will know how to defend it." By an almost unanimous vote, the Council of 500 sent Tarbé's report to be buried in the colonial committee.[30]

The republicans now went on the offensive. Etienne Laveaux, the former military commander in Saint-Domingue, demanded to know how Vaublanc dared to compare "the Blacks who defended, reestablished and saved the colony and the good citizens who stayed there, with the rebels and the émigrés whom the British government supports in order to completely destroy our colonies and our maritime commerce?" Joseph Eschassériaux argued that there was no possibility of mounting an expedition to occupy the colony by force. According to him, "The voice of [Jean-Jacques] Rousseau, of [Gabriel Bonnot de] Mably, [Guillaume Thomas François] Raynal, will not have been heard in vain, across the seas, even in the caves, in the hearts of savages. . . . That voice will stop the lawmaker who, conspiring against humanity, would have the sacrilegious audacity to force a man back into the chains of another, and the cruel owner who would treat another man as his property." Garran-Coulon made a point-by-point defense of Sonthonax's conduct and cited documents showing the connections between the white colonists in Paris and Maximilien Robespierre's allies that had resulted in the execution of Brissot, Claude Milscent, and other advocates of abolition.[31] The *Ami des Loix* backed up the republican deputies by warning that "after having done away with the freedom of the Negroes, [the Clichyens] will attack the freedom of the whites."[32]

Although the republicans in the legislature had gained the upper hand over their adversaries, the Directory, to which the Clichyens had succeeded in electing one of their allies in place of a member who had rotated off, decided not to seek a confrontation over the colonial issue. When letters from Sonthonax and Raimond arrived in France bearing reassuring news about the situation in the colony, the Directors decided to declare their mission accomplished and to recall them. For some weeks, the five-member Directory remained deeply divided about whether to seek a broader agreement with the more moderate Clichyens. Decisions made at the beginning of the revolutionary month of messidor V appeared to point toward a compromise. When the Council of 500 proposed to send new agents to Saint-Domingue to save the colony from "the furors of anarchy,"[33] the Directory responded by naming Joseph Hédouville, a military man who had gained his reputation by pacifying the rebellion in France's Vendée region, for the position, a choice that satisfied the advocates of the white colonists. Together with the dismissal of the proabolitionist navy minister Laurent Truguet, Hédouville's nomination seemed to portend a sharp turn in France's colonial policy, and perhaps in the government's overall orientation.

No one grasped the significance of the 1797 parliamentary debates about the colonies better than Toussaint Louverture. Acting military governor of Saint-Domingue since the departure for France of his former superior Laveaux at the end of 1796, Louverture saw the Clichyen victory in the spring elections as a potential threat to the Black population's freedom but also as an opportunity to rid himself of the white commissioner Sonthonax and put himself forward as a potential ally of the French conservatives. In a forty-four-page report to the Directory that one biographer has described as "a magnificent piece of creative fiction" and that was summarized in several Paris newspapers, Louverture purported to transcribe dialogues between himself and Sonthonax in which the latter had supposedly urged the Black general to join him in declaring Saint-Domingue independent and in massacring the remaining white population. This allowed Louverture to assert his confidence that France would stand by the principle of emancipation and to present himself as the defender of French authority.[34]

At the time when he wrote his denunciation of Sonthonax, in which he dismissed the danger from the colonial lobby in France, Louverture had not yet seen the Clichyens' speeches denouncing the consequences of emancipation in Saint-Domingue and, among other things, supporting his mixed-race political rivals in the colony. Once he realized the seriousness of the colonists' offensive, however, he sent to France a "refutation of some assertions in a speech given in the Legislative Body on 10 prairial, Year V, by Vienot Vaublanc," which was published in Paris in October 1797. Louverture now cast himself as a defender of the rights the Blacks had been granted in 1794 and 1795 against the evil intentions of the white colonial party whose influence he had previously accused Sonthonax of exaggerating.

In reading Vaublanc's speech, Louverture wrote, "I suffered at seeing my intentions misrepresented on every page . . . and the political existence of my brothers menaced." He reminded the French public that "it was the Blacks who, when France was in danger of losing this colony, used their bodies and their weapons to preserve it," and he answered the Clichyens' racist arguments by saying that the Blacks' lack of education did not justify the idea that they should be treated as "a class separate from the rest of the human race." Vaublanc had tried to argue that the violence in Saint-Domingue showed that the Blacks were unfit for freedom. What would he say, Louverture asked, if "a voice was raised in Saint-Domingue, and said to the French people, 'You have committed all these crimes, and you have no excuse, because, more educated, more civilized than us, you should have avoided them.'"[35]

If the whites would sincerely accept the freedom of the Blacks, Louverture promised, they "would see a growing love and attachment in the hearts of these men, which they have never ceased to cherish for the whites in general and for their former masters in particular, despite all their efforts to put them back into slavery and bring back to Saint-Domingue the reign of tyranny." But, he warned, if an army was sent to force the Blacks into slavery, "then, with the constitution in one hand, they would defend the liberty it guarantees." The population of Saint-Domingue, he warned, would "always rather be buried in the ruins of their country rather than to see the return of slavery."[36] Louverture's prophetic address was an eloquent expression of the Black population's determination to defend their freedom.

Louverture's pamphlets injected him directly into metropolitan politics. Once he had decided to compel Sonthonax to return to France, the Black general clearly knew that his position was going to become a subject of controversy in Paris. Louverture himself would never set foot in France until he was brought there as a prisoner in 1802, but from 1797 to the moment of his arrest, the question of how to deal with his growing power was as burning an issue in French politics as the fate of the rights promised to the Black population by the decrees of 1794 and 1795. Even as his actions raised increasing doubts about his intentions, Louverture bombarded the Directors and the navy minister with letters denouncing his critics and asserting his unswerving devotion to France. The "Louverture question" divided French officials, but it also pitted whites who supported abolition against each other, with Etienne Laveaux taking the side of his former comrade in arms and Sonthonax vehemently opposing him, and it also divided the Black and mixed-race deputies from the colonies, most of whom came to side with Sonthonax.[37]

Ironically, 18 fructidor Year V (4 September 1797), the date on which Louverture's pamphlet against Sonthonax was published in Cap Français, was also the date on which the three staunchest republican members of the French Directory staged a coup against the Clichyen faction whose favor the Black general had once hoped to win over. Earlier in the summer, when the Directory appointed Hédouville and dismissed Truguet, it had appeared as though a majority of its members were seeking a compromise with the Clichyens. After several months of mounting political tension in Paris, however, three of its members, Barras, Rewbell, and Louis-Marie Larevellière-Lépeaux, finally decided to resort to force to quash the conservative opposition. Having assured themselves of support from the army, the *triumvirs* expelled and arrested the leading Clichyen legislative deputies and their two more moderate colleagues and silenced the newspapers that supported them. Louis Gustave Le Doulcet de Pontécoulant, one of the conservative deputies targeted in what came to be known as the coup d'état of 18 fructidor, was sure that it was the revelation, during the colonial debate in prairial, that centrist deputies like Thibaudeau would stand up for the heritage of the republic that convinced the *triumvirs* that their move would succeed. "It was from that moment that one can date the irreconcilable hatred and the project of vengeance that the majority of the Directory developed for all those who had fought against it," he wrote in his memoirs.[38]

Backed by Napoleon Bonaparte, who sent one of his closest subordinates to Paris to direct the military aspect of the operation, the coup d'état of 18 fructidor V staved off the counterrevolutionary threat to the republic, but at the price of seriously undermining its claim to be a constitutional regime. Those Clichyens who did not take flight in time were exiled to Guiana, arriving as prisoners in a colony whose formerly enslaved Blacks were now free citizens.

The coup of fructidor inaugurated a new phase of the Revolution, which historians call the Second Directory. Sure of firm support from a legislature purged of its more conservative members, the reconstituted Directory embraced policies that recalled the radical phase of the Revolution. The governments in the "sister republics" the French had sponsored in the Netherlands, Italy, and Switzerland were purged of their more moderate members and brought into line with the new policy in Paris, although the Dutch successfully resisted French pressure to abolish slavery in their overseas colonies.[39]

Colonial policy was one of the main areas in which the Second Directory demonstrated its new militancy. A commission to review the contested elections in Saint-Domingue was appointed on the day of the coup, with the abolitionists Grégoire and Eschassériaux as members, and a week later the deputies from the colony's North Province were seated.[40] By the end of October 1797, Eschassériaux was ready to present the longest and most detailed law concerning the colonies passed during the entire period of the Revolution. Eventually approved on 12 nivôse Year VI (1 January 1798), the law was meant to fulfill the promise made in 1795 that France's republican constitution in its entirety would be extended to its overseas possessions. The task was not a simple one, Eschassériaux told his colleagues. "A people still unaccustomed to the art of living in society has to be instructed about the laws, taught to govern itself," and "men of different colors [had] to be brought together and united." Nevertheless, if the task could be accomplished, "humanity, the entire generation of the friends of liberty, are there to bless your memory if you have the good fortune to succeed."[41]

Before the fructidor coup, the Clichyens had tried to characterize the Blacks as "Africans" rather than French, but Eschassériaux was emphatic about their status as citizens. The Blacks might have been born in Africa, but they had been transported against their will and had been forced to work the land, and France should therefore be "regarded as their native land" and they should enjoy the same rights as other French citizens. But the law he proposed also reflected some hesitation about treating them like whites in metropolitan France. Its terms insisted on the obligations that went along with citizenship. "If they make agriculture flourish, if they serve in the armies, if they are engaged in some mechanical occupation, the fatherland will include them among the citizens of the Republic. But if they are a burden to it by their laziness, if they dishonor and trouble it by brigandage . . . it has the right to be severe, and to deprive them of the rights of citizenship, until . . . repentance brings them back to their work and their regular profession."[42] Although this language appears to justify claims like that of the historian Tessie Liu that republican France was at best prepared to treat the Blacks as "probationary citizens,"[43] Eschassériaux expressed confidence that most of the population would prove worthy to enjoy their rights. Defending the law in the Council of Elders two months later, the deputy Pierre Roger-Ducos reiterated the necessity of rewarding men who had fought for the country and added that policies should be adopted to enable formerly enslaved Blacks to acquire property of their own.[44]

Even though the fructidor purge had eliminated most of the spokesmen for the colonial lobby, there were still some objections to the proposed law. Eschassériaux warned, however, that the consequences of retreating from the principles adopted in 1794 and 1795 would be catastrophic. In words that would prove prophetic after Napoleon came to power, he exclaimed, "Do you think that it would be easy to force back under the yoke of their previous oppressors men who have been promised freedom for five years, who have defended it, who have enjoyed it? Would that not break all the ties that unite the colonies with the mother country, incite civil war, independence or enemy occupation, or else put into the hands of some new Spartacus the sword that would avenge this unfortunate land for so many broken promises, so many outrages?" The orators of the Directory period rarely matched the eloquence of their predecessors from the first years of the Revolution, but Eschassériaux's conclusion was one such occasion. "Representatives," he told his colleagues, "the freedom of peoples may be oppressed, but it does not reverse itself."[45]

The law of 12 nivôse VI provided an outline for the creation of a transatlantic, multiracial republican regime that would have been unique in the world. The deputies who passed it, however, did not fully understand the difficulties that stood in the way of its implementation. At the moment when the law was passed in

France, much of Saint-Domingue was a war zone, with the British still occupying the western part of the colony; even the basic task of defining the boundaries of the French-style *départements* into which the colony was supposed to be divided could not be carried out under the circumstances. Toussaint Louverture was locked in conflict with General Hédouville, the French agent who would have been responsible for putting the law into effect, and neither Louverture nor his mixed-race rival Rigaud had any desire to facilitate the installation of institutions that would limit their power. The outbreak of war between these two ambitious generals in mid-1799 put further obstacles in the way of any such project, and Napoleon's seizure of power in November of that year ended the metropolitan government's commitment to the law's objectives. The law of 12 nivôse VI was an expression of good intentions that were doomed to remain unfulfilled.

The policies embodied in the law of 12 nivôse VI were enthusiastically supported by the members of the Société des Amis des Noirs et des Colonies, which began meeting regularly in November 1797. The inspiration for the group came from surviving members of the Société des Amis des Noirs. Grégoire, Brissot's close friend François-Xavier Lanthenas, and the abolitionist author Benjamin Frossard all played active roles in the new association. They were joined by many of the deputies from the colonies; in December 1798 the Black legislator Pierre Thomany was elected as the society's president. Helen Maria Williams, an Englishwoman who had devoted herself to the revolutionary cause, was one of several female members. The society's members also included several government officials, notably Daniel Lescallier, the colonial expert and one-time supporter of Lafayette's prerevolutionary effort to introduce emancipation on his estates in Cayenne. For a time, the group actually held its meetings in the offices of the ministry of the navy and colonies.[46] As the society's bylaws, formally adopted in October 1798, acknowledged, the great goal of the abolition movement had been achieved: "The banner of freedom waves over all the plantations in our colonies . . . the question of the slave trade and the emancipation of the slaves is finally resolved for France; it is also for the whole world in all sensible and reasonable minds." The mission of the group was therefore to publicize the successes of the new regime in the colonies and to encourage the spread of "education, the sciences and the arts" among their populations. The group also hoped to work with abolitionists in other countries to promote the ending of the slave trade.[47]

The name chosen for the group indicated that the new society was in no way opposed to France's possession of overseas territories, and in fact its members showed as much interest in what came to be called the new colonialism as in the fate of the country's former slave colonies. Among the society's members, the most active promoter of this idea was the Swedish abolitionist C. B. Wadstrom. Inspired by the British effort to found a colony inhabited by free Blacks in Sierra Leone on the west coast of Africa, Wadstrom argued that Africa could become a source of sugar and the other tropical products Europeans craved even as the slave trade was eliminated. As present-day critics of the new colonialism have argued, the new colonialists combined the humanitarian idea of eliminating slavery with a conviction that Europeans had a right and even a duty to impose their own version of civilization on non-European peoples. In the nineteenth century, this idea of a *mission civilisatrice* (civilizing mission) would serve as a justification for the spread of French colonial rule in Africa and other parts of the world. Commenting on an article published by the society in the republican intellectual journal *La Décade philosophique* in the spring of 1798 that insisted on the need to export "moral and practical instruction" to the Africans, Bernard Gainot remarks that "there is a transformation from a missionary project to a pedagogical one. But the anthropological relationship remains the same: the European, and particularly the Frenchman, becomes the tutor to other parts of the world."[48]

Napoleon's expedition to Egypt, which set sail in May 1798, embodied the principles of the new colonialism. The French landed in Egypt promising to bring its population the benefits of European civilization, and a number of scientists and intellectuals from the same milieu as the membership of the Société des Amis des Noirs et des Colonies accompanied the soldiers. Meanwhile, back in France, the artist Anne-Louis Girodet was giving visual expression to the promise that the French Republic was prepared to treat men of all races equally. Girodet's striking portrait of the Black

Saint-Domingue deputy Belley, painted toward the end of 1797 and exhibited at the Salon, the official art exhibition, in the summer of 1798, showed its subject in his official legislator's uniform. Girodet's painting, "a profound political as well as pictorial accomplishment," according to art historian Darcy Grimaldo Grigsby, depicted Belley according to the conventions of formal European portrait painting, posing him next to a bust of Raynal, the author of the *Histoire de deux Indes*, with a verdant landscape in the background (figure 11).[49]

Girodet's portrait of Belley conveyed the profound transformation wrought by the policies adopted in 1794 and 1795 and confirmed by the passage of the law of 12 nivôse VI. Viewers could not miss the message that the man whose lustrous black skin Girodet emphasized was now a full-fledged member of the French national legislature. The relationship between Belley and the bust of Raynal has puzzled some commentators. The *Histoire de deux Indes* had warned of the possibility of a slave revolt; it had not foreseen the idea that enslaved Blacks could become equal citizens in a European polity. In the painting, Belley turns his back on Raynal's bust and slouches casually against the pedestal supporting it; there is no suggestion that he was expressing gratitude to the philosophe. Although his facial expression is hard to read, the Belley in the portrait seems fully at ease in his European clothes and, by implication, in the political role his dress reflected. Once Napoleon took power and banished Black deputies from the French legislature, Girodet's portrait vanished into obscurity. In the past few decades, the portrait of Belley has resurfaced and become a cultural icon, reproduced in innumerable books on the revolutionary era. Its current prominence signals a recognition of the significance of the events that allowed Belley to achieve the status of a French deputy and to command the attention of one of France's leading artists.

Girodet's portrait of Belley reflected the new reality created by the decree of 16 pluviôse and the subsequent laws that gave emancipated Blacks the rights of citizenship. The period's literature was slower to adjust to the new situation. In 1795 Madame de Staël, the daughter of the former minister Jacques Necker, whose salon brought together leading politicians and intellectuals from across the political spectrum, published her novella *Mirza*, which

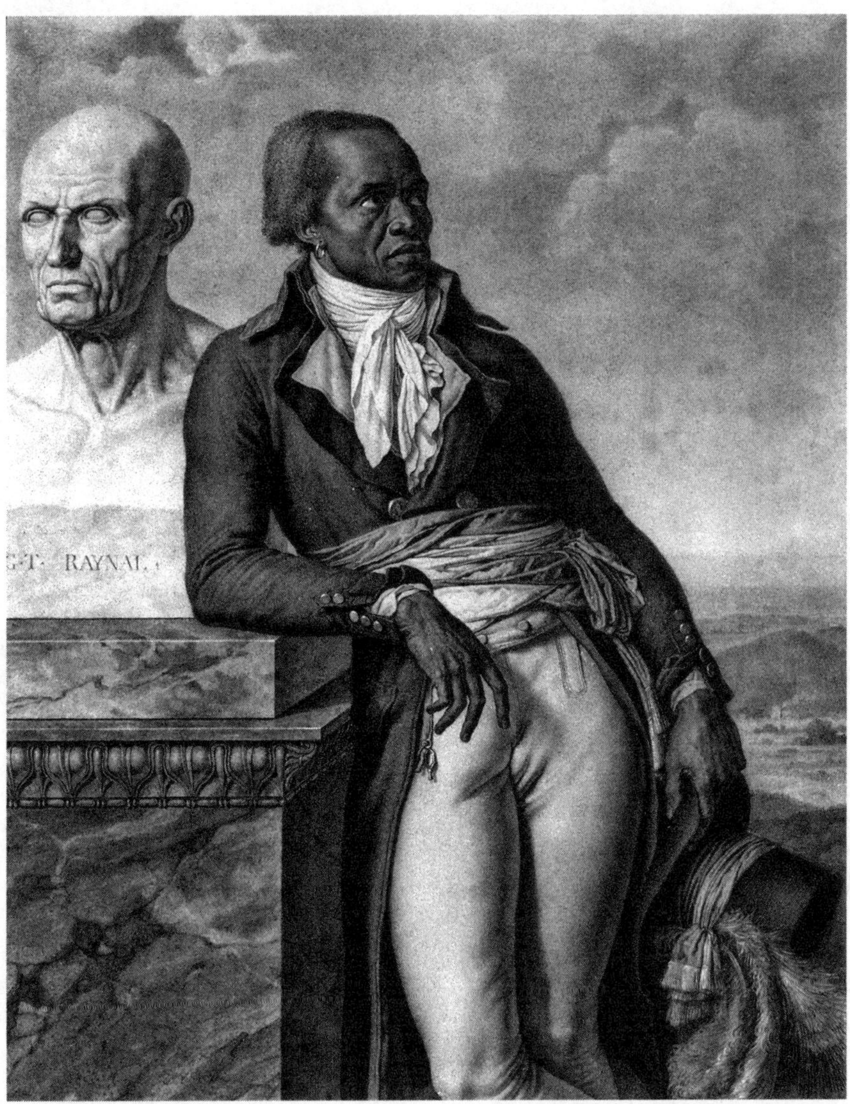

FIGURE 11: Anne-Louis Girodet's portrait of Jean-Baptiste Belley, a former slave who served in the French legislature from 1794 to 1798, has become an iconic representation of the dramatic changes brought about by the decree of 16 pluviôse. *Credit:* Anne-Louis Girodet de Roucy-Trioson, Jean-Baptiste Belley, 1797. The Art Institute of Chicago.

she had written in 1786, without updating its sentimental tale of star-crossed enslaved lovers. Charles-Antoine Guillaume Pigault-Lebrun's play *Le Blanc et le Noir*, performed in late 1795, and Jean-Baptiste Picquenard's novel *Adonis*, published in 1798 and quickly adapted for the stage, both recycled prerevolutionary tropes about noble slaves and goodhearted plantation owners who overcome racial differences. The plot of counterrevolutionary author Joseph Fiévée's 1798 bestseller *La Dot de Suzette* (Suzette's dowry) was more up-to-date: It featured a protagonist whose family fortune had been wiped out by the Saint-Domingue insurrection.[50]

Girodet's painting was finished just as Belley's term of office was ending; he left the Council of 500 and returned to Saint-Domingue after the spring elections in 1798. A few months earlier, both councils had marked the fourth anniversary of the abolition decree of 16 pluviôse Year II. The two speeches delivered in honor of the occasion, both given by white deputies representing Saint-Domingue, were in agreement in praising what the Convention had done, but their sharply divergent descriptions of the Black general Toussaint Louverture reflected the way in which controversies rooted in power struggles on the island were spilling over into metropolitan politics. In the Council of Elders, the deputy Martin Noël Brothier hailed Louverture as "one of these extraordinary men who prove that only liberty allows all talents to find their proper reward." In the Council of 500, however, Sonthonax, newly returned to France, accused Louverture of having become the instrument of a conspiracy organized by "counterrevolutionary priests who, in Saint-Domingue as in France, use all means to undermine liberty."[51] Sonthonax's accusations jolted other abolitionists, such as Grégoire, to whom Louverture had written asking for his help in recruiting Catholic priests for Saint-Domingue. Grégoire printed several of Louverture's letters in the *Annales de la Religion*, the journal of the "constitutional" prorepublican church, including a proclamation in which the Black general insisted that he had been "the defender of citizens of all colors" and that the colony owed its salvation to "the will of the God of armies."[52]

While the supporters of abolition became divided about the status of Toussaint Louverture, metropolitan politics took another swerve that, like all the many crises of the revolutionary decade, altered the atmosphere regarding the colonies. As a result of the coup d'état of 18 fructidor V, conservatives were sidelined during the parliamentary elections of April 1798, but a democratic "neo-Jacobin" movement scored unexpected successes. The Directors were no more willing to see themselves challenged from the left than they had been to accept the conservatives' success in the previous year's elections. On 22 floréal Year VI (11 May 1798), they staged another coup, purging a number of the neo-Jacobin deputies and installing regime loyalists in their place. Colonial issues had not figured significantly in the election campaign, but the defeat of the neo-Jacobins reduced enthusiasm for policies such as the full implementation of the law of 12 nivôse VI.

News from the Caribbean over the course of 1798 made it clear that in any event, laws passed in France were becoming steadily less relevant to the situation in the colonies. In Saint-Domingue, Louverture was increasingly acting like an independent ruler. In August 1798, ignoring the French agent Hédouville, he negotiated a treaty that ended the British occupation of the western part of the colony. When Hédouville objected, Louverture forced him to return to France. By this time, France was engaged in a "quasi-war" with the United States, but, in defiance of French policies, Louverture opened the colony's ports to American merchants. In mid-1799 the power struggle between Louverture and his mixed-race rival André Rigaud devolved into outright conflict, the "war of the South," which was still underway when Napoleon Bonaparte seized power in France in November of that year. Meanwhile, in Guadeloupe, turmoil broke out when a new French representative, Etienne Desfourneaux, arrived to replace Victor Hugues, whose partisans resisted his ouster, opening a period of instability there that persisted until Napoleon's forces arrived in 1802.[53]

While events in the colonies portended trouble for their integration into the French constitutional order foreseen by the law of 12 nivôse VI, there were also indications of resistance in France itself to the law's egalitarian principles. When the British turned over to the French a contingent of Black and mixed-race French officers captured during fighting in the Antilles, the navy minister, Eustache Bruix, who would subsequently become a major spokesman for Napoleon's policy of restoring slavery in 1802, refused to assign them to regular army units in accordance with their rank. Instead, he had them all held in a remote encampment at the Ile d'Aix on France's west coast. The Black Saint-Domingue deputy Etienne Mentor protested indignantly about their treatment: "It is less the bad conditions, the refusal to pay them, the privations of all sorts which have made them protest . . . than the contempt with which they are treated. The isolation from the white population in which they are being held affects them more than anything else." In retaliation for Mentor's complaints, Bruix evicted the Amis des Noirs et des Colonies from the meeting place in the ministry's offices that they had been using.[54]

Despite growing concerns about Louverture's actions and issues like Bruix's treatment of the Black troops, the Directory was still officially committed to the egalitarian policies enshrined in the decree of 16 pluviôse. Nevertheless, circumstances in some parts of the world tempted French officials to make compromises with the institution of slavery. Instructions to the governor of the French outpost of Gorée in Senegal at the beginning of 1799 reflected concern that the interruption of the slave trade had left the Caribbean colonies short of laborers. The government hoped that Africans could be persuaded to enroll voluntarily as contract laborers. The Directory planned to send a unit of Black troops to Senegal to demonstrate to the population there "how they would be treated if they joined us." The Directory recognized, however, that local rulers in Africa regarded the Blacks the French hoped to recruit as their property and would demand payment for them, thus seemingly reviving the practices of the slave trade. On the other side of the Atlantic, the governor of Guiana encouraged privateers to capture British slave ships. The Blacks in their cargoes were officially proclaimed free, but they were taken to French territory and forced to do plantation labor.[55]

On 16 pluviôse Year VII, the fifth anniversary of the passage of the Convention's abolition decree, the two legislative councils held what would turn out to be the last public celebrations of that law for some two hundred years. The Council of 500 turned the task of defining the event's significance over to Pierre Thomany, one of its Black members. His oration would be the last significant statement of the ideals embodied in the Convention's decree and the subsequent laws passed by the thermidorian Convention in the summer of 1795 and the Directory's law of 12 nivôse VI. Casting himself as the "voice of a race that was for too long unfortunate," Thomany evoked the "spectacle of two million men whom the most beautiful of holidays invites today to the liveliest celebration." Thanks to the law, the Blacks in France's colonies had been elevated from the "apathy, the kind of stupidity that characterized the slaves," and now enjoyed prosperity and happiness. France had no citizens "more devoted that those who have become free," and they could be counted on to support the war against the British. The only shadow in the picture sketched by Thomany was a reference to a few individuals who, "entrusted with commands, have disregarded the authority of the nation," an oblique condemnation of Toussaint Louverture and his rival Rigaud.[56] At the special meeting of the Société des Amis des Noirs et des Colonies in honor of the occasion, the Black deputy Etienne Mentor gave the principal speech, celebrating the "work of the Great Nation" in making sure that "posterity will only know through hearsay of the tyranny that weighed on the innocent and unfortunate African."[57]

These celebrations of abolition in 1799 took place as France was plunging into yet another grave political crisis. For four years, the republic's armies had enjoyed an almost unbroken streak of success, but in early 1799, an alliance led by Britain, Austria, and Russia suddenly threatened France's overextended forces. Enemy armies drove the French out of the Italian peninsula and staged a landing in the Netherlands, threatening the country from the north. As the specter of foreign troops crossing France's borders loomed, the spring elections once again went against the Directory, and this time the Directors were unable to find any way to elude the voters' verdict. Instead, the two councils staged a coup against the Directory, forcing the resignation of three of its members.

The result of this "coup d'état of 30 prairial Year VII" (18 June 1799) was a government sharply divided between two contradictory currents. On one side were the neo-Jacobins, a group that included Sonthonax and the Black deputies from Saint-Domingue, who argued for a return to the radical policies that had made France's victories in 1793–94 possible. Their influence on colonial policy was reflected in the replacement of the proslavery navy minister Bruix by Marc-Antoine Bourdon de Vatry, a member of the Amis des Noirs et des Colonies.[58] Opposing them were figures such as Emmanuel Sieyès, a member of the reconstituted Directory, who feared any recrudescence of radicalism and who were now convinced that the Constitution of 1795, with its provision for annual elections, was bound to create continuing political instability. Once military victories against the foreign coalition had ended the threat of an invasion, Sieyès began recruiting allies to plan yet another coup, one that this time would not simply change the political orientation of the government but fundamentally alter the constitution.

Knowing that he lacked the popularity to serve as the front man for such an enterprise, Sieyès set out to recruit a successful general to serve as a "sword" to lead the coup. He had already approached several candidates when France's most celebrated commander, Napoleon Bonaparte, unexpectedly appeared on the scene. For more than a year, Bonaparte had been in Egypt, stranded after the British destroyed the French fleet at the Battle of Aboukir in August 1798. Concerned about the news of French defeats in Europe and reports about the behavior of his wife, Josephine, Bonaparte abandoned his troops and sailed back to France. He quickly sized up the political situation in Paris and threw in his lot with Sieyès and his plotters. On 18 brumaire Year VIII (9 November 1799), the coup plan was put into operation. The "brumairians" persuaded the Council of Elders to invoke an emergency provision of the constitution calling for a special assembly of the legislature in the suburb of Saint-Cloud outside the capital. On the following day, despite a stumbling performance by Napoleon himself, the deputies were intimidated into giving Sieyès and Bonaparte authority to draft a new constitution. Among other things, the promise that citizens of the colonies would live under the same laws and enjoy the same liberties as the metropole was suddenly thrown into question.

CHAPTER TWELVE

Napoleon and the Reimposition of Slavery

COLONIAL ISSUES WERE not among the major concerns of the brumairian plotters, and no one knew what consequences the overthrow of the Directory might have in that sphere. The makeup of the provisional Consulate, the three-man body appointed to replace the Directory, could even have looked reassuring to supporters of abolition. One of them, Emmanuel Sieyès, had been a member of the Société des Amis des Noirs in 1789 and another, Pierre Roger-Ducos, had defended the law of 12 nivôse VI that extended the constitution to the colonies. It rapidly became clear, however, that the opinion that counted, on colonial issues and on all other matters, was that of Napoleon Bonaparte. Bonaparte quickly forced Sieyès to agree to a plan for a government in which the young general would occupy the position of "First Consul" with sweeping powers. Napoleon was now in a position to impose his will on all significant matters affecting the country.

The First Consul's career up to 1799 gave few indications of what colonial policies he might adopt. At the moment of his birth in 1769, his native island of Corsica in the Mediterranean, which had only been annexed to France one year earlier, was administered by the navy ministry, like the country's more remote colonies, and Corsicans were sometimes dismissed as "half-Africans" in the metropole. In his youth, Napoleon identified with Pasquale

Paoli, the legendary figure who had led a movement for the island's independence in the 1760s. As a teenager, he read Guillaume Thomas François Raynal's *Histoire de deux Indes* and even wrote a letter to the famous author. In the summer of 1789, as the Revolution was beginning in France, Napoleon composed a short story about a violent uprising against French rule in Corsica that included descriptions of bloodshed that prefigured the accounts of events in the Saint-Domingue uprising.[1]

Instead of throwing himself into a movement for Corsican independence after 1789 that might have paralleled events in the Caribbean, however, Napoleon soon began to rise within the ranks of the French revolutionary army. The victories he won in Italy in 1796 made him the most famous French general. His wife, Josephine, whom he married that same year, was a Creole woman from a slaveholding family in Martinique and knew other colonists in Paris. In 1794, when she had been in prison, expecting to be executed, she wrote a letter to her children reminiscing about her family's plantation and expressing sympathy for its enslaved Blacks, "these unfortunates excluded from the common lot of the human race," but in 1807, when she inherited the property and 123 slaves from her mother, she did nothing to change their situation, and there is no evidence that she ever tried to influence Napoleon's views on slavery.[2]

The French invasion of Egypt in 1798 provided Napoleon with his first personal experience of the non-European world. For Napoleon, invading Egypt was above all an opportunity to acquire personal glory by following in the footsteps of Alexander the Great and Julius Caesar, but he also identified himself with the ideas of the "new colonialism" supported by the members of the Société des Amis des Noirs et des Colonies, who saw a chance to spread European civilization to a backward part of the world. Slavery existed in Egypt, although in a very different form from that in the French colonies: Enslaved people in Egypt were primarily domestic servants rather than plantation laborers, and the sharp racial distinctions that characterized the colonial world did not exist. Napoleon took no steps to abolish the institution, and when he returned to France in 1799, he brought with him an Egyptian servant who remained with him for the rest of his career.

The question of Napoleon's personal attitude toward race and slavery has been debated furiously since the publication of Yves Bénot's pathbreaking *La Démence coloniale sous Napoléon* in 1992, which documented the extent of the First Consul's eventual commitment to the restoration of slavery in Saint-Domingue and Guadeloupe. In his polemical work *Le Crime de Napoléon*, published during the celebrations of the two hundredth anniversary of Napoleon's reign in 2005, Claude Ribbe characterized Napoleon as "the first racist dictator in history." Ribbe's work drew a heated response from Thierry Lentz, the longtime director of France's Institut Napoléon, and his collaborators Pierre Branda and Chantal Lheureuse-Prévot. They argued the government's policies were shaped "more by the First Consul's indifference with regard to the question of the Blacks than by his 'racism,' which was less pronounced, in any case, than that of most of his contemporaries." Philippe Girard has emphasized the "pragmatic, post-ideological" nature of Napoleon's policies and the fact that he never issued explicit orders for the reimposition of slavery in Saint-Domingue, although he concedes that "slavery seemed to have his preference." Thomas Pronier, however, has argued that Napoleon consciously filled his administration with advocates for the restoration of slavery and that "all that he did, all that he attempted but could not realize for reasons connected to the balance of military force, all reflected a logic of restoration that necessarily included the restoration of slavery."[3]

The most frequently cited statement attributed to Napoleon on the subjects of race and slavery is a passage from the memoirs of Antoine Thibaudeau, a moderate republican politician whom Napoleon appointed to the Conseil d'Etat, the body created soon after his seizure of power with the responsibility of drafting legislation. Thibaudeau claimed to have been present during an exchange between Napoleon and Laurent Truguet, who had been minister of the navy from 1795 to 1797, in which the First Consul, provoked by Truguet's opposition to the decision to maintain slavery in Martinique once it was returned by the British, gave free rein to his prejudices. "I am for the whites, because I'm white; I don't have any other reason, and that one is good enough," Napoleon supposedly said.

> How could one have given freedom to the Africans, to men who were completely uncivilized, who didn't even know what a colony was, what France was? It is obvious that those who were for the freedom of the Blacks wanted slavery for the whites. But do you think that if the majority of the Convention had realized what it was doing, and had known the colonies, that it would have freed the Blacks? Undoubtedly not, but few people were in a position to foresee the results, and a sentiment of humanity always has a powerful effect on the imagination. But to hold to those principles now! That can't reflect good faith; it can only be *amour propre* and hypocrisy.[4]

Jean Jacques Régis de Cambacérès, another former Convention deputy who was appointed as the permanent Second Consul once the new constitution was implemented at the end of 1799, also attributed definite racial prejudices to Napoleon. In his memoirs, he commented that Napoleon "had contempt for the Negroes, although he preferred them to the men of mixed race, whom he didn't like any better." Cambacérès himself was an opponent of abolition, but according to his account, Napoleon's own views on slavery were somewhat more nuanced. "The First Consul was convinced that the freedom of the Blacks should be the reward for their submission, that this benefit had to be given gradually, and that in the meantime the colonial system ought to be kept the way it was before the Revolution," Cambacérès recalled.[5]

A somewhat different picture of Napoleon's views on slavery in the early months of his regime comes from notes taken by Pierre-Louis Roederer, a former revolutionary legislator who had occasionally sided with the abolitionists in the National Assembly but later became an active participant in the brumaire coup. In August 1800, when the former colonial administrator François Barbé-Marbois argued that slavery should be reintroduced in Saint-Domingue, Roederer recorded Napoleon as responding, "The question is not to know whether it is good to abolish slavery, but whether it is good to abolish freedom in the free part of Saint-Domingue. I am convinced that the British would take over the island, if the Negroes were not loyal to us on account of their interest in their freedom. They will make less sugar, perhaps, but they will make it for us, and they will serve us as soldiers if necessary."

Napoleon went on to explain that he would adopt whatever policy would help him establish his authority, saying that it was by "making myself Muslim" that he had conquered Egypt and that it was by courting Catholics that he had ruled in Italy. "So, I will talk about liberty in the free part of Saint-Domingue; I will confirm slavery in the Ile de France . . . reserving the right to temper and limit slavery where I maintain it; to reestablish order and to introduce discipline, in places where I maintain liberty."[6]

Whatever Napoleon's personal attitudes about race and slavery may have been when he came to power in 1799, there is no doubt that he meant to regain firm control over France's overseas territories and reestablish the country's status as a world power. Discussions about sending officials to the colonies to assert the new government's authority began immediately, although the ongoing war with Britain made it impossible to plan for the dispatch of troops. In negotiations with Spain in 1800, France obtained the return of the vast Louisiana Territory in North America that the monarchy had ceded after its defeat in the Seven Years' War in 1763. Napoleon had a grandiose vision in which Louisiana would supply the French sugar islands with the foodstuffs they needed, making trade with the United States unnecessary and allowing the restoration of the plantation economy that had been destroyed during the Revolution.

At first, however, Napoleon understood that his options in the Caribbean were limited. While the war with Britain continued, France's hold on its most important overseas possession depended on Toussaint Louverture and his Black soldiers. Louverture's actions in the two years before Napoleon's seizure of power had raised alarms in Paris, but French officials continued to hope that, despite the Black general's "reprehensible conduct," particularly his negotiation of agreements with the British and the Americans and his ouster of the Directory's agent Joseph Hédouville, his loyalty to France remained basically intact.[7] Just at the moment when Napoleon came to power in November 1799, news of the outbreak of the "war of the South," the armed conflict between Louverture's forces and those of his rival André Rigaud that devastated the colony until the middle of the year 1800, reached Paris. This development reinforced the impression that the emancipation of the Blacks had led to a state of total disorder.[8]

During the first month of the new regime, the consuls encouraged Pierre Forfait, the new navy minister, to gather as much information as he could about the conditions in the colonies, and especially Saint-Domingue. They wanted answers to basic questions: What was the population of the island after the "enormous losses" it had suffered? How many troops did Louverture and Rigaud have, and which side, if either, should the government support? The white colonists Forfait met with were divided on these issues. The former civil commissioner Léger-Félicité Sonthonax denounced both the rival generals and said that it would be necessary to send a military expedition "to rescue the colony from the profound anarchy that devours it, and to take power away from the misled or guilty ones who have seized it."[9] The white deputy Louis Rallier, on the other hand, urged support for Louverture, since he had the backing of the Black population. Louverture "should be treated carefully, because he has great power; but at the same time he deserves consideration, because he has made an excellent use of that power."[10]

The first clear sign of the direction in which Napoleon intended to steer France's colonial policy came a month after the brumaire coup, with the publication of the new French constitution of Year VIII. As the conservative daily *Publiciste* noted with approval, "The constitution is not preceded this time by any declaration of rights. The danger of these vague and abstract principles that everyone comments on and interprets as they like, and which, in the hands of the factious, are always dangerous weapons against all solid institutions, has finally been recognized."[11] The omission of any acknowledgment of natural rights meant that, for the first time since the passage of the Declaration of the Rights of Man in 1789, there was no explicit language in the French constitution that could be cited against the institution of slavery. The new constitution's only reference to the colonies was its laconic article 91: "The regime of the French colonies is determined by special laws." With this single sentence, Napoleon's regime abrogated the constitutional provisions adopted in 1795 and spelled out in the law of 12 nivôse VI that put the inhabitants of the country's overseas territories under the same laws as those of the metropole. As a result of this provision, deputies representing the colonies were expelled from France's legislative assemblies. It would be many decades before another deputy of African descent would be seated in a French legislature.

Although article 91 put the colonies outside the framework of the constitution, it did not specify the nature of the "special laws" to be applied to them. A proclamation from the new Consuls addressed to "the citizens of Saint-Domingue" on 4 nivôse VIII sought to reassure the Black population, promising that "the sacred principles of the liberty and equality of the Blacks will never suffer, among you, any attack or modification" and reminding the "brave Blacks" that "the French people are the only ones who recognize your freedom and the equality of your rights." The proclamation's justification of the new constitutional arrangement, however, copied language that had often been used by advocates of slavery, asserting that the "difference of climates, . . . of habitudes, of customs, of interests, the differences in the soil, in the crops, in the products, require various modifications" in the laws.[12] The official from the navy ministry's colonial bureau who drafted the proclamation privately recommended the abrogation not only of the laws of 16 pluviôse II abolishing slavery and 12 nivôse VI guaranteeing constitutional rights in the colonies but even the law of 4 April 1792 on the rights of free people of color.[13]

Napoleon was already making it clear that the question of what the "special laws" for the colonies would look like was not going to be settled by public debate. The legislative assemblies created by the new constitution were limited to considering laws presented to them by the government, and a decree issued on 27 nivôse VIII banned all but thirteen specified newspapers in Paris and subjected them to police supervision. The members of the Consulate's assemblies were chosen by Napoleon, Sieyès, and their henchmen. In the first years of the regime, there was a certain amount of political diversity among them: Henri Grégoire, who was not only a veteran abolitionist but also a critic of Napoleon's religious policy, was a member of the Senate, and several other abolitionist activists, such as Joseph Eschassériaux and the economist Jean-Baptiste Say, were named to the Tribunate or the Legislative Body. Regardless of their race, however, none of the men who had represented the colonies during the Directory were named to the new assemblies. Napoleon seems to have had a particular dislike for Sonthonax. He was ordered arrested, although the police minister Joseph Fouché, who had come to know him during the Convention's hearings on his conduct in 1795, apparently protected him.[14]

While the deputies who had represented the colonies during thermidor and the Directory were purged, a number of former members of the proslavery colonial lobby were able to return to political life. Médéric Louis Élie Moreau de Saint-Méry, who had taken refuge in the United States in 1793, had already come back to France in 1798, thanks to the intercession of his friend Charles Maurice de Talleyrand, named foreign minister in 1797.[15] Once the Consulate was installed, Moreau de Saint-Méry was appointed to the Conseil d'Etat. The deputies from the Club de Clichy who had been banished in the coup d'état of 18 fructidor V were allowed to return, and some of them, like Barbé-Marbois, were soon appointed to important political positions. In 1801 Pierre-Victor Malouet, who might well have been considered a traitor because of his role in negotiating the treaty that led to the British occupation of France's Caribbean colonies in 1793, was able to come back to Paris and to publish his views on colonial matters. The message was clear: Having defended slavery and racial hierarchy during the revolutionary years was no obstacle to inclusion in the new political elite.

The first decision that Napoleon took that directly concerned the issue of slavery involved the Mascarene Islands, where the decree of 16 pluviôse II had never been implemented. The consensus of the officials in the navy ministry was that it was necessary to assure the white colonists there that the "disastrous laws" that had been applied in the Caribbean would not be introduced in the Indian Ocean.[16] Napoleon's policy in the Mascarenes alarmed Toussaint Louverture. Recognizing that Napoleon's proclamation to the "brave Blacks" of Saint-Domingue applied only to that colony, Louverture told Charles Vincent, the French military officer who brought the document to the colony, "It is not a freedom based on circumstances, conceded only to us, that we want; it is the unqualified adoption of the principle that all men, red, Black, or white, cannot be the property of his fellow man. We are free because of our struggle, and because we are stronger. The consul has maintained slavery on Bourbon island, and we too will become his slaves if he is strong."[17]

Although Napoleon's decision about slavery in the Mascarenes was not publicized and open discussion of colonial issues was severely limited, the navy minister Forfait continued to solicit the thoughts of a wide variety of figures interested in them. During the first two years of the Consulate, he collected numerous memoranda, some of them several hundred pages long, expressing ideas about the proper policies to be adopted with regard to slavery, especially in Saint-Domingue. The most valiant advocate of maintaining the policy of abolition and the granting of citizenship to the Blacks in the colonies was the former navy minister Truguet. He warned Napoleon against listening to the advice of the former white plantation owners who remained "fanatics of slavery." A sincere commitment to maintaining the freedom of the Blacks, "the true people, the only real people of our Antilles," would win the loyalty of Toussaint Louverture and "men formerly subject to whipping, who wanted to be free and now are so; who conquered their freedom by themselves, without help, and who have defended it against the united forces of the British and the Spanish."[18]

Surprisingly, several former slave-owning colonists joined Truguet in urging the recognition of the Blacks' freedom. The most unexpected case was that of Pierre-François Page, who, along with his colleague Augustin Brulley, had worked tirelessly to send advocates of abolition to the guillotine in 1793 and 1794. "At the time I was completely opposed to the emancipation of the Negroes, [and] to the suppression of the slave trade," he wrote. "Now men and things have taken on a new look, and everything requires us to adopt new ideas and new measures." Paul Alliot, another ex-colonist, was sure that the formerly enslaved Blacks were now "loyal and very attached to the government which has given them freedom," and that any attempt to force them back into slavery would mean resorting to "the atrocious method of destruction," which would leave the colony without workers and also cost the lives of thousands of soldiers.[19]

Just as surprising as the views expressed by former defenders of slavery like Page and Alliot were the opinions of some of the former advocates of abolition. Louis Dufay, whose speech on 16 pluviôse II had provoked the National Convention's decree abolishing slavery, now denounced the outcome of that measure. "For a long time, one has been too liberal and too tolerant toward the Blacks and the men of color, they have been treated too well, everything they have done has been accepted," he complained. The military commanders in Saint-Domingue "reign like sovereigns, like the nabobs in India . . . the soldiers obey them and are their slaves." The ordinary members of the Black population, he claimed, "are still in slavery, the freedom established by the law of 16 pluviôse II and by the constitution exists only for the chiefs and for some vagabonds and brigands who steal and pillage without fear of punishment." Toussaint Louverture, according to Dufay, had become a despot and the colony "is truly a land of abomination and desolation . . . it is lost forever if the government does not hasten to remedy so many ills."[20]

The overwhelming majority of the memoranda that ended up in Forfait's files agreed with Dufay in describing the situation in Saint-Domingue as unacceptable, although their authors were divided about the best remedy for the situation. For the first time since the defeat of the Clichyens in 1797, however, some authors felt confident that they could send demands for the outright restoration of slavery to high-ranking government officials. One writer called the law of 16 pluviôse II "disastrous" and asked, "Was it wise to suddenly break their chains and abandon them to the intoxication that inevitably occurs in any people who realize for the first time that there is no more restraint on their actions and their inclinations?" The idea that the different races could live together peacefully in the colony, he insisted, was a delusion: The Blacks remained "tigers thirsty for blood." To make up for the population losses suffered since the beginning of the 1791 uprising, the slave trade needed to be reopened.[21]

The memoranda that flooded into the navy ministry were confidential, but advocates of slavery were now confident that they could also make their case in public and even, as in the case of the author of one tract released in 1800, dedicate their works to the First Consul. C. Belu's *Des colonies et de la traite des nègres* was as unyielding in its advocacy of slavery, the slave trade, and racial hierarchy as any of the literature published in the first years of the Revolution. Slavery was justified, Belu insisted, because Blacks were inherently inferior to other races: "Their abilities do not exceed the boundaries that nature seems to have prescribed for them; in general they are limited to satisfying their physical needs." Belu not only demanded the reopening of the slave trade; he also provided detailed instructions for its conduct and the management of African captives during the Middle Passage.[22]

Proslavery advocates could proceed in the knowledge that they did not have much to fear from the defenders of abolition and racial equality. The *Décade philosophique*, a periodical that reflected the views of moderate liberals and advocates of the new colonialism, did publish occasional articles critical of slavery, but it devoted more attention to publications that suggested the possibility of integrating Africa into the European economy.[23] *Zorada*, a sentimental novel about the sad fate of a mixed-race woman caught up in the Saint-Domingue uprising published in 1801, contained passages critical of slavery but also evoked the "torrents of blood" spilled by the Blacks. Other works of fiction, such as René Perrin's *L'Incendie du Cap, ou le Règne de Toussaint-Louverture*, denounced the "horde of ferocious Africans whom inappropriate pity has freed from the restraints of slavery."[24]

Throughout the first year and a half of the Consulate, from the beginning of 1800 through the summer of 1801, Napoleon's officials continued to propose plans for reestablishing metropolitan control in the colonies and to debate about how to deal with Toussaint Louverture, whose victory over Rigaud became known in Paris toward the end of the summer of 1800. The minister Forfait urged caution until France was actually in a position to send substantial armed forces to the colonies, and he forwarded to Napoleon letters from Colonel Vincent, who was convinced that "only Toussaint can save everything, that the government must give him the strongest signs of confidence." Meanwhile, General Jean Joseph Sahuguet, who hoped to be appointed to command a French expedition to Saint-Domingue, wanted authority to "fix the limits of civil freedom for individuals who, brought up as slaves, only ceased to be so thanks to the disorders of anarchy" and who "can only be controlled by fear."[25]

French victories in Europe in 1800 put Napoleon in a position to dictate a favorable peace on the continent, but as long as the British controlled the seas, there was still no immediate prospect of undertaking serious measures in the colonies. An unsigned memorandum about the outcome of the civil war in the colony concluded that "Toussaint no longer has any rivals" and asked whether it would not be better to "tolerate what one cannot prevent, and make use of Toussaint's pride itself, as a powerful and useful instrument to bring things back to a better state?" The memorandum's author proposed that the French government should congratulate Louverture on his success and tell him "to protect the properties and the persons of all the colors, to uphold the liberty of the Blacks, and [to make] good use of that liberty for the benefit of agriculture."[26]

At the beginning of 1801, Napoleon seemed ready to adopt such a policy. One issue that particularly concerned him, however, was the rumor that Louverture, having asserted his control over the French colony of Saint-Domingue, was now preparing to occupy the neighboring Spanish colony of Santo Domingo. During the Directory years, the French government had decided against exercising its right to replace the Spanish under the terms of the Treaty of Basel signed in 1795, and Napoleon was even more determined to keep Santo Domingo, where slavery still prevailed, out of Louverture's hands. Instructions given in January 1801 to the French general whom Napoleon hoped to send to represent the French in Santo Domingo told him "to reassure all the white property owners about the views of the French government, which, chastened by the misfortunes of the French part of the island, will not give unlimited freedom to men unlikely to make good use of it," words that spoke loudly about Napoleon's opinion on the situation in Saint-Domingue. These instructions did concede that the French part of the island would be governed "with and by the Negroes," and the general (who never managed to take up his post) was told to act respectfully toward Louverture, but he was firmly commanded to make sure that no "army of Negroes" crossed the boundary between the two colonies.[27]

Two months later, Napoleon drafted a letter to Toussaint Louverture. Had it been sent, it would have informed the Black general that Napoleon was appointing him as captain general of the French colony. "The government could not give you any greater proof of its confidence in you. Employ your entire influence to maintain the peace, to encourage agriculture. Discipline and organize the national guards and the paid troops, so that the government will be able to rely on their courage and their efforts as one more means to triumph over our enemies," Napoleon wrote.[28] Before this letter could be sent, however, news arrived in Paris that Louverture had defied French instructions and occupied Santo Domingo. Napoleon's letter was never sent; instead, planning began for the dispatch of a military expedition to the Caribbean, to be launched as soon as negotiations with the British, who were under pressure to come to terms with France once their Austrian allies had made peace, were concluded.

Despite the best efforts of Colonel Vincent, who did everything he could to ward off a break between Louverture and Napoleon, the Black strongman proceeded to further provoke the First Consul by ordering the drafting of a constitution for Saint-Domingue. Louverture justified his decision by referring to article 91 of Napoleon's own constitution, which had stated that the colonies were to be governed by "special laws." Since the French government had not issued any such laws for Saint-Domingue, he claimed that he was merely filling the vacuum. Louverture's constitution proclaimed that "there can be no slaves in this territory; servitude is abolished within it forever. All men who are born here live and die free and French," a restatement of the principles incorporated in the laws of 16 pluviôse II and 12 nivôse VI that Napoleon's own constitution had abrogated. The speaker appointed to deliver the official response to Louverture at the ceremony for the presentation of the constitution, an event celebrated in a nineteenth-century Haitian engraving, specifically mentioned the "immortal decree of 16 pluviôse II" (figure 12).[29] Vincent, sent by Louverture to deliver the document to France, warned him that it would be regarded in France as a "manifesto against the French government," especially since it had already been printed and publicly proclaimed in Saint-Domingue, but Louverture persisted in his decision. In his cover letter to Napoleon, he complained that the First Consul had refused to answer any of his earlier letters. This was a further provocation to Napoleon, since it made it seem as though Louverture considered himself Napoleon's equal.[30]

The French press published Louverture's constitution, and the *Mercure de France*, an organ of the conservative Catholic party that

FIGURE 12: Toussaint Louverture's decision to issue his own constitution for the French colony of Saint-Domingue, depicted in a nineteenth-century engraving by Haitian artist Guillaume Guillon Lethière, helped inspire Napoleon's decision to send a military expedition to reassert French control over the territory. *Credit:* Library of Congress, LC-USZ62-7861.

was eagerly anticipating the conclusion of Napoleon's treaty with the Church, even noted approvingly that Louverture intended to make Catholicism the only publicly recognized religion in the colony and to outlaw divorce.[31] However, Napoleon had already decided that Louverture needed to be removed from power. The navy minister Forfait, who had expressed reservations about the wisdom of a military expedition, was replaced by Daniel Decrès, a hard-liner fully committed to the idea.[32] During his exile on Saint-Helena, Napoleon claimed that the enactment of Louverture's constitution left no room for compromise. "From that moment on, there was nothing to think about; the Black chiefs were ungrateful Africans and rebels. . . . The honor and the interest of France required that they be reduced to nothing."[33]

The conclusion of the peace negotiations between France and Britain in October 1801 obliged Napoleon to make a decision about the future of slavery in Martinique. The British had maintained the institution there, and Napoleon feared that their white colonists might resist the return of French authority if they thought that that situation might change. After the conclusion of the preliminary agreement that became the Treaty of Amiens when it was officially signed on 25 March 1802, Napoleon instructed Decrès to inform the planters in Martinique that "they have nothing to fear with regard to the freedom of the Negroes, who will be kept in their present condition." While promising that in the colonies where slavery had been abolished, "everyone is free and everyone will remain free," Napoleon announced, "Martinique has kept slavery, and slavery will be kept there. It has cost humanity too much to try a new revolution in this locality." Encouraged by the signs that France would soon have publicly acknowledged slave colonies again, entrepreneurs in Nantes and other ports began preparing to send ships to Africa to restart the slave trade.[34]

Despite this public assertion that there could be different policies on slavery in different colonies, Napoleon was clearly thinking about ways to restrict, if not to abolish, the freedom of the Black populations in Saint-Domingue and Guadeloupe, as a letter to his foreign minister Talleyrand, written in mid-November 1801, shows. Talleyrand needed to know how to explain to the British government the purpose of the French expedition to the Caribbean, since the dispatch of such a large fleet and so many soldiers was bound to raise alarms in London. Napoleon replied that if he was forced to delay the expedition, he would "be obliged to recognize Toussaint, to give up Saint-Domingue, and to constitute them as French," which, he argued, would create a permanent threat to the British colonies in the region. Instead, he stressed, he had decided to "annihilate the government of the Blacks in Saint-Domingue" in order to "stamp out, in all parts of the world, any germ of disquiet and troubles." Although Napoleon's letter did not explicitly mention slavery, the implication was clear: Black freedom in any Caribbean colony was a menace to slavery everywhere, and Napoleon intended to eliminate that danger.[35]

More ambiguous was the letter Napoleon prepared to be delivered to Toussaint Louverture once the expedition that was being prepared arrived in Saint-Domingue. Napoleon's plan called for this letter to be delivered to Louverture by the latter's two sons, who had been enrolled in the colonial school established under the Directory. Although Napoleon's letter praised many of the things Louverture had done, its content made it clear that his days in charge of the colony were over. The constitution Louverture had issued "contains [provisions] that are contrary to the dignity and the sovereignty of the French people, of which Saint-Domingue is just a part," Napoleon wrote. He expressed hope that Louverture would submit to his instructions, but if he resisted, the Black leader would be "digging a precipice under his feet, which, in swallowing you up, would contribute to the misfortunes of these brave Blacks, whose courage we admire and whom we would regret having to punish as rebels." As far as the "freedom of the Blacks" was concerned, Louverture should remember that "in all the countries where we have been, we have given [liberty] to the people who did not have it," an assurance not entirely convincing to anyone who was aware of the harsh measures Napoleon had taken to impose his authority in Italy and Egypt.[36]

Whether or not he was already planning to eventually reinstate slavery in Saint-Domingue and Guadeloupe, Napoleon knew better than to even raise the suggestion in his letter to Louverture or in the proclamation he prepared for the man he was appointing to replace the Black leader. Victoire-Emmanuel Leclerc, the young general appointed to command the expedition to Saint-Domingue—he was also Napoleon's brother-in-law, married to the First Consul's sister Pauline—was sent on his way bearing a proclamation promising to uphold emancipation that he was instructed to print and distribute as soon as he arrived, both in French and in Creole. "Whatever your origin and your color, you are all French, all free and all equal before God and before the Republic," the proclamation read. To this Leclerc added his own proclamation, assuring the population that the government's declaration "assures to the Blacks the freedom for which they have fought so hard, [and] to commerce and agriculture the prosperity without which there would be no colonies."[37]

Along with these proclamations, however, Leclerc was also carrying a set of secret instructions from Napoleon that had a very different tone and that make it clear that the First Consul had come to the same conclusion as the proslavery pamphleteer of 1797 who had recommended deliberately deceiving the Blacks until military control of the colony was established. According to these instructions, Leclerc's operation was to unfold in three phases. In the first days after his troops came ashore in Saint-Domingue, they were to occupy all the key positions in the colony. During this phase, Louverture was to be treated with respect, and the other generals in Louverture's army were to be assured that they would keep their commands. As soon as possible, however, Leclerc was to force Louverture onto a ship bound for France, along with his subordinates. If the top generals did not submit peacefully, they were to be declared traitors to the country and eliminated. In the final phase covered in Leclerc's instructions, every Black who had held any responsible position in the colony and any white who had collaborated with Louverture were to be deported. At this point, "all the Negroes, whatever party they belong to, must be disarmed and sent back to field work."[38]

Leclerc's secret instructions did not mention the word "slavery," and in fact they promised that "the French nation will never put men it has recognized as free into irons. Thus all the Blacks will live in Saint-Domingue as they do presently in Guadeloupe," where the system of forced labor imposed by Victor Hugues was still in effect. Nevertheless, the program Napoleon outlined made it clear that all Blacks who had profited from opportunities to elevate themselves above the status of plantation laborers were to be deprived of their positions. The order to deport any Black who had obtained a military rank above that of captain meant the dismissal of the officers who had defended the colony against the British. The secret instructions also targeted whites who had accommodated themselves to the multiracial society that had grown up under Louverture's rule. "Any individual who mentions the rights of the Blacks, who have shed so much white blood, will be sent back to France, regardless of his rank and his services," Leclerc was told. Napoleon's instructions were particularly venomous with regard to white women who had "prostituted themselves to Negroes." In his conversations with his aide Emmanuel de Las Casas on Saint-Helena, Napoleon stated clearly that his intention had been to "deprive the population of its leaders," rendering the Blacks incapable of defending their rights.[39]

As the military expedition to the Caribbean was being prepared, advocates for slavery unleashed a vigorous propaganda campaign in the metropole. A half century before the publication of Arthur de Gobineau's *Essay on the Inequality of the Human Races* in 1855, usually called the foundational text of modern race theories, the outpouring of anti-Black literature that coincided with the Napoleonic expeditions established overt racism as an accepted element of French public discourse. Proslavery and racist authors did not have to fear much opposition from the abolitionist camp. Weakened by the deaths of several of its leading members, the Directory-era Société des Amis des Noirs et des Colonies ceased to meet even before the brumaire coup. In early 1802 Grégoire told the members of the Pennsylvania Society for the Abolition of Slavery that he could not publish his book *The Literature of the Negroes*, which he said he had already completed, because "our printers think that the favorable time for circulating this work, and of course for printing it is not yet come"; it would not appear until 1808.[40] François-René Chateaubriand, the literary sensation of the moment, distilled the case against the Blacks into one sentence in his best-selling *Genius of Christianity*, an apologia for the Catholic faith timed to appear just as Napoleon's Concordat with the Church was allowing the resumption of public worship in early 1802. "Who would still dare plead the Blacks' case after the crimes they have committed?" Chateaubriand asked. Reviewing his work, the *Décade philosophique* responded that "any reasonable man, any man with feelings, any friend of humanity" would do so, but its objection was drowned out by the barrage of defenses of slavery.[41]

In fairness to Chateaubriand, whose father had been a slave-ship captain, his declamation was part of a passage that also expressed some sympathy for the condition of enslaved Blacks. Other writers who rushed into print in the early months of 1802 showed no such ambivalence. Malouet, who had played such a large role in opposing abolition during the first years of the Revolution, republished his earlier works in favor of slavery, adding a preface in which he deplored the idea that "a Black, a mule-driver who grew up a slave, disputes the sovereignty of Saint-Domingue with the hero who brought peace to Europe." Events in the colony had shown, Malouet exclaimed, that "the freedom of the Blacks means their domination! It's the massacre or the enslavement of the whites, the burning of our fields, our cities. . . . These Blacks have evidently forfeited the right to freedom: let them go back under the yoke!" He was no more sympathetic to the mixed-race population: "The mulattos have been atrocious . . . in general this class needs to be kept in subordination." And he had no hesitation in calling for the resumption of the slave trade, reviving the claim that the Blacks were more oppressed in Africa than in the Caribbean colonies.[42] Another Saint-Domingue colonist, Jean Barré de Saint-Venant, warned that the Blacks "have defeated their former masters, they have outraged them, they have torn them to pieces; punishments and force are the only means left to obtain obedience from the present generation, and above all to get them back to work."[43] Several publications took aim specifically at Toussaint Louverture, "a man who has grown up committing the most execrable crimes, covered with innocent blood, despised, abhorred by all nations."[44]

Malouet and Barré de Saint-Venant did not engage directly with the question of whether Blacks were an inherently inferior race, but several other writers had no such hesitations. Jean Jacques Virey, a naturalist whose works continued to be cited as authoritative throughout the first half of the nineteenth century, published the first version of his *Histoire naturelle du genre humain* (Natural history of the human race) in 1801. "Are we even really sure that his race is the same as ours," Virey asked, "with so many differences that are organic, fundamental, striking, and more conclusive even than his color?" He did, however, question whether "the difference of color, and the limited intelligence of the Negro, have somehow justified this enormous abuse of our power" represented by slavery. Still, he concluded in a slightly later publication, "the Negro is and always will be a slave; interest requires it, policy supports it, and his own nature submits to it almost without resistance."[45]

The most violent of the racist polemics issued in 1802 was Louis-Narcisse Baudry Deslozières's *Les Egarements du Nigrophilisme* (The errors of Negrophilia), which was dedicated to Napoleon's wife, Josephine, "the first lady of the French Republic . . .

who has all the sensibility of a Creole," and whom Napoleon himself later admitted "had some influence" on the policy he adopted in the Caribbean.[46] Baudry Deslozières, Moreau de Saint-Méry's brother-in-law, would presumably not have dared to evoke Josephine's Creole origins unless he had been confident that his gesture would be tolerated. Over and over again, Baudry Deslozières repeated that "the Negro is a species degraded by nature, who has never been anything on his own, and who is good only to serve as a tool for agriculture." In Africa, he asserted, "they are without principles, and I would even say without those primitive conceptions that announce the possibility of human understanding, and those of reasonable sentiments."[47]

Even though the number of Blacks living in France was still very small, Baudry Deslozières was obsessed with the dangers of racial mixing. He warned of the danger to "the pure blood of the French . . . a little more, and this mixture, already too common, will denature the national character, and we will see . . . mulattos in morals as well as in physique. One nation will be substituted for another, and I dare say that this replacement will not compensate the world for our loss." The measures Baudry Deslozières wanted to see taken in the Caribbean colonies were as extreme as his racial ideas. At a moment when it was not yet clear whether Napoleon intended to fully reverse the freedom granted to the Blacks in Saint-Domingue, Baudry Deslozières declared that "the system of establishing liberty in one island, and slavery in another, would cause the most terrible political inconveniences." As far as the treatment of the Blacks was concerned, he wrote that "the Negroes . . . have declared themselves our natural enemies so many times that they are no longer worthy of our pity. . . . They must be expelled or put in chains."[48]

While proslavery writers in France were venting their bile at the Blacks whom their country had declared citizens in 1794, the twenty thousand soldiers in Leclerc's expedition and the seven thousand commanded by Antoine Richepance were storming ashore in Saint-Domingue and Guadeloupe. Although they encountered strong resistance, both forces succeeded in gaining control of strategic points. Despite these initial successes, Leclerc's confidential letters to France indicated from the start that he was short of men, money, and supplies. The official letters from him and the naval commander Louis-Thomas Villaret-Joyeuse published in the *Moniteur*, however, gave an optimistic picture of the situation. Summing up the situation after the first week of major military engagements, Villaret-Joyeuse claimed, "Eight days have sufficed to carry out all these operations . . . and guaranteed to France, in a very short time, the conquest and possession of its best colony." The public was not necessarily convinced: Police reports on the conversations in Paris cafés quoted rumors that disease was decimating the French army and that whites were being massacred.[49] Nevertheless, by the beginning of April, Napoleon was ready to proceed with the step he had heretofore hesitated to take: the repeal of the law of 16 pluviôse II and the legal reinstitution of slavery.

Although there had been many indications that Napoleon was leaning in that direction, he had had reasons to delay any public announcement. He certainly understood that news of such a move in France, even if it was ostensibly limited to maintaining slavery in colonies such as Martinique where the law of 16 pluviôse had never been implemented, would be understood in Saint-Domingue and Guadeloupe as a threat to the Black population's freedom. By April 1802, however, with French troops on the ground in those colonies, it seemed safe to proceed. News of anything done in Paris would not arrive in the Caribbean for at least another month and a half, by which time, Napoleon assumed, Black resistance would be crushed, a calculation that proved accurate in Guadeloupe but disastrously wrong in Saint-Domingue. The imminent return of Martinique to French control, promised in the Treaty of Amiens, was another reason why action seemed necessary: Unless the emancipation law was repealed, the whites there would not be confident that the slavery system would remain intact. An attempt to maintain slavery in some colonies but not in others was bound to create uncertainty everywhere: Neither slaveholders nor emancipated Blacks would trust the government's intentions.

On 7 April 1802 Napoleon met with representatives of the port cities of Bordeaux, Nantes, and Marseille and assured them that "soon they will be able to devote themselves to the same business that they used to practice," including the slave trade.[50] On 27 April 1802 Napoleon ordered the Conseil d'Etat to prepare laws for the colonies, as well as a measure to bar Black persons from entering metropolitan France. The Conseil d'Etat responded with two proposals. One, meant for Martinique and the Mascarenes, declared flatly that the laws passed during the Revolution would not be applied to them, that the laws in effect in 1789 would be reinstated, and that the slave trade could resume. A second law, meant for Saint-Domingue and Guadeloupe, divided the Black population into two groups. Those who had been legally free before the passage of the law of 16 pluviôse or who had fought to defend French territory would remain free. All others "will be subject to regulations that will assign them to landowners to aid them in agricultural work, determine their salary, and include all the provisions necessary to prevent vagabondage and insubordination." It was a proposal to effectively reinstate slavery in all but name.[51]

As the first favorable reports from Leclerc's expedition were arriving in Paris, the navy minister Decrès pressed Napoleon to "take the axe . . . to the terrible laws of 16 pluviôse II, 4 brumaire [IV] and 12 nivôse VI." These laws were, he said "long ago abrogated in the minds of all the statesmen of the Republic, [but] they nevertheless have the most disastrous effect on the imaginations of those who are most affected by them," the white colonists. At a minimum, he wanted a clear statement that slavery and the slave trade would be maintained in the colonies being returned by the British, but he hoped that they could then be extended to the other colonies. Even "those who in their ideology would be opposed won't dare express their disapproval," he added. "It will be enough, to silence them, to tell them that the law is necessary and let's see whether you prefer to be French or cosmopolitan."[52]

Napoleon could have enacted these measures as decrees, but he wanted them to have the authority of laws passed by the national legislature, just as the law of 16 pluviôse II had been. The law reauthorizing slavery was part of a series of measures that indicated how rapidly his regime, although still officially called a republic, was moving in the direction of the empire that would be created in 1804. Just before the introduction of the law on slavery, the assemblies had been asked to approve the establishment of the Legion of Honor, which was widely seen as a step toward the creation of a privileged body resembling the nobility of the ancien régime, and on 10 May 1802, ten days before the passage of the slavery law, the Conseil d'Etat approved the holding of a plebiscite to decide whether Napoleon should be declared First Consul for Life. Napoleon knew that there would be some opposition to these measures in the legislature, although he was sure he could count on his loyalists to approve them. In the case of the Legion of Honor, the government's official newspaper, the *Moniteur*, was even allowed to publish speeches calling the proposal "a law that attacks the bases of public liberty," and to reveal that the final vote on the measure in the Tribunate had been only fifty-six in favor, with thirty-eight opposed.[53]

In contrast to the debate on the Legion of Honor, in the case of the law reauthorizing slavery, only the speeches of Napoleon's spokesmen were made public. They faced a unique challenge: Representing a government whose official stationery still bore the motto "Liberty—Equality," they had to argue for a law whose clear purpose was to deprive the Black inhabitants of France's colonies of those rights. In making the case for the government's decision, Napoleon's spokesmen drew on the legacy of justifications of slavery made during the revolutionary debates, but they also introduced some new arguments. Opening the discussion in the Tribunate on 28 floréal X, the councilor of state André Julien Dupuy repeated familiar tropes about the necessity of different laws in "these distant countries, where the inescapable difference between civilized men and those who are not . . . demands great differences in the civil and political status of persons." In the colonies where slavery had never been abolished, it had to be maintained. In those where the Revolution had abolished it, "we must hasten to substitute for seductive theories a restorative system whose details are linked to circumstances, vary according to them, and are left to the wisdom of the government."[54]

Two days later, Pierre Adet, a veteran colonial official who had opposed the pluviôse decree in 1794, delivered what would prove to be the last of the revolutionary era's major orations on the subject of slavery. In a speech that ran over two issues of the *Moniteur*, he began by saying that slavery, like war, was something that thinking people had long condemned, but that every society had engaged in. Then he shifted to a new argument: If France wanted to be fully recognized as a part of the family of civilized European nations, it had to show that it had recovered from the excesses of the Revolution and was no longer trying to propagate ideas that undermined their common interests. "Can a nation . . . let loose among [the nations of the world] a contagious germ as communicable by its nature as rapid in its spread and as disastrous in its effects?" Adet asked. "Now that France has restored itself with glory to the place that it occupies in the European family, it should return to the spirit of family and coordinate its institutions . . . with those of other peoples, in order to preserve that harmony of principles that tends to . . . perpetuate the peace so necessary to the welfare of all nations."[55]

Adet went on to say that the history of the Revolution in France had shown that even in a civilized country, men had often "confounded the excesses of license, and the cruelties of a brutal tyranny, with the noble prerogatives of liberty." How could one then expect men "whose reason is still in the shadows of infancy" to successfully make the transition from slavery to freedom? "Let us leave it to time alone the task of preparing and carrying out the changes in the organization of the colonies that humanity calls for, but that policy should not impose in a violent fashion," he concluded. If he was speaking to a less enlightened assembly, he added, he would show that slavery was "in the interest of the Blacks themselves." Events had demonstrated that when they had been granted freedom, they had "terrified the world with scenes of bloodshed and carnage" before "falling back into the chains of their own kind."[56]

From slavery, Adet turned to the slave trade. He admitted that if one contemplated the spectacle of Black prisoners being torn away from their native country, pity would dictate its abolition. But, he told the legislators, they could not give in to their emotions. Resorting to a comparison that no doubt seemed appropriate under Napoleon's rule, he told them that it was their duty to emulate generals who did not hesitate to order soldiers into battle, knowing that many of them would have to die to secure a victory. Even if France prohibited the slave trade, other countries would continue to engage in it, and the Africans would be no better off. True, the British were debating the abolition of the slave trade, but the reformers were encountering firm resistance from its defenders.

Nodding to the ideas of the new colonialism, he held out the hope that the development of civilization in Africa would someday render the slave trade unnecessary, but in the meantime, all that could be done was to try to make the treatment of captives more humane.[57]

In the last section of Adet's speech, he justified the government's demand that it be authorized to issue laws for the colonies by decree, without further consultation with the legislature. "The situation of the colonies requires a power that is prompt, energetic and severe, as variable in its measures as are the events whose consequences it needs to foresee or forestall." It was therefore necessary to set aside article 91 of the constitution, which, while it stated that the colonies were not subject to the constitution, still implied that they would be governed by laws rather than by arbitrary edicts. Although Adet did not say so, his language clearly opened the door to the reimposition of slavery in Saint-Domingue and Guadeloupe if circumstances permitted. But, he assured the legislators, they could trust the government to exercise a "paternal authority" that would make each colony "a great family." The situation in the colonies would soon "offer nothing to the philosopher, to the friend of humanity, except touching scenes of patriarchal life, which the benevolent man will be able to contemplate with so much delight for his mind and his heart."[58]

No member of the Tribunate asked to speak in response to the government's presentation, and the tribunes then voted fifty-four to twenty-seven to approve the government's proposition, a result very similar to the vote for the Legion of Honor two days earlier.[59] The number of "no" votes on both propositions indicated that there was some serious opposition to both of these laws, but the opponents of slavery were not allowed to express their concerns outside the Tribunate's meeting hall. The action then moved to the larger Legislative Body, whose rules dictated that its members voted on proposals forwarded from the Tribunate but were not allowed to debate them. A tribune from the Gironde department that was so vitally interested in the resumption of colonial trade presented the familiar arguments about the economic importance of the colonies and the indispensability of enslaved labor in the tropics. Admiral Eustache Bruix conceded that "one can lament that a portion of the human race is condemned by nature or by social institutions to servile labor and slavery," but urged the legislators to remember that "Sparta with its helots, Rome with its slaves, knew, cherished, adored liberty."[60]

The final speaker, Michel Regnault Saint-Jean d'Angély, reminded his audience that the deputies of the National Assembly of 1789–91 in which he had sat had never tried to abolish slavery. "No one has greater respect than I for that Society of the Friends of the Blacks, almost all of whom the revolutionary scythe has cut down, and among whom I counted some most honorable friends," he claimed, but even they had wanted to avoid "the violent upheavals, of which its existence and its publications were the source or the pretext." A few years earlier, under the Directory, Eschassériaux had proclaimed that liberty did not reverse itself. Regnault replied that, during revolutions, "one yields to enthusiasm that carries one away, rather than to reason that sets limits. . . . But when the revolution is over . . . wisdom consists in looking behind oneself, and in returning to the point that [reason] has marked out for us. Then it is necessary, just, honorable to retrograde." Hadn't the three years of the Consulate "retrograded to calm, to peace, to order, to stability, to happiness, to true glory?" By a roll-call vote of 211 to 63, the legislators passed the law of 30 floréal X (figure 13).[61]

With the passage of that law, the long series of legislative discussions about slavery and race that had punctuated the French Revolution, starting with the debates about the admission of colonial deputies in June 1789 and continuing through every successive phase of the Revolution up to the Consulate, came to an end. In August 1789, when the Declaration of the Rights of Man was passed, Honoré Gabriel Riqueti de Mirabeau had written that if its principles were taken seriously, "there cannot be, either in France, or in any other territory under France's laws, any men except *free men*, except *men equal to one another*."[62] In 1799 Napoleon had eliminated the declaration, leaving no constitutional provision that could be cited to oppose the reinstitution of slavery. Although the short, dry text of the law of 30 floréal X concealed its full import, the speeches given by Napoleon's spokesmen had made its significance clear. Claiming to be enacted "in the name of the French people" and with the approval of the legislature, the law stated that "in the colonies returned to France in execution of the treaty of

LOI

Relative à la traite des Noirs et au régime des Colonies.

Du 30 Floréal, an X de la République une et indivisible.

Au nom du peuple français, Bonaparte, premier Consul, proclame loi de la République le décret suivant, rendu par le Corps législatif le 30 floréal an X, conformément à la proposition faite par le Gouvernement le 27 dudit mois, communiquée au Tribunat le même jour.

DÉCRET.

Art. I.er Dans les colonies restituées à la France en exécution du traité d'Amiens, du 6 germinal an X, l'esclavage sera maintenu conformément aux lois et réglemens antérieurs à 1789.

II. Il en sera de même dans les autres colonies françaises au-delà du Cap de Bonne-Espérance.

III. La traite des noirs et leur importation dans lesdites colonies, auront lieu, conformément aux lois et réglemens existans avant ladite époque de 1789.

IV. Nonobstant toutes lois antérieures, le régime des

(2)

colonies est soumis, pendant dix ans, aux réglemens qui seront faits par le Gouvernement.

Collationné à l'original, par nous président et secrétaires du Corps législatif. A Paris, le 30 Floréal, an X de la République française. *Signé* Rabaut le jeune, *président;* Thiry, Bergier, Tupinier, Rigal, *secrétaires.*

Soit la présente loi revêtue du sceau de l'État, insérée au Bulletin des lois, inscrite dans les registres des autorités judiciaires et administratives, et le ministre de la justice chargé d'en surveiller la publication. A Paris, le 10 Prairial, an X de la République.

Signé Bonaparte, *premier Consul.* Contre-signé, *le secrétaire d'état,* Hugues B. Maret. Et scellé du sceau de l'État. Vu, *le ministre de la justice,* signé Abrial.

Vu par le Ministre de la Marine et des Colonies, pour être exécutoire dans les colonies,

FIGURE 13: The decree of 30 floréal Year X, passed by the French legislature at Napoleon's request, authorized the continuation of slavery in colonies where the decree of 16 pluviôse had never been applied. Arguments by Napoleon's spokesmen implied that slavery would also be restored in Saint-Domingue and Guadeloupe, two colonies where it had been abolished after 1794. *Credit:* Wikimedia Commons.

Amiens . . . slavery will be maintained in accordance with laws and regulations prior to 1789." The Code Noir was thus reinstated, both in the Caribbean and in the Mascarenes. The slave trade was also reestablished. As for the colonies where the law of 16 pluviôse II had been implemented, their situation was left, for ten years, to the discretion of the government.[63]

Technically, this did not amount to a declaration that slavery would be reintroduced in places where it had been abolished, but Napoleon now had authority to do so if he wished. In view of the resources that were being invested in the expeditions to Saint-Domingue and Guadeloupe and the propaganda campaign against Blacks flooding the metropole, there could be little doubt about his intentions. In a letter to Leclerc at the beginning of July, Napoleon repeated his insistence on the elimination of all Black military officers. "Once the Blacks have been disarmed and the principal generals sent to France, you will have done more for commerce and European civilization than has been achieved in the most brilliant campaigns. . . . Rid us of these gilded Africans, and we will have nothing more to desire."[64]

The passage of the law of 30 floréal X ensured the continuation of slavery in Martinique and the smaller islands around it and in the Mascarenes. Victor Hugues, who had been dispatched to Cayenne in 1801, promptly restored the institution there, using the same ruthless methods with which he had controlled Guadeloupe from 1794 to 1798. Only on that island and in Saint-Domingue was there any question about whether the Black population would be forced back into slavery after enjoying legal freedom for eight years. Forwarding the text of the law to Leclerc, navy minister Decrès pointed out that it was not immediately applicable to Saint-Domingue, where it was still necessary to proceed cautiously. To "precipitously destroy this idol of liberty, in whose name so much blood has flowed up to now," would be premature. "For some time to come, vigilance, order, discipline in agriculture and the military needs to take the place of explicit slavery." But once the Blacks had been able to recognize "the difference between a usurped and tyrannical yoke and that of a legitimate owner, interested in their preservation, then the moment will have come to put them back in their original condition, from which it was so unfortunate to have removed them." In the meantime, however, it was urgent to start rebuilding the colony's workforce by permitting the reopening of the slave trade. Leclerc was authorized to give purchasers "the formal assurance that they have acquired the right of full property" over any captives they acquired, a promise that meant that there could once again be enslaved people in Saint-Domingue.[65]

Public reaction to the law of 30 floréal X in France was muted. At the moment when the law was enacted, news reports from the Caribbean made it hard to judge whether the military expeditions sent to those two islands were succeeding. News of Toussaint Louverture's surrender and his subsequent arrest had not yet reached Paris, but there were rumors of heavy casualties among the troops. According to one police bulletin, the colonial students in the school set up during the Directory "say that the love of independence will multiply the forces of the Negroes, and that they will not be so cowardly as to renounce the advantages of the conquest that they have made." Only in early June 1802, when Leclerc's report that Toussaint Louverture had abandoned the struggle and agreed to retire to one of his plantations and that the Blacks were returning to the plantations was published, did the public become convinced that Saint-Domingue was under control.[66]

Aside from official dispatches from Leclerc and admiral Villaret-Joyeuse, which maintained an upbeat tone that contrasted sharply with Leclerc's confidential letters, the press carried little news about the expedition. Leclerc implored Napoleon to "prohibit the publication in French journals of any insults to the Blacks" because it would undermine his efforts to establish his authority.[67] In the weeks leading up to the passage of the law, the *Décade philosophique*, which had strongly supported the Société des Amis des Noirs et des Colonies during the Directory, joined the official press in denouncing Toussaint Louverture and dismissing rumors that the Blacks were going to be reenslaved. When the law of 30 floréal X was passed, the journal published the text, without any commentary. The conservative *Mercure de France*, responding to a British newspaper that called the law "anti-Christian," defended the measure, asking whether, "in order to honor a religion that breathes peace and humanity, it would have been necessary to unleash in Martinique, in Sainte-Lucie, in the Ile de France, a race whose behavior has only been too well tested, [and] sacrifice to inevitable ruin and massacre the whites of these colonies, whose prosperity would be replaced by the devastations, the atrocities, the barbarities that Saint-Domingue owes to the Amis des Noirs!"[68]

Returning to the subject later in the summer, at a time when press reports still made it appear that resistance in Saint-Domingue had been subdued, the *Mercure* openly justified slavery and the slave trade. "This conclusion is shocking, I admit, and will make many readers pause," the magazine wrote. "In adopting it, one has to be prepared to bear the weight of the condemnations accumulated over sixty years . . . and even to seem to reject this great argument of 'humanity.'" Nevertheless, the author continued, "we have to admit (and it is easier since the discovery of the facial angle [the pseudoscientific claim put forward by Petrus Camper that the angle from the brow to the chin was more animal-like in Blacks than in whites] that these men of an inferior nature, whom we would call children if they had the charm and the perfectibility, are born to be eternally dependent on our reason and our intelligence."[69]

The reinstitution of slavery in the colonies was accompanied by a series of measures aimed at Black people in the metropole. A decree issued on 29 May 1802 exiled all those living in France to two remote departments in the south of the country. Black military men were assigned to three special units commanded by white officers that were to be based on islands off the coast.[70] At the end of September, the government published a law, approved several months earlier, that banned Blacks and mulattos from entering the metropole. There was an exception for domestic servants of whites, a provision that undid the ancien régime's "freedom principle" by suggesting that there could be enslaved people on French soil. Valentin de Cullion, a former Saint-Domingue slave owner who had been the spokesman for the Leopardins when they addressed the National Assembly in the fall of 1790, applauded the measure in his virulently racist *Examen de l'esclavage*, hoping that it would put an end to the "scandal" of well-dressed Blacks walking the streets of Paris, whose presence threatened "French blood in all its purity." A few months later, a government circular forbade marriages between Blacks and whites. In the meantime, the navy minister Decrès had come personally to announce the expulsion of the Black students from the interracial school founded by the abbé Jean-Baptiste Coesnon. One of the students later described the scene in a letter to Louverture's sons: "The minister Decrès came to the institution, had all the Americans gathered in the courtyard and spoke to them harshly. The government would no longer provide for their education, it had already done too much for creatures like us." The former students would be trained for agricultural or mechanical occupations, the only ones "that reason allows for individuals of this color."[71]

Although the passage of the law of 30 floréal X evoked little visible opposition in France, it had a devastating effect in Saint-Domingue. Long before the news of the law reached him, Leclerc had found it impossible to carry out the plans laid down in his secret instructions. Instead of being able to arrest the Black generals who had initially fought against him, he found himself forced to incorporate them and their men into his own army to replace the thousands of white troops lost to disease. In mid-June he succeeded in arresting and deporting Toussaint Louverture, but he was now dependent on Louverture's lieutenants Jean-Jacques Dessalines and Henri Christophe, whose intentions he thoroughly distrusted, to combat the Black insurgents in the mountains who were continuing to fight for their freedom.[72] Two months later, at the beginning of August, when Leclerc received the news of the law of 30 floréal X, he wrote angrily to Napoleon, "I had begged you, citizen Consul, not to do anything that could make [the Blacks] fear for their freedom, until the moment when I was ready. . . . Suddenly there has arrived here the law that authorizes the slave trade with the colonies. . . . In addition, General Richepance has issued a decree to reestablish slavery in Guadeloupe. In this situation, citizen Consul, the moral force that I had acquired here is destroyed, I cannot achieve anything by persuasion, I have nothing left but force, and I don't have the means for that."[73] Richepance had acted on his own initiative, but he had correctly anticipated Napoleon's reaction to the news that resistance in Guadeloupe had been largely crushed. On 16 July 1802 Napoleon had issued a decree reestablishing slavery on that island.[74]

Faced with what he recognized as an impossible situation, Leclerc pleaded to be relieved of his command, telling Napoleon that by the time he left, he hoped that "the colony will be in a condition to receive the regime that you want to give it, but it will be up to my successor to take the last step, if you think it is appropriate"—or, in other words, to announce the reestablishment of slavery. For his part, he added, he would not take any action that would contradict the public proclamation he had issued promising the Blacks that he would maintain their freedom. Two months later, at the beginning of October, as the Black generals began to turn against him, Leclerc wrote despairingly to Napoleon that the only way to retain French control of Saint-Domingue would be to "destroy all the Negroes in the mountains, men and women, sparing only the children under age 12, to destroy half of those in the plains and to not leave in the colony a single man of color who has worn an officer's epaulette."[75]

A few weeks after Leclerc wrote this horrifying letter, the yellow fever that had ravaged his white troops claimed his own life and prevented him from attempting the genocidal policy he had suggested. Meanwhile, Napoleon was treating Toussaint Louverture with brutal vindictiveness. As soon as the ship that carried him to France arrived, he was separated from his family and rushed to the Fort de Joux, a prison in the cold Jura Mountains of northeastern France. During his confinement, Louverture composed a lengthy protest recounting all that he had done to maintain French authority in Saint-Domingue and asserting that it had been his military obligation to oppose Leclerc's unannounced eruption in the colony. He complained that he had been subjected to "treatment that had never been employed even against the worst criminals. No doubt, I owe this treatment to my color, but did my color prevent me from serving my country with zeal and fidelity?" he demanded.[76]

Louverture's impassioned defense never reached Napoleon; the Black general died in April 1803. Napoleon's vindictiveness also extended to the Black deputies whose presence in the French legislature had embodied the policies of racial equality adopted during the Revolution, even those who had opposed Louverture. Jean-Baptiste Belley, the subject of Anne-Louis Girodet's famous portrait, was arrested in 1802 and died three years later. The deputies Jean-Baptiste Mills and Jean-Louis Annecy were deported to the island of Elba and died there in 1807.[77] Meanwhile, on the other side of the Atlantic, the white former deputy Louis Dufay, whose speech had set the stage for the passage of the decree of 16 pluviôse and who had returned to Saint-Domingue with the Leclerc expedition, met an equally grim fate: He was apparently one of the victims of the massacre of French whites ordered by Jean-Jacques Dessalines, Louverture's successor as the leader of the resistance to the French, after the declaration of Haitian independence in 1804.[78]

In Saint-Domingue, the French fought on for another year under Leclerc's successor, Donatien Rochambeau, but the resumption of the war with Britain in April 1803, which ended any possibility of further reinforcements for the army, doomed the effort to force the Black population back into slavery. With coldblooded realism, Napoleon cut his losses, writing off his troops and abandoning his dream of an empire in the Americas. The foreign minister

Talleyrand was instructed to offer the Louisiana Territory to the United States, a decision Napoleon might not have had to make if he had not been so determined to restore slavery. Years later, during his exile in Saint-Helena, Napoleon admitted that "it was a great mistake to have tried to subjugate [the colony] by force." In his telling, however, it was not his fault: "He had only yielded to the opinion of the Conseil d'Etat and that of his ministers, who were influenced by the outcries of the colonists, who formed a large party in Paris."[79] The faithful Las Casas, who recorded Napoleon's words, did not remind him that it was he who had appointed the members of the Conseil d'Etat and the ministers and allowed the colonists to wage their propaganda campaign.

Epilogue

NAPOLEON'S REINSTITUTION OF slavery and the subsequent defeat of the French expedition to Saint-Domingue had profound, if contradictory, consequences. On 1 January 1804 what had been the most prized French colony proclaimed itself the independent nation of Haiti. Haiti became the first country in the world to make the permanent abolition of slavery its guiding principle, but it also found itself a pariah state, forced to fight for decades for recognition of its sovereignty and portrayed, in a hostile white-dominated world, as proof of the incapacity of Black people to create a functioning society of their own. While the existence of Haiti was a rebuke to slavery and racism, France under Napoleon demonstrated that progress in the recognition of human rights could be reversed, even where those rights had been most emphatically proclaimed. The country that had been the center of the European Enlightenment and in which the Declaration of the Rights of Man and Citizen had been hailed as a sacred document now became the only country where the abolition of slavery was undone. Slavery and racial hierarchy were maintained in the other French colonies, and in the metropole itself, openly racist laws targeted even Blacks who had fought in the country's armies.

What might have happened if France had not abandoned the vision of a transatlantic, multiracial polity embodied in the laws passed during the 1790s is impossible to say. To be sure, that vision was never entirely implemented. Nevertheless, as Léon Deschamps, the first historian to make a serious study of the Revolution's colonial legislation, wrote in 1891, at the moment when Napoleon chose to repudiate abolition, "our colonies . . . had everything that would have made them prosperous . . . administrative autonomy, freedom of trade, freedom of labor and of persons. If this tradition had been maintained, our history during the nineteenth century would have been completely different."[1] As a result of Napoleon's decisions, France, which had gone beyond the northern American states by abolishing slavery altogether and declaring Blacks full citizens, forfeited its claim to be "the country of the rights of man" and became instead a bulwark of slavery and a hothouse for the propagation of racist ideas. After 1807, when Parliament, following eighteen years of debate, finally approved William Wilberforce's motion to ban the slave trade, Britain claimed the moral high ground in the struggle against slavery. A quarter century later, in 1833, the British granted freedom to the enslaved Blacks in their colonies. Contrary to the warnings of its opponents, the law was implemented without much violence and without undermining British control of its colonies or the British economy. The lesson seemed clear: The gradual approach to abolition adopted in Britain had succeeded, unlike the more radical measures adopted by the French revolutionaries in the 1790s.

This view, which put the gradualist approach to abolition at the center of histories of that movement for many decades, did not do justice to the important consequences of the French Revolution's contribution to the cause. The revolutionaries had demonstrated, nearly forty years before the British law of 1833, that slavery could in fact be abolished—not just gradually and in places where whites had an overwhelming numerical majority, such as the northern states of America, but in true "slave societies" such as Saint-Domingue and Guadeloupe. The French revolutionary abolitionists' campaign affirmed that the abolition of slavery and racial hierarchy was a necessary consequence of the universalist principles of the Declaration of the Rights of Man and Citizen, as Honoré Gabriel Riqueti de Mirabeau had so forcefully argued in August 1789. As the opponents of abolition came to realize, defending slavery against the compelling force of the abolitionists' arguments required either denying the existence of natural rights or else denying the humanity of Black people. Napoleon, by imposing a constitution without a declaration of rights and by reinstating slavery, embraced both of these positions. In the long run, however, the appeal of the ideals of liberty and equality proved too strong, not only in France but in the United States and in the other countries where slavery was eventually abolished. In 1848, when another revolution finally ended the era of monarchy in France and revived the democratic and egalitarian ideals of 1789, one of the first actions of the government it established was to abolish slavery in the remaining French colonies.

Another important outcome of the French Revolution's policies was to provide the Black population of Saint-Domingue with the experience that eventually allowed them to defend their freedom against France itself. The Haitian Revolution is often described as a thirteen-year struggle against French rule, but in fact, from 1794, when the news of the decree of 16 pluviôse II reached the island, until 1802, when Napoleon's forces arrived, the colony's population were "free and French," as the constitution Toussaint Louverture issued in 1801 proclaimed. By 1802, Louverture and his lieutenants had had the chance to hone their military and political skills as they rose through the ranks of the French military and administration. Ordinary members of the population learned to think of themselves as individuals with rights. Had Saint-Domingue come under the domination of the Spanish and British, who both launched invasions of its territory in 1793, it would certainly have evolved in a very different direction from the one that ultimately resulted in the creation of Haiti.

The French Revolution's confrontation with the issues of slavery and race, even if it failed to bring about the end of those injustices, was thus an important episode in the wider battle over these issues. The period's debates on these issues were also a major aspect of the French Revolution. They punctuated every period of the movement, from the opening days of the National Assembly when the question of admitting deputies from the colonies was thrashed out until the sessions of the Napoleonic legislature during the Consulate in which Napoleon's spokesmen justified the reestablishment of slavery. In many cases, the stands revolutionary politicians took on colonial issues changed the course of their lives. From the beginning of the Revolution, Jacques-Pierre Brissot was the "friend of the

Blacks," and a single phrase—"Perish the colonies!"—defined Maximilien Robespierre for much of his revolutionary career. Antoine Barnave sacrificed his standing among the "patriots" by his defense of slavery, and Napoleon sealed his repudiation of the principles of liberty and equality with his decree reestablishing slavery.

It was not only members of the revolutionary assemblies who took sides in the period's debates about "the affair of the colonies." Both the abolitionists and the defenders of the colonial system had supporters throughout the country. Colonial issues divided Jacobin clubs and mobilized journalists such as Claude Milscent and Léger-Félicité Sonthonax. Julien Raimond was the first man of African descent to become a recognized participant in metropolitan politics. The issues of slavery and race galvanized authors and playwrights such as Olympe de Gouges, artists such as Anne-Louis Girodet, and obscure figures such as the diarist and investor Célestin Guittard de Floriban. The crowds who gathered outside the National Assembly's meeting hall during the epic debate of May 1791 and who attended the great festival celebrating the abolition of slavery at Notre-Dame in February 1794 show that there was genuine public engagement with these matters.

In assessing the importance of the French Revolution's confrontation with slavery, it is also important to remember that those who engaged themselves on behalf of racial equality and abolition during the French Revolution did so at great risk to themselves. No one ever paid a more eloquent tribute to the devotion of France's opponents of slavery than the great mid-nineteenth-century Haitian historian Beaubrun Ardouin. "As we recall that at the moment when general liberty was proclaimed in Saint-Domingue" in the summer of 1793, he wrote, "Brissot and the Girondins, these devoted friends of the Blacks, languished in the prisons of the Terror, and that a month later their heads fell under the lethal blade of that bloody epoch, we ask ourselves whether Haitians do not owe eternal regrets for the death of these gallant revolutionaries who, through their writings, through the triumph of their opinions, assured the triumph of our rights?"[2] White abolitionists in other countries never faced such mortal risks.

Courageous as many of them were, the French revolutionary abolitionists were also human beings whose flaws sometimes undermined their efforts on behalf of racial justice. Whether Mirabeau was bribed to soften his much-anticipated denunciation of the slave trade in 1790 may never be known. Brissot's poor political judgment proved fatal to him and his most loyal allies and came close to scuttling the antislavery movement altogether. Few of the abolitionists saw their efforts on behalf of the victims of slavery as part of a campaign for the rights of all oppressed groups. Pierre Chaumette, who organized the grand ceremony celebrating the abolition of slavery in February 1794, is mentioned most often nowadays in histories of the French Revolution for his vehement speech against rights for women, delivered just a few months earlier. Julien Raimond blamed both white and mixed-race women for undermining his efforts to dismantle racial hierarchy. Claude Milscent had no love for Jews, "these machines . . . who have learned only to calculate the misery and the needs of their fellows."[3] Henri Grégoire, the religiously inspired defender of the rights of both Blacks and Jews, followed traditional Catholic teaching about women's roles. Perhaps only the philosophe Condorcet, who argued for the rights of Blacks, women, and Jews, truly embodied the universalist notion of human rights that some historians would like to find in the French Revolution, but his devotion to abstract ideals made him an inept politician.

Beaubrun Ardouin's tribute to the French revolutionary abolitionists was one of the rare recognitions of their importance published during the nineteenth century and the first half of the twentieth. Napoleon's spokesman Michel Regnault Saint-Jean d'Angély, speaking at a moment when it was still assumed that France was about to regain control of Saint-Domingue, set the tone for discussions of the issue for decades to come. He acknowledged the "good faith" of the reformers and expressed sorrow for those who had been executed, but he insisted that it was their writings that were responsible for the "violent upheavals" that had beset the colonies.[4] Once the catastrophic outcome of the Leclerc expedition became clear, the former colonists and military officers who had participated in the unsuccessful campaign delivered even harsher verdicts on the culpability of the Société des Amis des Noirs.

The few opponents of slavery who managed to get their arguments into print in Napoleonic France found themselves on the defensive. The economist Jean-Baptiste Say, who had been a member of the Société des Amis des Noirs et des Colonies, strongly condemned the cruelty of slavery in his *Traité d'économie politique*, first published in 1803, but he undercut one of the strongest antislavery arguments by calculating that slave labor was in fact more profitable than the employment of free workers. Grégoire's *De la littérature des Nègres*, published at the height of the Napoleonic empire in 1808, was the most eloquent treatise in favor of abolition to appear during the period. Grégoire valiantly refuted the racist theories that had become so prominent after 1800, but he carefully avoided any mention of the law of 16 pluviôse II and insisted that he and the other Amis des Noirs had always advocated "a gradual approach that would have brought about the good without upheaval."[5]

At the Congress of Vienna following Napoleon's defeat in 1814, the French successfully bargained for the return of their overseas slave colonies and for an assurance that the other powers would allow France to reconquer Saint-Domingue. The veteran proslavery advocate Pierre-Victor Malouet was appointed as navy minister, a clear signal of the government's intention to maintain slavery, and agents were sent to Haiti to attempt to persuade the rulers of the two rival states that had emerged there to allow a return of French rule.[6] During his brief return to power in 1815, Napoleon tried to court liberal opinion by announcing the abolition of the slave trade, imitating what the British had done in 1807, but the Battle of Waterloo ended his reign before his decree could have any effect. The British extracted a promise from the restored Bourbon king Louis XVIII to join them in suppressing the slave trade, but for many years the French did little to enforce this ban.

By the beginning of the 1820s, the French government grudgingly recognized that reconquest of their former colony was no longer a practical possibility. The decision to recognize Haiti's independence in 1825, in exchange for a hefty indemnity for the French colonists who had owned property there, caused a noisy controversy, with many former plantation owners objecting to what they regarded as an unjust abrogation of their property rights.[7] Vivid scenes in Victor Hugo's first novel, *Bug-Jargal*, published in 1826, introduced a new generation of readers to images of the violence of the 1790s that derived from colonists' accounts. How memories of the revolutionary era continued to haunt French imaginations was shown when silk workers in Lyon staged the first major proletarian uprising in 1831. In an article that shaped visions of metropolitan class conflict for many years, a conservative journalist warned that "each manufacturer lives . . . like the planters of the colonies in the midst of their slaves, one against a hundred, and the Lyon revolt is a sort of uprising of Saint-Domingue."[8]

Organized advocacy for the improvement of conditions for the enslaved Blacks in the remaining French colonies and for the rights of free people of color resumed in the early 1820s. The Société de la morale chrétienne, a group led by liberal aristocrats and members of France's Protestant minority, formed a committee to promote gradual emancipation in 1822, and Cyrille Bissette, a free man of color from Martinique convicted for agitating for rights for his group in 1824, became the face of a movement for that cause. The July Revolution of 1830 led to the replacement of the Bourbon dynasty by the "bourgeois monarchy" of Louis-Philippe and the elevation of several members of the Société de la morale chrétienne to important political positions. The new king remained opposed to any significant reforms in the colonies, however, even after the British government mandated the abolition of slavery in 1833. Although the French slave colonies that had been recovered after 1815 had much less economic importance than the prerevolutionary sugar islands, their white elites continued to resist any change in their institutions, often citing the events of the 1790s to underline the danger of abolition.[9]

By the beginning of the 1840s, the abolitionist cause in France found a new spokesman: Victor Schoelcher. In *Des colonies françaises: De l'abolition immédiate de l'esclavage*, published in 1842, he broke with the more cautious advocates of abolition by calling for an immediate, as opposed to a gradual, ending of slavery. The British experience had shown that the institution could be abolished without sparking violence, and indeed Schoelcher argued that only its definitive dismantlement would create the conditions for a stable and prosperous colonial society. Schoelcher understood, however, that he needed to distance himself from the revolutionary-era abolitionists who were widely blamed for inciting the Saint-Domingue uprising. He was careful not to evoke the decree of 16 pluviôse II, which he mentioned only in passing.[10]

By the mid-1840s, pressure for some movement in the direction of abolition in the French colonies grew. Extensive debates in the French legislature resulted in the passage in 1845 of a law that made vague promises about ameliorating the treatment of enslaved people.[11] The revolution of 1848, which overthrew Louis-Philippe's regime, provided an opportunity for more radical measures. The provisional government that replaced the king immediately appointed Schoelcher to lead a commission charged with preparing an abolition law. The 1848 law, like the legislation passed fifty years earlier, declared the immediate end of slavery. It promised the Black populations of the French colonies full citizenship, including the rights to vote and hold office, and it granted the colonies representation in France's legislature. The biggest difference between the 1848 law and its revolutionary predecessor was the promise of an indemnity to be paid to former slave owners. Even though the members of Schoelcher's commission stated that human property had never been legitimate, they conceded that slavery had been authorized by the state and that private individuals who had taken advantage of that situation deserved some compensation.[12]

By the time the news of the 1848 abolition law reached the Caribbean colonies, popular unrest in Martinique had already led officials there and in Guadeloupe to promise the Black population their freedom. Even though colonial property owners succeeded in imposing regulations intended to force former slaves to continue working on their plantations rather than making themselves into independent peasant farmers, the 1848 law ended debate about the legitimacy of slavery in the French empire. In French collective memory, Victor Schoelcher's success in abolishing the institution peacefully largely erased memories of the earlier effort made during the revolutionary period. Schoelcher's remains were transferred to the Panthéon, France's shrine to its great historic figures, in 1949; statues to him have been erected in several places; and a number of French public schools bear his name.

The legacy of the racism that had taken root in French thought during the revolutionary era was harder to dispel than the institution of slavery. In 1855, just seven years after the passage of the

Schoelcher law, Arthur de Gobineau published his *Essay on the Inequality of the Huma Races*, destined to become the bible of white racists throughout the Western world. Although Gobineau did not comment explicitly on the recently passed French emancipation law, he dismissed the history of Haiti since its independence as "nothing but a long story of massacres" and praised the whites in the southern United States because they did not hesitate to force their enslaved Blacks "down to the level of the soil they work for them."[13]

Belated as it was, coming almost seventy years after the French law of 1794, the end of slavery in the United States after the Civil War finally made it possible to argue that the common values of the world's progressive countries now condemned that institution, in contrast to what Napoleon's henchmen had asserted to justify its reestablishment in 1802. Cuba and Brazil, the last two strongholds of slavery in the Americas, finally ended it in 1886 and 1889 respectively. Ironically, the freeing of the descendants of Africans forcibly taken across the Atlantic coincided with the high tide of European imperialism in Africa itself, a movement partly justified, according to its promoters, by the claim that it was eliminating the practices of slavery that had continued to exist there. In France, the democratic and republican regime of the Third Republic, established in 1875, followed in the footsteps of the revolutionary-era advocates of a "new colonialism" by portraying its acquisition of vast territories in sub-Saharan Africa as part of a "civilizing mission." At the same time, however, the behavior of the French toward the Black populations in their colonies often reflected the racial prejudices that had been articulated during the revolutionary and Napoleonic eras.

While the second abolition of slavery in France in 1848 was regularly commemorated and Victor Schoelcher made into an emblematic figure, the first abolition of slavery during the Revolution was largely forgotten. Even historians sympathetic to the cause of abolition, such as the socialists Louis Blanc in the 1850s and Jean Jaurès at the end of the nineteenth century, still included dramatic evocations of the violence of the slave uprising of 1791 in their works. Although both of those authors praised the efforts of the abolitionists of the Revolution's early years, with Jaurès calling the debate of May 1791 "one of the great economic and social battles of that time, between racial pride and the idea of equality, between the Rights of Man and property understood as the consecration of slavery," neither of them even mentioned the decree of 16 pluviôse II.[14] For more conservative historians, the revolutionaries' debates about colonial issues, if they were mentioned at all, were demonstrations of the movement's unrealistic idealism. Particularly once France's nineteenth-century colonial empire became a source of national pride, evocations of the loss of Saint-Domingue were painful, and the fact that that loss had occurred during what was otherwise remembered as the most brilliant period of the reign of the country's greatest hero, Napoleon, made discussions of it doubly awkward.

Léopold Senghor and Aimé Césaire, two leading figures in the Francophone "Négritude" movement of the mid-twentieth century, were pioneers in recognizing the significance of the French Revolution's contribution to abolition, and in particular the importance of the decree of 16 pluviôse II. After France's liberation from German occupation in 1945, when there were hopes that the country was ready to convert its imperial territories into full-fledged partners in a "French Union," Senghor published an article praising the Declaration of the Rights of Man as an expression of "French universalism" that necessarily promised equality to all human beings. "It was the Society of the Friends of the Blacks, to which all the leading philosophers belonged, that applied the principle to the colonial domain and the domain of practice," he added. "It is [that society] that, in the end, brought about the vote for the abolition of slavery on 4 February 1794."[15] Aimé Césaire, who represented Martinique in the French National Assembly from 1945 to 1993, played a leading role in the passage of the law that made France's "old" colonies, those that had been part of the empire in the revolutionary period, *départements* like those of metropolitan France, thus finally fulfilling the promise of the law of 12 nivôse VI. Like Senghor, Césaire recognized the importance of the abolition law of 16 pluviôse II. In his history of the French Revolution and the colonies, he wrote, "The abolition of slavery was a logical consequence of the Revolution, but it took violent pressure on the historical actors to get them to play their role as they should have."[16]

As Césaire was writing in 1961, France was adjusting to the loss of almost all of its other overseas possessions. One reaction to this situation was a tendency to erase the history of the French empire from national consciousness. The enormously influential seven-volume exploration of French national memory edited by Pierre Nora in the 1980s, *Les Lieux de mémoire* (Sites of memory), for example, did not include any discussion of the colonies.[17] As the bicentennial of the French Revolution approached in the 1980s, academic historians in France and elsewhere explored almost every other dimension of the event, but it was left to an outsider, Yves Bénot, a longtime activist in anticolonial movements, to take the initiative of publishing what can fairly be called the first book-length account of the revolutionary abolition movement in French since Deschamps's 1898 volume. Bénot's *La Révolution française et la fin des colonies* and *La Démence coloniale sous Napoléon* opened a new era of research that has made it impossible for serious scholars to neglect the colonial dimension of the French Revolution.[18] The explosion of studies about the Haitian Revolution, most of it by English-language scholars, took off at approximately the same time and has made it clear that that movement had a dynamic of its own, a recognition that has added to the challenges of explaining events in the metropole.

Since the 1990s, it is not only scholars in France who have come to pay more attention to the country's historical involvement with slavery. In 1998 the commemoration of the 150th anniversary of the 1848 law abolishing slavery for the second time provoked a movement, particularly among descendants of formerly enslaved people from Martinique, Guadeloupe, Guiana, and Réunion, for public recognition of this aspect of the country's past. One result of this campaign was the passage, in 2001, of the "Taubira law," named after Christiane Taubira, a legislator from French Guiana, which declared slavery and the slave trade "crimes against humanity" and mandated the teaching of the history of France's involvement with them in the schools. The date on which the Taubira law was passed, 10 May, is now a national holiday commemorating the victims of slavery. Later, 23 May, the anniversary of the public march in 1998 that launched the movement for recognition of those victims, was also declared a day of remembrance, and the entire month of May is now a time of frequent public programs and exhibitions devoted to the subject.[19]

The city of Nantes, once the major French slaving port, has been a center of efforts to bring the history of the country's involvement with slavery to light. In 1992 the mayor of the city, Jean-Marc Ayrault, who would later become president of the French government's official Fondation pour la mémoire de l'esclavage (Foundation for the Memory of Slavery), sponsored the first public exhibition devoted to the history of the slave trade, "Les Anneaux de la mémoire." In 2012 a permanent memorial to the victims of slavery was inaugurated on the banks of the Loire River, where slaving ships once departed on their voyages to Africa. Nantes's city history museum, located in the historic palace of the dukes of Brittany, has an extensive permanent exhibition explaining how thoroughly engagement with slavery permeated the city's life for two centuries, from the beginnings of the slave trade in the 1600s to the days of the illegal trade in the 1800s.[20]

As one stands before the glass-fronted cases in the Nantes museum exhibiting iron shackles that were once used to subdue enslaved captives, one is reminded of the cruelty of the institution that the abolitionists of the French Revolution worked to end. Portraits like those of the elegantly dressed Nantes slave trader Dominique Deurbroucq and his wife, Marguerite, both shown being waited on by their Black servants, are testimony to the wealth that slavery generated in France and that its beneficiaries fought so hard to defend. Everyday objects like a tobacco snuffbox in the form of an enslaved woman show how the victims of slavery were dehumanized and how people in the metropole were so desensitized to the issue that they found demeaning depictions of its victims amusing.[21] It was against those practices and attitudes that Brissot, Mirabeau, Condorcet, Grégoire, Milscent, and their allies raised their voices. Theirs was a war of words, less violent than the struggles of Vincent Ogé, Toussaint Louverture, and the thousands of Black men and women who took up arms to fight against slavery and racism in the French colonies. Without the actions of the free men of color and the enslaved Blacks in the Caribbean, abolitionists in France would not have won the victories they did in the 1790s. But without the impact of the French abolitionists' words, the ending of slavery would never have come to be seen, not as a defeat for France, but as a triumph for the principles of liberty and equality that the French Revolution so eloquently proclaimed to the world.

ACKNOWLEDGMENTS

THIS BOOK REPRESENTS the culmination of research carried out over three decades, ever since a reading of novelist Madison Smartt Bell's *All Souls' Rising* (1995) inspired my interest in the French Revolution's confrontation with the issues of race and slavery. Along the way, I have benefited from the advice and encouragement of many colleagues, many of whom I have also been fortunate to count as friends. David Geggus and Norman Fiering's invitation to present my first scholarly paper on this subject at the John Carter Brown Library's conference "The World of the Haitian Revolution" in 2004 allowed me to meet Yves Bénot, Jean Casimir, Jacques de Cauna, Elizabeth Colwill, Laurent Dubois, Ada Ferrer, Carolyn Fick (whom I had known as a graduate student in Paris in the 1970s, long before I came to appreciate the importance of the topic she was researching), John Garrigus, David Geggus, Malick Ghachem, Sue Peabody, Dominique Rogers, Ashli White, and others. Even before that memorable conference, I had met Marcel Dorigny and Alyssa Sepinwall because of our shared interest in the career of the abolitionist Henri Grégoire. Others who have stimulated my thinking on this topic include the late Trevor Burnard, Andy Cabot, Lauren Clay, Myriam Cottias, Vincent Cousseau, Manuel Covo, Marlene Daut, Daniel Désormeaux, Seymour Drescher, Miriam Franchina, Julia Gaffield, Bernard Gainot, Doris Garraway, Olivier Gliech, Sudhir Hazareesingh, Patrice Higonnet, Lynn Hunt, Jonathan Israel, Darrell Meadows, Graham Nessler, Claire Payton, Frédéric Régent, Marie-Jeanne Rossignol, Pierre Serna, Jeffery Stanley, Sonia Taleb, Timothy Tackett, Patrick Travens, and Damien Tricoire. My colleagues at the University of Kentucky, a number of whom are scholars of slavery and abolition in other contexts, have also contributed important insights, particularly Vanessa Holden, Hilary Jones, Gerald Smith, and Amy Murrell Taylor. I would also like to acknowledge the participants in the National Endowment for the Humanities Summer Seminars that I directed at the

Newberry Library in 2001 and 2006, as well as the students in my classes on the French and Haitian Revolutions at the University of Kentucky and Brown University, who helped sustain my conviction about the importance of this subject.

Research fellowships at the John Carter Brown Library (2005), the Institute for Advanced Studies (2006), and the National Humanities Center (2012–13) and visiting appointments at the Ecole des Hautes Etudes en Sciences Sociales and the Institut de l'Histoire de la Révolution française (2006) facilitated research for this book, as did financial support from the T. Marshall Hahn, Jr. and William T. Bryan endowed professorships at the University of Kentucky. I am grateful to the staffs of the Archives nationales de France, the Bibliothèque nationale de France, the Newberry Library, the John Carter Brown Library, the Bibliothèque historique de la Ville de Paris, the Institut de l'Histoire de la Révolution française, and the University of Kentucky Libraries, where the Special Collections Department and the Interlibrary Loan office were especially helpful.

I am grateful to Stanford University Press for permission to reuse some material from my article "Saint-Domingue, Slavery and the Origins of the French Revolution," in *From Deficit to Deluge*, edited by Thomas Kaiser and Dale Van Kley (Stanford, CA: Stanford University Press, 2011), 220–48. Thanks to Cambridge University Press for permission to reuse some material from chapter 10 of my book *You Are All Free: The Haitian Revolution and the Abolition of Slavery* (Cambridge: Cambridge University Press, 2010), and to *French Historical Studies* for allowing me to reuse parts of my article "Thermidor, Slavery, and the 'Affaire des colonies,'" which appeared in that journal, vol. 38 (2015): 61–82. Unless otherwise indicated, all translations from other languages are my own.

Many thanks to my hardworking agent, Peter W. Bernstein, for help in developing this book; to the three anonymous readers of the manuscript; and to Priya Nelson and Emma Wagh at Princeton University Press for guiding me through the editorial and production process.

This book is dedicated to the memory of my friend Marcel Dorigny (1948–2021), whose passion for the complicated and fascinating story of the French Revolution's struggles about slavery went together with a boundless appreciation for the cultural contributions of the people of the French Antilles and Haiti, in the past and in the present. Evenings spent with him, his wife Marie-Odile, and his circle of friends in his apartment on the rue Marx-Dormoy recreated the atmosphere of the salons of the French Enlightenment where the ideas that contributed to the abolition of slavery were first articulated.

NOTES AND A NOTE ON SOURCES

Full citations of all sources used are included in the first note for each archival document or printed work. A bibliography of sources cited can be accessed at https://press.princeton.edu/books/hardcover/9780691246925/the-first-emancipation?srsltid=AfmBOor2qJ6ZiMjZAVUpIS8CGb1hmIhl5-8NKBv3tqTTHp8S1-u5UZXv.

Introduction

1. *Archives parlementaires de 1787 à 1860, recueil complet des débats législatifs et politiques des chambres françaises: Première série (1787–1799)*, ed. Jérôme Madival et al. (Paris: P. Dupont, 1862–) (hereafter AP), 84:283.

2. *Courier de Provence*, no. 30 (20–21 August 1789): 3–4; emphasis in original.

3. On the circumstances leading up to Sonthonax and Polverel's emancipation decrees in Saint-Domingue, see Jeremy D. Popkin, *You Are All Free: The Haitian Revolution and the Abolition of Slavery* (New York: Cambridge University Press, 2010), 269–79.

4. Two classic works on the abolition movement are David Brion Davis, *The Problem of Slavery in the Age of Revolution, 1770–1823* (Ithaca, NY: Cornell University Press, 1975); and Seymour Drescher, *Abolition: A History of Slavery and Antislavery* (New York: Cambridge University Press, 2009). A more recent French work that gives more coverage to events in that country is Olivier Grenouilleau, *La Révolution abolitionniste* (Paris: Gallimard, 2016).

5. Jeremy D. Popkin, *Facing Racial Revolution: Eyewitness Accounts of the Haitian Uprising* (Chicago: University of Chicago Press, 2007); Popkin, *You Are All Free*; Jeremy D. Popkin, *Concise History of the Haitian Revolution*, 2nd ed. (Boston: Wiley Blackwell, 2021). For an overview of recent scholarship on the Haitian Revolution, see Jeremy D. Popkin, "The Haitian Revolution Comes of Age: Ten Years of New Research," *Slavery and Abolition* 42, no. 2 (2021): 382–401.

6. "Toussaint Louverture, general of the king's army, to Monsieur Chanlatte the younger, criminal, traitor and liar," 27 August 1793, Archives Nationales (hereafter AN), CC 9 A 8.

7. For an argument against attributing too much significance to the Revolution's colonial debates, see David A. Bell, "Questioning the Global Turn: The Case of the French Revolution," *French Historical Studies* 37, no. 1 (2014): 1–24.

8. On the implications of placing the Haitian Revolution alongside the American and French Revolutions, see Jeremy D. Popkin, "Un-Silencing the Haitian Revolution and Redefining the Revolutionary Era," in *The Atlantic World: Essays on Slavery, Migration and Imagination*, 2nd ed., ed. Willem Klooster and Albert Padula (London: Routledge, 2018), 230–50.

9. Myriam Cottias, "Les vingt ans de la loi Taubira," *Cahiers d'histoire*, no. 151 (2021): 167–78.

10. Yves Bénot, *La Révolution française et la fin des colonies* (Paris: La Découverte, 1987); Florence Gauthier, *Triomphe et mort du droit naturel en Révolution 1789-1795-1802* (Paris: Presses Universitaires de Paris, 1992); Jean-Daniel Piquet, *L'Emancipation des Noirs dans la Révolution française (1789–1795)* (Paris: Karthala, 1995); Tessie P. Liu, *A Frail Liberty: Probationary Citizens in the French and Haitian Revolutions* (Lincoln: University of Nebraska Press, 2022).

11. "Adresse à l'Assemblée générale de la partie française de St. Domingue, par MM. les citoyens de couleur, de la Grande Rivière Ste. Suzanne et autres quartiers malheureusement enveloppés dans le funeste evenement du 23 aoust dernier," AN, D XXV 1, d. 4, n.d. but probably 10 or 11 Dec. 1791. On Louverture's labor policy, see "Forced Labor Decree," in *Toussaint Louverture*, ed. George F. Tyson (Englewood Cliffs, NJ: Prentice Hall, 1973), 51–56.

12. See, for example, Marie-Jeanne Rossignol, *Noirs et Blancs contre l'esclavage. Une alliance antiesclavagiste ambiguë aux Etats-Unis 1754–1830* (Paris: CIRESC, 2022), 16.

13. Serge Daget, "Les Mots esclave, nègres, Noir, et les jugements de valeur sur la traite négrière dans la littérature abolitionniste française de 1770 à 1845," *Revue française d'histoire d'outre-mer* 60, no. 221 (1973): 511–48.

14. For a study of one of these individuals, see Huguette Krief, *Le Métis révolutionnaire: Barbault-Royer, homme de lettres et voyageur engagé* (Paris: Classiques Garnier, 2021).

Chapter One

1. Sue Peabody, *"There Are No Slaves in France": The Political Culture of Race and Slavery in the Ancien Régime* (New York: Oxford University Press, 1996), 29, 31.

2. Gillian Weiss, "Infidels at the Oar: A Mediterranean Exception to France's Free Soil Principle," *Slavery and Abolition* 32, no. 3 (2011): 397–412; Paul Walden Bamford, "The Procurement of Oarsmen for French Galleys, 1660–1748," *American Historical Review* 65, no. 1 (1959): 31–48.

3. Peabody, *"There Are No Slaves,"* 31.

4. Quoted in Michael Harrigan, *Frontiers of Servitude: Slavery in Narratives of the Early French Atlantic* (Manchester: Manchester University Press, 2018), 173. On the history of slavery in the French empire, see Frédéric Régent, *La France et ses esclaves: De la colonisation aux abolitions (1620–1848)* (Paris: Grasset, 2007).

5. Paul W. Bamford, "French Forest Legislation and Administration, 1660–1789," *Agricultural History* 29, no. 3 (1955): 100.

6. Quoted in Lauren R. Clay, "'Cruel Necessity': Capitalism, the Discourse of Sympathy, and the Problem of the Slave Trade in the Age of Human Rights," *Slavery and Abolition* 37, no. 2 (2016): 256–83, 269. On the drafting of the Code Noir, see Malick W. Ghachem, *The Old Regime and the Haitian Revolution* (New York: Cambridge University Press, 2011), 43–75.

7. "The 'Code Noir' (1685)," trans. John Garrigus, Washington State University, accessed 21 May 2025, https://s3.wp.wsu.edu/uploads/sites/1205/2016/02/code-noir.pdf.

8. Garrigus, "'Code Noir.'"

9. "Le Code noir: Recueil d'édits, déclarations et arrêts concernant les esclaves nègres de l'Amérique," L'aménagement linguistique dans le monde, accessed 21 May 2025, https://www.axl.cefan.ulaval.ca/amsudant/guyanefr1685.htm.

10. Jean-Baptiste Labat, *Nouveau Voyage aux isles de l'Amérique* trans. John Garrigus, in Garrigus, "'Code Noir.'"

11. Pierre-François de Charlevoix, *Histoire de l'Isle Espagnole ou de Saint-Domingue* (1730–34), quoted in Andrew S. Curran, *The Anatomy of Blackness: Science and Slavery in an Age of Enlightenment* (Baltimore: Johns Hopkins University Press, 2011), 53–54.

12. Jean-Baptiste Labat, *Nouveau Voyage aux Antilles* (Paris: Delespine, 1741), 3:406, quoted in Doris Garraway, *The Libertine Colony: Creolization in the Early Caribbean* (Durham, NC: Duke University Press, 2005), 140.

13. Labat, *Nouveau Voyage aux isles.*

14. Robert Harms, *The Diligent: A Voyage Through the Worlds of the Slave Trade* (New York: Basic Books, 2002), xiii.

15. Caroline Le Mao, ed., *Mémoire noire, histoire de l'esclavage: Bordeaux, La Rochelle, Rochefort, Bayonne* (Abbeville: Mollat, 2020), 9.

16. Erick Noël, *Etre noir en France au XVIIIe siècle* (Paris: Tallandier, 2006), 146–48.

17. Peabody, *"There Are No Slaves,"* 15–16; Noël, *Etre noir*, 69–70.

18. Peabody, *"There Are No Slaves,"* 18–22.

19. Peabody, *"There Are No Slaves,"* 23–40.

20. Jacques Savary de Bruslons, *Le Parfait Négociant* (Paris: Veuve Etienne, 1736), 229.

21. Jean-François Melon, *Essai politique sur le commerce* (n.p., 1734), 64, 69, 71.

22. Richard Cantillon, *Essay on the Nature of Trade in General*, ed. Henry Higgs (London: Frank Cass, 1959), pt. 1, ch. 11, https://oll.libertyfund.org/title/higgs-essay-on-the-nature-of-trade-in-general-higgs-ed.

23. Peabody, *"There Are No Slaves,"* 74; Pierre Bardin, *Joseph Sieur de Saint-Georges: Le Chevalier Noir* (Paris: Guenegaud, 2008), 53; Miranda Spieler, "Slave Voice and the Legal Archive," in *Hearing Enslaved Voices: African and Indian Slave Testimony in British and French America, 1700–1848*, ed. Sophie White and Trevor Burnard (London: Routledge, 2020), 181.

24. Trevor Burnard and John Garrigus, *The Plantation Machine: French Saint-Domingue and British Jamaica* (Philadelphia: University of Pennsylvania Press, 2016), 203–15, 211.

25. Robert Louis Stein, *The French Slave Trade in the Eighteenth Century: An Old Regime Business* (Madison: University of Wisconsin Press, 1979), 39.

26. Le Mao, *Mémoire noire*, 42; Burnard and Garrigus, *Plantation Machine*, 250.

27. [Banastre Tarleton], "Mémoire sur la traitte des Negres, et sur le commerce de Liverpool à la cöte de Guinée et aux Indes occidentales," AN, D XXV 86, d. 829.

This is an excerpt from Tarleton's testimony to the British parliamentary committee looking into the slave trade in 1789.

28. Benoît Jullien, "Pour étudier la traite et l'esclavage: Les archives de la Région Nouvelle-Aquitaine," in Le Mao, *Mémoire noire*, 275–91, 283.

29. Stein, *French Slave Trade*, 67–69.

30. Eric Saugera, *Bordeaux, port négrier: Chronologie, économie, idéologie XVIIe–XIXe siècles*, new ed. (Paris: Karthala, 2002), 87–110.

31. On the French sugar industry, see Robert Louis Stein, *The French Sugar Business in the Eighteenth Century* (Baton Rouge: Louisiana State University Press, 1988), 135–46.

32. Emma Rothschild, *An Infinite History: The Story of a Family in France over Three Centuries* (Princeton, NJ: Princeton University Press, 2021), 14, 52, 55, 104–5, 106–7, 108–9.

33. Louis Lezin de Milly, *Discours prononcé le 20 février [1790] par M. de Milly, Américain, citoyen de Paris, avocat en parlement, l'un des commissaires nommés par le district de Filles Saint-Thomas, pour l'examen de la Question relative à la liberté et à l'abolition de la traite des Nègres* (Paris: Didot jeune, 1790), 34.

34. Dominique Barbier, *Le Dernier Seigneur d'Arsy: Louis-Marthe de Gouy d'Arsy* (Paris: self-published, 2019), 48.

35. Vincent Cousseau, "Etre esclave dans les colonies françaises," in Le Mao, *Mémoire noire*, 157–80, illustration on 162; Burnard and Garrigus, *Plantation Machine*, 44–47, illustrations on 46–47; Krystel Guadlé, *L'Abîme: Nantes dans la traite Atlantique et l'esclavage coloniale* (Bain-de-Bretagne: Musée d'histoire de Nantes, 2021), 166, 178, 179.

36. "Manuscrit d'un voyage de France à Saint-Domingue, à la Havanne et aux Unis états [*sic*] d'Amérique," John Carter Brown Library, Codex Fr. 20, pt. 1, pp. 6–7; Michel Rodigneaux, *Victor Hugues: L'Ambition d'entrer dans l'histoire, 1762–1826* (Paris: SPM, 2017), 45; René Levasseur, *Mémoires de R. Levasseur (de la Sarthe) ex-Conventionnel*, ed. Michel Vovelle (1829–31; Paris: Messidor / Editions sociales, 1989), 426.

37. Bardin, *Sieur de Saint-Georges*, 95.

38. Noël, *Etre noir*, 134.

39. Peabody, *"There Are No Slaves,"* 113–29, 119.

40. Saugera, *Bordeaux, port négrier*, 291; Noël, *Etre noir*, 100–114.

41. Noël, *Etre noir*, 115–16, 123, 134, 157.

42. Sara E. Johnson, *Encyclopédie Noire: The Making of Moreau de Saint-Méry's Intellectual World* (Chapel Hill: University of North Carolina Press, 2023), 41.

43. Jennifer Palmer, *Intimate Bonds: Family and Slavery in the French Atlantic* (Philadelphia: University of Pennsylvania Press, 2016), 131–52.

44. Thomas Jefferson to Paul Bentalou, 25 August 1786, in *The Papers of Thomas Jefferson*, ed. Julian Boyd (Princeton, NJ: Princeton University Press, 1954), 10:296.

45. Rothschild, *Infinite History*, 82.

46. Jean Tarrade, "L'Administration coloniale en France à la fin de l'Ancien Régime: Projets de réforme," *Revue historique* 219 (1963): 103–25, 114.

47. Médéric Elie Moreau de Saint Méry, *Loix et constitutions des colonies françoises de l'Amérique*, 6 vols. (Paris: Moreau de Saint-Méry, 1784–90), 6:655–57.

48. Pierre Céleron de Blainville, letter, 8 May 1785, quoted in Gabriel Debien, *Les Esclaves aux Antilles Françaises (XVIIe–XVIIIe siècles)* (Basse-Terre: Sociétés d'histoire de la Guadeloupe et de la Martinique, 1974), 486.

Chapter Two

1. See Jean Ehrard, *Lumières et esclavage: L'Esclavage colonial et l'opinion publique en France au XVIIIe siècle* (Brussels: André Versaille, 2008), 27–32.

2. Montesquieu, *Esprit des lois*, bk. 15, ch. 1, in *Oeuvres complètes* (Paris: Seuil, 1964), 618.

3. Montesquieu, *Esprit des lois*, bk. 15, ch. 5, p. 620.

4. Montesquieu, *Esprit des lois*, bk. 15, ch. 7, p. 620.

5. Montesquieu, *Esprit des lois*, bk. 15, ch. 17, p. 623.

6. Montesquieu, *Esprit des lois*, bk. 15, ch. 18, p. 623.

7. Michel Figeac, "Pour ou contre l'esclavage: Un débat clivant au sein des élites portuaires," in Le Mao, *Mémoire noire*, 205–22, 209.

8. Chevalier de Jaucourt, "Traite des Nègres," in Denis Diderot and J. L. R. d'Alembert, *Encyclopédie, ou Dictionnaire raisonné des sciences, des arts, et des métiers*, 17 vols. (Paris: Briasson, 1751–1765), 16:532.

9. Samuel Formey, "Nègre," in Diderot and D'Alembert, *Encyclopédie*, 11:76; Denis Diderot, "Humaine Espèce," in Diderot and D'Alembert, *Encyclopédie*, 8:344.

10. "Nègres, commerce," in Diderot and D'Alembert, *Encyclopédie*, 11:79; Le Romain, "Nègres, considérés comme esclaves dans les colonies de l'Amérique," in Diderot and D'Alembert, *Encyclopédie*, 11:80–81.

11. Voltaire, *Traité de métaphysique*, in vol. 12 of *Oeuvres*, quoted in Pierre Boulle, *Race et esclavage dans la France de l'Ancien Régime* (Paris: Perrin, 2007), 28.

12. Christopher L. Miller, *The French Atlantic Triangle: Literature and Culture of the Slave Trade* (Durham, NC: Duke University Press, 2008), 428–29n62.

13. Jean-Jacques Rousseau, *Contrat social*, bk. 3, ch. 15, in *Oeuvres complètes* (Paris: Gallimard, 1964), 3:431. For a vehement critique of Rousseau's attitude toward Blacks and slavery, see Laurent Estève, *Montesquieu, Rousseau, Diderot: Du genre humain au bois d'ébène: Les silences du droit naturel* (Paris: UNESCO, 2002), 133–202. For a discussion of Rousseau's longest and most detailed discussion of slavery, incorporated in an unfinished novel, see Jeremy D. Popkin, "Émile in Chains: Rousseau, Algerian Captivity, and Hegel's *Phenomenology*," in *Mediterranean Slavery and World Literature*, ed. Mario Klarer et al. (London: Routledge, 2020), 294–311.

14. Quoted in Michèle Duchet, *Anthropologie et histoire au siècle des Lumières* (1971; Paris: Albin Michel, 1995), 162.

15. Victor Riqueti, marquis de Mirabeau, *L'Ami des hommes ou Traité de la population* (Avignon, 1756), 3:147.

16. *Journal de Commerce*, May 1759, cited in Pernille Røge, *Economists and the Reinvention of Empire: France in the Americas and Africa, c. 1750–1802* (Cambridge: Cambridge University Press, 2015), 97.

17. Clay, "'Cruel Necessity,'" 268.

18. [Jean Bellon de Saint-Quentin], *Dissertation sur la Traite et le Commerce des Nègres* (n.p., n.p., 1764), 69.

19. Jacques-Philibert Rousselot de Surgy, *Mélanges intéressants et curieux, ou Abrégé d'histoire naturelle, morale, civil et politique de l'Asie, l'Afrique, l'Amérique, et des terres polaires* (Paris: Lacombe, 1766), 10:164–66.

20. Sieyès quoted in William H. Sewell Jr., *A Rhetoric of Bourgeois Revolution: The Abbé Sieyès and "What Is the Third Estate?"* (Durham, NC: Duke University Press, 1994), 153–54. See also Angus H. Brown, "Republican Nostalgia, the Division of Labour, and the Origins of Inequality in the Thought of the Abbé Sieyès," *Intellectual History Review*, December 2022, https://doi.org/10.1080/17496977.2022.214977.

21. Simon-Henri-Nicolas Linguet, *Théorie des lois civiles* (Paris: Fayard, 1984 (orig. 1767)), 441, 582–83.

22. Linguet, *Théorie des lois civiles*, 514, 516.

23. Linguet, *Théorie des lois civiles*, 597, 599, 610, 612, 613.

24. Pierre-Samuel du Pont de Nemours, *Ephémérides du citoyen* (1771), 6:178–246, reprinted in *Analyse des Papiers Anglois*, 25 April 1788, 3 May 1788, 522–23.

25. Caroline Oudin-Bastide and Philippe Steiner, *Calcul et morale: Coûts de l'esclavage et valeur de l'émancipation (XVIIIe–XIXe siècle)* (Paris: Albin Michel, 2015), 52–54.

26. Jean François de Saint-Lambert, *Ziméo*, in *Les Saisons: Poème*, new ed. (1767; Paris: Pissot, 1785), 303, 311. On Tacky's Rebellion, see Vincent Brown, *Tacky's Revolt: The Story of an Atlantic Slave War* (Cambridge, MA: Harvard University Press, 2020).

27. Saint-Lambert, *Ziméo*, 304, 306.

28. On de Gouges's and de Staël's works, see Doris Y. Kadish and Françoise Massardier-Kenney, eds., *Translating Slavery: Gender and Race in French Women's Writing, 1783–1823* (Kent, OH: Kent State University Press, 1994).

29. Elisabeth Badinter and Robert Badinter, *Condorcet (1743–1794): Un intellectuel en politique* (Paris: Fayard, 1988), 199–200; Johnson, *Encyclopédie Noire*, 15.

30. Gary Kates, *The Books That Made the European Enlightenment: A History in 12 Case Studies* (London: Bloomsbury Academic, 2022), 301.

31. Doris Y. Kadish, "Translation in Context," in Kadish and Massardier-Kenney, *Translating Slavery*, 26–61, 45.

32. Bibliothèque de l'Arsenal, Fonds Mercier, Ms. 15801 (1), doc. 244.

33. The question of the authorship of the antislavery passages in the various editions of the *Histoire philosophique* has spawned an extensive literature in recent decades. For summaries of the debate, see Carminella Biondi, "L'Apport antiesclavagiste de Pechméja et de Diderot à l'*Histoire des deux Indes*," in *Guillaume Thomas Raynal: Les Colonies, l'esclavage et la Révolution française*, ed. Marcel Dorigny (Paris: Société française d'histoire des outre-mers, 2015), 49–64; and Ann Thomson, "Colonialism, Race and Slavery in Raynal's *Histoire des deux Indes*," *Global Intellectual History* 2017, no. 3 (2017): 251–67.

34. Pierre-Samuel du Pont de Nemours, *Ephémérides du citoyen* (1772), 3:184, quoted in Edward Derbyshire Seeber, *Anti-Slavery Opinion in France During the Second Half of the Eighteenth Century* (New York: Burt Franklin, 1937), 94.

35. [Guillaume Thomas Raynal], *Histoire philosophique et politique des établissemens et du commerce des Européens dans les deux Indes*, 6 vols. (Amsterdam, 1770), 4:119, 155. Citations to the *Histoire des deux Indes* are from the digital versions available on the University of Chicago's ARTFL web site : https://artflsrv03.uchicago.edu/philologic4/raynal/.

36. *Histoire des deux Indes* (1770), 4:156; Guillaume Thomas Raynal, *Histoire philosophique et politique des établissements et du commerce des Européens dans les deux Indes*, 3rd ed., 10 vols. (Geneva: Pellet, 1780), 3:1780.

37. [Guillaume Thomas Raynal], *Histoire philosophique et politique des établissements et du commerce des Européens dans les deux Indes*, 2nd ed., 7 vols. (La Haye, 1774), 4:226; (1780), 3:204–5.

38. Quoted in Laurent Dubois, *Avengers of the New World* (Cambridge, MA: Harvard University Press, 2004), 57.

39. *Histoire des deux Indes* (1770), 4:173–74; (1774), 4:226; (1780), 3:204.

40. Condorcet, *Vie de Monsieur Turgot* (London, 1786), 65.

41. Badinter and Badinter, *Condorcet*, 17–18. On Brissot's condemnation of whippings in school, see Régis Coursin, *Jacques-Pierre Brissot: Sociologie historique d'une entrée en révolution* (Rennes: Presses Universitaires de Rennes, 2023), 30.

42. Condorcet, "Remarques sur les pensées de Pascal," in *Oeuvres de Condorcet*, ed. A. Condorcet O'Connor and M. F. Arago (Paris: Didot, 1847; repr., 1968), 3:635–62, 644, 647.

43. [Condorcet], *Réflexions sur l'esclavage des nègres, par M. Schwartz, pasteur du Saint-Evangile à Bienne, membre de la société économique de B****** (Neufchâtel: Société Typographique, 1781), 1.

44. Condorcet, *Réflexions sur l'esclavage des nègres*, 35.

45. Duchet, *Anthropologie et histoire*, 154. Condorcet added a reference to the Pennsylvania law in the 1788 edition of his pamphlet.

46. Jacques Necker, *De l'administration des finances de la France* (n.p., n.p., 1784), 1:317–18.

47. Nicolas Bergier, *Traité historique et dogmatique de la vraie religion* (Paris: Moutard, 1780), 11:472; Nicolas Bergier, "Esclavage," in *Encyclopédie méthodique: Théologie* (Paris: Panckoucke, 1790), 1:671. On Bergier's attitude toward slavery and race, see Patrick Graille and Andrew Curran, "Un apologiste abolitionniste: L'Abbé Bergier et les Négres de 1767 à 1789," *Société française d'Etude du Dix-Huitième Siècle*, no. 48 (2016): 517–32.

48. Marie-Pierre Le Hir, "Feminism, Theater, Race," in Kadish and Massardier-Kenney, *Translating Slavery*, 65–83; Françoise Massardier-Kenney, "Staël, Translation, and Race," in Kadish and Massardier-Kenney, *Translating Slavery*, 135–45.

49. Nicolas Baudeau, "Nègres," in *Dictionnaire encyclopédique du commerce* (Paris: Panckoucke, 1783–84), 3:321; Jean-Nicolas Démeunier, "Nègres," in

Dictionnaire d'economie politique et diplomatique (Paris: Panckoucke, 1788), 3:413; Nicolas Bergier, "Esclavage" and "Nègres," in Bergier, ed., *Dictionnaire de théologie* (Paris: Panckoucke, 1788), 1:668–71; 2:746–50.

50. Emilien Petit, *Traité sur le gouvernement des esclaves* (Paris: Knapen, 1777), 2:29; [Emilien Petit], *Observations sur plusieurs assertions extraites littéralement de l'Histoire Philosophique des Etablissements des Européens dans les deux Indes, édition de 1770* (Amsterdam: Knapen, 1776), 223–24.

51. M. R. Hilliard d'Auberteuil, *Considérations sur l'état présent de la colonie française de Saint-Domingue* (Paris: Grangé, 1776), 1:130–32.

52. David Duval-Sanadon, *Discours sur l'esclavage des nègres, et sur l'idée de leur affranchissement dans les colonies* (Amsterdam: Hardouin et Gattey, 1786), 123–24.

53. [Pierre-Victor Malouet], *Essai sur l'administration de St. Domingue* (n.p., n.p., 1785), 38–39. Malouet claimed the authorship of the *Essai* in the introduction to a republication of his various writings about the colonies published during the Napoleonic regime: Pierre-Victor Malouet, *Collection de mémoires sur les colonies, et particulièrement sur Saint-Domingue* (Paris: Baudouin, An X [1802]), 4:54.

54. A. A., "Mulâtres," in *Supplément à l'encyclopédie* (Amsterdam: M. M. Rey, 1776), 3:973–74.

55. On the role of Black authors in American debates, see Manisha Sinha, *The Slave's Cause: A History of Abolition* (New Haven, CT: Yale University Press, 2016), 42–47; and Edward J. Larson, *American Inheritance: Liberty and Slavery in the Birth of a Nation, 1765–1795* (New York: W. W. Norton, 2023), 69–76.

56. Julien Raimond, mémoires (1783–86), AN, Col. F 3 91, fols. 177–92. I would like to thank John Garrigus for sharing his transcription of these documents with me.

57. Jean François de Saint-Lambert, "Réflexions sur les moyens de rendre meilleur l'état des Nègres et des affranchis de nos colonies," in Duchet, *Anthropologie et histoire*, 181–87, 181, 187.

58. Lafayette to Washington, 5 February 1783, cited in https://founders.archives.gov/documents/Washington/99-01-02-10575 (accessed 7 July 2025).

59. J. Hector St. John de Crèvecoeur, *Lettres d'un cultivateur américain* (Paris: Cuchet, 1784), 1:xv–xix, 2:361–78.

60. François Jean de Beauvoir, marquis de Chastellux, *Travels in North-America, in the Years 1780, 1781, and 1782* (French ed., 1786; London: Robinson, 1787), 2:295.

61. Thomas Jefferson, *Notes on the State of Virginia*, in *The Life and Selected Writings of Thomas Jefferson*, ed. Adrienne Koch and William Peden (New York: Modern Library, 1994), 255–62, 279.

62. [Jean-Nicolas Démeunier], *L'Amerique indépendante, ou les différentes constitutions des treize provinces qui se sont érigées en républiques, sous le nom d'Etats-Unis de l'Amérique* (1786; Gand: De Goesin, 1790), 1:193–94. Jefferson had furnished Démeunier with the passage he incorporated into the work in a letter of 26 June 1786. Jefferson, Thomas, 1743–1826, Miscellany, Electronic Text Center, University of Virginia Library.

63. Filippo Mazzei, *Recherches historiques et politiques* (Paris: Fouillé, 1786–88), 2:14, 127, 4:131, 140.

64. Jacques-Pierre Brissot, *Examen critique des voyages dans l'Amérique septentrionale, de M. le Marquis de Chatellux* (London, 1786), 95, 90, 99.

Chapter Three

1. Jean Egret, *The French Prerevolution, 1787–1788*, trans. Wesley D. Camp (1962; Chicago: University of Chicago Press, 1977), 4.

2. Minutes of the Société Gallo-Américaine, John Carter Brown Library, Codex fr. 15, 9 January, 6 March, 3 April 1787.

3. On the reasons for historians' neglect of Brissot, see Pierre Serna, "Le pari politique de Brissot ou lorsque le Patriote Français, l'Abolitionniste Anglais et le Citoyen Américain sont unis en une seule figure de la liberté républicaine," *La Révolution française* no. 5 (2013).

4. The standard edition of Brissot's memoirs is Jacques-Pierre Brissot, *Mémoires (1754–1793)*, 2 vols., ed. Claude Perroud (Paris: Picard, 1911), supplemented by Jacques-Pierre Brissot, *Correspondance et papiers*, ed. Claude Perroud (Paris: Picard, 1912). Perroud did not have access to the Brissot papers donated to the Archives Nationales in the 1980s, which include the draft of Brissot's trial defense in 446 AP 13–14. Comparison of that document with the published *Mémoires* shows that it is the source for much of the content of the latter, but there are some significant differences between the two.

5. Leonore Loft, *Passion, Politics, and Philosophie: Rediscovering J.-P. Brissot* (Westport, CT: Greenwood, 2002), xviii; Jonathan Israel, *Revolutionary Ideas: An Intellectual History of the French Revolution from "The Rights of Man" to Robespierre* (Princeton, NJ: Princeton University Press, 2014), 478.

6. Serious scholarship on Brissot began with Eloise Ellery, *Brissot de Warville: A Study in the History of the French Revolution* (1915; New York: Burt Franklin, 1970). The prominent American Enlightenment scholar Robert Darnton's widely read article "The Grub Street of Style of Revolution: J.-P. Brissot, Police Spy," *Journal of Modern History* 40, no. 3 (1968): 301–27, put a serious dent in Brissot's reputation by alleging that he had been a spy for the police in the years before the Revolution. Simon Burrows, "The Innocence of Jacques-Pierre Brissot," *Historical Journal* 46, no. 4 (2003): 843–71, critiques Darnton's claim. Suzanne d'Huart, *Brissot: La Gironde au pouvoir* (Paris: Robert Laffont, 1986), the first scholarly biography of him in French, called him an "enigmatic man," a "superficial" writer, an orator who lacked "the gift of eloquence." Bette Oliver, *Jacques Pierre Brissot in America and France, 1788–1793* (Lanham, MD: Lexington Books, 2016), is the only biography that concentrates on Brissot's role during the Revolution. The most recent study of Brissot, Régis Coursin, *Jacques-Pierre Brissot: Sociologie historique d'une entrée en révolution* (Rennes: Presses Universitaires de Rennes, 2023), acknowledges the sincerity of his idealism but concludes that he lacked the political judgment necessary to survive in the revolutionary environment.

7. Brissot, *Correspondance et papiers*, 349.

8. Jérôme Pétion, "Notice sur Brissot," in *Charlotte de Corday et les Girondins, pièces classées et annotées*, by M. Charles Vatel, 3 vols. (Paris: Plon, 1864–72), 2:231.

9. Marie Jeanne Phlipon Roland de la Platière, *Mémoires de Madame Roland*, ed. C. A. Dauban (Paris: Plon, 1864), 230; letter of 23 July 1792, AN, 446 AP 8.

10. British committee to Brissot, 27 August and 4 November 1787, in *La Société des Amis des Noirs*, ed. Marcel Dorigny and Bernard Gainot (Paris: Editions UNESCO, 1998), 63–64; Brissot to Joseph Wood and James Philips, 13 October 1787, Cambridge University, St. John's College Library, Special Collections, Clarkson Papers, folder 1–5, doc. 2.

11. Jacques-Pierre Brissot, "Notes relatives au plan de conduite pour les députés du peuple aux Etats-Généraux de 1789," appendix to Brissot, *Plan de conduite pour les députés du peuple aux Etats-généraux de 1789* (Paris, 1789), 27. On Lafayette's purchase of several plantations in the French colony of Cayenne (today's French Guiana), see Albert Krebs, "La Fayette et le problème de l'esclavage," *Annuaire-Bulletin de la Société de l'histoire de France* (1956–57): 49–60; and David Allen Harvey, *Tropical Despotisms: Enlightened Reform in the French Caribbean* (Ithaca, NY: Cornell University Press, 2024), 187–91.

12. Jefferson to Brissot, 11 February 1788, in Dorigny and Gainot, *Amis des Noirs*, 94.

13. Dorigny and Gainot, *Amis des Noirs*, 68.

14. Translated articles on slavery in issues of the *Analyse de papiers anglois* before the first meeting of the Amis des Noirs included "Troisième mélanges sur l'esclavage: Morceau tiré des *Principes de philosophe morale et politique*," originally published in *Universal Magazine*, July 1787 (24 January 1788); "Plan pour abolir entièrement l'esclavage des Negres, dans les possessions Britanniques" (31 January 1788); and "Suite du fragment sur l'abolition de l'esclavage des Nègres" (15 February 1788).

15. Brissot, *Mémoires*, 2:38.

16. [Jacques-Pierre Brissot], *Discours sur la nécessité d'établir à Paris une société pour concourir, avec celle de Londres, à l'abolition de la traite & de l'esclavage des Nègres* (Paris, 1788), reprinted in *La Révolution française et l'abolition de l'esclavage* (Paris: Editions d'histoire sociale, 1968), 6:3–4.

17. Catherine Duprat, *"Pour l'amour de l'humanité": Le Temps des philanthropes: La Philanthropie parisienne des Lumières à la monarchie de Juillet* (Paris: CTHS, 1993), 125.

18. Marcel Dorigny, "La Société des Amis des Noirs: Antiesclavagisme et lobby colonial à la fin du siècle des Lumières (1788–1792)," in Dorigny and Gainot, *Amis des Noirs*, 40.

19. [Brissot], *Discours sur la nécessité*, 5, 9, 24–25.

20. [Brissot], *Discours sur la nécessité*, 6, 14.

21. [Brissot], *Discours sur la nécessité*, 23.

22. [Brissot], *Discours sur la nécessité*, 26, 28, 31.

23. *Journal de Paris*, 25 February 1788.

24. Amis des Noirs, session of 18 March 1788, in Dorigny and Gainot, *Amis des Noirs*, 109.

25. Dorigny and Gainot, *Amis des Noirs*, 139.

26. For an overview of Condorcet's life, see Badinter and Badinter, *Condorcet.* The detailed analyses of Condorcet's thought in Keith Baker, *Condorcet, from Natural Philosophy to Social Mathematics* (Chicago: University of Chicago Press, 1975), and Rolf Reichardt, *Reform und Revolution bei Condorcet* (Bonn: Röhrscheid, 1973), both neglect his involvement in the campaign against slavery. Emma Rothschild, *Economic Sentiments: Adam Smith, Condorcet, and the Enlightenment* (Cambridge, MA: Harvard University Press, 2001), gives more attention to the subject.

27. Badinter and Badinter, *Condorcet*, 80.

28. Brissot, *Patriote françois*, 10 October 1789.

29. Dorigny and Gainot, *Amis des Noirs*, 163.

30. Dorigny and Gainot, *Amis des Noirs*, 136–37.

31. "Mémoire au roi," April 1788, in "Journal Historique du Comité colonial de St. Domingue, t. I," Library of Congress, Ms. MMC 2671, pp. 6–35, 18–20. This explicit defense of slavery was omitted from the version of the letter to the king, dated 31 May 1788, that was included with the documents the colonists eventually submitted in support of their demand for representation in the Estates General in 1789, from which most mentions of slavery were deleted (AN, B III 135). The marquis Gouy d'Arsy, who took the lead in the campaign for representation in the Estates General, published a highly condensed version of some of these documents in 1788: Louis-Marthe Gouy d'Arsy, *Lettre du comité colonial de France, au comité colonial de Saint-Domingue; contenant le journal historique de toutes les assemblées, délibérations, démarches & opérations de la commission nommée par les colons résidans à Paris; d'après les pouvoirs de ceux résidans dans la colonie, depuis le 15 Juillet 1788, époque de la nomination de la Commission jusqu'à ce jour* ([Paris, 1788]).

32. Médéric Elie Moreau de Saint-Méry, *Mémoire justificatif pour M. Moreau de Saint-Méry* (Paris: Baudouin, 1790), 14–16. On Moreau de Saint-Méry, see Anthony-Louis Elicona, *Un colonial sous la Révolution en France et en Amérique: Moreau de Saint-Méry* (Paris: Jouve, 1934); Dominique Taffin, ed., *Moreau de Saint-Méry ou les ambiguités d'un créole des Lumières* (Martinique: Société des Amis des Archives et de la Recherche sur le Patrimoine culturel des Antilles, 2006); and Johnson, *Encyclopédie Noire.*

33. Moreau de Saint-Méry, *Mémoire justificatif*, 10, 35. On the Cercle des Philadelphes, see James E. McClellan, *Colonialism and Science: Saint-Domingue in the Old Regime* (Baltimore: Johns Hopkins University Press, 1992).

34. *Journal de Paris*, 1 March 1788; *Mercure de France*, 22 March 1788. The *Essai sur l'administration des colonies françaises* (Paris: Monory, 1788), which mentioned slavery only in one footnote, is attributed to an otherwise unknown colonist named Bleschamps.

35. Moreau de Saint-Méry, *Mémoire justificatif*, 17.

36. Edna Hindie Lemay, *Dictionnaire des constituants 1789–1791* (Paris: Universitas, 1991), 1:422–23. On Gouy d'Arsy's involvement with the Compagnie des eaux, see Jean Bouchary, *L'Eau à Paris à la fin du XVIIIe Siècle: La Compagnie des eaux de Paris et l'entreprise de l'Yvette* (Paris: Marcel Rivière, 1946), 95, 99–103.

37. "Lettre adressée au roi par les propriétaires planteurs &c de la colonie de St. Domingue," 31 May 1788, AN, B III 135.

38. "Lettre adressée au roi," 5, 9–10, 17–18.

39. Amis des Noirs, session of 19 August 1788, in Dorigny and Gainot, *Amis des Noirs*, 175.

40. "Journal Historique du Comité colonial de St. Domingue, t. I" (Sept. 1788), Library of Congress, Ms. MMC 2671; AN, B III 135, pp. 77–78; Gouy d'Arsy, address to the "people" of Saint-Domingue, 30 September 1788, AN, D XXV 13, document hors chemise.

41. "Journal historique," session of 9 September 1788, Library of Congress, Ms. MMC 2671, p. 124. On Reynaud, see Lemay, *Dictionnaire des constituants*, 2:804.

42. "Journal historique," session of 26 September 1788, Library of Congress, Ms. MMC 2671, p. 180. Further discussions of Mirabeau's possible role in supporting the colonists occurred on 11 October, 16 October, and 25 October 1788.

43. "Journal historique," October 1788, Ms. MMC 2671, pp. 175–76, 187, 210, 213–14.

44. Duc de Castries, *Mirabeau* (Paris: Fayard, 1960), 271–75.

45. Lucas de Montigny, cited in Marcel Dorigny, ed., *Les Bières flottantes des négriers: Un discours non prononcé sur l'abolition de la traite des Noirs (novembre 1789–mars 1790)* (Saint-Etienne: Publications de l'Université de Saint-Etienne, 1999), 38.

46. "Journal historique," session of 25 October 1788, Library of Congress, Ms. MMC 2671, p. 224.

47. Malouet to Gouy d'Arsy, 4 November 1788, in "Journal historique," 242–43.

48. "Copie de la requête en forme de protestation contre les démarches faites à Paris pour obtenir l'admission aux Etats Généraux, des députés de la colonie," AN, B III 35, pp. 565–74.

49. Marquis de Paroy to Larchevesque-Thibaud, 21 September 1788, in Blanche Maurel, *Cahiers de doléances de la colonie de Saint-Domingue pour les Etats-généraux de 1789* (Paris: Librairie Ernest Leroux, 1933), 138.

50. La Luzerne, *Mémoire envoyé le 18 juin 1790, au comité des rapports de l'Assemblée nationale, par M. de Luzerne, ministre et secrétaire d'état* (Paris: Imprimerie royale, 1790), 5–11.

51. "Mémoire instructif remis aux notables par MM. les commissaires de la colonie de Saint-Domingue sur le régime et l'importance de cette colonie," n.d. but November 1788, in AN, B III 135, p. 344.

52. Ambassador Dorset to Duke of Leeds, 2 April 1789, in *Despatches from Paris, 1784–1790*, ed. Oscar Browning (London: Offices of the Society, 1910), 2:181.

53. On the Society of Thirty, see Daniel L. Wick, "A Conspiracy of Well-Intentioned Men" (PhD diss., University of California–Davis, 1977). Wick lists the group's members on 45–48.

54. Robert Blanc, *Un pasteur du temps des Lumières: Benjamin-Sigismond Frossard (1754–1830)* (Paris: Honoré Champion, 2000), 47, 72.

55. Malouet to Gouy d'Arsy, 4 November 1788, in "Journal historique," Library of Congress, Ms. MMC 2671, n.p.

56. Benjamin-Sigismond Frossard, *La Cause des esclaves nègres et des habitans de la Guinée, portée au tribunal de la justice, de la religion, de la politique* (Lyon: Aimé de la Roche, 1789), vol. 2.

57. Frossard, *La Cause des esclaves nègres*, 2:v–vi.

58. *Journal de Lyon*, 31 December 1788, quoted in Blanc, *Un pasteur du temps*, 118; Dorigny and Gainot, *Amis des Noirs*, 224.

59. [Jacques-Pierre Brissot], *Mémoire sur les Noirs de l'Amérique septentrionale, lu à l'Assemblée de la Société des Amis des Noirs, le 9 février 1789* (Paris: Bureau du Patriote françois, 1789), reprinted in *La Révolution française et l'abolition de l'esclavage*, vol. 7, no. 3.

60. Jacques-Pierre Brissot, *Plan de Conduite pour les Députés du Peuple aux Etats-Généraux de 1789* (Paris: n.p., 1789).

61. Dorigny and Gainot, *Amis des Noirs*, 194 (27 January 1789), 196 (3 February 1789), 213 (31 March 1789); [Condorcet], *Au Corps électoral, contre l'esclavage des Noirs* (1789; Paris: Éditions d'histoire sociale, 1968), vol. 6, no. 7–8.

62. *Observations présentées à l'assemblée de MM. les electeurs de la partie du Nord de Saint-Domingue, par M. Bacon de la Chevalerie, représentant de la paroisse de Limonade, le 27 janvier 1789, au Cap-Français* (Paris: Quillau, 1789), 2. Other pro-planter pamphlets intended to influence the Estates General elections included *Premier recueil de pièces intéressantes, remises par les commissaires de la colonie de Saint-Domingue, à MM. les notables, le 6 Novembre 1788* (n.p., n.d.) and *Extrait du registre des délibérations du comité colonial de St.-Domingue, séant à Paris: Du 21 mars 1789* (n.p., n.d.).

63. Guy Chaussinand-Nogaret, *Mirabeau* (Paris: Seuil, 1982), 137.

64. Hans-Jürgen Lüsebrink, "Le rôle de Raynal et la réception de l'Histoire des deux Indes pendant la Révolution française," in *Lectures de Raynal: "L'Histoire des deux Indes" en Europe et en Amérique au XVIIIe siècle*, ed. Hans-Jürgen Lüsebrink and Manfred Tietz (Oxford: Voltaire Foundation, 1991), 87.

65. Lemay, *Dictionnaire des constituants*, 2:497, 628.

66. Badinter and Badinter, *Condorcet*, 262–65; Elisabeth Badinter, ed., *Correspondance inédite de Condorcet et Mme Suard, M. Suard et Garat (1771–1791)* (Paris: Fayard, 1988), 249–50.

67. Brissot, *Correspondance et papiers*, 233n.

68. Lemay, *Dictionnaire des constituants*, 1:278.

69. Moreau de Saint-Méry, *Mémoire justificatif*, 19.

70. Lucie Maquerlot, "Rouen et Le Havre face à la traite et à l'esclavage: Le Mouvement de l'opinion (1783–1794)," in *Esclavage, résistances, abolitions*, ed. Marcel Dorigny (Paris: Editions du CTHS, 1999), 165–83, 173.

71. AP, 1:754 (Amiens, Third Estate).

72. AP, 3:736 (Melun, clergy).

73. AP, 4:36 (Mont-de-Marsan, Third Estate), 3:760 (Metz, clergy).

74. AP, 5:525 (Reims, clergy).

75. AP, 3:662 (Mantes, noblesse).

76. AP, 3:659–60 (Mantes, clergy).

77. AP, 5:525 (Reims, Third Estate).

78. In addition to the Mantes clergy, the clergy of Alençon urged the Estates General to grant the group official recognition. AP, 1:710.

79. Marcel Dorigny, "The Abbé Grégoire and the *Société des Amis des Noirs*," in *The Abbé Grégoire and His World*, ed. Jeremy D. Popkin and Richard H. Popkin (Dordrecht: Kluwer, 2000), 29–30. On the role of religious arguments in antislavery debates during the Revolution, see Jeremy D. Popkin, "Religion and Anti-Slavery in Revolutionary France and Saint-Domingue," *Slavery and Abolition* 46, no. 1 (2025): 84–99.

80. AP, 5:357, 2:643.

81. AP, 2:676.

82. AP, 5:182.

83. AP, 5:289, 182.

84. AP, 5:275.

85. Dorigny and Gainot, *Amis des Noirs*, 217–18 (7 April 1789).

86. AP, 2:401, 3:484, 3:534, 4:97, 5:348, 5:600.

87. AP, 4:97.

88. *Réponse à l'écrit de M. Malouet, sur l'esclavage des nègres* (1789; Paris: Éditions d'histoire sociale, 1968).

89. *Journal de Paris*, 11 April 1789, letter of Malouet, 2 April 1789; *Journal de Paris*, letter of 22 April 1789.

90. Jacques-Pierre Brissot, *Mémoire aux Etats-Généraux: Sur la nécessité de rendre dès ce moment la presse libre, et surtout pour les journaux politiques* (Paris, 1789); Mirabeau, prospectus for *Etats-Généraux* (Paris: Le Jay, 1789).

Chapter Four

1. Olivier Gliech, *Saint-Domingue und die Französische Revolution: Das Ende der weißen Herrschaft in einer karibischen Plantagenwirtschaft* (Cologne: Böhlau, 2011), 230. This figure, based on an examination of the documents about compensation payments made to former plantation owners in 1826, does not include the colonial deputies who were eventually seated; it also excludes deputies who may have had property or relatives in Martinique, Guadeloupe, or the Mascarene Islands.

2. *Supplement* to *Journal de Paris*, 14 May 1789, viii. Aside from the subsidy to the slave trade, Necker claimed that other royal subventions to commerce amounted to 3.8 million livres a year; the slave traders were thus receiving 39 percent of all the money the government was giving to promote trade.

3. *Supplement to Journal de Paris*, 14 May 1789, xvii; Wilberforce quote in *New Annual Register*, 1789, 156.

4. *Supplement* to *Journal de Paris*, 14 May 1789, xxvii.

5. Jacques-Pierre Brissot, "Aux Etats Géneraux sur les plans de M. Necker," AN, 446 AP 13–14.

6. Prosper Boissonnade, *Saint-Domingue à la veille de la Révolution et la question des la représentation coloniale aux Etats-Généraux (janvier 1788–7 juillet 1789)*

(Paris: Paul Geuthner, 1906), 219–22; *Requête présentée au Etats-Généraux du royaume, le 8 juin 1789, par les députés de l'Isle Saint-Domingue* (n.p., n.p., 1789) ; Jacques-Antoine Creuzé-Latouche, *Journal des Etats généraux et du début de l'Assemblée nationale 18 mai–29 juillet 1789*, ed. Jean Marchand (Paris: Henri Didier, 1946), 75.

7. Adrien Duquesnoy, *Journal d'Adrien Duquesnoy*, ed. Robert de Crèvecoeur (Paris: A. Picard, 1894), 1:81.

8. Duquesnoy, *Journal d'Adrien Duquesnoy*, 1:91; Pierre-Paul Nairac, "Etats généraux de 1789: Ordre du tiers Etat," Archives de l'Eure, V F 63, p. 57, entry for 14 June 1789. I would like to thank Timothy Tackett for lending me a photocopy of Nairac's manuscript chronicle.

9. *New Annual Register*, 1789, 154, 159.

10. *Journal de Paris*, 10 June 1789.

11. Dorigny and Gainot, *Amis des Noirs*, 229 (16 June 1789).

12. [Condorcet], *Sur l'admission des députés des planteurs de Saint-Domingue, dans l'Assemblée nationale* (June 1789; Paris: Editions d'histoire sociale, 1968), 163.

13. For the dating of Brissot's *Plan de conduite*, see Dorigny and Gainot, *Amis des Noirs*, 224.

14. J. P. Brissot de Warville, *Réflexions sur l'admission, aux Etats-Généraux, des députés de Saint-Domingue* (n.p., n.d.), 10, 32.

15. Jacques-Pierre Brissot, "Note sur l'admission des planteurs," in appendix to *Plan de conduite*, 23.

16. Brissot, "Note sur l'admission," 24–25; Elbridge Gerry quoted in Sean Wilentz, *No Property in Man: Slavery and Antislavery at the Nation's Founding* (Cambridge, MA: Harvard University Press, 2019), 62. For Mirabeau's appropriation of the line, see *Lettres à mes commettans*, 26–27 June 1789.

17. Brissot, *Refléxions sur l'admission*, 34–35.

18. *Point du jour*, 21 June 1789. The marquis de Ferrières gave a shorter account of Gouy d'Arsy's speech in a letter to his wife on 22 June 1789, in Marquis de Ferrières, *Correspondance inédite (1789, 1790, 1791)*, ed. Henri Carré (Paris: Armand Colin, 1932), 72.

19. *Point du jour*, 21 June 1789.

20. *Point du jour*, 22 June 1789; *Journal des Etats généraux*, 1:169. Gouy d'Arsy had prepared a lengthy justification of the colonists' demands: *Précis sur la position actuelle de la députation de Saint-Domingue, aux Etats-Généraux* (Versailles, 20 June 1789).

21. Count based on press accounts published by the *Courier de Provence*, the *Point du jour*, the *Journal des Etats généraux*, the *Journal de Paris*, and the *Assemblée nationale: Bulletins de correspondance réunies des clergé et de la Sénéchaussée de Rennes*, as well as those recorded in Creuzé-Latouche's diary.

22. *Point du jour*, 28 June 1789.

23. *Point du jour*, 28 June 1789; *Journal des Etats généraux*, 1:260; *Assemblée nationale: Bulletins de correspondance réunies des clergé et de la Sénéchaussée de Rennes*, 1 July 1789; *Journal de Paris*, 29 June 1789.

24. *Point du jour*, 28 June 1789.

25. Dorigny and Gainot, *Amis des Noirs*, 235.

26. *Lettres à mes commettans*, 7–12 June 1789, 2; *Lettres à mes commettans*, 26 June 1789. The *Archives parlementaires* includes Mirabeau's phrase in its account of his speech on 3 July 1789, but other summaries of his remarks on that occasion do not mention it.

27. Nairac, "Etats généraux de 1789," 94–95, entry for 27 June 1789.

28. *Point du jour*, 4 July 1789.

29. *Journal des Etats généraux*, 1:331–32.

30. One of two brothers both elected to the Estates General, Dominique-Joseph Garat served briefly as minister of justice and then minister of the interior after the proclamation of the Republic in 1792, and was later a minor member of the Idéologue group during the Directory period. Lemay, *Dictionnaire des constituants*, 1:386–88.

31. *Lettres à mes commettans*, no. 16, 5–6, 16.

32. *Lettres à mes commettans*, no. 16, 18–19.

33. *Point du jour*, 4 July 1789.

34. *Point du jour*, 5 July 1789.

35. AP, 4 July 1789, 8:189.

36. *Aux colons de Saint-Domingue* (Paris: Cellot, 1789), 16, 19.

37. Creuzé-Latouche, *Journal des Etats généraux*, 183; *Journal des Etats généraux*, 1:349–51.

38. Francisque Mège, ed., *Gaultier de Biauzat, député du tiers-état aux Etats-Généraux de 1789: Sa vie et sa correspondance* (Clermont-Ferrand: Michel Bellet et fils, 1890), 2:160 (entry for 4 July 1789).

39. Sieyès to Brissot, 4 July 1789, in Brissot, *Correspondance et papiers*, 237.

40. Mitchell Bennett Garrett, *The French Colonial Question, 1789–1791* (Ann Arbor: George Wahr, 1918), 16.

41. *Patriote françois*, 12 August 1789.

42. *Courier de Provence*, 3–5 August 1789, 19.

43. Moreau de Saint-Méry, *Mémoire justificatif*, 21; Antoine-François Delandine, *Troisième mémorial historique des Etats généraux* (Paris, 1789), 164; *Journal de Paris*, 3 August 1789.

44. Honoré Gabriel Mirabeau, *Aux Bataves*, in *La Déclaration des droits de l'homme et du citoyen*, ed. Stéphane Rials (Paris: Hachette, 1988), 519.

45. Emmanuel Sieyès, *Instruction donnée par S.A.S. le duc d'Orléans à ses représentants aux bailliages*, cited in Rials, *Déclaration des droits*, 539; Condorcet, *Declaration des droits*, in Rials, *Déclaration des droits*, 549.

46. Jacques-Pierre Brissot, 1 May 1789, in Rials, *Déclaration des droits*, 563.

47. Declaration of rights from the *cahier de doléances* of the Third Estate of Nemours, in Rials, *Déclaration des droits*, 552.

48. Sieyès, *Déclaration des droits du citoyen français*, in Rials, *Déclaration des droits*, 596, emphasis in original.

49. Guy-Jean-Baptiste Target, in Rials, *Déclaration des droits*, 610.

50. Charles-François Bouche, in Rials, *Déclaration des droits*, 687; François Louis LeGrand de Boislandry, in Rials, *Déclaration des droits*, 727.

51. Alexis-François Pison de Galland, in Rials, *Déclaration des droits*, 719; Pétion, in Rials, *Déclaration des droits*, 726.

52. Jean-Paul Rabaut Saint-Etienne, in Rials, *Déclaration des droits*, 672, 679–82.

53. Pierre-Victor Malouet, speech of 1 August 1789, in AP, 8:322–23.

54. Jeremy D. Popkin, "Declarations of Rights," in *The Cambridge History of Rights*, vol. 4, *The Eighteenth and Nineteen Centuries*, ed. Dan Edelstein and Jennifer Pitts (Cambridge: Cambridge University Press, 2025), 200–227.

55. "Copie de la lettre écrite par MM. les députés de Saint-Domingue, à leurs constituans au Cap," dated Versailles, 12 August 1789, in *Patriote françois*, 2 March 1790.

56. *Courier de Provence*, 20–21 August 1789, 3.

57. *Courier de Provence*, 20–21 August 1789, 3–4.

58. *Courier de Provence*, 20–21 August 1789, 4–5.

59. *Patriote françois*, 24 August 1789.

60. *Affiches américaines* (Port-au-Prince edition), 11 November 1789.

Chapter Five

1. *Patriote françois*, 11 November 1789.

2. The most extensive analysis of the first French constitution is François Furet and Ran Halévi, *La Monarchie républicaine: La Constitution de 1791* (Paris: Fayard, 1996), which, however, says almost nothing about the issues of slavery and the colonies.

3. The two sides of the debate are represented by David Waldstreicher, *Slavery's Constitution: From Revolution to Ratification* (New York: Hill and Wang, 2009), which emphasizes the ways in which the Constitution protected slavery; and Wilentz, *No Property in Man*, which argues that the Constitution was meant to facilitate eventual abolition. The debates that took place in the states as well as at the Constitutional Convention are covered in Edward J. Larson, *American Inheritance: Liberty and Slavery in the Birth of a Nation, 1765–1795* (New York: Norton, 2023).

4. Condorcet to Brissot, 15 August 1789, in *Condorcet: Lettres inédites à Brissot (1784–1791)*, ed. Virginie Martin and Nicolas Rieucau (Paris: Société française d'étude du dix-huitième siècle, 2024).

5. Procès-verbaux de la Société correspondante des Colons [Club Massiac], 20 August 1789, AN, D XXV 85, d. 818.

6. An old study by Gabriel Debien, *Les Colons de Saint-Domingue et la Révolution: Essai sur le Club Massiac (août 1789–août 1792)* (Paris: Armand Colin, 1953), exaggerates the success of the club in uniting the proslavery forces. Sonia Taleb, "Une relecture des origines du Club Massiac, entre Saint-Domingue et metropole, 1788–1790," *La Révolution française* 27 (January 2025), https://journals.openedition.org/lrf/8997, emphasizes the opposition between the colonial deputies in the National Assembly and the majority of the club members.

7. On du Chilleau's decision, see Manuel Covo, *Entrepôt of Revolutions: Saint-Domingue, Commercial Sovereignty, and the French-American Alliance* (New York: Oxford University Press, 2022), 75–79.

8. Quoted in Joseph Letaconnoux, "Le Comité des députés extraordinaires des manufactures et du commerce de France et l'oeuvre économique de l'Assemblée constituante (1789–1791)," *Annales Révolutionnaires* 6 (March–April 1913): 155, 156; Jean-Michel Deveau, *Le Commerce rochelais face à la Révolution* (La Rochelle: Rumeur des Ages, 1989), 67. On the lobbying efforts of the French merchant community, see Lauren Clay, "Liberty, Equality, Slavery: Debating the Slave Trade in Revolutionary France," *American Historical Review* 128, no. 1 (2023): 89–119; and Marcel Treille, *Le Commerce de Nantes et la Révolution* (Paris: Sirey, 1908).

9. Thomas Clarkson, *The History of the Rise, Progress, and Accomplishment of the Abolition of the African Slave-Trade by the British Parliament* (London: Longman, Hurst, Rees and Orme, 1808), 2:134.

10. Nairac, letter of 3 September 1789, in Deveau, *Commerce rochelais*, 135–36.

11. Duval-Sanadon, letter of 24 August 1789, AN, D XXV 85, d. 822.

12. Procès-verbaux, 28 August 1789, AN D XXV 85, d. 818 (comment by Gouy d'Arsy); *Réponse des députés des manufactures et du commerce de France: Aux motions de MM. De Cocherel et de Reynaud, députés de l'isle de Saint-Domingue à l'Assemblée nationale* (Paris, 1789), 24; Begouën, letter of 24 December 1789, quoted in Maquerlot, "Rouen et Le Havre," 173.

13. Quoted in Gabriel Debien, *Gens de couleur libres et colons de Saint-Domingue devant la Constituante (1789–mars 1790)* (Montreal: Revue d'Histoire de l'Amérique française, 1951), 14.

14. "Procès-verbaux . . . Club Massiac," 26 August 1789, AN, D XXV, d. 818.

15. "Procès-verbaux . . . Club Massiac," 7 and 9 September 1789, AN, D XXV, d. 818.

16. *Extrait du procès-verbal de l'Assemblée des citoyens-libres et propriétaires de couleur des isles et colonies françoises, constituée sous le titre de Colons américains* (Paris, 1789), 3.

17. *Cahier, contenant les plaintes, doléances & réclamations des citoyens-libres et propriétaires de couleur, des isles et colonies françoises* (Paris, 1789), 1–2, 5, 7, 13.

18. *Extrait du procès-verbal de l'Assemblée des citoyens-libres et propriétaires de couleur des Isles et Colonies françoises, constituée sous le titre de Colons américains* (Paris, 22 September 1789).

19. *Adresse à l'Assemblée-Nationale, pour les citoyens-libres de couleur, des isles et colonies françoises* (Paris, 18 October 1789).

20. *Patriote françois*, 24 October 1789 (National Assembly session of 22 October); AP, 9:478 (22 October 1789).

21. Nairac, letter of early December 1789, in Deveau, *Commerce rochelais*, 159.

22. *Patriote françois*, 12 August 1789.

23. *Patriote françois*, 24 August 1789.

24. *Patriote françois*, 1 September 1789.

25. Condorcet to Brissot, 7 September 1789, in Martin and Rieucau, *Condorcet*.

26. Clarkson, *History of the Rise*, 2:141.

27. Clarkson to Mirabeau, 14 November 1789, Fonds Mirabeau, 102, Musée-Bibliothèque Paul Arbaud, Aix-en-Provence. I would like to thank Lauren Clay for sharing her photographs of these documents with me.

28. Letter from Nantes, 21 November 1789, AN, D XXV, d. 824.

29. Nairac, letter of 24 November 1789, quoted in Dorigny, *Bières flottantes*, 16–17.

30. Letter drafted by Duval-Sanadon, 3 October 1789, AN, D XXV, d. 824.

31. "Mémoire adressé par les ministres du Roi à l'AN," in AP, 9:592. The AP dates this memorandum to 27 September 1789, but other references make it clear that it was sent in late October.

32. Dorigny and Gainot, *Amis des Noirs*, 245; *Patriote françois*, 26 November 1789.

33. Copy of letter of Mosneron, 16 November 1789, AN, D XXV 86, d. 825.

34. AP, 10:352 (session of 1 December 1789).

35. Henri Grégoire, *Mémoire en faveur des gens de couleur ou sang-mêlés de St. Domingue, et des autres isles françoises de l'Amérique, adressé à l'Assemblée nationale* (Paris: Belin, 1789). On the beginnings of Grégoire's interest in colonial and racial issues, see Marcel Dorigny, "Grégoire et le combat contre l'esclavage pendant la Révolution," in *Grégoire et la cause des Noirs (1789–1831): Combats et projets*, ed. Yves Bénot and Marcel Dorigny (Paris: Société française d'histoire d'outre-mer, 2000), 52–53.

36. *Patriote françoise*, 5 December 1789 (National Assembly session of 3 December 1789).

37. AP, 10:363 (National Assembly session of 3 December 1789).

38. Club Massiac to Société des Colons de Bordeaux, 15 December 1789, AN, D XXV 86, d. 825.

39. Dorigny and Gainot, *Amis des Noirs*, 249 (session of 4 December 1789).

40. Grégoire, *Mémoire en faveur*, 17–25.

41. Grégoire, *Mémoire en faveur*, 45, 31, 32, 36, 35.

42. Jean Vinot-Préfontaine, "Un curé de Paris sous la Révolution: Sébastien-André Sibire (1742–1823)," *Revue des Etudes historiques* 99 (1932): 128–29.

43. Sébastien-André Sibire, *L'Aristocratie negrière, ou Réflexions philosophiques et historiques sur l'esclavage et l'affranchissement des Noirs* (Paris: Lesclapart, 1789), reprinted in *La Révolution française et l'abolition de l'esclavage*, 2:98, 28, 14–15.

44. *Réclamations des nègres libres, colons américains* (n.p., n.p., 1789), 1.

45. [Médéric Elie Moreau de Saint-Méry], *Observations d'un habitant des colonies, sur le mémoire en faveur des gens de couleur, ou sang-mêlés, de Saint-Domingue & des autres isles françoises de l'Amérique* (Paris, 16 December 1789). Moreau de Saint-Méry acknowledged his authorship of this pamphlet in his *Mémoire justificatif*, 30. On Moreau de Saint-Méry's daughter, see Johnson, *Encyclopédie Noire*, 25-26.

46. Olympe de Gouges, "Reflections on Negroes" (1788), trans. Sylvie Molta, in Kadish and Massardier-Kenney, *Translating Slavery*, 84. On Olympe de Gouges's views on slavery and on the significance of the performance of her play in December 1789, see Anaïs Cécile Pedron, "Olympe de Gouges, anti-esclavagiste et anticolonialiste?," in *Les Lumières, l'esclavage et l'idéologie coloniale, XVIIIe–XXe siècles*, ed.

Pascale Pellerin (Paris: Classiques Garnier, 2020), 155–79; and Jean-Claude Halpern, "L'Esclavage sur le scene révolutionnaire," *Annales historiques de la Révolution française*, nos. 293–94 (December 1993): 409–20.

47. Samuel Pierre David Joseph de Missy, letter of 26 December 1789, in *Lettres inédites d'un armateur rochelais: 1789*, ed. de Richemond (La Rochelle: Siret, 1889), 20; *Actes des Apôtres* 1, no. 15:10.

48. *Moniteur universel*, 31 December 1789.

49. Olympe de Gouges, "Réponse au Champion américain," in Kadish and Massardier-Kenney, *Translating Slavery*, 270.

50. Jean Lecointe-Marsillac, *Le More-Lack, ou Essai sur les moyens les plus doux & les plus équitables d'abolir la traite & l'esclavage des Nègres d'Afrique, en conservant aux Colonies tous les avantages d'une population agricole* (London: Prault, 1789), 279–81. For Brissot's comment, see *Patriote françois*, 14 January 1790.

51. Joseph Lavallée, *Le Nègre comme il y a peu de blancs* (Paris: Buisson, 1789).

52. Léon Deschamps, *Histoire de la question coloniale en France* (Paris: Plon, 1891), 357.

53. *Gazette universelle*, 12 April 1790; *Gazette de Paris*, 1 April 1790.

54. *Actes des Apôtres* 1, no. 15:10; Hélène Maspero-Clerc, *Un journaliste contre-révolutionnaire: Jean-Gabriel Peltier (1760–1825)* (Paris: Société des Etudes Robespierriestes, 1973), 12–13.

55. Address from the Colons de Bordeaux, September 1789, AN, D XXV 85, d. 823.

56. Henry Romberg to Club Massiac, 5 September 1789, AN, D XXV 85, d. 823.

57. Pierre Bernadeu, "Tablettes manuscrites, nov. 1789, sept. 1793," entries for 6 December 1789 and 7 February 1790, Bibliothèque municipale de Bordeaux, Micr. 1698/5-6-7.

58. Letter from Nantes, 21 November 1789, AN, D XXV 85, d. 823; Grenouilleau, *Révolution abolitionniste*, 380.

59. Clay, "Liberty, Equality, Slavery," 102–3; Brissot to Clarkson, 14 February 1790, Cambridge University, St. John's College Library, Special Collections, Clarkson Papers, Folder 8.

60. *Affiches americaines*, 28 October 1789; letter from the slaves of Martinique, in *Slave Revolution in the Caribbean*, 2nd ed., ed. Laurent Dubois and John Garrigus (Boston: Bedford / St. Martin's, 2017), 54–55.

61. *Gazette universelle*, 2 December 1789, 9 December 1789, 23 December 1789, 5 January 1790.

62. *Patriote françois*, 2 January 1790.

63. *Patriote françois*, 15 February 1790; Maissemy to Club Massiac, 27 February 1790, AN, D XXV 85, d. 826.

64. *Adresse de l'Armée patriotique bordelaise, à l'Assemblée nationale* (n.p., n.p., 1790), 2.

65. Fernand Gerbaux and Charles Schmitt, *Procès-verbaux des Comités d'agriculture et de commerce* (Paris: Imprimerie nationale, 1906), 1:153 (19 January 1790).

66. Chaussinand-Nogaret, *Mirabeau*, 232.

67. Mosneron de l'Aunay, "Discours sur les colonies et la traite des noirs," 26 February 1790, in François-Alphonse Aulard, *La Société des Jacobins: Recueil de documents pour l'histoire du Club des Jacobins de Paris,* 6 vols. (Paris: Jouaust, 1889–97), 1:9.

68. Jean-Baptiste Nairac, letter of 2 March 1790, quoted in Dorigny, *Bières flottantes,* 25.

69. Dorigny, *Bières flottantes,* 51, emphasis in original.

70. Vicomte de Mirabeau, undelivered address to the National Assembly, in AP, 12:75.

71. Dorigny, *Bières flottantes,* 58, 94.

72. Dorigny, *Bières flottantes,* 107, 109, 110, 111.

73. Dorigny, *Bières flottantes,* 111.

74. *Patriote françois,* 2 March 1790; Treille, *Commerce de Nantes,* 102; Nairac, quoted in Dorigny, *Bières flottantes,* 25; Duquesnoy, *Journal,* 2:440 (4 March 1790).

75. *Gazette universelle,* 2 March 1790 (National Assembly session of 1 March).

76. *Patriote françois,* 3 March 1790 (session of 2 March); AP, 12:6 (3 March 1790).

77. Quoted in Treille, *Commerce de Nantes,* 104.

78. *Patriote françois,* 5 March 1790.

79. Duquesnoy, *Journal,* 2:439 (4 March 1790).

80. On Barnave's connections to the colonial milieu, see Souad Degachi, *Barnave Rapporteur du comité des Colonies (1789–1791)* (Révolution Française.net Editions, September 2007), https://revolution-francaise.net/editions/barnave_colonies_degachi2.pdf.

81. Nairac, letter of 6 March 1790, in Deveau, *Commerce rochelais,* 202.

82. *Gazette universelle,* 10 March 1790.

83. AP, 12:72–73 (session of 8 March 1790). For Barnave's rough draft, see John Hardman, *Barnave: The Revolutionary Who Lost His Head for Marie-Antoinette* (New Haven, CT: Yale University Press, 2023), 165.

84. *Gazette universelle,* 9 March 1790.

85. Duquesnoy, *Journal,* 2:444 (8 March 1790).

86. *Gazette universelle,* 10 March 1790; Louise Elisabeth Croy d'Havre, duchesse de Croy, *Mémoires de madame la duchesse de Tourzel,* ed. duc de Cars (Paris: Plon-Nourrit, 1904), 76; *Moniteur universel,* 9 March 1790; Club Massiac, letter of 10 April 1790, AN, D XXV 85, d. 828; Nairac, letter of 8 March 1790, in Deveau, *Commerce rochelais,* 202–3.

87. *Patriote françois,* 9, 10 March 1790; Bernadeu, "Tablettes," 76 (9 March 1790).

88. Clay, "Liberty, Equality, Slavery," 117.

89. *Réclamation des citoyens de couleur des isles & colonies françoises; sur le décret du 8 mars 1790* (Paris, March 1790), 14.

90. AP, 12:383 (28 March 1790).

Chapter Six

1. Brissot, letter of 13 March 1790, in *Correspondance et papiers*, 249.

2. Data from Trans-Atlantic Slave Trade database, consulted 29 September 2023, https://www.slavevoyages.org/voyage/database.

3. Dorigny and Gainot, *Amis des Noirs*, 280 (22 March 1790); *Seconde Adresse à l'Assemblée nationale, par la Société des Amis des Noirs* (Paris, 1790), reprinted in *La Révolution française et l'abolition de l'esclavage*, vol. 7, no. 8, p. 3.

4. Jérôme Pétion, *Discours sur la traite des Noirs* (Paris: Desenne, April 1790), 70; "Adresse de la commune du Havre," 5 June 1790, AN, D XXV 85, d. 831.

5. *Détail des circonstances relatives à l'inauguration du monument placé le 20 juin 1790 dans le Jeu de Paume de Versailles, par une société des patriotes* (Paris: Révolutions de Paris, 1790), 22.

6. Clarkson, *History of the Rise*, 2:149; Ogé interrogation, 18 December 1790, AN, D XXV 58, d. 574; *Adresse à l'Assemblée nationale, des citoyens de couleur, réunis à Paris, sous le titre de colons américains* (Paris, 5 July 1790), AN, Col. F 3 195, Papers of Moreau de Saint-Méry.

7. Gliech, *Saint-Domingue und die Französische Revolution*, 261–75.

8. *Affiches américaines*, 1 May 1790 (Saint-Marc, 28 April 1790), 6 May 1790 (Saint-Marc, 28 April 1790).

9. "Extrait des registres de l'assemblée-générale de la Partie Française de Saint-Domingue," 28 May 1790, AN, Col. F 3 195, Papers of Moreau de Saint-Méry; *Affiches américaines*, 3 June 1790 (Saint-Marc, 28 May 1790).

10. "Extrait des registres des délibérations du Comité de la partie de l'Ouest de St. Domingue séant au Port-au-Prince," 2 June 1790, AN, Col. F 3 195, Papers of Moreau de Saint-Méry.

11. [Antoine Louis Thomassin de Peinier], *Proclamation de M. le Gouverneur Général, concernant les troubles de la colonie* (Port-au-Prince: Mozard, 29 July 1790), AN, Col. F 3 195, Papers of Moreau de Saint-Méry.

12. On the *Léopard* mutiny, see Jeremy D. Popkin, "Sailors and Revolution: Naval Mutineers in Saint-Domingue, 1790–1793," *French History* 26 (December 2012): 460–81.

13. Club Massiac, sessions of 25, 28, 29 July 1790, AN, D XXV 86, d.829.

14. *Gazette universelle*, 31 July, 4 August 1790.

15. "Lettre des citoyens de couleur à M. le président de l'Assemblée nationale," 1 August 1790, in AN, D XXV 86, d. 829.

16. "Colonies françaises," *Révolutions de Paris*, 18–25 September 1790, 519–24.

17. AP, 19:93 (20 September 1790), 19:275 (27 September 1790), 19:336 (30 September 1790).

18. AP, 19:570, 568 (12 October 1790). For Barnave's reassurance to the Léopardins, see Degachi, *Barnave Rapporteur*, 87.

19. *Patriote françois*, 13 October 1790; Jérôme Pétion, *Discours sur les troubles de Saint-Domingue* (Paris: Imprimerie du Patriote françois, 14 October 1790); Henri Grégoire, *Lettre aux Philanthropes, sur les malheurs, les droits et les réclamations des*

Gens de Couleur de Saint-Domingue, et des autres îles françoises de l'Amérique (Paris: Belin, 1790), 7.

20. *Révolutions de Paris*, 9–16 October 1790. On Sonthonax's authorship, see Bénot, *Révolution française*, 130.

21. Jacques-Pierre Brissot, *Lettre de J. P. Brissot à M. Barnave, sur ses rapports concernant les colonies, les décrets qui les ont suivis, leurs conséquences fatales; sur sa conduite dans le cours de la révolution; sur le caractère des vrais démocrates; sur les bases de la constitution, les obstacles qui s'opposent à son achèvement, la nécessité de la terminer promptement, etc.* (Paris: Desenne, 1790), 6, 18, 88.

22. Quoted in E. D. Bradby, *The Life of Barnave* (Oxford: Clarendon, 1915), 1:294.

23. AP, 21:125–26 (29 November 1790); Henri Joucla, *Le Conseil supérieur des Colonies et ses antécédents* (Paris: Editions du Monde moderne, 1927), 233–34.

24. Baron de Beauvois, *Idées sommaires sur quelques règlements à faire par l'Assemblée coloniale* (Cap François: Batilliot, 1790), 6–7, emphasis in original.

25. [Guillaume-François de Mahy de Corméré], *Des Noirs et des blancs, ainsi que de quelques effets résultans du mélange des races dans l'espèce humaine* (Paris: Potier de Lille, 1791), 9.

26. On the Cercle social, see Gary Kates, *The Cercle Social, the Girondins, and the French Revolution* (Princeton, NJ: Princeton University Press, 1985).

27. On Fauchet, see Caroline Chopelin-Blanc, *De l'apologétique à l'Eglise constitutionnelle: Adrien Lamourette (1724–1794)* (Paris: Honoré Champion, 2009), 305–7.

28. Fauchet, in *Bouche de fer*, no. 15 (November 1790), 227.

29. Fauchet, in *Bouche de fer*, no. 15 (November 1790), 238.

30. Julien Raimond, *Observations sur l'origine et les progrès du préjugé des colons blancs contre les hommes de couleur; sur les inconvéniens de le perpétuer; la nécessité, la facilité de le détruire; sur le projet du Comité colonial, etc.* (Paris: Belin, Desenne, Bailly, 26 January 1791), 1, 13.

31. Raimond, *Observations sur l'origine*, 22–23.

32. Anacharsis Cloots, *Anacharsis à Paris, ou, Lettre de Jean-Baptiste Cloots à un prince allemand* (Paris, 6 October 1790), 5, 27. On Cloots and his October 1790 pamphlet, see Roland Mortier, *Anacharsis Cloots, ou l'utopie foudroyée* (Paris: Stock, 1995), 154.

33. The original manuscript version of Moreau de Saint-Méry's notes on the meetings of the colonial committee are in Archives nationales d'outre-mer, microfilm 87 MIOM 95. I would like to thank Manuel Covo for sharing his photographs of these documents with me. We subsequently discovered that these documents were published in Joucla, *Conseil supérieur*. Citations are to Joucla's book. Moreau de Saint-Méry, session of 29 January 1791, in Joucla, *Conseil supérieur*, 259.

34. Bernadeu, "Tablettes," 20 December 1790; *Réimpression de l'ancien Moniteur*, 32 vols. (Paris: Bureau central, 1840–45), 6:702, 749 (24, 29 December 1790).

35. On Ogé's movement, see John Garrigus, "Vincent Ogé *jeune* (1757–1791): Social Class and Free Colored Mobilization on the Eve of the Haitian Revolution," *Americas* 68 (2011): 33–62.

36. Bernadeu, "Tablettes," 20 December 1790; *Patriote françois*, 5, 15 January 1791; *Révolutions de Paris*, 25 December 1790–1 January 1791.

37. Médéric Elie Moreau de Saint-Méry, *Considérations présentées aux vrais amis du repos et du bonheur de la France, à l'occasion des nouveaux mouvemens de quelques soi-disant Amis-des-Noirs* (Paris: Imprimerie nationale, 1791), 26, 28; *Perfidie du systême des Amis des Noirs* (Nantes, 1791), 3.

38. Joucla, *Conseil supérieur*, 262 (session of 3 February 1791); Moreau de Saint-Méry, *Considérations présentées*, 47–48.

39. Jules Solime Milscent, in *Abeille Haytienne: Journal politique et littéraire*, no. 12 (16 January 1818): 8.

40. *Motion présentée au Comité provincial de la Partie du Nord de Saint-Domingue, par M. Milscent de Mussé*, AN, Col. F 3 194, Papers of Moreau de Saint-Méry.

41. "A Messieurs de l'Assemblée générale de la partie Française de Saint-Domingue, séant à Saint-Marc," in [Claude Milscent], *Adresse à l'Assemblée nationale par les hommes de couleur libres de Saint-Domingue* (Paris, 1791), 31.

42. *Journal du département de Maine et Loire, par les Amis de la Constitution d'Angers*, 9 March 1791.

43. *Patriote françois*, 25 March 1791. The responses of a number of Jacobin clubs were published as *Lettres des diverses sociétés des Amis de la Constitution qui réclament les droits de Citoyen actif en faveur des hommes de couleur des colonies* (1791), reprinted in *La Révolution française et l'abolition de l'esclavage*, vol. 4.

44. Quoted in Michael L. Kennedy, *The Jacobin Clubs in the French Revolution: The First Years* (Princeton, NJ: Princeton University Press, 1982), 207; "Lettres de diverses sociétés des Amis de la Constitution, qui réclament les droits de Citoyen actif en faveur des hommes de couleur des colonies," in Etienne Clavière, *Adresse de la Société des Amis des Noirs, à l'Assemblée nationale, à toutes les villes de commerce, à toutes les manufactures, aux colonies, à toutes les sociétés des Amis de la Constitution*, 2nd ed. (Paris: Desenne and Bailly, 10 July 1791), 209–305.

45. "Réponse aux deux lettres des amis des noirs," *Patriote françois*, 8 April 1791.

46. [Claude Milscent de Mussy], "Envoi de M. d. M., propriétaire américain," *Bouche de fer* (19, 24 April 1791), 165–66, 222–27.

47. *Patriote françois*, 30 April 1790; *Gazette universelle*, 29 April 1791.

48. AP, 25:335–40 (23 April 1791); Joucla, *Conseil supérieur*, 314 (session of 27 April 1791).

49. Joucla, *Conseil supérieur*, 305 (session of 26 April 1791).

50. Joucla, *Conseil supérieur*, 310–11 (session of 27 April 1791).

51. *Gazette universelle*, 12 May 1791.

52. Unsigned letter, AN, 446 AP 10, Brissot Papers, n.d.

53. AP, 25:636 (7 May 1791).

54. AP, 25:638–40 (7 May 1791).

55. "Supplément nécessaire à l'adresse des amis des noirs, en faveur des hommes de couleur: Distribué le 11 Mai 1791, à l'Assemblée nationale," in Clavière, *Adresse de la Société*, 208.

56. AP, 25:740–42. For the proposal to abolish slavery that was not allowed to be put forward, see Jean-Louis Viefville des Essarts, *Discours et projet de loi pour l'affranchissement des nègres ou l'adoucissement de leur régime et réponse aux objections des colons* (Paris: Imprimerie nationale, 1791), in AP, 25:760–88.

57. AP, 25:743–44 (11 May 1791); Gouy d'Arsy, "Louis-Marthe de Gouy, député à l'Assemblée nationale, à ses commettants," in AP, 25:306.

58. AP, 25:746–49 (11 May 1791).

59. AP, 25:750, 752 (11 May 1791).

60. AP, 25:755 (11 May 1791).

61. *Mercure universel*, 19 May 1791 (Jacobin Club, 11 May 1791).

62. Maximilien Robespierre, *Oeuvres de Maximilien Robespierre* (Paris: Société des Etudes Robespierristes, 1912–2007), 7:348; AP, 26:15, 26–27 (12 May 1791).

63. "Louis-Marthe de Gouy, député à l'Assemblée nationale, à ses commettants," in AP, 31:306.

64. AP, 26:47 (13 May 1791).

65. AP, 26:49, 60 (13 May 1791).

66. On Robespierre's involvement with colonial issues in general, see Bernard Gainot, "Robespierre et la question coloniale," in *Robespierre: Portraits Croisés*, ed. Michel Biard and Philippe Bourdin (Paris: Armand Colin, 2012), 79–94; and Jean-Daniel Piquet, "Robespierre et les colonies entre la politique et les principes (janvier 1791–juillet 1794)," Amis de Robespierre, 30 January 2023, https://www.amis-robespierre.org/?Robespierre-et-les-colonies-entre-la-politique-et-les-principes-janvier-1791.

67. AP, 26:50, 52, 59, 60 (13 May 1791); *Révolutions de France et de Brabant*, no. 78 (May 1791): 599; *Gazette de Paris*, 17 May 1791; *Annales patriotiques*, 14 May 1791 (13 May 1791).

68. "Louis-Marthe de Gouy, député à l'Assemblée nationale, à ses commettants," in AP, 31:308; AP, 26:61 (13 May 1791).

69. *Mercure universel*, 16 May 1791 (Jacobins, 13 May 1791). Cf. Aulard, *Société des Jacobins*, 2:414–15; and Robespierre, *Oeuvres*, 7:366.

70. AP, 26:66–69 (14 May 1791).

71. "Louis-Marthe de Gouy, député à l'Assemblée nationale, à ses commettants," in AP, 31:309; AP, 26:89 (15 May 1791).

72. *Gazette universelle*, 16 May 1791 (National Assembly session of 15 May 1791).

73. AP, 26:93 (15 May 1791).

74. Robespierre, *Oeuvres*, 7:369, 371 (15 May 1791).

75. George Granville Leveson-Gower, *The Despatches of Earl Gower, English Ambassador at Paris from June 1790 to August 1792*, ed. Oscar Browning (Cambridge: Cambridge University Press, 1885), 87.

76. Quoted in Hardman, *Barnave*, 225; *Révolutions de France et de Brabant*, no. 78 (mid-May 1791), 596.

77. For a discussion of this image, see Florence Gauthier, *L'Aristocratie de l'épiderme: Le Combat de la Société des Citoyens de Couleur, 1789–1791* (Paris: Editions du CNRS, 2007), 308–21.

78. *Patriote françois*, 16 May 1791.

79. *Mercure universel*, 22 May 1791 (Jacobin Club meeting of 16 May 1791).

80. Henri Grégoire, "Lettre aux citoyens de couleur et Nègres libres de Saint-Domingue," in Clavière, *Adresse de la Société*, 306, 311.

81. Albert Meynier, *Un représentant de la bourgeoisie angevine à l'assemblée nationale constituante et à la Convention nationale: L.-M. La Reveillière-Lépeaux (1753–1795)* (Angers: Germain et Grassin, 1905), 239; *Le Creuset*, 27 July 1791.

82. "Lettre des commissaires des citoyens de couleur en France, a leurs frères et commettans dans les îles français," in Clavière, *Adresse de la Société*, 317.

83. Pierre Labuissonnière to [Julien Raimond], 27 August 1791, AN, 446 AP 9, Brissot Papers.

84. AP, 26:123 (16 May 1791).

85. Gouverneur Morris, *A Diary of the French Revolution* (Boston: Houghton Mifflin, 1939), 2:183 (16 May 1791); Levenson-Gower, *Despatches*, 88 (20 May 1791).

86. AN, D XXV 89, register 2, meeting of 20 May 1791; Joucla, *Conseil supérieur*, 344–47 (sessions of 23 and 24 May 1791); Louis-Marthe Gouy d'Arsy, *Louis-Marthe de Gouy, député à l'Assemblée nationale, à ses commettans* (Paris, May 1791), 28.

87. "Pétition des négocians, capitaines de navires, citoyens de la ville du Havre," 23 May 1791, in *Journal général de politique et de littérature*, 16 June 1791; *Adresse présentée à l'Assemblée nationale, sous le nom du Commerce du Havre* (n.p., n.p., 1791).

88. AP, 27:670–71 (2 July 1791); Treille, *Commerce de Nantes*, 122–23.

89. *Extrait du registre des délibérations de la Chambre du commerce de la ville de Bordeaux; et adresses des, &c., &c., &c.* (n.p., n.p., 1791), 5, 19; *Patriote françois*, 25 May 1791.

90. *Chronique de Paris*, 19 May 1791; *Feuille du Jour*, 30 May 1791.

91. "Lettre des citoyens de couleur et nègres libres, à Jean-Baptiste Cloots," *Bouche de fer* (9 June 1791); "Réponse de l'Orateur du genre humain, aux citoyens de couleur & nègres libres," *Chronique de Paris*, 18 June 1791.

92. *Extrait des proces-verbaux de l'Assemblée nationale, relativement à l'état des personnes dans les colonies* (Paris: Imprimerie nationale, 1791), 4, 5, 8; AP, 27:237 (15 June 1791).

93. Quoted in Ellery, *Brissot de Warville*, 176.

94. AN, D XXV 89, register 2, 1 July 1791.

95. *Courrier politique et littéraire du Cap-Français*, 7 July 1791; Blanchelande, letter of 3 July 1791, AN, C 9 A 167.

96. *Gazette universelle*, 7 September 1791 (National Assembly session of 5 September 1791), 9 September 1791.

97. *Le Creuset*, 11, 18 September 1791; Aulard, *Société des Jacobins*, 3:126 (12 September 1791); Jacques-Pierre Brissot, *Discours sur la nécessité de maintenir le décret rendu le 15 mai 1791, en faveur des hommes de couleur libres* (Paris, 1791). An address in the name of the Jacobin Club, dated 16 July 1791, was signed by Robespierre, Pétion, Brissot, Carra, François-Xavier Lanthenas, Clavière, and Raimond, among others. Aulard, *Société des Jacobins*, 3:21–24 (16 July 1791); Jean-Daniel Piquet, "Un

Discours inédit de l'abbé Grégoire sur le décret du 15 mai 1791, 'Discours de M. Grégoire sur la révocation du décret relatif aux gens de couleur,'" *Annales historiques de la Révolution française*, no. 363 (Jan. 2011), 175-83.

98. AP, 31:253–59 (23 September 1791).

99. AP, 31:274 (24 September 1791).

100. AP, 31:277 (24 September 1791).

101. *Annales patriotiques*, 26 September 1791; AP, 31:442 (28 September 1791).

102. Barnave to Marie-Antoinette, 25 September 1791, in *Correspondance de Marie-Antoinette (1770–1793)*, ed. Evelyne Lever (Paris: Tallandier, 2005), 616–17; *Patriote françois*, 25 September 1791.

Chapter Seven

1. "Copies de différentes lettres sur les événements de Saint-Domingue," AN, D XXV 46, d. 435. Grégoire had been elected as a bishop of the constitutional church at the end of the National Assembly's session.

2. Frédérique Beauvois, *Between Blood and Gold: The Debates over Compensation for Slavery in the Americas*, trans. Andrene Everson (2013; New York: Berghahn, 2017), 27.

3. AN, D XXV 89, sessions of 22 and 23 October 1791; *Gazette universelle*, 24 October 1791.

4. Letter from Cayes, 31 August 1791, AN, D XXV 46, d. 435.

5. Documents in AN, D XXV 46, d. 435.

6. AN, D XXV 46, d. 435.

7. Grégoire, in *Journal des débats de la société des amis de la Constitution*, no. 61 (16 September 1791), cited in Piquet, "Discours inédit de l'abbé Grégoire," 177.

8. C. J. Mitchell, *The French Legislative Assembly of 1791* (Leiden: Brill, 1988), 203.

9. At least 169 of the 745 deputies initially affiliated with the Feuillants, whereas only 52 were known members of the Jacobins. Mitchell, *French Legislative Assembly*, 15.

10. Aulard, *Société des Jacobins*, 3:134 (16 September 1791), 3:192 (16 October 1791).

11. J. P. Collot d'Herbois, *L'Almanach du Père Gérard* (Paris: Imprimerie du Patriote françois, 1792), 27–28.

12. *Gazette universelle*, 25 November 1791.

13. AN, D XXV 89, session of 5 November 1791.

14. AP, 35:455–56 (27 October 1791).

15. AP, 35:456, 522–25 (27, 30 October 1791)

16. [Claude Milscent], *Sur les troubles de Saint-Domingue* (Paris: Imprimerie du Patriote françois, 1791), 4, 12, reprinted in *Patriote françois*, 23 November 1791, and *Morning Chronicle*, 12 December 1791.

17. AP, 35:63 (14 November 1791).

18. *Courier de la Gironde*, 1 January 1792; AP, 35:118 (17 November 1791), 35:261 (20 November 1791).

19. Jeremy D. Popkin, "Port-au-Prince and the Collapse of French Imperial Authority, 1789–1793," *French Historical Studies* 44, no. 1 (2021): 70–71.

20. "Copies des lettres de MM. Millet, Cougnacq-Mion, Chesneau de la Mesgrière, Lebugnet, La Gourgue, de Sainte-James, commissaires de l'Assemblée générale de la Partie française de St. Domingue près la Métropole, commencé le 17 8bre 1791," AN, D XXV 76.

21. AP, 35:454–67 (30 November 1791).

22. AP, 35:467–68 (30 November 1791); *Annales patriotiques*, 1 December 1791.

23. Mayor of Tonneins to commissioners, 5 December 1791, AN, D XXV 63, d. 631.

24. Jacques-Pierre Brissot, *Discours de J. P. Brissot, député, sur les causes des troubles de Saint-Domingue, prononcé à la séance du premier décembre 1791* (Paris: Imprimerie nationale, 1791), 3, 4, 6, 48, 49, 51, 53, 58.

25. Brissot, *Discours de J. P. Brissot*, 59–60, 67, 70.

26. Jean-François Michon-Dumaret [Dumarais], in AP, 35:548 (3 December 1791).

27. AP, 35:614, 605, 543 (6 and 3 December 1791). Charles Tarbé delivered reports from the colonial committee on 10 December 1791, 11 January 1792, and 29 February 1792, setting off renewed debates each time.

28. *Ami du Peuple*, 2 November 1791.

29. Camille Desmoulins, *Jean [sic] Pierre Brissot démasqué* (Paris, 1792), 39.

30. Olympe de Gouges, "Preface to *The Slavery of the Blacks*," quoted in Dubois and Garrigus, *Slave Revolution*, 97.

31. Mathieu Blanc-Gilli, *Observations importantes sur les troubles de Saint-Domingue* (Paris: Imprimerie nationale, 1791), 3, 4; Armand-Guy Kersaint, *Suite des moyens proposés à l'assemblée nationale, pour rétablir la paix et l'ordre dans les colonies* (Paris: Cercle social, 1792), 5, 21.

32. Julien Raimond, in Kersaint, *Suite des moyens*, 9–15n.

33. Claude Milscent, *Du régime coloniale* (Paris: Cercle social, 1792), 16, 23, 30.

34. *Patriote françois*, 26 January 1792.

35. Jean-François and Biassou, letter to the civil commissioners, 9 December 1791, AN, D XXV 1, d. 4; English translation in Dubois and Garrigus, *Slave Revolution*, 87–89.

36. AN, D XXV 76, 11 February 1792.

37. Lever, *Correspondance de Marie-Antoinette*, 735, 769.

38. Brissot speech, in AP, 40:212 (21 March 1792).

39. *Annales patriotiques*, 24 March 1792 (Legislative Assembly session of 22 March 1792); *Patriote françois*, 24 March 1792 (Legislative Assembly session of 23 March 1792).

40. AN, D XXV 76, letter of 26 March 1792; Mathieu Dumas, in AP, 40:366 (22 March 1792); Vaublanc, in AP, 40:441 (24 March 1792).

41. AP, 40:449–55 (24 March 1792).

42. AP, 40:487 (26 March 1792); *Patriote françois*, 13 March 1792 (Milscent) and 31 March 1792 (Garran-Coulon).

43. Condorcet, *Révision des travaux de la première legislature. Janvier, Février, Avril et Juin 1792*, in Condorcet, *Oeuvres de Condorcet*, ed. A. Condorcet and M. F. Arago (Paris: Firmin Didot, 1847), 10:422.

44. Stanhope to Condorcet, 3 April 1792, in *Patriote françois*, 9 April 1792.

45. AP, 41:412–13 (10 April 1792), 41:500 (11 April 1792); AN, D XXV 76, letter of 11 April 1792.

46. *Révolutions de Paris*, 7–14 April 1792. On Chaumette's navy service and his involvement with the *Révolutions de Paris*, see Nicole Bossut, *Chaumette, porte-parole des sans-culottes* (Paris: Editions du CTHS, 1998), 29–32, 57–61.

47. Roume, letter of 10 May 1792, AN, D XXV 2, d. 17.

48. AP, 40:708–9 (30 March 1792).

49. *Courier de la Gironde*, 3 April 1792; AP, 41:55 (1 April 1792), Oise; AP, 41:97 (2 April 1792), Seine-Inférieure; AP, 41:101 (3 April 1792), Allier and Nord; AP, 41:318 (7 April 1792), Charente; AP, 41:364 (8 April 1792), Pas-de-Calais; AP, 42:60 (18 April 1792), Côte-d-Or; AP, 42:307 (23 April 1792), Côtes-du-Nord; AP, 42:314 (23 April 1792), Finistère; AP, 42:505 (29 April 1792), Vendée.

50. Marcel Dorigny, "Sonthonax et Brissot: Le cheminement d'une filiation politique assumée," in *Sonthonax: La première abolition de l'esclavage: La Révolution française et la Révolution de Saint-Domingue*, new ed., ed. Marcel Dorigny (Paris: Société Française d'histoire d'outre-mer, 2005), 35; Robert Louis Stein, *Léger Félicité Sonthonax: The Lost Sentinel of the Republic* (Rutherford, NJ: Fairleigh Dickinson University Press, 1985), 42.

51. Popkin, *You Are All Free*, 88; Ailhaud to National Convention, 22 January 1793, AN, D XXV 12, d. 112.

52. Brissot, draft letter, 19 June 1792, AN, 446 AP 13, Brissot Papers. It is not known whether this letter was ever sent.

53. Raimond, letter of 18 June 1792, AN, D XXV 13, d. 127.

54. Letter of Dubourg and Félix Ouvière, *Revue du Patriote*, 19 June 1792.

55. Raimond, letter of 18 June 1792, AN, D XXV 13, d. 127.

56. *Revue du Patriote*, 7, 19 June 1792.

57. AN, D XX 76, session of 20 July 1792.

58. *Revue du Patriote*, 14 June 1792.

59. Debien, *Les Colons de Saint-Domingue et la Révolution* , 376; Elicona, *Un colonial sous la Révolution*, 123–24; Charles Frostin, "L'Intervention britannique à Saint-Domingue en 1793," *Outre-Mers* 49, no. 176–77 (1962): 310–11.

60. AN, D XX V 76, sessions of 25 July 1792 (Page) and 16 August 1792 (Brulley). A third member of the delegation disappeared soon after reaching Paris.

61. AP, 48:358, 361 (18 August 1792); *Créole patriote*, 19 August 1792.

Chapter Eight

1. AN, D XXV 76, 23, 25, 28 August 1792.

2. *Patriote françois*, 4 September 1792.

3. Joseph Lequinio, *Les Préjugés détruits*, 2nd ed. (Paris: Cercle social, 1 January 1793), 165–75.

4. AP, 49:428–29 (7 September 1792); *Créole patriote*, 9 September 1792. On the Legion des Américains, see Bernard Gainot, *Les Officiers de couleur dans les armées de la république et de l'empire (1792–1815)* (Paris: Karthala, 2007), 33–54.

5. Page to Larchvevseque-Thibaud, 11 August 1792, AN, D XXV 68, d. 685.

6. On the strategies of the various émigré factions, see Frostin, "L'Intervention britannique."

7. AN, D XXV 71, d. 712, document dated 23 April 1793.

8. AN, D XXV 63, d. 639, 10 December 1792; *Créole patriote*, 25 September 1793.

9. On Legrand, see *Jean-Baptiste-Bernard Le Grand, sécretaire-garde des archives de la Commission de Saint-Domingue, à la Convention nationale* (Paris, 1794).

10. Brulley to mother, 7 November 1792, AN, D XXV 71, d. 712.

11. [Augustin-Jean Brulley], *Précis des manoeuvres contre-révolutionnaires opérées dans la partie française de Saint-Domingue* (Paris: Duplain, 1792); Pierre-François Page, *Discours historique sur la cause des désastres de la partie française de Saint-Domingue, établi sur pièces probantes, déposées au Comité Colonial* (Paris, 1792).

12. Page and Brulley, register, 11 February 1793, AN, D XXV 76; Raimond, letter of 21 March 1793, in Julien Raimond, *Lettres de J. Raimond à ses frères les hommes de couleur* (Paris: Cercle social, An II [1793]), 108.

13. *Créole patriote*, 31 October, 5 November 1792; Aulard, *Société des Jacobins*, 4:642 (4 January 1793).

14. *Créole patriote*, 21 September, 28 November 1792.

15. Julien Raimond, *Réflexions sur les véritables causes des troubles et des désastres de nos colonies, notamment sur ceux de Saint-Domingue; avec les moyens à employer pour préserver cette colonie d'une ruine totale; adressés à la Convention nationale; par Julien Raymond, colon de Saint-Domingue* (Paris, 1793), 5, 19, 20, 24, 26.

16. *Créole patriote*, 15 January 1793; Page and Brulley, register, 14, 15 January 1793, AN, D XXV 63, d. 639. The text of this play, which Milscent attributed to an author named Désaudrais, probably Charles-Emmanuel Guillaume de Saudray (1740–1832), does not seem to have survived.

17. *Créole patriote*, 8 February 1793.

18. *Créole patriote*, 8 February 1793; "Lettre de Jean-François, Biassou and Belair," first published in Joseph Cambefort, *Quatrième partie du mémoire justificative, de Joseph-Paul-Augustin Cambefort, colonel du régiment du Cap* (Paris, 1793), 4–11, and in *Créole patriote*, 9 February 1793. On the origins of the document, see Jeremy D. Popkin, "A Haitian Revolutionary Manifesto? New Perspectives on the 'Letter of Jean-François, Biassou, and Belair,'" *Slavery and Abolition* 43, no. 1 (March 2022): 3–19. For Roume's explanation of the letter's origin and how it ended up in Cambefort's hands, see Roume, "Réfutation des calomnies inventées contre le Cn. Roume," June 1793[?], AN, D XXV 3, d. 31.

19. *Créole patriote*, 9 February 1793.

20. *Créole patriote*, 11, 13, 19 February 1793.

21. *Bulletin des Amis de la Vérité*, 2 March 1793.

22. *Bulletin des Amis de la Vérité*, 23, 27 February and 2, 5, 13, 17, 27 March 1793.

23. Page and Brulley, register, 19 January 1793, AN, D XXV 63, d. 639; Sonthonax, "Relation officielle," 10 December 1792, AN, D XXV 5, d. 43. For the background to Sonthonax's action, see Popkin, *You Are All Free*, 101–20.

24. Page and Brulley, register, 30 January, 8 February 1793, AN, D XXV 64, d. 640.

25. On Sonthonax's and Polverel's actions in Saint-Domingue before the journée of 20 June 1793, which led them to issue their first emancipation offer, see Popkin, *You Are All Free*, 132–43. Sonthonax's letter of 11 February 1793 is in AN, AA 55, d. 1511.

26. Marc de Vissac, *Les Révolutionnaires du Rouergue* (Riom: E. Girard, 1893), 59, 133.

27. Minutes of colonial committee, 25 January, 4, 8 February 1793, AN, D* XVI 3-4-5; AP, 59:626 (National Convention session of 5 March 1793).

28. [Pierre-François Page and Augustin Brulley], *Développement des causes des troubles et désastres des colonies françaises, présenté à la Convention nationale par les commissaires de Saint-Domingue, sur la demande des comités de Marine & des Colonies, réunis, après en avoir donné communication aux Colons résidens à Paris, & convoqués, à cet effet, le 11 juin 1793, l'an 2e de la République* (Paris, 1793), 17, 30.

29. Brulley, testimony at Blanchelande trial, 5 April 1793, AN, D XXV 47, d. 444bis; Saint-Léger, testimony, in *Bulletin du Tribunal Criminel Révolutionnaire*, no. 9; *Nouvelles politiques*, 17 April 1793.

30. [Page and Brulley], *Développement des causes*, 53–86.

31. Julien Raimond, *Mémoire sur les causes des troubles et des désastres de la Colonie de Saint-Domingue, présenté aux comités de Marine et des Colonies, dans les premiers jours de juin dernier, par les citoyens de couleur, d'après l'invitation que leur en avoit été faite par les comités* (Paris: Cercle social, 1793), 61, 65; [Page and Brulley], *Développement des causes*, 40, 86, 88; AP, 60:301 (19 March 1793).

32. "Plan de Constitution présenté à la Convention nationale les 15 et 16 février 1793, l'an II de la République," Pt. 2, "Project de déclaration des droits naturels, civils et politiques des hommes," article 20, in Condorcet, *Œuvres de Condorcet*, eds. François Arago and Arthus O'Connor, 12 vols. (Paris: Firmin Didot, 1847–49), 12:420.

33. Robespierre, speech of 24 April 1793, in *Oeuvres*, 9:460.

34. Constitution of 1793, article 18, in *Les Constitutions de la France depuis 1789*, ed. Jacques Godechot (Paris: Flammarion, 1970), 81.

35. *Adresse à la Convention nationale, à tous les clubs et sociétés patriotiques, pour les Nègres détenus en esclavage dans les colonies Françaises de l'Amérique, sous le régime de la République* (Paris: Galletti, 17 May 1793), 14. On Labuissonnière, see Yves Bénot, "Un anti-esclavagiste kleptomane? En marge de l'affaire Milscent," *Dix-Huitième Siècle*, no. 22 (1990): 295–300.

36. *Journal des débats de la Société des amis de la Constitution séante aux Jacobins à Paris*, 5, 7 June 1793 (Jacobins, 3 June 1793).

37. AP, 66:57 (4 June 1793).

38. Bénot, "Anti-esclavagiste kleptomane?" On Chaumette's role in the abolitionist events in June 1793, see Bossut, *Chaumette*, 306–8.

39. Page and Brulley, register, 23 June, 3 July, 26 June 1793, AN, D XXV 76.

40. Page and Brulley, register, 15 July 1793, AN, D XXV 76; AP, 64:711 (16 May 1793), 69:39 (16 July 1793); *Nouvelles politiques*, 18 July 1793.

41. Letters of Page and Brulley, 11, 28 August 1793, AN, D XXV 54, d. 523; Julien Raimond, letter of 1 August 1793, in *Correspondance de Julien Raimond, avec ses frères de Saint-Domingue, et les pièces qui lui ont été adressés par eux* (Paris: Cercle social, An III [1794]), 123.

42. AP, 69:580 (27 July 1793); *Réimpression de l'ancien Moniteur*, 21 September 1793 (National Convention session of 19 September 1793).

43. On the events of 20 June 1793, see Popkin, *You Are All Free*, 189–216.

44. Toussaint Louverture, declaration, 8–27 August 1793, AN, AA 55, d. 1511. For the events leading from the crisis in June to the issuance of the emancipation decrees, see Popkin, *You Are All Free*, 217–79.

45. Page and Brulley, register, 24, 25, 31 August, 1 September 1793, AN, D XXV 76; *Créole patriote*, 29 August 1793.

46. Page and Brulley, register, 5 September 1793, AN, D XXV 76.

47. On the journée of 5 September 1793, see Jeremy D. Popkin, *A New World Begins: The History of the French Revolution* (New York: Basic Books, 2019), 356–58.

48. AN, D* 16 3–4, entries for 11, 23 September 1793; Page and Brulley, register, 25, 26 September, 6 October 1793, D XXV 76; [Pourçain] Martel, *Rapport général sur les déportés des colonies françoises, par le citoyen Martel, membre du comité de Marine* (Paris: Imprimerie nationale, 1793), 16, 34.

49. Page and Brulley, register, 6 October 1793, AN, D XXV 76.

50. *Moniteur universel*, 17 October 1793.

51. Abel A. Louis, *Janvier Littée: Martiniquais premier député de couleur membre d'une assemblée parlementaire française (1752–1820)* (Paris: L'Harmattan, 2013), 138–42.

52. Page and Brulley, register, 13, 16 October, 1 brumaire II (22 October 1793), 2 brumaire II (23 October 1793), AN, D XXV 76; *Bulletin du Tribunal Criminel Révolutionnaire*, no. 40.

53. Brissot, manuscript, n.d., AN, 446 AP 13–14.

54. *Nouvelles politiques*, 27 October 1793; *Créole patriote*, 10e jour, An II (1 October 1793); Page and Brulley, register, 9 brumaire II (30 October 1793), AN, D XXV 76; *Bulletin du Tribunal Révolutionnaire*, nos. 41, 61.

55. Robespierre, speech of 27 brumaire II (17 November 1793), in *Oeuvres*, 10:173–74; Page and Brulley, register, 27 brumaire II, AN, D XXV 76.

56. Page and Brulley, register, 5 frimaire II (25 November 1793), AN, D XXV 76.

57. *Bulletin du Tribunal Révolutionnaire*, nos. 75–76 (Mme. Roland), 67 (de Gouges); Page and Brulley, register, 6, 7, 8 frimaire II (26, 27, 28 November 1793), AN, D XXV 76; Gérard Walter, ed., *Actes du Tribunal révolutionnaire* (Paris: Mercure de France, 1968), 310.

58. Raimond, interrogation, 4 frimaire II (24 November 1793), and Brulley, denunciation, 15 frimaire II (5 December 1793), AN, D XXV 77, d. 547.

59. Page and Brulley, register, 17 frimaire II (7 December 1793); 2 nivôse II (22 December 1793).

60. Page and Brulley, register, 17 frimaire II (7 December 1793), AN, D XXV 76.

61. Page and Brulley, register, 11, 13 nivôse II (31 December 1793, 2 January 1794), AN, D XXV 76.

62. *Créole patriote*, 16 frimaire II (6 December 1793), 11 nivôse II (31 December 1793) (Jacobins, 8 nivôse II [28 December 1793]).

63. *Créole patriote*, 11, 12 nivôse II (31 December 1793, 1 January 1794) (Jacobins, 8 nivôse II [28 December 1793]); testimony of Jean Rochefort, 12 nivôse II (31 December 1793), AN, D XXV 56, d. 554.

64. Condorcet, *Esquisse d'un tableau historique des progrès de l'esprit humain* (Paris: Flammarion, 1988), 268, 271.

Chapter Nine

1. Honoré Guérin to Brulley, 10 pluviôse II (29 January 1794), AN, D XXV 71, d. 713.

2. Page and Brulley, register, 6 pluviôse II (25 January 1794), AN, D XXV 76.

3. For the certification of the men's election in Saint-Domingue, see AN, D 1 ¶ 39, d. 283; and AP, 84:265–66. On the challenges they faced in getting to France, see *Lettre écrite de New-Yorck par les députés de Saint-Domingue, à leurs commettans* (Paris: Imprimerie nationale, 1794); Piquet, *Emancipation des Noirs*, 321–31; Popkin, *You Are All Free*, 320–23; and Matthieu Carlot, "Des chemins périlleux: Le Voyage des conventionnels des colonies vers Paris (1793–1794)," *Annales historiques de la Révolution française*, no. 380 (June 2015): 3–24. On Genet's report, see Andy Cabot, "Le Rapport Genet (1793) sur la Bataille du Cap français: Aux sources d'un texte anti-esclavagiste," *La Révolution française* 27 (January 2025), https://doi.org/10.4000/1346b.

4. Dufay to Sonthonax and Polverel, 4 December 1793, AN, D XXV 6, d. 54, and D XXV 16, d. 158.

5. On Danton's activities during these crucial months, see Loris Chavanette, *Danton et Robespierre: Le Choc de la Révolution* (Paris: Humensis, 2021), 309–42.

6. Quoted in Jean-Charles Benzaken, *Louis Pierre Dufaÿ: Conventionnel abolitionniste et colon de Saint-Domingue, 1752–1804* (Paris: SPM, 2015), 185.

7. Louis Pierre Dufay, *Sur les députés, et autres, connus sous le nom de la Gironde* (Paris: Pain, 1795), 2.

8. Page and Brulley, register, 6, 7 pluviôse II (25, 26 January 1794), AN, D XXV 25, 76.

9. Dufay and Mills to Convention, 12 pluviôse II (31 January 1794), AN, D XXV 57, d. 563.

10. Page and Brulley, register, 14 pluviôse II (2 February 1794), AN, D XXV 76.

11. AP, 84:256–57. For a discussion of the sources for the reconstruction of this Convention session, see Yves Bénot, "Comment la Convention a-t-elle voté l'abolition de l'esclavage en l'An II?," *Annales historiques de la Révolution française*, nos. 293–94 (July 1993): 349–61.

12. AP, 84:257.

13. Benzaken, *Louis Pierre Dufaÿ*, 39–44, 99, 124, 127–28.

14. *Moniteur universel*, 18 pluviôse II (6 February 1794).

15. Dufay, *Sur les députés*, 3.

16. Dufay, speech of 16 pluviôse II (4 February 1794), in AP, 84:282.

17. [Louis Pierre Dufay], *Rélation détaillée des événemens malheureux qui se sont passes au Cap depuis l'arrivée du ci-devant général Galbaud, jusqu'au moment où il a fait bruler cette ville et a pris la fuite* (Paris: Imprimerie nationale, An II [1794]), 55.

18. Dufay, *Sur les députés*, 3.

19. AP, 84:277.

20. AP, 84:278. Records show that Belley had owned at least two female slaves, one of whom had been branded with his name. Jean-Louis Donnadieu, "Derrière le portrait, l'homme: Jean-Baptiste Belley, dit 'Timbaze,' dit 'Mars' (1746?–1805)," *Bulletin de la Société d'Histoire de la Guadeloupe* 170 (2015): 40–41.

21. AP, 84:278. For a detailed account of the events in Saint-Domingue after June 1793, see Popkin, *You Are All Free*, 189–288.

22. AP, 84:279; Cabot, "Le Rapport Genet."

23. AP, 84:282–83.

24. AP, 84:283.

25. AP, 84:283.

26. Dominique Joseph Garat, *Mémoires sur la Révolution, ou Exposé de ma conduite dans les affaires et dans les fonctions publiques* (Paris: J. J. Smits, An III [1795]), 192.

27. AP, 84:284. The versions of Danton's speech printed at the time differ somewhat. For an analysis of the significance of these differences, see Jean-Daniel Piquet, "Le Discours abolitionniste de Danton (16 pluviôse An II)," *Revue d'histoire et de philosophie religieuses* 90, no. 3 (2010): 353–77.

28. *Nouvelles politiques*, 17 pluviôse II (5 February 1794) (National Convention session of 16 pluviôse II [4 February 1794]).

29. Levasseur, *Mémoires*, 422; Henri Grégoire, *Mémoires*, ed. Hypollite Carnot (1831; Paris: Editions de Santé, 1989), 81.

30. AP, 84:284–85.

31. *Journal de Paris*, 18 pluviôse II (6 February 1794) (National Convention session of 17 pluviôse II [5 February 1794]); AP, 84:283, 326. There is some uncertainty about whether Grégoire spoke on the issue on 16 pluviôse or on the following day, or on both occasions.

32. *Annales de la Révolution*, 18 pluviôse II (6 February 1794).

33. AP, 84:326–27.

34. Robespierre, "Discours sur les principes de morale politique qui doivent guider la Convention Nationale dans l'administration intérieure de la

République," in AP, 84:330–37; Stein, *Léger-Félicité Sonthonax*, 111–12; Albert Mathiez, *Études sur Robespierre (1754–1794)*, ed. Georges Lefebvre (Paris: Éditions sociales, 1958), 146.

35. Mondou to Brulley, 20 pluviôse II (8 February 1794), AN, D XXV 71, d. 713; Captain Sherlock, speech to convention, *Moniteur universel*, 22 pluviôse II (10 February 1794) (National Convention session of 20 pluviôse II); Adrien de La Salle, proclamation of 8 October 1793, AN, D XXV 19, d. 187.

36. Luc-André Biarnais, "Images et représentations raciales de l'administration: La Délivrance des passeports à Nantes et La Rochelle durant la Révolution française," in Pellerin, *Les Lumières, l'esclavage*, 294.

37. *Moniteur universel*, 22 pluviôse II (10 February 1794) (Jacobins, 16 pluviôse II [4 February 1794]).

38. *Créole patriote*, 20 pluviôse II (8 February 1794) (National Convention session of 20 pluviôse II); *Moniteur universel*, 22 pluviôse II (10 February 1794) (National Convention session of 20 pluviôse II).

39. Antoine Piis, *Chansons patriotiques par le citoyen Piis* (Paris: Théâtre du Vaudeville, An II [1794]), 36.

40. *Créole patriote*, 25 pluviôse II (13 February 1794) (Commune session of 21 pluviôse II [9 February 1794]).

41. *Journal de la Montagne*, 20 pluviôse II (8 February 1794) (Commune session of 18 pluviôse II [6 February 1794]); *Moniteur universel*, 21 pluviôse II (National Convention session of 20 pluviôse II); *Journal de la Montagne*, 25 pluviôse II (13 February 1794) (Commune session of 21 pluviôse II [9 February 1794]).

42. *Discours prononcé par le citoyen Chaumette, au nom de la Commune de Paris, le décadi 30 pluviôse, l'an II de la République française . . . à la fête célébrée à Paris, en réjouissance de l'abolition de l'esclavage* (Paris: Imprimerie nationale, An II [1794]), 17, 2, 10.

43. Entry for 18 February 1794, in *Journal de Célestin Guittard de Floriban, bourgeois de Paris sous la Révolution*, ed. Raymond Aubert (Paris: Editions France-Empire, 1974), 320–21; *Moniteur universel*, 2 ventôse II (20 February 1794) (National Convention session of 30 pluviôse II [18 February 1794]).

44. *Discours, de la citoyenne Lucidor F. Corbin, Créole, Republicaine, prononcée par elle même au Temple de la Raison, l'An 2e de la Liberté* (Paris: Coutubrier, 1794); *Hymne des citoyens de couleurs, par la Citoyenne Corbin; Créole et Républicaine* (Paris: n.p., 1794). On Lucidor Corbin, see Pierre Bardin, "Lucidor, ancien esclave, et sa fille Marie-Thérèse, à Paris," *Genealogie et Histoire des Caraïbes*, 16 July 2009 (https://www.ghcaraibe.org/bul/ghc227/som227.html).

45. Official report, quoted in Jean-Claude Halpern, "Les Fêtes révolutionnaires et l'abolition de l'esclavage en l'An II," in *Les Abolitions de l'esclavage, de L. F. Sonthonax à V. Schoelcher: 1793, 1794, 1848*, ed. Marcel Dorigny (Vincennes: Editions UNESCO, 1995), 190–91, 195; number of addresses in Gauthier, *Triomphe et mort*, 237; Bordeaux delegations in *Moniteur universel*, 13 ventôse II (3 March 1794) (National Convention session of 17 ventôse II [7 March 1794]); report on Bordeaux ceremony in *Courrier républicain*, quoted in Saugera, *Bordeaux, port négrier*, 116; Jean-Daniel

Piquet, "Le Comité de Salut Public et les fêtes sur la liberté des Noirs: Châlons-sur-Marne, Lyon, l'Etre Suprême à Paris," *Annales historiques de la Révolution Française*, no. 316 (1999): 349.

46. *Père Duchêne*, 2 ventôse II (20 February 1794).

47. *Feuille du Salut public*, 17 pluviôse II (5 February 1794).

48. *Nouvelles politiques*, 1 ventôse II (19 February 1794).

49. *Créole patriote*, 16 pluviôse II (4 February 1794).

50. *Révolutions de Paris*, 11–24 pluviôse II (30 January–12 February 1794).

51. Sculpture head in Musée Nissim de Camando, originally from the collection of the duc d'Orléans. The Metropolitan Museum of Art in New York has a small-scale model of the original sculpture group, created by the artist Houdon, showing that it depicted a Black servant bathing her white mistress.

52. Claude Wanquet, *La France et la première abolition de l'esclavage, 1794–1802* (Paris: Karthala, 1998), 301–10.

53. Régent, *La France*, 252.

54. *Philadelphia General Advertiser*, 30 April 1794; *Moniteur universel*, 29 ventôse II (14 March 1794) (House of Commons session of 25 February 1794); "An Act for establishing regulations respecting Slaves arriving in this island, or resident therein, except such as are imported directly from the coast of Africa," 31 May 1794, Laws of Enslavement and Freedom in the Anglo-Atlantic World, University of New Brunswick Libraries, https://slaveryandfreedomlaws.lib.unb.ca/laws/tobago-1794; Jervis quoted in Frédéric Régent, "Pourquoi faire l'histoire de la Révolution par les colonies?" in *Pour quoi faire la Révolution?*, ed. Jean-Luc Chappey et al. (Marseille: Agone, 2012), 70.

55. *New-Jersey Journal*, 16 October 1793; also in *Columbian Gazetteer* (New York), *Daily Advertiser* (New York), *New York Journal and Patriotic Register*, *Weekly Register* (Norwich, CT), *Farmer's Library* (Rutland, VT), and *Vermont Gazette* (Bennington).

56. *American Star / Etoile Américaine*, 3 May 1794.

57. *Gazette of the United States*, 1 May 1794.

58. *Minutes of the Proceedings of the Second Convention of Delegates from the Abolition Societies* (Philadelphia: Zachariah Poulson, 1795), 30.

Chapter Ten

1. AN, D*16 3-4-5, entry for 17 pluviôse II.

2. Page and Brulley, register, 18 pluviôse II (6 February 1794), AN, D XXV 76.

3. Page and Brulley, register, 18, 24, 27 pluviôse II (6, 12, 15 February 1794), AN, D XXV 76; Belley speech, AP, 84:471 (National Convention session of 20 pluviôse II [8 February 1794]).

4. *Moniteur universel*, 21 ventôse II (11 March 1794) (National Convention session of 19 ventôse II [9 March 1794]).

5. *Moniteur universel*, 20, 21 ventôse II (10, 11 March 1794) (National Convention session of 19 ventôse II [9 March 1794]).

6. Jean-Baptiste Belley, *Belley, de Saint-Domingue, représentant du peuple, à ses collègues* (Paris: Pain, 1794), 4; Duny, letters of 17 prairial II (5 June 1794) and 19 floréal II (8 May 1794), AN, D XXV 76, d. 757.

7. Page and Brulley to Couthon, 16 prairial II (4 June 1794), AN, D XXV 81, d. 794.

8. Tribunal révolutionnaire, 29 floréal II (18 May 1794), AN, D XXV 56, d. 554; Yves Bénot, "L'Affaire Milscent," *Dix-Huitième Siècle* 21 (1989): 311, 316–18.

9. Barbier, *Seigneur d'Arsy*, 162; Darline Gay Levy, *The Ideas and Careers of Simon-Nicolas-Henri Linguet* (Urbana: University of Illinois Press, 1980), 328–33.

10. Bossut, *Chaumette*, 465–77; Mathiez, *Études sur Robespierre*, 146.

11. "Manuscrit d'un Voyage de France à Saint-Domingue, à la Havanne et aux Unis états [*sic*] d'Amérique," John Carter Brown Library, Codex Fr. 20, pt. 2, p. 50.

12. *Réimpression de l'ancien Moniteur*, 7 thermidor II (25 July 1794) (Tribunal révolutionnaire, 2 thermidor II [20 July 1794]).

13. Stein, *Léger Félicité Sonthonax*, 112.

14. *Adresse à la Convention nationale* (Paris: Laurens aîné, 2 fructidor II [19 August 1794]). On the colonists' propaganda efforts and the responses to them, see Alex Fairfax-Cholmeley, "Colonial Factions and Pamphlet Warfare: Writing Histories of Saint-Domingue and France During the Thermidorian Reaction, 1794–1795," *French Historical Studies* 47 (2024): 36–69.

15. Raimond, letter of 14 vendémiaire III (5 October 1794) from Evêché prison, AN, D XXV 82, d. 802; Julien Raimond, *Lettre d'un citoyen, détenu pendant quatorze mois, et traduit au Tribunal révolutionnaire, au Citoyen C. B***, représentant du peuple, en réponse à une question importante* (Paris: Imprimerie de l'Union, An III [1795]); J.-P. Garran-Coulon, *Rapport sur Julien Raimond, fait au nom de la Commission des Colonies et des Comités de Salut public, de législation et de la marine réunis, le 24 floréal de l'an 3 de la République, par. J. Ph. Garran, député par le département du Loiret* (Paris: Imprimerie nationale, prairial An III [1795]).

16. *Réimpression de l'ancien Moniteur*, 7 fructidor II (24 August 1794) (National Convention session of 5 frucidor II [22 August 1794]), 12 vendémiaire III (3 October 1794) (National Convention session of 9 vendémiaire III [30 September 1794]).

17. On these hearings, usually known as "the trial of Sonthonax" even though they were not a judicial procedure, see Stein, *Léger Félicité Sonthonax*, 114–19; and Yves Bénot, "Le Procès Sonthonax ou les *Débats entre les accusateurs et les accusés dans l'affaire des colonies* (an III)," in Dorigny, *Sonthonax*, 55–63. The proceedings of the inquiry were published as *Débats entre les accusateurs et les accusés dans l'affaire des colonies*, 9 vols. (Paris: Imprimerie nationale, 1795). Guillois, *Analyse des débats, entre les accusateurs et les accusés, dans l'affaire de la colonie de Saint-Domingue, conformément aux décrets de la Convention Nationale; par le citoyen Guillois, l'un des tachygraphes nommés par la Convention Nationale, pour recueillir les débats* (Paris: Chevet, [1795]), provides a convenient summary of the debates, despite its author's strong bias in favor of the proslavery colonists.

18. J.-P. Garran-Coulon, *Rapport sur les troubles de Saint-Domingue, fait au nom de la Commission des colonies, des Comités de Salut public, de Législation, et de Marine, réunis*, 4 vols. (Paris: Imprimerie nationale, 1797–98).

19. *Journal de correspondance de Paris à Nantes, et du département de la Loire Inférieure*, supplement to no. 13, vol. 8 (n.d.), letter of 22 February [1791].

20. Guillois, *Analyse des débats*, 21.

21. Popkin, *You Are All Free*, 189–216.

22. Benoît Gouly, *Vues générales sur l'importance du commerce des colonies* (Paris, 1794), 46, 29n, 54. On Gouly, see Claude Wanquet, "Un 'Jacobin' esclavagiste, Benoît Gouly," *Annales historiques de la Révolution française*, nos. 293/294 (July–December 1993): 445–68.

23. *Réimpression de l'ancien Moniteur*, 11 frimaire III (1 December 1794) (National Convention session of 9 frimaire III (29 November 1794).

24. Letter from P. Bayonne, Lorient, 10 pluviôse III (29 January 1795), in *Réimpression de l'Ancien Moniteur* (Paris: Bureau Central, 1840–45), vol. 23, 22 pluviôse III (10 February 1795). It is significant that this letter identifies Toussaint Louverture by his prerevolutionary name rather than by the new sobriquet he had adopted in August 1793; its author clearly knew something about Louverture's past. Saint-Michel and Saint-Raphaël were towns on the border with the Spanish colony of Santo Domingo.

25. *Moniteur*, 19 pluviôse III (7 February 1795) (National Convention session of 16 pluviôse III [4 February 1795]).

26. Pelet, report of 4 pluviôse III (23 January 1795), in *Réimpression de l'Ancien Moniteur*, 8 pluviôse III (27 January 1795).

27. Gouly, speech of 24 pluviôse III (12 February 1795), in *Reimpression de l'Ancien Moniteur*, 27 pluviôse III (15 February 1795).

28. *Réimpression de l'Ancien Moniteur*, 29 pluviôse III (17 February 1795) (National Convention session of 26 pluviôse III [14 February 1795]).

29. Letter from Cayenne, 15 October 1794, in *Nouvelles politiques*, 19 germinal III (8 April 1795).

30. Dufay, speech of 12 messidor III (30 June 1795), in *Réimpression de l'Ancien Moniteur*, issues of 15 and 16 messidor III [3 and 4 July 1795]).

31. *Réimpression de l'Ancien Moniteur*, 20 messidor III (8 July 1795) (National Convention session of 17 messidor III [5 July 1795]).

32. *Réimpression de l'Ancien Moniteur*, 20 messidor III (8 July 1795) (National Convention session of 17 messidor III [5 July 1795]). In the *Moniteur* account, the two deputies who most strongly insisted on the principle of equality are identified as "Fermont" and "Garrand." There were no deputies of those names, and, in view of their other interventions on the subject, it seems clear that the speakers were Defermon and Garran-Coulon.

33. *Réimpression de l'Ancien Moniteur*, 22 messidor III (10 July 1795) (National Convention session of 19 messidor III [7 July 1795]).

34. On the constitutional laws concerning the colonies during the Directory period, see Bernard Gainot, "La Constitutionalisation de la liberté générale sous le Directoire," in Dorigny, *Les Abolitions de l'esclavage*, 213–29.

35. On this debate, see Wanquet, *La France*, 239–47.

36. Defermon, speech of 5 thermidor III (24 July 1795), in *Réimpression de l'Ancien Moniteur*, 10 thermidor III (29 July 1795).

37. Defermon, speech.

38. Defermon, speech.

39. Lecomte de la Seine-Inférieure, speech of 5 thermidor III (23 July 1795), in *Réimpression de l'Ancien Moniteur*, 11 thermidor III (29 July 1795).

40. Albert Sorel, *L'Europe et la Révolution française* (Paris: Plon-Nourrit, 1908), 4:321, 369.

41. Boissy d'Anglas, speech to Convention, 17 thermidor III (4 August 1795), in *Réimpression de l'Ancien Moniteur*, vol. 26, 23 thermidor II (10 August 1795).

42. Boissy d'Anglas, speech.

43. "Constitution du 5 fructidor an III," 22 August 1795, title I, article 6, https://www.conseil-constitutionnel.fr/les-constitutions-dans-l-histoire/constitution-du-5-fructidor-an-iii. According to article 7, Saint-Domingue was to be divided into between four and six departments, while the other colonies would each constitute a single department. The "départementalisation" of Saint-Domingue was in fact never carried out, and deputies were chosen on the basis of the colony's three prerevolutionary provinces (North, West, and South). Since most of the West was occupied by the British until the spring of 1798, no elections were ever held there. After many disputes, some of them related to the purge of deputies following the coup of 18 fructidor An V, a total of eleven deputies, six representing the North Province and five the South, were finally seated. Bernard Gainot, "La Députation de Saint-Domingue au corps législatif du Directoire," in Dorigny, *Sonthonax*, 95–110.

44. Dufay, memorandum, 16 August 1795, in Moreau de Saint-Méry papers, AN, Col. F 3 267, cited in Benzaken, *Louis Pierre Dufay*, 341–48.

45. On the tensions inherent in this policy in the twentieth century, see Gary Wilder, *The French Imperial Nation-State: Negritude and Colonial Humanism Between the Two World Wars* (Chicago: University of Chicago Press, 2005).

46. Gauthier, *Triomphe et mort*, 252; Miranda Frances Spieler, *Empire and Underworld: Captivity in French Guiana* (Cambridge, MA: Harvard University Press, 2012). Spieler asserts that the drafters of the Constitution of 1795 intended to "make constitutional rule overseas impossible" and contends that the Convention "sought to obscure rather than amplify the rights of former slaves" (52).

47. Popkin, *Concise History*, 77–79.

48. Boissy d'Anglas, letter in *Patriote françois*, 15 May 1791.

Chapter Eleven

1. On the laws providing relief for refugees from Saint-Domingue, see Marcel Grandière, "Les Refugiés et les déportés des Antilles à Nantes sous la Révolution," *Bulletin de la Société d'histoire de la Guadeloupe*, nos. 33–34 (1977): 3–171.

2. *Journal historique et politique de la marine et de des colonies*, 21 vendémiaire V (12 October 1796).

3. *Réimpression de l'Ancien Moniteur*, 9 pluviôse IV (29 January 1796) (Council of 500, 4 pluviôse IV [24 January 1796]).

4. Dufay to Laveaux, 23 May 1796, quoted in Beaubrun Ardouin, *Etudes sur l'histoire de Haïti, suivies de la vie du général J.-M. Borgella* (Paris: Dezobry and E. Magdeleine, 1853), 3:38.

5. *Reimpression de l'Ancien Moniteur*, 9, 10 pluviôse IV (29, 30 January 1796) (Council of 500, 4 pluviôse IV [24 January 1796]; Council of Elders, 5 pluviôse IV [25 January 1796]); *Reimpression de l'Ancien Moniteur*, 12 nivôse, 16 pluviôse IV (2 January, 5 February 1796) (Council of 500, 8 nivôse [29 December 1795], 8 pluviôse IV [28 January 1796]).

6. Frédéric Régent, *Esclavage, métissage, liberté: La Révolution française en Guadeloupe 1789–1802* (Paris: Grasset, 2004), 288–89; Popkin, *Concise History*, 79; colonist's protest, 15 nivôse V (4 January 1797), in AN, AF III 207, d. 945; Fourcroy to Carnot, 16 brumaire IV (7 November 1795), AN, AF III 209, d. 955.

7. Bernard Gainot, "Un projet avorté d'intégration républicaine: L'Institution nationale des colonies (1797–1802)," *Dix-Huitième Siècle*, no. 32 (2000): 373; Dufay to Toussaint Louverture, n.d., New York Public Library, Manuscripts Division.

8. *Reimpression de l'Ancien Moniteur*, 10 thermidor IV (28 July 1796).

9. Bernard Gainot, "Le Général Laveaux Gouverneur de Saint-Domingue député néo-Jacobin," *Annales historiques de la Révolution française*, no. 278 (October–December 1989): 445.

10. Baco, letter of 14 frimaire V (4 December 1796), in *Moniteur universel*, 24 frimaire V (14 December 1796). On Baco and Burnel's mission, see Claude Wanquet, "La Tentative de Baco et Burnel d'application de l'abolition aux Mascareignes en 1796," in Dorigny, *Les Abolitions de l'esclavage*, 231–40.

11. [Jean-Baptiste Laplace], *Réflexions sur la colonie de Saint-Domingue, ou Examen approfondi des causes de sa ruine, et des mesures adoptées pour la rétablir; terminées par l'exposé rapide d'un plan d'organisation propre à lui rendre son ancienne splendeur; adressés au Commerce et aux Amis de la prospérité nationale*, 2 vols. (Paris: Garnery, An IV [1796]). On Laplace, see Jean-Charles Benzaken, "Qui est l'auteur de l'*Histoire des désastres de Saint-Domingue* publié à Paris en l'an III?," *Revue de l'Institut Napoléon*, no. 204 (2012): 118–37, which corrects an earlier misidentification in Jean-Charles Benzaken, "Who Was the Author of *L'Histoire des désastres de Saint-Domingue*, published in Paris in the Year III?," *French History* 23, no. 2 (2009): 261–67.

12. [Laplace], *Réflexions sur la colonie*, 1:149, 150, 153, 175.

13. [Laplace], *Réflexions sur la colonie*, 1:185.

14. [Laplace], *Réflexions sur la colonie*, 1:188, 190, 249.

15. [Laplace], *Réflexions sur la colonie*, 2:99.

16. [Laplace], *Réflexions sur la colonie*, 2:168.

17. [Laplace], *Réflexions sur la colonie*, 2:170–72; *De l'affranchissement des noirs, ou Observations sur la loi du 16 pluviôse, an deuxième, et sur les moyens à prendre pour le rétablissement des colonies, du commerce et de la marine* (n.p., n.d.), 29.

18. [Laplace], *Réflexions sur la colonie*, 2:196, 198, 202, 236, 248.

19. Louis Rallier, *Observations sur Saint-Domingue, par Rallier, député d'Ille et Vilaine, membre du Conseil des Anciens* (Paris: Imprimerie nationale, ventôse An IV [1796]), 8–10, 22.

20. Rallier, *Observations sur Saint-Domingue*, 13–14, 20–21; Louis Rallier, *Suite des observations sur Saint-Domingue, par Rallier, membre du Conseil des anciens* (Paris: Baudouin, An IV [1796]), 4, 20–21, 22.

21. Pascale Pellerin, "Colonialisme et esclavage dans les journaux du Directoire," in Pellerin, *Les Lumières, l'esclavage*, 297–315.

22. [Pierre] Marec, *Rapport fait au nom de la Commission des Colonies-Occidentales, sur la situation de l'isle Saint-Domingue* (Paris: Imprimerie nationale, 11 ventôse An V [1 March 1797]), 4, 64, 103, 142. On the incident in Cayes, see Manuel Covo, "Le Massacre de fructidor an IV à Saint-Domingue: Violence et politique de la race sous le Directoire," *Annales historiques de la Révolution française*, 395 (2019): 143–70.

23. *Républicain des colonies*, 10, 15 germinal V (30 March, 4 April 1797); Gainot, "La Députation de Saint-Domingue," 97.

24. *Message: Extrait du registre des délibérations du Directoire exécutif du 3 floréal V* (Paris: Imprimerie nationale, An V [1797]), 3, 12.

25. *Républicain des colonies*, 5 floréal V (24 April 1797); *Message: Extrait du registre des délibérations du Directoire exécutif du 19 floréal V* (Paris: Imprimerie nationale, An V [1797]), 5. On the *Républicain des colonies*, see Bernard Gainot, "Bottu, Le Républicain des colonies (1797)," *Annales historiques de la Révolution française*, nos. 293/94 (July–December 1993): 431–44.

26. Vincent-Marie Vienot-Vaublanc, *Discours sur l'état de Saint-Domingue et sur la conduite des agens du Directoire, prononcé par Vienot-Vaublanc: Séance du 10 prairial an 5* (Paris: Imprimerie nationale, 1797), 1.

27. Vienot-Vaublanc, *Discours sur l'état*, 9, 15, 24.

28. *Réimpression de l'Ancien Moniteur*, 16 prairial V (4 June 1797) (Council of 500, 11 prairial V [30 May 1797]), 28:719; Louis-Thomas Villaret-Joyeuse, *Discours de Villaret-Joyeuse . . . sur l'importance des colonies et les moyens de les pacifier* (Paris: Imprimerie nationale, An V [1797]), 4, 9–10.

29. Police report, 18 prairial V (6 June 1797), quoted in Stein, *Léger Félicité Sonthonax*, 179–80.

30. *Moniteur universel*, 21 prairial V (9 June 1797) (Council of 500, 15 prairial V [3 June 1797]); A. C. Thibaudeau, *Mémoires sur le Directoire et le Consulat* (Paris: Baudouin frères, 1824), 1:185.

31. Etienne Laveaux, *Réponse d'Étienne Laveaux, général de division, ex-gouverneur de Saint-Domingue, aux calomnies que le citoyen Vienot Vaublanc . . . s'est permis de mettre dans son discours prononcé dans la séance du 10 Prairial dernier* (Paris: J. F. Sobry, 1797), 11; Joseph Eschassériaux, *Opinion d'Eschassériaux aîné, sur les moyens de rétablir les Colonies* (Paris: Imprimerie nationale, 1797), 15; J.-P. Garran-Coulon, *Opinion de J. Ph. Garran sur les dénonciations formées contre les agens du Directoire, à Saint-Domingue* (Paris: Imprimerie nationale, An V [1797]), 19–20.

32. *Ami des Loix*, 2 messidor V (20 June 1797).

33. *Moniteur universel*, 8, 9 messidor V (26, 27 June 1797).

34. Toussaint Louverture, *Extrait du rapport adressé au Directoire exécutif par le citoyen Toussaint Louverture, général en chef des Forces de la République française à Saint-Domingue* (Cap-Français: P. Roux, An V [1797]); a manuscript copy of Louverture's denunciation of Sonthonax is in AN, AF III 210, d. 961. For the description of the report as "creative fiction," see Sudhir Hazareesingh, *Black Spartacus: The Epic Life of Toussaint Louverture* (New York: Farrar, Straus and Giroux, 2020), 115; and for a demonstration of the implausibility of Louverture's accusations, see Stein, *Léger Félicité Sonthonax*, 169–70.

35. Toussaint Louverture, *Réfutation de quelques assertions d'un discours prononcé au Corps législatif le 10 prairial, an cinq, par Vienot Vaublanc* (n.p., n.d.), 1, 5, 6, 7.

36. Louverture, *Réfutation de quelques assertions*, 10, 11, 32.

37. On the division among the colonial deputies about Louverture, see Bernard Gainot, "Les Représentants de couleur de Saint-Domingue dans les assemblées de la Première République," *La Révolution française*, no. 27 (2025): 20–25, https://doi.org/10.4000/13467.

38. Louis Gustave Le Doulcet de Pontécoulant, *Souvenirs historiques et parlementaires du comte de Pontécoulant, ancien pair de France*, ed. L. A. Le Doulcet, marquis de Pontécoulant (Paris: Michel Lévy, 1861), 1:166.

39. Angelie Sens, "La Révolution batave et l'esclavage: Les (Im)possibilités de l'abolition de la traite des noirs et de l'esclavage (1780–1814)," *Annales historiques de la Révolution française*, no. 326 (2001): 65–78.

40. Gainot, "La Députation de Saint-Domingue," 98.

41. *Moniteur universel*, 2 brumaire VI (23 October 1797) (Council of 500, 1 brumaire VI [22 October 1797]).

42. *Moniteur universel*, 3 brumaire VI (24 October 1797) (Council of 500, 1 brumaire VI [22 October 1797]).

43. Liu, *Frail Liberty*, 8.

44. *Moniteur universel*, 3 brumaire VI (24 October 1797) (Council of 500, 1 brumaire VI [22 October 1797]); *Moniteur universel*, 12 nivôse VI (1 January 1798) (Council of Elders, 4 nivôse VI [24 December 1797]).

45. *Moniteur universel*, 3 brumaire VI (24 October 1797) (Council of 500, 1 brumaire VI [22 October 1797]).

46. On the history of the Société des Amis des Noirs et des Colonies, see Bernard Gainot, introduction to Dorigny and Gainot, *Amis des Noirs*, 301–27; and Bernard Gainot, "Helen-Maria Williams, médiatrice culturelle dans la Décade philosophique," *La Révolution française* 1 (2017), https://doi.org/10.4000/lrf.1754.

47. Société des Amis des Noirs et des Colonies, "Reglement," in Dorigny and Gainot, *Amis des Noirs*, 383–85.

48. Bernard Gainot, "La Décade et la 'colonisation nouvelle,'" *Annales historiques de la Révolution Française*, no. 339 (January 2005): 111.

49. Darcy Grimaldo Grigsby, *Extremities: Painting Empire in Post-revolutionary France* (New Haven, CT: Yale University Press, 2002), 22.

50. Germaine de Staël, "Mirza," in Kadish and Massardier-Kenney, *Translating Slavery*, 146–56; Charles-Antoine Guillaume Pigault-Lebrun, *Le Blanc et le Noir, drame en quatre actes et en prose* (Paris: Mayeur and Barba, An IV [1796]); Jean-Baptiste Picquenard, *Adonis suivi de Zoflora et de documents inédits*, ed. Chris Bongie (Paris: L'Harmattan, 2006); Joseph Fiévée, *La Dot de Suzette* (Paris, 1798). On the stage version of *Adonis*, see Halpern, "L'Esclavage," 418.

51. *Moniteur universel*, 20 pluviôse VI (8 February 1798) (Brothier speech, Council of Elders, 16 pluviôse VI [4 February 1798]), 18–19 pluviôse VI (6–7 February 1798) (Sonthonax speech, Council of 500, 16 pluviôse VI); *Publiciste*, 17 pluviôse VI (5 February 1798).

52. *Annales de la Religion*, 8 (1797–98):140.

53. Régent, *Esclavage, métissage, liberté*, 375–79.

54. Etienne Mentor, *Dernier mot d'Etienne Mentor, représentant du peuple, à Etienne Bruix, ministre de la marine et des colonies* (Paris: n.p., 1798), 8. On this affair, see Gainot, *Officiers de couleur*, 81–100.

55. Christian Schefer, *Instructions générales données de 1763 à 1870 aux gouverneurs et ordonnateurs des établissements français en Afrique Occidentale* (Paris: Société française d'histoire d'outre-mer, 1921, 1927), 1:170–73; Miranda Spieler, "Abolition and Reenslavement in the Caribbean: The Revolution in French Guiana," in *The French Revolution in Global Perspective*, ed. Suzanne Desan, Lynn Hunt, and William Max Nelson (Ithaca, NY: Cornell University Press, 2013), 135–42.

56. Thomany speech, 16 pluviôse VII (4 February 1799), in *Moniteur universel*, 21 pluviôse VII (9 February 1799); Laveaux speech in *Moniteur universel*, 22 pluviôse VII (10 February 1799).

57. "Compte rendu de la cérémonie commemorative du décret d'abolition," *Chronique universelle*, 29 pluviôse VII (17 February 1799), quoted in Dorigny and Gainot, *Amis des Noirs*, 393–94.

58. Gainot, *Officiers de couleur*, 100.

Chapter Twelve

1. Philip Dwyer, *Napoleon: The Path to Power* (New Haven, CT: Yale University Press, 2007), 45–46, 63.

2. Sainte-Croix de la Roncière, *Joséphine impératrice des Français, reine d'Italie* (Paris: chez l'auteur, 1934), 257–58; Christophe Pincemaille, "Rompre avec un silence: Joséphine et l'esclavage," https://musees-nationaux-malmaison.fr/chateau-malmaison/actualite/rompre-avec-un-silence-josephine-et-lesclavage.

3. Yves Bénot, *La Démence coloniale sous Napoléon* (Paris: La Découverte, 1992); Claude Ribbe, *Le Crime de Napoléon* (Paris: Privé, 2005); Thierry Lentz, Pierre Branda, and Chantal Lheureuse-Prévot, *Napoléon, l'esclavage et les colonies* (Paris: Fayard, 2006), 104; Philippe Girard, "Napoleon Bonaparte and the

Emancipation Issue in Saint-Domingue, 1799–1803," *French Historical Studies* 32 (2009): 606; Thomas Pronier, "L'Implicite et l'explicite dans la politique de Napoléon," in *Rétablissement de l'esclavage dans les colonies françaises: Aux origines d'Haïti*, ed. Yves Bénot and Marcel Dorigny (Paris: Maisonneuve et Rose, 2003), 67. Bénot added significant detail to his 1992 book in an article, "Le 18 brumaire, un enjeu colonial?," in *Du Directoire au Consulat*, vol. 3, *Brumaire dans l'histoire du lien politique et de l'Etat-nation*, ed. Jean-Pierre Jessenne (Lille: Publications de l'Institut de recherches historiques du Septentrion, 2001), 243–55. A critical assessment of Napoleon's policies was offered in a collective volume published in 2021: Suzanne Dracius, ed., *La Faute à Bonaparte?* (Martinique: Idem, 2021). Lentz and Branda updated their treatment of the subject in a special issue of *Napoleonica: La Revue* on "Napoléon et l'esclavage," 2, no. 49 (2024).

4. Antoine Thibaudeau, *Mémoires sur le Consulat* (Paris: Baudouin, 1827), 120–21.

5. Jean Jacques Régis de Cambacérès, *Mémoires inédits* (Paris: Perrin, 1999), 1:586–87.

6. Pierre-Louis Roederer, *Autour de Bonaparte: Journal du comte P.-L. Roederer, ministre et conseiller d'état*, ed. Maurice Vitrac (Paris: Daragon, 1909), 16.

7. Bruix to Directory, 7 nivôse VII (28 December 1798), AN, AF III 210.

8. Letter from Cap Français, 8 vendémiaire VIII (30 September 1799), in *Publiciste*, 10 frimaire VIII (1 December 1799), and *Moniteur*, 11 frimaire VIII (2 December 1799).

9. Sonthonax interview, 17 frimaire VIII (8 December 1799), AN, C 9 B 18.

10. Rallier to Bonaparte, 21 frimaire VIII (12 December 1799), AN, AF 1212, no. 6.

11. *Publiciste*, 27 frimaire VIII (18 December 1799).

12. Proclamation of 4 nivôse VIII (25 December 1799), in *Moniteur universel*, 7 nivôse VIII (28 December 1799).

13. Granet, letter of 12 nivôse VIII (2 January 1800), AN, AF IV 1187.

14. Stein, *Léger Félicité Sonthonax*, 184–86.

15. Elicona, *Un colonial sous la Révolution*, 215–20.

16. AN, AF IV 1187, memorandum of pluviôse VIII; Wanquet, *La France*, 531–57; Bénot, *Démence coloniale*, 32–24.

17. Charles-Humbert-Marie de Vincent, *Observations du général du génie Vincent sur les deux premières notes rapportées dans une collection de mémoires pour servir à l'histoire de France sous Napoléon* (Paris: Pélicier, 1824), 10–11, quoted in Hazareesingh, *Black Spartacus*, 227. On Charles Humbert Vincent, see Christian Schneider, "Le Colonel Vincent, officier du génie à Saint-Domingue," *Annales Historiques de la Révolution française*, no. 329 (2002): 101–22.

18. Truguet to Napoleon, letters of 19 nivôse VIII (9 January 1800), AN, AF IV 1187.

19. Page, "1er Mémoire: Notes pour servir au gouvernement dans ses combinaisons politiques et législatives relativement aux colonies," n.d., AN, AF IV 1212, no. 7; Alliot, letter of 19 prairial VIII (8 June 1800), AN, CC 9 A 27.

20. Dufay, doc. 44, n.d., AN, AF IV 1212.

21. Gautier d'Auxonne, n.d., AN, AF 1212, no. 21.

22. C. Belu, *Des colonies et de la traite des nègres* (Paris: Guilleminet, An IX [1800]), 24, 48–51, 34.

23. On the *Décade philosophique*'s policy during this period, see Bénot, *Démence coloniale*, 238–50.

24. *Zorada, ou la Créole, histoire récente, publiée par Emilie J. . . . t.* (Paris: Vatar-Jouannet, 1801), 2:27; René Perrin, *L'Incendie du Cap, ou le Règne de Toussaint-Louverture* (Paris: Marchand, 1802), xi.

25. Forfait, summary of reports from Saint-Domingue and letters from Vincent, AN, AF IV 1187; Vincent letter, 28 prairial VIII (17 June 1800), AN, CC 9 A 28; Sahuguet to Bonaparte, 3rd jour complémentaire VIII, AN, AF IV 1187.

26. Memorandum, 27 vendémiaire IX (19 October 1800), AN, CC 9 A 28.

27. Instructions for General Combis, 14 January 1801, Correspondance de Napoléon Ier, Institut Français de Vienne, http://www.histoire-empire.org.

28. Napoléon Bonaparte, *Correspondance de Napoléon Ier*, ed. Jean-Baptiste Philibert Vaillant (Paris: Imprimerie Impériale, 1858–70), 7:61.

29. Toussaint Louverture, "Constitution of the French Colony of Saint-Domingue," in Dubois and Garrigus, *Slave Revolution*, 159; *Bulletin Officiel de Saint-Domingue*, 19 messidor XI (8 July 1801).

30. Louverture to Napoleon, 27 messidor IX (16 July 1801), AN, AF IV 1213.

31. *Mercure de France*, 1 brumaire X (23 October 1801). A version of Louverture's constitution, translated from an article in an American newspaper, had been published in the *Moniteur* on 11 vendémiaire X (3 October 1801), and the official version was printed on 23 vendémiaire X (25 October 1801).

32. "Decrès," in Georges Six, *Dictionnaire biographique des généraux et amiraux français de la Révolution et de l'Empire: 1792–1814*, 2 vols. (Paris: Librairie historique et nobiliare, 1934) 1:305–6.

33. Comte de Montholon, *Mémoires pour servir à l'histoire de France, sous Napoléon, écrits à Sainte-Hélène, par les généraux qui ont partagé sa captivité* (Paris: Firmin Didot, 1823), 3:193.

34. Napoléon to Decrès, 7 October 1801, in *Correspondance de Napoléon Ier*, 7:277, 330; Eric Saugera, "Introduction," *Outre-Mers*, no. 408–9 (2020): 21–48.

35. Napoleon to Talleyrand, 13 November 1801, in *Correspondance de Napoléon Ier*, 7:319–20. See also Marlene Daut, *Awakening the Ashes: An Intellectual History of the Haitian Revolution* (Chapel Hill: University of North Carolina Press, 2023), 166–67.

36. Napoleon to Toussaint Louverture, 27 brumaire X (18 November 1801), in *Lettres du Général Leclerc, commandant en chef de l'armée de Saint-Domingue en 1802*, ed. Paul Roussier (Paris: Société de l'histoire des colonies françaises, 1937), 307–9.

37. Roussier, *Lettres du Général Leclerc*, 62–65.

38. Roussier, *Lettres du Général Leclerc*, 263–72.

39. Roussier, *Lettres du Général Leclerc*, 272–74; Emmanuel de Las Casas, *Mémorial de Saint-Hélène*, 4 vols. (Paris: Garnier, 1823), 2:523.

40. On the deaths of François-Xavier Lanthenas and C. B. Wadstrom, see Gainot, introduction to Dorigny and Gainot, *Amis des Noirs*, 323, 325; Grégoire to

Pennsylvania Society for the Abolition of Slavery, 2 March 1802, in Dorigny and Gainot, *Amis des Noirs*, 395.

41. François-René Chateaubriand, *Le Génie du christianisme*, 4 vols. (Paris: Migneret, 1802), 1:189; *Décade philosophique*, 10 messidor X (29 June 1802).

42. Malouet, *Collection de mémoires*, 4:46–47, 52, 72.

43. Jean Barré de Saint-Venant, *Des colonies modernes sous la zone torride, et particulièrement de celle de Saint-Domingue* (Paris: Rochot, 1802), 91.

44. [Louis Dubroca], *La Vie de Toussaint-Louverture, chef des noirs insurgés de Saint-Domingue* (Paris: Dubroca, 1802), 44. Another pamphlet, *Vie privée politique et militaire de Toussaint-Louverture, par un homme de sa couleur* (Paris: Magasin de librairie, 1801), was somewhat less hostile to him.

45. Jean Jacques Virey, *Histoire naturelle du genre humain: ou recherches sur ses principaux fondemens physiques et moraux* (Paris: Dufart, 1801), 1:201, 2:120; Jean Jacques Virey, "Nègre," in *Nouveau dictionnaire d'histoire naturelle appliquée aux arts* (Paris, 1803), 15:440. On Virey, see Jean-Claude Halpern, "Le Nègre et l'Européen: Virey ou l'anthropologie bavarde," in Bénot and Dorigny, *Rétablissement de l'esclavage*, 523–35.

46. Gaspard Gourgaud, *Talks of Napoleon at St. Helena*, trans. Elizabeth Wormeley Latimer (Chicago: A. C. McClurg, 1903), 112.

47. Louis-Narcisse Baudry Deslozières, *Les Egarements du Nigrophilisme* (Paris: Migneret, 1802), 95.

48. Baudry Deslozières, *Egarements du Nigrophilisme*, 38, 29, 186–87.

49. Villaret-Joyeuse, letter of 28 pluviôse X (17 February 1802), in *Moniteur*, 2 germinal X (23 March 1802); police report, 4 April 1802, in François Aulard, *Paris sous le Consulat* (Paris: L. Cerf, 1903–9), 2:828.

50. Saugera, "Introduction."

51. Bonaparte, *Correspondance de Napoléon Ier*, 7:444–46.

52. Decrès to Napoléon, 1 floréal X (21 April 1802), AN, AF IV 1190.

53. Savoy-Rollin speech, in *Moniteur*, 30 floréal X (20 May 1802) (Tribunate, 28 floréal X [18 May 1802]).

54. Dupuy, in *Moniteur*, 28 floréal X (18 May 1802) (Tribunate, 27 floréal X [17 May 1802]).

55. Adet speech, in *Moniteur*, 30 floréal X (20 May 1802) (Tribunate, 29 floréal X [19 May 1802]).

56. Adet, speech, in *Moniteur*, 30 floréal X (20 May 1802) (Tribunate, 28 floréal X (18 May 1802).

57. Adet speech, in *Moniteur*, 1 prairial X (21 May 1802) (Tribunate, 29 floréal X [19 May 1802]).

58. Adet speech, in *Moniteur*, 1 prairial X (21 May 1802) (Tribunate, 29 floréal X [19 May 1802]).

59. *Journal des Débats*, 20 May 1802 (Tribunate, 29 floréal X [19 May 1802]).

60. Speeches of Jaubert and Bruix, in *Moniteur*, 3 prairial X (23 May 1802) (Legislative Body, 30 floréal X [20 May 1802]).

61. *Moniteur*, 3 prairial X (23 May 1802) (speeches in Legislative Body, 30 floréal X [20 May 1802]).

62. *Courier de Provence*, 20–21 August 1789, 3–4; emphasis in original.

63. Text of law of 30 floréal X, in Bénot and Dorigny, *Rétablissement de l'esclavage*, 563.

64. Napoleon to Leclerc, 1 July 1802, in *Correspondance de Napoléon Ier*, 7:641.

65. Decrès to Leclerc, 25 prairial X (14 June 1802), in Roussier, *Lettres du Général Leclerc*, 285.

66. Police reports, 31 May 1802, 11, 12 June 1802, in Aulard, *Paris sous le Consulat*, 3:107; Leclerc, letter of 18 prairial [*sic:* floréal] X (7 June 1802), in *Moniteur*, 24 prairial X (13 June 1802).

67. Leclerc, letter of 17 floréal X (6 June 1802), in Roussier, *Lettres du Général Leclerc*, 146.

68. *Décade philosophique*, 10, 30 floréal X (30 April, 20 May 1802); *Mercure de France*, reprinted in *Journal des Débats*, 7 June 1802.

69. *Mercure de France*, 5 thermidor X (24 July 1802).

70. Gainot, *Officiers de couleur*, 167.

71. [Valentin de Cullion], *Examen de l'esclavage en général, et particulièrement de l'esclavage des nègres dans les colonies françaises de l'Amérique* (Paris: Desenne et Maradan, An XI [1802]), 1:143–44n. The text of the law, which was dated 13 messidor X (2 July 1802), was published in the *Moniteur* on 9 vendémiaire XI (1 October 1802). The Paris prefect of police issued instructions for enforcing the law on 3 brumaire XI (25 October 1802) (*Moniteur*, 8 brumaire XI [30 October 1802]). On the prohibition of mixed marriages, see Louis-Charles-Antoine Allemand, *Traité du mariage et de ses effets* (Riom, 1846–47), 1:130. For the closing of the school, see Gainot, *Officiers de couleur*, 161.

72. Leclerc to Napoleon, 17 prairial X (6 June 1802), in Roussier, *Lettres du Général Leclerc*, 161–62.

73. Leclerc to Napoleon, 18 thermidor X (6 August 1802), in Roussier, *Lettres du Général Leclerc*, 202.

74. Frédéric Régent, "Le Rétablissement de l'esclavage et du préjugé de couleur en Guadeloupe (1802–1803)," in Bénot and Dorigny, *Rétablissement de l'esclavage*, 289; Jean-François Niort and Jérémy Richard, "A propos de la découverte de l'arrêté consulaire du 16 juillet 1802 et du rétablissement de l'ancien ordre colonial (spécialement de l'esclavage) à la Guadeloupe," *Bulletin de la Société d'Histoire de la Guadeloupe*, no. 152 (January–April 2009): 31–59.

75. Leclerc to Napoleon, 21 thermidor X (9 August 1802), 15 vendémiaire XI (7 October 1802), in Roussier, *Lettres du Général Leclerc*, 208, 256.

76. Toussaint Louverture, *Mémoires du général Toussaint Louverture*, ed. Daniel Desormeaux (Paris: Classiques Garnier, 2011), 140.

77. Jean-Louis Donnadieu, "Derrière le portrait, l'homme: Jean-Baptiste Belley, dit 'Timbaze,' dit 'Mars' (1746?–1805)," *Bulletin de la Société de l'histoire de la Guadeloupe*, no. 170 (2015),46–47; Gainot, "Représentants de couleur," 29.

78. Jean-Charles Benzaken, "Louis-Pierre Dufay, député abolitionniste et homme d'affaires avisé. Esquisse biographique," *Annales historiques de la Révolution française* no. 368 (2012), 85.

79. Las Casas, *Mémorial de Saint-Hélène*, 2:523.

Epilogue

1. Deschamps, *Histoire de la question*, 370. On Deschamps, see Gérard Boëldieu, "Léon Deschamps," in *Le Maitron: Dictionnaire biographique du mouvement ouvrier et social*, 2 September 2012, https://maitron.fr/spip.php?article141639. Among other things, Deschamps pressed to have a street in the city of Le Mans, where he taught for many years, named after René Levasseur, the Convention deputy who introduced the motion to abolish slavery on 16 pluviôse II.

2. Ardouin, *Etudes sur l'histoire*, 2:260–61.

3. *Créole patriote*, 6 July 1792.

4. Regnault Saint-Jean d'Angély, speech of 30 floréal X (20 May 1802), in *Moniteur universel*, 3 prairial X (23 May 1802).

5. Jean-Baptiste Say, *Traité d'économie politique* (Paris: Crapelet, 1803), 1:214–28; Henri Grégoire, *De la littérature des Nègres* (Paris: Maradan, 1808), 281.

6. On French policy in the first years of the Restoration, see Jean-François Brière, *Haïti et la France: La Rêve Brisée* (Paris: Karthala, 2008), 57–76.

7. Brière, *Haïti et la France*, 126–40.

8. Saint-Marc Girardin, in *Journal des Débats*, 8 December 1831.

9. On the French abolitionist movement after 1815, see Lawrence C. Jennings, *French Anti-Slavery: The Movement for the Abolition of Slavery in France, 1802–1848* (Cambridge: Cambridge University Press, 2000).

10. Victor Schoelcher, *Des colonies françaises: De l'abolition immédiate de l'esclavage*, ed. Lucien Abénon (1842; Paris: Editions du CTHS, 1998), 175.

11. Jennings, *French Anti-Slavery*, 202–28.

12. On the abolition of 1848, see Jennings, *French Anti-Slavery*, 275–84; and Jean-Pierre Sainton, "De l'état d'esclave à 'l'état de citoyen': Modalités du passage de l'esclavage à la citoyenneté aux Antilles françaises sous la Seconde République," *Outre-mers*, no. 338–39 (2003): 47–82. On the limitations of the 1848 law, see Silyane Larcher, *L'Autre citoyen: L'Idéal républicain et les Antilles après l'esclavage* (Paris: Armand Colin, 2014).

13. Joseph Arthur Gobineau, *Essai sur l'inégalité des races humaines* (1855; Paris: Firmin-Didot, 1884), 1:49, 2:530.

14. Jean Jaurès, *Histoire socialiste de la Révolution française*, rev. ed., ed. Albert Mathiez (Paris: Editions Sociales, 1938), 3:239.

15. Léopold Senghor, "Vues sur l'Afrique noire ou assimiler, non être assimilés," in *Négritude et humanisme* (Paris: Seuil, 1964), 41.

16. Aimé Césaire, *Toussaint Louverture: La Révolution française et le problème colonial* (Paris: Présence Africaine, 1961), 197.

17. Pierre Nora, ed., *Les Lieux de mémoire*, 7 vols. (Paris: Gallimard, 1984). On the way in which France obscured the memory of its colonial past, see Todd Shepard, *The Invention of Decolonization: The Algerian War and the Remaking of France* (Ithaca, NY: Cornell University Press, 2006).

18. On the career of Yves Bénot (whose original name was Edouard Helman), see Marcel Dorigny, "Yves Bénot (1920–2005)," *Annales Historiques de la Révolution française*, no. 339 (2005): 151–54.

19. On the background to the Taubira law and its results, see Cottias, "Les vingt ans"; Sébastien Ledoux, "'Devoir de mémoire': The Post-Colonial Path of a Post-National Memory in France," *National Identities* 15 (2013): 239–56; and Simon Férelloc, "The Taubira Law," Manifest, 17 January 2023, https://www.projectmanifest.eu/the-taubira-law-en-fr/.

20. The museum has published a lavishly illustrated catalog of its permanent exhibition: Krystal Guadlé, *L'Abîme: Nantes dans la traite atlantique et l'esclavage colonial 1707–1830* (Bain-de-Bretagne: Musée d'histoire de Nantes, 2021). See also the guide to the historic exhibition in the Musée d'Aquitaine, *Bordeaux au XVIIIe siècle: Le Commerce Atlantique et l'esclavage* (Bordeaux: Le Festin, 2010).

21. Guadlé, *L'Abîme*, 146, 121, 124, 130–31.

INDEX

Page numbers in *italics* refer to figures.